SURPRISED
BY THE
VOICE
OF
GOD

Also by Jack Deere

Surprised by the Power of the Spirit

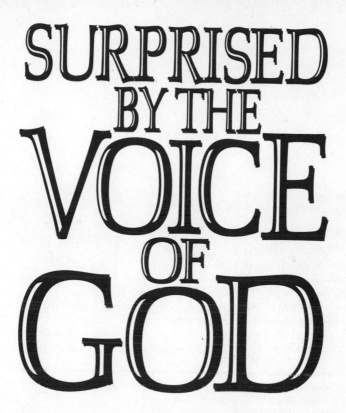

SURPRISED BY THE VOICE OF GOD

How God Speaks Today Through Prophecies, Dreams, and Visions

JACK DEERE

ZondervanPublishingHouse
Grand Rapids, Michigan

A Division of HarperCollinsPublishers

Surprised by the Voice of God
Copyright © 1996 by Jack S. Deere

Requests for information should be addressed to:

ZondervanPublishingHouse
Grand Rapids, Michigan 49530

Library of Congress Cataloging-in-Publication Data
    Surprised by the voice of God : how God speaks today through prophe-
cies, dreams, and visions / Jack Deere
        p.   cm.
    Includes bibliographical references (p.   ).
    ISBN: 0-310-22558-2 (softcover)
    1. Gifts, Spiritual.   2. Prophecies.   3. Dreams—Religious aspects—
Christianity.   4. Visions.   5. Deere, Jack.   I. Title.
    BT767.3.D38   1996   96-8380
    234'.13—dc20
    CIP

Printed in the United States of America

98 99 00 01 02 03 /❖ DC/ 10 9 8 7 6 5 4 3 2

For Paul Cain,
Who has endured rejection like a true prophet,
loving enemies, doing good to those who hate, blessing
those who curse, praying for those who mistreat.
A friend who sticks closer than a brother,
A mentor who is like his Master,
A father who delights in his children.
I thank my God every time I remember you
(Philippians 1:3).

Contents

WHO HEARS HIS VOICE?

THE WORD AND THE SPIRIT

Acknowledgments

Once again, I must thank the people at Zondervan for their skill in helping to bring this book to completion. I am also grateful for the extraordinary patience and kindness they showed me during the numerous delays necessitated by a move and a new pastorate on my part. I especially want to thank Dr. Stan Gundry, Jack Kuhatschek, and Rachel Boers for their help.

I also wish to thank my dear friends, who read the manuscript at various stages and made valuable suggestions, Prof. Wayne Grudem, Reed Grafke, Dudley Hall, Dr. Sam Storms, Ken Gire, and John and Claire Hughes. And thanks to my assistant and loyal friend, Lara Gangloff, who not only typed the manuscript, but assisted in other ways too numerous to mention.

My wife Leesa not only read the entire manuscript, offering valuable suggestions and corrections, but she also lived many of the experiences contained in this book. Her prayers, insights, and ability to hear the voice of God have enriched both this book and my own life. And thanks to my sons, Craig and Scott, and my daughter, Alese, for their love and prayers.

Launching Out

1

Surprised by the Voice of God

He sat there before me, the ideal image of the all-American boy. Robert was young, handsome, intelligent, impeccably dressed in a suit and tie, and spiritual. He was an elected leader of his seminary class, headed for a promising pastoral career. He was also in the bondage of a terrible, merciless evil he had hidden from everyone, for he knew if he shared his darkness with anyone, he would be immediately and irrevocably ruined.

So for years Robert lived the life of a religious hypocrite. The irony was that he didn't want to be a hypocrite, and he didn't really want to sin. Although he hadn't confessed his sin to any leader, he had tried all of the "spiritual prescriptions" his religious teachers had given him through the years, but they never seemed to work for him. He was trapped. He felt utterly condemned and hopeless.

It was amazing how well he had hidden it all—the sin, the guilt, the condemnation, the hopelessness. Years of practice had taught him how to attend church and prayer meetings—even how to conduct religious services and write theological papers—without betraying the state of his soul. He was convinced no one would ever know. No one *could* ever know.

But Robert was wrong. Someone did know, and in spite of this knowledge, he loved Robert. He loved Robert even though Robert had long since lost the capacity to feel that love in any meaningful way. Robert's *only* hope lay in that love, and in the sudden exposure of his private darkness, an exposure the mercy of the Lord Jesus Christ was about to grant him. Evil becomes impotent in the presence of the mercy of the Savior. Unwittingly, almost comically, Robert was poised to fall into the limitless mercy of God's Son. Like the woman at the well, he was about to be surprised by the voice of God. And so was I.

It began earlier that afternoon while I was sitting at my desk in my seminary office pondering what was wrong with contemporary theological education. A knock at the door interrupted my thoughts. Robert pushed his face through the door and asked if he could "have just a minute of my time"—which translated usually means, "I am here to take up the rest of your afternoon if you will give me the slightest encouragement."

I was Robert's Hebrew professor, and Robert had come to my office to ask for mercy for a late assignment. He began to offer a long and unnecessary excuse for his tardy work—unnecessary because, in my way of thinking, seminary students already had enough pressure on them without professors demanding everything be handed in on time; I had already decided to accept the late assignment. Wishing to appear courteous, I patiently listened to the superfluous explanation.

That's when it happened, something I had never experienced before. Or if I had experienced it, I certainly didn't remember it. As I was listening to Robert, he faded away and in his place I *saw* the word "PORNOGRAPHY" in large, capital, block letters. *What is happening to me?* I thought. *There is no way this student is into pornography. I must be making this up.* But why would I make up something I thought to be an impossibility?

I realized I was having what some believers call "a word of knowledge." It wasn't intuition; knowledge about Robert was being given to me by the Spirit of God. He was the last student I would have suspected of being addicted to pornography. Yet now I was sure, well almost sure, he was under its power.

For months, I had been praying for God to speak to me like this, asking him to impart to me supernatural knowledge about people so that I might minister to them more effectively. For months, I had been longing to experience the supernatural ministry of Jesus. Now at last it was finally beginning to happen. God was telling me supernaturally about the sin of one of my students.

All I needed to do was confront Robert so he could confess his sin and be forgiven. It seemed simple, but what if it wasn't that simple? What if Robert denied he had any attraction to pornography? Worse, I could just see myself bungling the confrontation so badly that Robert would leave my office in anger and tell other students, "Don't go into Professor Deere's office, the guy's a pervert hung up on pornography." Worse still, what if news of such a bungled confrontation reached the president's office? What if he called me into his office and asked, "Did you accuse one of our students of an addiction to pornography?" I would be forced to admit that I had. I could just hear the president saying, "On what basis did you make this accusation?"

"Uh, a vision."

"A what?"

"Well, er, uh, a kind of vision, you know."

"You had a vision!"

In my circles, in those days, visions weren't exactly in vogue. In fact, having a vision could have been grounds for dismissal, or at least a trip to the faculty psychiatrist's office. As these cold realities began to settle on me, my enthusiasm for my newly found "word of knowledge" ministry began to sputter.

Was it really worth the risk? Was it worth being humiliated? I decided not to say anything. Yet, I had been praying for months for God to speak to me like this. A harsh legalistic thought entered my mind. *If this is God speaking to me and I don't say anything to Robert, God may never speak to me like this again.* It seemed like, one way or another, I was going to offend someone. Whom would I offend, man or God? Not really a difficult choice, unless you are in that embarrassing position. I decided to obey God—at least sort of.

I took a weak stab at confronting Robert by interrupting his excuse for his late assignment and asking, "Excuse me, but have you been struggling with anything lately?"

"No, not at all. Why do you ask?" came the confident reply.

"Oh, no reason really—anyway, what were you saying?" That was as much risk as I was going to take that day for God and my fledgling "word of knowledge" ministry. As soon as I made the decision not to say any more to Robert, the vision came back. This time the word "pornography" started blinking on and off. Sounds crazy, doesn't it? I was beginning to think so myself. On the other hand, maybe God was letting me know he was really serious about this confrontation. There was only one way to find out.

I interrupted Robert again, "Are you sure you don't have any guilt you haven't been able to get rid of?"

"No," he replied. This time he looked offended. "Why are you saying this? Why are you asking me this?"

I apologized, saying that I wasn't really sure why I was asking. I decided to shut up and just listen. But the word came back! I wondered if this was going to be like the blood on Macbeth's hands, the "spot" that wouldn't go away until he finally made his confession. My last thought was, *This had better be worth the risk.* I looked Robert straight in the eyes and blurted out, "Are you into pornography?"

When I looked into his eyes, I knew two things. First, he was into pornography. Second, he was going to deny it. "Wait a minute," I said. "Before you say anything, let me tell you something. Since you have been sitting in my office, I think God has been telling me you are into pornography. If you are, I will never tell anyone your name, and I will not get you dismissed from seminary or your church because of this. And finally, I think the Lord has been telling me this because he wants to set you free. And he wants to start today."

Robert was stunned. He turned his eyes away and hung his head. "I was," he confessed.

"When was the last time you bought a magazine?"

"Last week."

"How long has this been going on?"

"Since I was thirteen or fourteen."

He said after he had become a Christian in his later teenage years, he had not been able to give up the addiction to pornography. He had never been able to tell anybody about it because he feared being rejected. He thought he was the only Christian in his circle with this sin. He was wrong, of course, but he never knew that. I talked to him about the mercy and forgiveness of Christ. I told him about the power of the blood of Jesus to destroy these kinds of addictions. Hope, by the Holy Spirit, began to enter into Robert's heart for the first time in a long, long while.[1] I walked over to him and put my hand on his shoulder to pray. When I asked the Lord Jesus to intensify his presence with us, Robert grew visibly uncomfortable. I removed my hand and said, "There is more here than pornography, isn't there?"

"I'm so ashamed," he replied on the verge of tears. It took him the longest time to begin. Finally, in a barely audible whisper, Robert began to confess things I would not put into print. Pornography was only the tip of the iceberg. Robert was in the grip of an evil power far stronger than he. He had been trying for years to battle this evil power with his own discipline and willpower, and he had been steadily losing ground. Without going into more detail, let me say that when Robert left my office after confession and prayer, he was a new person.

I saw him later that night in front of the seminary library. He ran up to me, threw his arms around me, and hugged me. He almost shouted, "I'm a new person! I'm a new person! Something has left me; I feel lighter. I don't think I'll ever go back into that bondage again."

Over the years I lost touch with Robert. But for the remainder of my time in seminary I stayed in contact with him, and as far as I know, he lived a clean life, free of his former bondage.

Outside of my conversion, this is the first time I remember hearing the voice of God in a blatantly supernatural way. Has this kind of thing become an everyday occurrence for me? No. But it is surprisingly common. What is more, I have come to expect that voice to speak to me, especially when I am attempting to minister to someone in Jesus' name. I have found that if I expect his voice, if I really *need* his voice, and if I am diligent in learning how to recognize his voice, he speaks to me regularly and sometimes in amazing ways. In fact, I have come to count on the voice of God to such a degree that I can no longer conceive of trying to live the Christian life without it.

When we expect and need his voice, even the simplest form of ministry can become an occasion for a supernatural communication from God. Years ago, when I was serving on the staff of the Vineyard Christian Fellowship in Anaheim, California, some home group leaders brought to me a young, single woman who had been having nightmares. For the last three months Rhonda had been experiencing these nightmares every single night. For several reasons, both she and her home group leaders thought the nightmares were demonic in origin. They asked me to pray for her.

As I began to pray, the name "Don" kept coming to mind. I stopped praying and asked, "Does the name Don mean anything to you?" Her face lost its color and seemed to retreat behind a veil of shame. I said, "It does mean something to you, doesn't it? And it's bad. Can you talk about it?"

"I don't think so."

Gently I told her I thought God was telling us the nightmares were connected with Don. God seemed to be indicating that whatever she had buried in darkness had to be brought to the light before these nightmares would go away. She would have to find the courage to tell us about Don before we could pray effectively for her. I encouraged her to tell her home group leaders about him as soon as she felt the freedom to do so. If she wanted me to be involved at that time, I would be happy to help. We said good-bye, and Rhonda went away ashamed and disappointed. But her nightmares did not go away. Later that week her home group leaders called and said she was ready to talk, could they bring her in?

Here is the story she related to me. Three months earlier one of her girlfriends had taken her to meet a man named Don. The three of them met in Don's house and began to drink. Eventually, the women became drunk and ended up committing sexual immorality with him. Rhonda related the shame and humiliation she felt the next day after the alcohol had worn off. The nightmares started the next night. Later she discovered Don was deeply involved in the occult. In addition to the sexual defilement, he had been able to impart an evil spirit to this young woman. When she confessed this and repented, we were able to pray for her, and immediately the nightmares stopped.

If these stories strike you as strange and even a little scary, I can sympathize with you. At one time I would have had the same reaction. For me the "normal" Christian life used to mean believing the right doctrine, helping out at church, trying to be a good person through regular times of reading the Bible and praying, and witnessing when the opportunity arose. I did not believe in any real revelation from God apart from the Bible. I didn't think I needed it. I was busy trying to live the Christian life out of discipline rather than passion. I couldn't figure out why so often prayer and Bible study took on the character of a religious duty rather than a conversation with a person with whom I was deeply in love.

Looking back on that time, I realize now that so much of the Bible actually seemed unreal to me. I had relegated many experiences in the Bible to the distant, unrepeatable past. It had become for me primarily a book of doctrines and abstract truths about God. I loved the doctrines of the Bible and its literary beauty, but I shared very few experiences with the people of the Bible.

Unlike me, the people of the Bible heard God speak in a variety of ways. He spoke through an audible voice, through dreams, visions, circumstances, fleeces, inner impressions, prophets, angels, and other ways, as well as through Scripture. These things were so common in New Testament times that Paul had to give detailed instructions to the Corinthians concerning the use of prophecy, tongues, words of wisdom, words of knowledge, and discernment of spirits (1 Cor. 12–14). The author of Hebrews even underscored the importance of hospitality, reminding his readers that by showing hospitality "some people have entertained angels without knowing it" (Heb. 13:2). He believed that in his day angelic visits were still possible!

I didn't have to be a theological genius to read the Bible and figure out God used to speak in many different ways to his people. But after God wrote the Bible, he apparently went mute, or so it seemed to me, for the only way I could hear him speak was through his book. On a practical level, I acted as though the Holy Spirit was some kind of impersonal force who provided the church with a vague, ill-defined, general guidance. Many believers seem to be in the same predicament today.

Back when I held those views, if Robert had come into my office, he would have gone out unhelped. The same with Rhonda. I would have been happy to pray for her nightmares, but nothing would have happened because I would not have been able to hear God say the name "Don." In Robert's case and in Rhonda's, a single word from God was the key to revealing their hidden sin and setting them free. Neither Robert nor Rhonda had the courage to tell anyone about their sin. Shame and the fear of rejection had overpowered their hearts. They had lost their confidence in the power of the blood of Jesus. But when they realized God was supernaturally revealing their sin in order to set them free, the Holy Spirit infused their hearts with hope, and they found the courage to expose their sin. We serve a God who specializes in bringing "to light what is hidden in darkness" (1 Cor. 4:5). When

Jesus comes again, he will do this on a terrifying scale. But even now, he comes to us individually with his revealing ministry . . . *if we have ears to hear.*

The God of the Bible reveals much more to us than the sins of others. He speaks about many things. Sometimes we fail to hear him because he says more than we want to hear. Sometimes we fail to hear him because we are ignorant of the varied ways in which he speaks. And sometimes we fail to hear him because his voice is drowned out by competing voices that masquerade as God's voice, throwing us into confusion.

Besides the voice of God, there are at least three other voices that speak to us: the voice of our emotions; the voice of darkness, that is, the devil and his demons; and the voice that comes through the pressure we feel from family, friends, and others. Sometimes we mistake these three voices for the voice of God. This raises the important question, "How do you know when the voice is God's and not another's?"

This book is about the voice of God and how to hear it. Although at times it may not be easy to hear his voice, hearing it isn't as complicated as you might think.

This is not an academic book. I have not written it for professional theologians. I have tried to write a practical book for ordinary Christians who want to hear God's voice above the clamor of everyday life. The still, small voice that spoke to Elijah in the cave is far more powerful than many of us realize. It can keep us from being bound by tradition or driven by circumstance. The voice can give us more than our own abilities to understand the Bible. Many Christians have wandered into a spiritual wilderness devoid of passion and power. Those who hear and obey the voice of God will escape that wilderness or see it changed into a garden.

And who knows what beauty will come out of that garden? Or what fruit?

2

The Problem of the Unreal Bible

When I was seventeen, I became born again. *Really* born again. Overnight, a rebellious, reckless, immoral kid began to pursue Jesus with all his heart. Immediately, I picked up a good habit that has also become a life-long habit—I began to read the Bible on a regular basis. I can't remember how it happened, but I also acquired another habit, a bad one. It was this: When I read the stories of the people of the Bible, I did not expect their experiences to be like mine. They were special people living in special times. Their experience of God was unique; mine wasn't. Mine was more *normal*, whatever that meant. So I read and memorized the Bible, never expecting much of what I read to ever be reproduced in my life. I don't know when or who taught me to read the Bible like this.

My friend John Wimber, though, can remember exactly when he was taught to read the Bible like this. He was twenty-nine. He and his wife, Carol, had just recently accepted Christ at a home Bible study. Until then, John had managed to live his whole life with almost no exposure to church, the Bible, or religious people. Christianity was a whole new experience for him, but in recent weeks he had come to love the Bible and began to devour the New Testament.

The man who led the Wimbers to Christ told them they should begin attending church. The next Sunday, Carol dutifully got their four children ready for the family's first worship experience. Even though they had never done it before, they instinctively knew what to do—they got up late, had an argument, and drove to church angry. Without realizing it, they had already fallen into the typical Sunday-morning pattern for American churchgoing families.

Arriving late, they sat toward the back. The congregation sang a few hymns with outdated melodies. The singing was so out of tune it hurt John's ears. (Wimber was and is a gifted musician. He had been the arranger and producer of the early music for the Righteous Brothers.) The minister proceeded to deliver a rather passionless forty-minute sermon, and church was over. As soon as they were outside, John started to light up a cigarette, but Carol made him put it back. "Do you see anybody else smoking around here? You're not supposed to smoke at church," she chided. In those days John was a chain-smoker, and he thought it strange that no one else was smoking; in fact, the whole experience seemed strange to him. But he decided to come back, because he had been told Christians were supposed to go to church—no matter how boring it was.

So the Wimbers became churchgoers. John also became a voracious Bible-reader. Unlike church, the Scriptures excited him. They filled him with hope and longing. They brought him into contact with a God who could do anything, even raise the dead. He began to notice a significant difference between the church he attended on Sunday and the Bible he read every day. The Bible seemed normal. The church seemed weird. This impression was strengthened when, after a Sunday service, one of the elders looked across the lawn and, figuring John was a newcomer, walked over to him and said, "Brother, have you been washed in the blood?" With a quizzical look on his face John replied, "Yuk, when do they do that around here?"

Finally, after weeks of reading a miraculous Bible and attending monotonous religious services, John walked up to one of the lay leaders and asked, "When do we get to do the stuff?"

"What stuff?" asked the leader.

"You know, the stuff here in the Bible," said John, as he opened the New Testament and pointed to the Gospels. "You know, like the stuff Jesus did—raising people from the dead, healing the blind and the paralyzed, you know, that stuff."

"Well, we don't do that anymore," the man said.

"You don't?"

"No."

"Well, what do you do?" asked John.

"What we did this morning."

"For that I gave up drugs?" John was incredulous that the experience of the people of God today was so different from the experience of the people in the Bible. However, church leaders were able to get him over his disappointment. The key was just not to expect too much.

So it was in the early weeks of John's born-again experience that he was taught to read the Bible and consciously not expect its experiences to be repeated in his life. Many Christians today read the Scriptures that same way. Though we believe all of the experiences in the Word of God are real, to us they have become *unreal*, causing us to have to "spiritualize" or "tone down" the applications of much of what we read.

COULD EUTYCHUS BE RAISED TODAY?

When I was a seminary student, I had to write a paper on Acts 20:7–12. This is the passage where the young man named Eutychus fell asleep during one of Paul's sermons and fell to his death out of a third story window. Paul went down to the pavement, raised the young man from the dead, and returned to his sermon. For weeks I studied this text, looking for its theological significance. I searched for hidden meanings in the details of the story. I tried to discover Luke's literary and theological purpose for including the story in the book of Acts, and his purpose in putting it in that precise place in the narrative. I never once considered there might actually be a literal, practical application of this story for today's church. In my mind there was an irreconcilable divorce between the experiences of the people of the Bible and our own experiences. Besides, what practical relevance could the raising of Eutychus have today? It wasn't until years later I was to find out.

In November of 1991, I was speaking at an interdenominational conference in Atlanta. There were about 1,200 people present when I stood up that evening to speak. The theme of my message was that God is still healing and doing miracles in today's church. I had just started to speak when Clement Humbard, an older man sitting in about the seventh pew on my right, collapsed and slid to the ground. Someone said, "I think he's dead." How would you like to have been in charge of that service?

I had just begun to speak on the subject of healing and miracles, and someone died! At first I was so scared I thought I might die too. What would you do if someone died at the beginning of your message on healing? What was going on here? Did the Lord want to give us a vivid illustration of his power to heal? Was this the devil coming to taunt us and challenge the notion that God could heal today? Was this God's judgment on a man, as in the case of Ananias and Sapphira (Acts 5)? Whatever it was, it was about to cause one preacher in the room to succumb to an anxiety attack. After the initial shock wore off, I asked all the people in the room to pray that God would raise this man up. Someone ran to call the paramedics. When I got to him, I could not find his pulse and his skin was already turning blue. We carried his limp body to the back of the church and placed him on a couch in the foyer. Several of us laid hands on him and began praying for him. By the time the paramedics got there, he had not only begun to breathe, but was able to stand up under his own power. Several people there, including a nurse, were sure this man had died and been brought back to life.

I don't know whether Clement Humbard really did die that night. I don't know if our prayers helped bring him back to life. I only know that, when I returned to the pulpit, the story of Eutychus had a great deal more relevance for me than it had about twenty years earlier. Until that night, Acts 20:7–12 had been part of the unreal Bible in my experience. Now I understood God intended the raising of Eutychus to be relevant to the church of our day.

HEROES LIKE US

The problem with the unreal Bible is not a new one. It was in the first-century church as well. James wrote:

> Is any one of you sick? He should call the elders of the church to pray over him and anoint him with oil in the name of the Lord. And the prayer offered in faith will make the sick person well; the Lord will raise him

up. If he has sinned, he will be forgiven. Therefore confess your sins to each other and pray for each other so that you may be healed. The prayer of a righteous man is powerful and effective (5:14–15).

Apparently, James could feel the skepticism of some of his readers. They might have been thinking something like this: *It is all well and good for you to say that, James. After all, you are the Lord's brother. You and the other apostles saw the Lord do these kinds of things, and we know that you have done them, but how can you expect us to pray for people and see the same kinds of miracles? We're just ordinary folk. But you, you are a special person. These kinds of things happen to special people. Surely you don't think God would use us to do miracles, do you?* Here's how James answered these objections. He promised his readers God would use them to heal sick people (5:14–16),[1] and then he offered them a biblical illustration of a miracle from Old Testament times. He wrote:

Elijah was a man just like us. He prayed earnestly that it would not rain, and it did not rain on the land for three and a half years. Again he prayed, and the heavens gave rain, and the earth produced its crops (James 5:17–18).

At first glance James' reasoning doesn't seem very convincing because he picks one of the Old Testament's most supernatural prophets. You can almost hear the critics replying, "But Elijah was a special man, living in a special time." James' point is just the opposite. He says that "Elijah was a man *just like us.*" James meant that Elijah demonstrated the same kind of instability and inconsistency seen in our lives today. After calling fire down from heaven, and then praying down a heavy rain to end a three-and-a-half-year drought, Elijah became filled with fear and ran from the woman Jezebel (1 Kings 18:3). He became so despondent that he prayed for God to take his life. Later, when God came to retrieve him, Elijah's conversation with God demonstrated he was filled with self-pity and self-centeredness (1 Kings 19:10). That's why Elijah is such a powerful illustration. His prayers were used to accomplish miracles, even though he was a man *just like us.*

James was encouraging his readers to read a *real* Bible and to believe it. Don't write off the experiences of a person like Elijah by thinking he was a special man who lived in a special time. According to James, these same things can happen to us today.

The author of Hebrews had a similar way of applying the Bible. He wrote, "Do not forget to entertain strangers ..." (Heb. 13:2a). Now listen to the motivation he gave his readers for being hospitable, " ... for by doing so some people have entertained angels without knowing it" (v. 2b). This is exactly what happened to Abraham in Genesis 18. Angelic visitations did not stop in Abraham's time. What happened then, happens today—just read your Bible. This is the spirit in which the New Testament authors used the Old Testament. These weren't the only special people or the only special times. *Anyone who knows God is a special person living in a special time.*

HOW NOT TO READ THE BIBLE

So many of us have been conditioned to read the Bible in terms of *our experience* rather than in terms of the experience of the people in the Bible. If we don't hear God's voice today in special ways, we assume he is not speaking in special ways anymore. If we don't see miracles today, we assume he's not doing miracles anymore. Yet the Bible is filled with dreams, visions, miracles, and many other supernatural experiences. Liberal churchgoers simply deny that these things ever happened. They say these stories are myths that were never meant to be taken literally, they were just meant to illustrate great theological truths.

Many conservative churchgoers are appalled anyone would ever read the Bible like this. They want nothing to do with the rationalistic unbelief of liberals. They are certain every miracle in the Bible took place just as it's recorded. Yet when it comes to applying the Bible to today's experience, many conservatives are filled with the same kind of unbelief as the liberals. For many orthodox Christians, the Bible is a book of abstract truths about God rather than a guide into the supernatural realm of God's power.

Two sad effects invariably result from reading the Bible in such a de-supernaturalizing manner. First, we experience very little of God's supernatural power. Why? Because we have neither the faith to pray for miracles nor the confidence that God can speak to us in any supernatural way. Why do we lack faith?

Because our method of reading the Bible has taught us not to expect these things. This leaves us with a moralistic version of Christianity that believes discipline is the key to the spiritual life. *Our* discipline. Mix that discipline with a little help from God, and it causes us to be better people while we are on the way to heaven. For example, we might study the book of Proverbs and try to discern principles for raising our children, but we never learn how to pray with the kind of faith that delivers a homosexual son from his homosexuality or a teenage daughter from drugs. Beyond taking us to heaven, we don't expect too much from God. And usually we get what we expect.

The second result of de-supernaturalizing the Bible is described by Dallas Willard:

> The other problem that arises when we do not understand the experience of biblical characters in terms of our own lives is that we simply stop reading the Bible altogether. Or else we take it "in regular doses," choking it down like medicine because someone told us that it would be good for us, though we really do not find it to be so.
>
> The open secret of many "Bible believing" churches is that only a very small percentage of their members study the Bible with even the degree of interest, intelligence, or joy they bring to bear on their newspapers or *Time* magazine. In my opinion, based on considerable experience, this is primarily because they do not and are not taught how to understand the experience of biblical characters *in terms of their own experience.*[2]

I could not agree with Professor Willard more. I was the pastor of a Bible church for a number of years. During that time I did not believe God spoke in any reliable way except through the Bible, nor did I believe he was doing miracles or healings today. My number-one prescription for the people was, "Read your Bible every day." The most frequent confession I heard from my church members in those years was, "I don't read my Bible."

It is hard to read a book every day that tells how God supernaturally intervenes in the daily lives of his children, and yet see no practical relevance for these supernatural phenomena in our present experience. Once the supernatural element is taken out of the Bible, it becomes merely a moralistic life guide. And God becomes a remote God who helps his people, but not very much.

The Bible is more than a theological treatise. It is a guide to dynamic encounters with a God who works wonders. The Bible was given to us that we might hear God's voice and respond to that voice with life-changing faith. Yet it is all too common for Bible-believing people to read the Bible without ever hearing that voice.

ARE WE FOLLOWING THE PHARISEES?

The Pharisees read, studied, and memorized the Bible more than most churchgoing people today will ever do, but unlike Moses and the other Old Testament heroes, they could not hear God's voice. Jesus said the Pharisees never heard his Father's voice at any time (John 5:37). The Pharisees claimed to be looking for the coming Messiah, but they never really expected the Old Testament examples of supernatural phenomena to be repeated in their lifetime. They had a theoretical belief in the supernatural—they believed in angels and the resurrection of the body—but expected nothing supernatural in their own lives. They did not listen for God's voice apart from the Scriptures, and they never heard his voice in the Scriptures.

A word of caution here: Please don't make the mistake of thinking that since the Pharisees weren't Christians, you and I can't repeat their sins today. Any Christian can fall into sin. The Pharisees are the New Testament's monumental warning of what can happen to religious people when they become proud. There is no more effective way to drown out the voice of God than through the noise of pride. And no believer is exempt from the sin of religious pride.

There are a number of examples from the New Testament that show us that God still speaks today in ways other than the Bible—examples from the lives of Jesus, the apostles, and others. It would be easy to discount these examples by saying these were special people living in special times. But this would be a very *unbiblical* way of reading the Bible. A more biblical way is to think of Jesus as our supreme example of both how to live and how to minister.

Think of the apostles as James said to think of Elijah, "as men like us who prayed earnestly." Consider the possibility of angelic visitations as suggested in Hebrews 13:2. Remember what Paul said of the miracles and judgments that happened to the Israelites in the wilderness, "These things happened to them as examples and were written down as warnings for us, on whom the fulfillment of the ages has come" (1 Cor. 10:11). The miracles of the Bible are still examples and warnings for contemporary Christians.

Most of my life I've read the Bible more like a Pharisee than a New Testament Christian. Most of my life I've made the mistake of believing God for too little. For the rest of my life, if I have to make a mistake, it's going to be believing God for too much. But how can you believe an omnipresent, omniscient, omnipotent God for too much, especially when he himself says, "Everything is possible for him who believes" (Mark 9:23)?

The Voice of God
in the Bible and History

3

Jesus and the Voice of God

In the words of a sad country song, Myra Wattinger "was down on her luck and down on her love." Alone and penniless, she wandered through the South Texas towns of the 1940s, finally getting a job caring for an elderly man. The pay was pitiful, but at least she had the security of a place to sleep and food to eat.

Myra had a history of what psychiatrists today would call "rejection." She and her husband had recently divorced. Although he was prosperous, he refused to give her any money. Her parents had died when she was an adolescent, so she had no one to turn to for help.

As Myra sat in the house watching her elderly employer sleeping, she thought her life had sunk as low as it could go. Sadly, she was wrong. The devil had planned a new torment for her, something that would even bring her to the point of killing herself. One day, while the old man was sleeping, she found herself alone in the house with one of his sons. The son, an alcoholic, had previously made sexual advances toward Myra. Although Myra had made it clear she found him and his actions repulsive, on this day he was determined not to be refused. He raped her.

Nothing in Myra's short difficult life came close to the humiliation of that afternoon's violation. *How God must hate me,* she thought. *Why else had he let this happen? What had she done to make him so angry?*

Whenever she tried to talk to God about her situation, she heard nothing from him. It could have been the turmoil of her emotions, or the fact that she had no real history of conversation with God, that kept her from hearing his tender comforts and promises. But Myra didn't ponder either of these options. Instead, she concluded that God had abandoned her.

Sometimes when things can't get any worse, they, in fact, do. The incidence of pregnancy in forcible rape is incredibly low, less than three pregnancies out of every hundred rapes. Myra's body defied those odds. It seemed to her God had gone out of his way to add one last torment to her misery—to have her become pregnant through the rape. God was forcing her to carry the drunken brute's child.

Even if Myra had been able to support a child, she had no intention of supporting *this* child. She had been forced to endure the humiliation of the rape, but she was not going to let the rapist, or even God, force her to endure the humiliation of the pregnancy. It just wasn't fair. She shouldn't have to suffer any more consequences from that horrible afternoon. She decided to kill the baby.

But her doctor wouldn't cooperate. Quickly, Myra found out that in South Texas in the 1940s it was not easy to get an abortion from a physician. She still thought the best course of action would be to kill the baby with or without the help of a doctor—without anyone's help if it had to be that way.

These were the thoughts battling for the control of Myra's mind on a spring afternoon in 1943, as she trudged back home from the physician's office. Sitting on the back porch of the home where she had been raped, a new option came to her mind— suicide. Just at the point when the thought of suicide seemed to promise the quickest end to her pain, there came an urge from somewhere deep within her spirit to pray. She looked up to heaven and cried out, "Lord, I am carrying this child, and I don't know what to do."

She was never really sure afterward if the voice was audible or not. It was, however, as clear as any voice she had ever heard. God said to her, "Have this baby. It will bring joy to the world."

Those two, short divine sentences dispelled all thoughts of suicide and abortion. Heaven's words have a power that no voice from hell can match. When Myra heard those words, not only did her destructive thoughts leave, but the joy of heaven entered into her soul and crowded out the depression and anguish. She was convinced God would give her a baby girl whom she would call Joy, for according to God, this baby girl would bring joy to the world.

On October 9, 1943, Myra brought her baby into the world in the charity ward of St. Joseph's hospital in Houston, Texas. Things began to go wrong immediately. Myra almost died in childbirth. The baby turned out to be a boy and not a girl as she had thought. The next few years were not easy for Myra or her young son. They were often separated, with the boy in a foster home.

Over the following years, the son showed no promise at all for fulfilling his heavenly destiny of bringing joy to the world. He did become a Christian in his early teenage years, but showed no promise for Christian work. In fact, he was so incredibly shy he simply could not speak in any kind of public setting.

The summer after the young man graduated from high school he went to a revival meeting, and, on the last night of the revival meeting—a Friday night—he *heard* God calling him to preach. It was as clear as an audible voice, although no one else would confirm it. They all knew this young man was not gifted for any sort of public ministry.

On Monday he went back to work at the chemical plant. Most of the men who worked at the plant were not Christians. Their conversation was filled with profanity, dirty jokes, and sexual references about their wives and mistresses. While this talk had never bothered the young man before, what had happened to him on the previous Friday night made all of the obscenity unbearable. As he listened to the men on the job and then again at lunch, where two hundred of the workers gathered around two flatbed trailers, the young man was overcome by compassion for the workers and filled with anger at the sin separating them from Christ. Suddenly, without realizing what he was doing, he jumped up on one of the flatbed trucks, and shouted to all two hundred of his coworkers, "Listen to me!" The men stopped chewing on their sandwiches and stared in amazed silence.

"I am just a boy out here trying to learn how to be a man. All you men are teaching me is how to talk filthy, think filthy, live filthy, be filthy! Men, I wouldn't talk about a dog the way most of you talk about your wives. But God loves you. And he gave Jesus to die for you." This was the introduction to the young man's first sermon. Pipe fitters, insulators, craftsmen, and their helpers sat stunned as they heard these words. As the young man continued to preach, the conviction of the Holy Spirit swept over them. When he stopped speaking, no one said a word. They just hung their heads and shuffled back to their jobs—without realizing a revival had just begun in their chemical plant. Over the next few weeks the young man had the privilege of leading many older workers to Christ. It became apparent to all that he was called to be an evangelist. Some thirty years later, that young man has been responsible for leading millions of people to believe in Jesus as their Lord and Savior.

His name is James Robison.

In the spring of 1943, his mother, Myra, was truly surprised by the voice of God saying, "Have this baby. It will bring joy to the world." Who would have ever thought a baby conceived through rape would bring joy to the world? Who would have ever thought that an incredibly shy young man who had no ability to speak in public would be responsible for introducing millions of people to Jesus Christ? What God said to Jeremiah could have also been said to James Robison: "Before I formed you in the womb I knew you, before you were born I set you apart; I appointed you as a prophet to the nations" (Jer. 1:5).

James, and others who knew him, objected to this call, just as Jeremiah did: "'Ah, Sovereign LORD,' I said, 'I do not know how to speak; I am only a child'" (Jer. 1:6). However, James was not being called *because* of his abilities but *in spite* of them, and for the sovereign purposes of God. His heavenly Father had saved his life with two short sentences spoken from heaven to a mother determined to kill him. And in due time the God who makes even the wrath of man praise him (Ps. 76:10 NASB) would give James the ability to fulfill his divine calling.[1]

Today it seems strange to many of us that God would speak so clearly and personally of a child's destiny at his conception, especially one conceived like Myra's baby. In the world of the Bible this was not so unusual. Many times God spoke at or before the birth of children, especially those children destined to play a prominent role in his kingdom.[2] This was certainly the case in the most famous of all the births in the Bible. Like the birth of Myra's son, this birth also occurred in "questionable" circumstances. Without the heavenly voice, no one would have ever guessed the role this Son was destined to play in his Father's kingdom.

THE BIRTH OF JESUS AND THE VOICE OF GOD

When it came time for God's Son to dwell on the earth, who could have foreseen that an elderly priest at the end of his ministry and his barren wife would have a significant role to play in the earth's greatest visitation? That's why God had to send the angel Gabriel to Zechariah and Elizabeth. Even with the majestic Gabriel standing before him, Zechariah could not believe the message that a special son would be given to him in his old age. It just wasn't possible for an old woman to have a child.

Zechariah made the mistake of asking Gabriel for a sign. The angel told him he would be struck mute until the birth of his son, John the Baptist, the forerunner of the Messiah (Luke 1:5–25). Although Zechariah was a godly man, he became an unwitting symbol of the religious leaders' response to the Messiah: They too would be dumbfounded and filled with unbelief, even in the presence of overwhelming supernatural evidence.

If it wasn't possible for an old woman to have a baby, how about a teenage virgin conceiving a son without a man's help? This was Gabriel's next message. But the biological impossibility of Gabriel's announcement wasn't the hardest part to believe. His word to the young virgin Mary contained what seemed the most outlandish spiritual absurdity ever uttered—a human womb was about to become the first home on earth for the Savior of the world. All of the fullness of God was about to be compressed into the womb of a teenager. Who could have ever imagined that God would stoop so low? Yet Mary believed Gabriel when he said, "For nothing is impossible with God" (Luke 1:37). These words would become the motto of Jesus' own ministry, and later, the motto of the New Testament church.

In addition to this, the birth of Jesus also teaches something very important about the voice of God.

Jesus Found Only by Divine Revelation

Even though nothing is impossible with God, no one could have guessed how he intended to send his Son to the earth. No one found the way to the baby Jesus without direct revelation from the Holy Spirit. Zechariah knew what was about to happen because the angel Gabriel told him. Mary knew her womb would become his first home on earth because of Gabriel's announcement. Elizabeth had to be filled with the Holy Spirit in order to recognize Mary was carrying the Lord Jesus. Joseph had to be told in a dream or he would have divorced Mary. The shepherds found their way to the child through an angelic announcement, and the Magi were guided to him by a star. Simeon and Anna were moved by the Holy Spirit to recognize him and speak prophetically of his mission. The most striking *absence* at the birth of Jesus was that of the current reigning religious intelligentsia. The Bible scholars of the day never made it to the manger.[3]

God was setting the pattern early for all to see: *no one would ever find their way to Jesus without direct, supernatural revelation.* Religious scholarship, human intelligence, political power, and social influence were all insufficient guides.

This divine pattern shows that even knowledge of the Bible is an insufficient guide to Jesus. After all, the Old Testament had prophesied the major events surrounding the birth of the Messiah. Matthew pointed out Isaiah had prophesied the Messiah would be born of a virgin. The religious leaders knew Micah had prophesied the Messiah would be born in Bethlehem. The Old Testament was clear that the Messiah would be persecuted. Matthew reminded his readers that the Old Testament, properly understood, prophesied the Messiah would be called out of Egypt just as Israel had been called out of Egypt at the time of Moses.[4]

But the Old Testament never said which virgin, where, or at what time. No one could understand the application of these prophecies without supernatural guidance. Even though the scribes knew the Messiah was to be born in Bethlehem, that knowledge ultimately proved worthless to them because it was not illumined by the Holy Spirit. The revelatory ministry of the Holy Spirit surrounding the birth of Jesus demonstrated that we are utterly dependent on the voice of God to find and recognize the Messiah. Everyone who got to the crib of Jesus had to be guided by something or someone greater than their own Bible knowledge. The birth of Jesus teaches us the need for supernatural guidance, regardless of our intellect or knowledge of the Bible.

The Humility of God

Another of the major lessons taught to us by the birth of Jesus is how utterly humble God is. The God who lives "in a high and holy place" (Isa. 57:15) made his first home on earth the womb of a young woman. He made his second home a stable—not the nice, warm manger scenes you see at Christmastime, but a crude, first-century, Palestinian stable filled with steaming piles of manure. The Light of the World entered Bethlehem in the dark of night. The Word of God became a speechless infant. The One destined to clothe a heavenly army in clean, white linen was wrapped in coarse strips of cloth. The Bread of Life was laid in the feeding trough of an animal. No one *expected* something like this of God, so most people couldn't *accept* it. No one could have imagined that the Creator of the universe would stoop so low, could be so humble.

God's humility is both a blessing and a very great problem for us. A blessing, because his humility leads him to fellowship with people as low as we are. A problem, because his humility leads him to come to us in ways that make it easy for us to reject him.[5] No one would have imagined God would enter the world in a stable, or that he would allow his Son to be born with the stigma of illegitimacy hanging over him.[6] No one would have thought the Son of God's first visit to his temple would be in the form of a helpless infant. All but two worshipers that day crowded past the little baby who one day would redeem them (Luke 2:21–38).

The relevance of the manner in which Jesus was born frequently escapes the church. The first two chapters of Matthew and Luke are not just nice stories given to make us feel warm and sentimental once a year at Christmas. The birth of Jesus shows us something of the very character of God and how he relates to his fallen creation. His highest purpose for the earth was birthed in a stable—his highest purposes are *still* being birthed in stables. Who would have ever thought Myra's little baby, conceived through a forcible rape, would grow up to love God and lead millions of people to Jesus? Yet without the voice of God, Myra might have killed her son, and the One who controls our destinies might have chosen another woman's baby to fulfill his purposes.

But Myra did hear and believe, just as Mary heard and believed. The humility of God surprised Myra just as it did Mary.

God's humility ought to surprise us too. God is so humble he doesn't mind the shame of the stable or the stigma of illegitimacy. Have you ever noticed God's preference for the humble, the lowly, and the afflicted (Isa. 57:15; 66:2)? Have you ever noticed how he resists the proud (Ps. 138:6; 1 Peter 5:5)? The humble will share the shame of the stable, but the proud won't even come near it. The birth of Jesus teaches us that the humble will be the first to hear the voice of God. Whether driven to it through desperate circumstances or having acquired it through careful cultivation, the quality of humility is essential for hearing the voice of God.

As we pass from the birth of the Messiah to look at Jesus the man, we will find the same themes emerging again: the necessity of supernatural revelation, and the requirement of humility to receive that revelation.

THE MINISTRY OF JESUS AND THE VOICE OF GOD

He was sitting at the front of the church, glaring at me. I was only five minutes into the message when I noticed him. Every time I looked at him, I was caught by his steely eyes. Everything about this older man, from his facial expression to his body language, showed contempt and disdain for me. Every time I looked at the second row on my left, I could visualize him saying to me, "You young, insolent know-it-all. You don't know what you are talking about." I was sure he was an unbeliever who had been forced to come to the meeting that night in order to please his wife. Perhaps he was even a member of an occult circle who had come specifically to disrupt the meeting.

It was the third night of a conference that had been going well until this point. Normally, things like this in the audience don't bother me. This night, though, the hatred I felt coming from this man was getting to me. After about thirty minutes of his nasty glare, I became a little desperate. I actually thought about stopping the meeting and speaking to him in public in front of everyone. I went from being irritated to being distracted. I finished the last part of the message by looking away from the man and staring at the people on my right

After the message was over, I was standing off to the side talking to some people. Out of the corner of my eye, I noticed him approaching me. I was overjoyed. *The Lord hath delivered him into mine hand,* I thought. I turned to face him. Now I would have a chance to pay him back for the solid hour of uninterrupted hostility he had directed toward me. Involuntarily, I clenched my fists.

When he got within three feet of me, the man had that same nasty look on his face. Both of his hands shot out at once. He grabbed my right hand, taking me by surprise. But instead of wrestling me to the floor, he actually shook my hand with both of his. He said, "I want to tell you what a blessing you have been to me. I prayed the prayer you suggested last night, and it was the first time in months I have had a peaceful night's sleep. You are like an angel sent from God."

I was dumbfounded. "Well, I could tell you were really into the message tonight," I said. "Tell me about yourself."

He told me his wife had prayed for him for years to become a Christian. About a year or so before, the Lord had answered her prayers, and he had been born again. After he had become a Christian, everything began to go wrong. He and his wife suffered severe financial problems, health problems, and other calamities. For the last few months, he had had severe insomnia. Satan had come almost immediately to challenge this man's conversion experience, and my new friend had been beaten up badly.

What I had interpreted as anger in the man's face and eyes was not anger, but pain. I had mistaken confusion and torment for hostility. I had looked at a man's face, which had nothing but affection for me, and read hostility into it. And what is worse, I had allowed my misreading to distract me from proclaiming the Word of God.

You want to know the funniest thing about that evening? The text of my sermon was:

> The Spirit of the LORD will rest on him—the Spirit of wisdom and of understanding, the Spirit of counsel and of power, the Spirit of knowledge and of the fear of the LORD—and he will delight in the fear of the LORD. He will not judge by what he sees with his eyes, or decide by what he hears with his ears; but with righteousness he will judge the needy (Isa. 11:2–4).

At the same time that I was encouraging everyone in the room to depend on the Holy Spirit rather than on their eyes for discernment and telling them how deceiving appearances can be, I was judging this man with my eyes! After that night, you could never convince me God doesn't have a sense of humor, or that I'm not capable of sinking into profound depths of spiritual blindness.

I believe that, if at any time during that sermon I would have asked God the source of this man's anger or pain, God would have graciously shown me I was not the cause of it. But I never stopped to ask. I allowed myself to be guided by what my eyes saw, and I thought I knew what was motivating this man. When you consider the pattern of Jesus' ministry, you will notice this is a mistake he never made.

Not by What His Eyes See

As shown above, appearances are not always what they seem, and our natural senses may frequently deceive us. This is why it is important to judge or evaluate by the Spirit rather than by relying solely on our senses.

The story of Jesus' encounter with the Samaritan woman at Jacob's well is a wonderful illustration of his ability to judge by the Spirit rather than by appearances (John 4:1ff.). When others looked at the Samaritan woman, they saw a woman with an immoral past. When Jesus looked at her, he saw a woman with deep spiritual thirst. He offered her Living Water to satisfy that thirst, but because she had no idea who he was, she misunderstood the offer.

Although her thirst was real, the woman's past was a barrier keeping her from the Living Water that was just within her reach. The past had to be dealt with before she could receive the water. "Go, call your husband and come back," Jesus said.

"I have no husband," she replied.

"You are right when you say that you have no husband. The fact is, you have had five husbands, and the man you now have is not your husband. What you have just said is quite true."

"Sir, I can see that you are a prophet . . ."

You know the rest of the story. She was so changed by this encounter with Jesus that through her testimony many of the Samaritans came to see Jesus and believed in him.

This is a typical example of the ministry of Jesus. He did not judge by what his eyes saw or his ears heard. Instead, *through the Spirit*, he saw this woman's spiritual thirst, that she had had five husbands, and that she was living in immorality with a sixth man. *Through the Spirit,* Jesus saw the steps necessary to bring this woman into the kingdom of God.

The Limitations of Jesus' Humanity

Some people feel such incidents from the life of Jesus are not valid examples of what our ministry ought to be like today. They say that Jesus was God, and he should be expected to function with omniscience. This is true, of course. Jesus was and is God— fully God and fully man. He is omniscient. He is also omnipresent and omnipotent. However, the Scriptures teach that Jesus restricted the use of these divine attributes when he took on the form of man (Phil. 2:6–11)[7].

This was what it meant for Jesus to become human. He could become hungry (Matt. 4:2), thirsty (John 19:28), and tired (John 4:6). His human body could only be in one place at a time. In his human nature, like other children, "Jesus grew in wisdom" (Luke 2:52). In his adult ministry, he learned things through natural means (John 4:3). He did not know the "day or hour" of his second coming (Matt. 24:36). Instead of depending on his own power for healing, he waited until "the power of the Lord was present for him to heal the sick" (Luke 5:17). And there were times when he allowed the unbelief of people to limit his healing ministry (Mark 6:1–6; Matt. 13:58). So even though Jesus was fully God, he took on the limitations of humanity in such a way that he did not heal, prophesy, or minister out of his own divine power.[8] But he did minister in power. From where did this power come?

The Source of Jesus' Power

The Scriptures are extraordinarily clear about the source of Jesus' power. His supernatural ability came from the Holy Spirit, who infused his humanity with grace, wisdom, and miraculous powers. The total dependence of the Messiah upon the Holy Spirit was prophesied by Isaiah (11:1–5; 42:1–4; 61:1–3). At his conception, it was the Holy Spirit who gave the Son of God his human body (Luke 1:35). At his baptism, the Holy Spirit came on him and remained on him (Matt. 3:16; John 1:32). At his temptation, he was led and empowered by the Holy Spirit to do battle with Satan. Luke wrote that Jesus was "led by the Spirit in the desert," and that he was also "full of the Holy Spirit" at the beginning of his conflict with Satan (Luke 4:1).

At the beginning of Christ's public ministry, both Luke and Jesus himself made it absolutely clear that the source of power in Jesus' ministry was not his deity, but rather his dependence on the Holy Spirit.

> Jesus returned to Galilee *in the power of the Spirit,* and news about him spread through the whole countryside. He taught in their synagogues, and everyone praised him. He went to Nazareth, where he had been brought up, and on the Sabbath day he went into the synagogue, as was his custom. And he stood up to read. The scroll of the prophet Isaiah was handed to him. Unrolling it, he found the place where it is written: *"The Spirit of the Lord is on me,* because *he has anointed me* to preach good news to the poor. He has sent me to proclaim freedom for the prisoners and recovery of sight for the blind, to release the oppressed, to proclaim the year of the Lord's favor." Then he rolled up the scroll, gave it back to the attendant and sat down. The eyes of everyone in the synagogue were fastened on him, and he began by saying to them, "Today this scripture is fulfilled in your hearing" (Luke 4:14–21).

This same testimony appears again in the middle of his ministry. Jesus said he cast out demons by "the Spirit of God" (Matt. 12:28). Matthew said on one occasion when a great crowd had followed Jesus that "he healed all their sick" (Matt. 12:15). At first glance, you might think Matthew attributed this healing power to the deity of Jesus, [9] but just a few verses later, Matthew said that this fulfilled the prophecy of Isaiah: "I will put my Spirit on him" (Matt.12:18 citing Isa. 42:1). After Jesus was resurrected and ascended, Peter summed up his ministry in the following way: "How God *anointed Jesus of Nazareth with the Holy Spirit and power,* and how he went around doing good and healing all who were under the power of the devil, because God was with him (Acts 10:38).

Thus the Old Testament prophets, Jesus himself, and his apostles all attribute the divine power in his ministry not to the uniqueness of his deity, but rather to the ministry of the Holy Spirit through him. Now let's take a closer look at the role of the Holy Spirit and divine revelation from the Father in Jesus' ministry.

THE DIVINE PATTERN FOR MINISTRY: HEARING IN ORDER TO SERVE

It was normal for Jesus to hear from his Father before he did or said things. Jesus said his ministry was guided by this great principle: He did what he saw his Father doing (John 5:19). This way of living did not originate with Jesus. It has always been God's ideal for his servants. Over fourteen hundred years earlier, God had taken Moses on a mountain where he showed him a heavenly vision of what the tabernacle was to look like. Then he warned him to make the earthly tabernacle according to the pattern he saw (Ex. 25:9, 40; Acts 7:44; Heb. 8:5). This has always been the best way to live and to minister—see it in heaven and copy it on earth. It is the essence of all sincere prayer—"Thy will be done, on earth as it is in heaven" (Matt. 6:10 NASB). No one can do God's will on earth unless God first reveals his will from heaven. He reveals, we copy. He initiates, we respond.

Jesus didn't originate this pattern, but he fulfilled it on a far grander scale than anyone could have ever imagined. Moses constructed an earthly tabernacle according to the heavenly pattern, but Jesus has constructed a spiritual temple, the church, which will never be overcome by the powers of darkness. He did this by following one simple principle for all life and ministry: he only did what he saw his Father doing.

John repeatedly emphasized this theme in his gospel. In his humanity, Jesus claims he can do nothing of himself, so he *judges* as he hears his Father judge (John 5:30). His *teaching* does not originate with himself but with his Father (John 7:16). He *speaks* only the words of his Father (John 8:28; 12:49–50; 14:10, 24). In short, he *does* exactly what his Father commands him (John 14:31). In every instance, he presents himself as a servant under orders in unbroken communion with his Father. And he does all of these things—judges, teaches, speaks, obeys—not out of his deity but by the Spirit who rests upon him without limit (John 3:34).

Even the Holy Spirit himself conforms to this same pattern. Jesus said that the Holy Spirit "will not speak on his own; he will speak only what he hears, and he will tell you what is yet to come" (John 16:13). Hearing God in order to serve God is the New Testament pattern, even for the Spirit of God.

Shouldn't it be the pattern for our lives as well?

Do we need to hear him any less?

JESUS, THE HOLY SPIRIT, AND US

Among all the servants of God, Jesus is indeed unique. He is unique because he is God. He is unique because he is the only human ever to obey God perfectly and live a sinless life. He is unique in that he did not simply announce the kingdom of God as other prophets did, but he brought the kingdom with him in his Person. He is unique in his authority within the kingdom: "All authority in heaven and on earth has been given" to Jesus (Matt. 28:18). He is unique in his atoning sacrifice on the cross and in his high priestly office.

He is not unique, however, in the source of power for his earthly ministry. His power to live a moral life and to minister miraculously is unequivocally attributed to the power of the Holy Spirit.

To be sure, Jesus made better use of the Holy Spirit's power than anyone before or after him. He was so reliant on the Spirit that he lived a sinless life. No one will ever duplicate that feat. But does that mean Jesus should not be our moral model? Of course not. If his moral perfection doesn't prohibit him from being our model of purity, why should his use of the Holy Spirit's power for hearing God and doing miracles preclude him from becoming our model for the miraculous?

Jesus *listened* to God, and then as one empowered by the Holy Spirit, he *spoke* and *acted*. He passed this same method of ministry on to his apostles, promising them he would send the Holy Spirit to empower them. The Holy Spirit would speak to them, teach them all things, bring all the words of Jesus to their remembrance, testify to Jesus, guide them into truth, and reveal the future to them (John 14:26; 15:26; 16:13). The end result was that the apostles heard

God in supernatural ways and worked miracles just as their Master had done. Jesus was their model for ministry.

But he wasn't only the model for the apostles. He was the model for all Christians. Stephen and Philip were "full of the Spirit" (Acts 6:3, 5; 7:55) like Jesus, so they too heard God in supernatural ways and worked miracles (Acts 6:8, 10; 7:56; 8:6–7, 13, 26, 29, 39).

What do we have in common with Jesus, the apostles, Stephen, Philip, Agabus and other New Testament prophets, and all the charismatically gifted believers in the New Testament churches like those at Corinth, Rome, Ephesus, Thessalonica, and elsewhere? According to the apostles, what we share with them is the *very same power* that gave them the supernatural ability to hear God and work miracles. Paul's prayer is that all Christians would come to recognize the inheritance that belongs to them through the presence of the Holy Spirit and know "his incomparably great power for us who believe. That power is like the working of his mighty strength, which he exerted in Christ when he raised him from the dead and seated him at his right hand in the heavenly realms" (Eph. 1:19–20).

Since we share the same Holy Spirit who empowered Jesus and his followers in the first century, why not let them be our models for what is possible in the Christian life? After all, on more than one occasion Jesus taught that "everything is possible for him who believes" (Mark 9:23; Matt. 21:21–22; Mark 11:23). Even the dead can be raised when we believe (John 11:40). I can't recall a place in the Bible where Jesus took back this teaching, nor can I think of a place where the apostles "toned it down" in their writings.

Dr. Gerald Hawthorne, Professor of Greek and New Testament Exegesis at Wheaton College, has studied every single New Testament reference concerning the Holy Spirit in the life and ministry of Jesus. His conclusion is worthy of full consideration.

> And as it was true of Jesus, so it is true of his followers: "As the Father has sent me, even so I send you" (John 20:21b). As Jesus was filled and equipped by the Spirit, so those who belong to Jesus are filled and equipped by the Spirit (Acts 2:4), or at least potentially so (Eph. 5:18). Just as it was true that this filling of Jesus enabled him to be and do the extraordinary, so it is true of those who

believe in him. The Acts of the Apostles (or "of the Holy Spirit"), to say the very least, was intended to show something of the nature of those things that God is able to do through people who yield themselves willingly to the influence of the Spirit. Through the Spirit those people of the very early church were enabled to preach boldly, convincingly, and authoritatively (Acts 2:14–41), to face crises and surmount obstacles with a courage and resoluteness and power they never dreamed they had (4:29–31), to cheerfully face persecution and suffering, and even to accept death with a prayer of forgiveness (5:40–41; 7:55–60), to heal the sick and raise the dead (9:36–41; 28:8), to arbitrate differences and bring about peace (15:1–35), to know where to go and where not to go, what to do and what not to do (16:6–10; 21:10–11), and so on.

There is no reason whatsoever to believe that what was true of those earliest Christians is any less true of Christians in this century. Surely contemporary crises are no less great, the pains of the world are no less meliorated, the challenges to one's strength, wisdom, patience, and love are no less demanding of resources beyond human resources than they were in the first century, and followers of Jesus today are no more sufficient for all these in and of themselves than were his followers yesterday. Furthermore, God's program of enabling people to burst the bounds of their human limitations and achieve the impossible is still in place and still effective—that program that involves filling people with his Spirit, filling them with supernatural power.[10]

Thus Professor Hawthorne concludes that Jesus is to be our model in *every area of life.* Can you think of a better model? Is there someone else who would be a better example of how we are to hear the voice of God?

If we reject Jesus, the apostles, and the New Testament churches as our models for hearing God today, then we are left with no biblical models for hearing him. Who then should we trust to show us how to hear his voice?

4

The New Testament Church and the Voice of God

A missionary who had a history of being persecuted—once he was almost beaten to death—had come to a new city to start up another work. This was his seventeenth year in the mission field. He was so effective in witnessing for Jesus in this new city that the enemies of the Gospel organized against him and began abusing him. He knew where all this was leading. Soon they were going to try to kill him.

He thought about the time he had almost been killed by a wild mob. He thought about other times when he had been beaten and tortured for the sake of the Gospel. Then he thought about the times he had escaped from different places just before a satanically energized crowd had been able to hurt him.

His work had been going well, no doubt about that. One of the major leaders of an opposing religion had even been won to Christ. But perhaps this was one of those times when the better part of wisdom dictated he flee so he could live to preach another day. He dwelled for a moment on the wounds which had almost been mortal and how painful they had been and how long the pain lasted and how long it had taken him to heal. He never wanted to go through that again. Perhaps he would leave soon.

That night when he fell asleep, Jesus appeared to him in a vision and told him not to be afraid. Some might try to attack him, but no one would be able to harm him—not this time. Jesus made it clear that there were many more people in this new city who were going to respond to the Gospel.

The missionary awoke the next morning, renewed and encouraged by the vision. It all happened just as the Lord said it would. The persecution intensified, but he was not harmed. Over the next eighteen months many were saved through his ministry. If it hadn't been for this vision, the missionary might have left. Or if he had stayed, he might have suffered unnecessary stress, worrying about his own safety. This missionary had learned long ago that he was not intelligent enough or godly enough to figure out things like this for himself. He knew how easy it was to be deceived by appearances and circumstances. Therefore, he had come to rely on the voice of the Lord, not only in the Bible, but in dreams and visions, in his human spirit, and in other ways. He had been surprised by God's voice in its many forms and had been saved by it more times than he could remember.

Occasionally, when one of my students or someone from the church would tell me a story like this, skepticism would automatically well up within my heart. My first question was usually, "Can this story be documented?" Most of the time, these kinds of stories could not be. So I simply dismissed them as having no relevance to the Christian life. The story I have just related, however, can be documented. Maybe you have already guessed the identity of this veteran missionary. This particular episode in his career is documented in Acts 18:1–18. The missionary was the apostle Paul. And the city in question was Corinth. I frequently use examples like this one to encourage people to believe that hearing God in dreams, visions, impressions, and in other ways is simply normal New Testament Christianity.

Some, though, object that this is not normal Christianity. They maintain that even though these kinds of revelatory experiences may happen once in a while, they are so infrequent they should not be considered important ways of listening to God. I used to think like that—until I started reading the book of Acts with an open mind. The book of Acts is incredibly important for our understanding of what it was like to be Christian in the early days of the church. It is made up of stories that illustrate how Christians lived immediately after Jesus had gone to the cross and been resurrected. The book of Acts doesn't deal in theories about

how the Christian life *should* be lived. It gives us realistic por-
trayals of how the first century Christians *actually* lived.

Let's survey the book of Acts to determine just how common
supernatural revelation was in the early church.

THE PREPARATION OF THE FIRST WITNESSES

At the beginning of Acts, the resurrected Lord and his eleven
apostles were standing on the Mount of Olives. Jesus had just finished telling them to wait in Jerusalem for the baptism of the Holy
Spirit. Their first question showed how little they understood their
apostolic mission, "Lord, are you at this time going to restore the
kingdom to Israel?" (Acts 1:6). That question drew the following
rebuke. "It is not for you to know the times or dates the Father has
set by his own authority" (Acts 1:7). The last time the apostles
asked a question like this it provoked a long discourse from Jesus
on his second coming and the end of the age (Matt. 24:4ff.). During
this discourse he had explicitly told them, "No one knows about
that day or hour, not even the angels in heaven, nor the Son, but
only the Father" (Matt. 24:36). He had already told them that their
question was out of bounds, but they asked it again anyway.

After promising them power from the Holy Spirit, he was
taken into heaven before their very eyes. Instead of returning to
Jerusalem, as he had instructed them, the apostles stood on the
Mount of Olives, gazing skyward. Two angels were sent to say to
them, "Men of Galilee ... why do you stand here looking into the
sky? This same Jesus, who has been taken from you into heaven,
will come back in the same way you have seen him go into
heaven" (Acts 1:11).

Think about the implications of this scene. The book of Acts
opens with supernatural communication, the resurrected Lord and
two angels speaking to the apostles. Right at the beginning of
church history, we are being taught that the church will be built by
supernatural revelation, not by cleverly devised human programs.
Not even the apostles were capable of designing an adequate blue-
print for the church. Although they had three and a half years of
special training by the best Teacher, they appear at the beginning
of Acts to have comprehended very little of their teacher's program
for redeeming the earth. They are divinely led back to Jerusalem to
wait for understanding and power to be given them.

THE EMPOWERING OF THE FIRST WITNESSES

Chapter 2 of the book of Acts tells the story of the empowering of the first witnesses. The chapter begins with an explosion of revelation—"Suddenly a sound like the blowing of a violent wind came from heaven and filled the whole house where they were sitting" (Acts 2:2). Wind is a common symbol of the power of the Holy Spirit to produce life.[1] The Spirit had come "suddenly," and "from heaven" to breathe life into the body of the infant church, just as God once breathed life into the lifeless body of the first man. The Spirit did not come in response to long years of planning and dedication on the part of God's people. No, the power of an indestructible life filled the room that day because God himself had sent the Spirit. The tongues of fire represented inspired, prophetic speech that would declare "the wonders of God" (Acts 2:11). All the supernatural phenomena in the upper room indicated that the proclamation of the church would be divinely inspired by heaven.

The sound of the wind and the sight of the fiery tongues attracted a huge crowd to the place where the 120 believers had just been filled with the Holy Spirit. Some in the crowd were both "amazed" by the supernatural phenomena and "perplexed"— they did not understand what it meant (Acts 2:12). Others missed the supernatural character of the event altogether and mocked the 120, thinking they were drunk (Acts 2:13).

Peter saw both the confusion and the skepticism. He "stood up with the Eleven, raised his voice and addressed the crowd" (Acts 2:14). The speech Peter gave the crowd was a prophetic proclamation inspired by the Holy Spirit.[2] The fulfillment of the ancient prophecy of Joel 2:28–32 had just begun. Peter began his speech by quoting this prophecy:

> In the last days, God says, I will pour out my Spirit on all people. Your sons and daughters will prophesy, your young men will see visions, your old men will dream dreams. Even on my servants, both men and women, I will pour out my Spirit in those days, and they will prophesy. I will show wonders in the heaven above and signs on the earth below, blood and fire and billows of smoke. The sun will be turned to darkness

and the moon to blood before the coming of the great
and glorious day of the Lord. And everyone who calls
on the name of the Lord will be saved (Acts 2:17–21).

In other words, the coming of the Holy Spirit inaugurated
an *age of revelation*. Instead of having only a few prophets in each
generation, now "your sons and daughters will prophesy."
Visions and dreams were now normal for the people of God.
There were no longer age, economic, or gender restrictions on
the Holy Spirit's revelatory ministry. He was to inspire both sons
and daughters, along with male and female servants, to prophesy and to understand revelatory phenomena. The Spirit was
coming in such power with diverse revelatory phenomena
because he was giving birth to a prophetic people. Just as the
Holy Spirit "overshadowed" a young Jewish girl so that the
Leader of all the prophets was conceived in her womb, so the
Holy Spirit now "overshadowed" the 120 so that the prophetic
church could be born—prophetic because its head is the King of
the prophets.

The prophetic birth of the church is symbolic of the fact that
God's program to redeem the earth could not have been thought
up by or executed by the plans of man. Acts 1 and 2 depict a
church birthed by revelation. These chapters teach us that apart
from supernatural revelation the church will never fulfill its
redemptive mission on the earth.

THE PATTERN UNFOLDS

Some Christians live all their lives without ever consciously
experiencing a direct communication from the Father, Son, Holy
Spirit, or one of the heavenly angels. They are so used to reading
the Bible in terms of their own experience that it is easy for them
to miss one of the book of Acts' most astonishing characteristics.
When they read it, their *lack of experience* with God's voice selec-
tively filters out Luke's emphasis on divine supernatural com
munication between God and his servants. They either miss or
refuse to consider the implications of Acts' startling repetition of
supernatural revelation.

With the exception of chapter 17, every chapter of Acts contains an example of, or a reference to, supernatural revelatory

communication from God to his servants. Consider the following examples:

Chapter 1. After his resurrection, Jesus appeared to the eleven (vv. 3–9). After Jesus ascended into heaven, angels came down and gave the eleven directions (vv. 10–11). Finally, Matthias was chosen by lot to take Judas' place. Presumably, God was supernaturally guiding the decision of the lot just as he did in Old Testament times (v. 26).

Chapter 2. A violent wind and tongues of fire swept in the room where the 120 were praying, and they all spoke in tongues (v. 2–4). Then Peter preached an inspired sermon, quoting the promise of prophetic ministry from Joel 2:28–32 (vv. 14ff.).

Chapter 3. The healing of the lame man at the temple gate called Beautiful revealed the glory of Christ (v. 13).

Chapter 4. Peter's defense of the Gospel and the apostles' ministry was an example of preaching inspired by the Holy Spirit and also a fulfillment of Jesus' own prophecy in Luke 12:11–12 and 21:12–15 (vv. 8ff.).

Chapter 5. Peter prophesied the death of Ananias and Sapphira (v. 3ff.). An angel freed the apostles from jail (vv. 19–20).

Chapter 6. Stephen performed miraculous signs and wonders and spoke so effectively by the Holy Spirit that no one could refute him (vv. 8, 10).

Chapter 7. In Stephen's final moments, the Lord Jesus revealed himself to Stephen so that he could actually see the Son of God standing at the right hand of the Father (v. 55).

Chapter 8. First an angel from heaven gave directions to Philip for ministry (v. 26), and then the Holy Spirit spoke to him directly, giving him further directions (v. 29). Finally, the Spirit himself carried Philip away to Azotus (v. 39).

Chapter 9. Jesus appeared to Saul and gave him the beginning of his commission on the Damascus road (vv. 3–6). Jesus spoke to Ananias and sent him to minister to Saul (vv. 10–16).

Chapter 10. An angel appeared in a vision to Cornelius and told him to send for Peter (vv. 4–6). In the meantime, God caused Peter to fall into a trance, gave him a vision, and declared to him that all foods were clean (vv. 10–16). The Holy Spirit spoke to Peter and told him to go with the three men Cornelius had sent (v. 19). While Peter was preaching to Cornelius, the Holy Spirit fell on Cornelius and all the Gentiles in his house so that all of them spoke in tongues (v. 46).

Chapter 11. The prophet Agabus correctly predicted a famine (v. 28).

Chapter 12. An angel visited Peter in his jail cell and delivered him from certain death (vv. 7–11).

Chapter 13. The Holy Spirit spoke to the church at Antioch, telling them to set apart Barnabas and Paul for a specific ministry (v. 2). On his first missionary journey, Paul accurately predicted a judgment against the sorcerer Elymas so that Elymas was blinded (vv. 9–12).

Chapter 14. While Paul was preaching at Lystra, there was a man sitting in the audience who had been lame from birth. Paul looked at him while he spoke and supernaturally saw that the man had faith to be healed. Paul told the man to stand up, and he was instantly healed (vv. 9–10).

Chapter 15. The Holy Spirit communicated to the apostles and elders in the Jerusalem council that it was good not to burden the Gentiles with the law (v. 28).

Chapter 16. On his second missionary journey, the Holy Spirit forbade Paul and his companions to preach the gospel in Asia (v. 6). The Holy Spirit also denied Paul and his companions permission to enter Bithynia (v. 7). Later on this journey Paul was given a vision of a man in Macedonia, beckoning them to come over and help (vv. 9–10). This proved to be the direction in which the Lord was leading Paul's missionary team. At Philippi the Lord specifically opened Lydia's heart to believe the Gospel Paul was preaching (v. 14).

Chapter 18. The Lord spoke to Paul in a night vision and told him that no one would harm him and that the Lord had many people in the city of Corinth (v. 9–11).

Chapter 19. Twelve believers at Ephesus, on whom Paul laid his hands, spoke in tongues and prophesied (v. 6).

Chapter 20. Paul spoke of the supernatural guidance of the Holy Spirit when he said he was compelled by the Spirit to go to Jerusalem (v. 22). He also said the Holy Spirit had warned him that suffering was waiting for him (v. 23). Paul gave a prophetic word to the Ephesian elders when they had gathered to meet him at Miletus that they would never see him again (v. 25).

Chapter 21. A number of believers urged Paul *through the Spirit* not to go to Jerusalem because they knew of the danger waiting for him there (v. 4). This chapter also records that Philip's four daughters were all prophetesses (v. 9). Agabus prophesied to

Paul that the Jews of Jerusalem would bind Paul and hand him over to the Gentiles (vv. 10–11).

Chapter 22. Paul retold the story of his conversion and how the Lord appeared to him on the Damascus road (vv. 6–16). He also told about his first visit to Jerusalem after his conversion when, in the temple, he had fallen into a trance in which the Lord warned him to leave Jerusalem and revealed he was sending him to the Gentiles (vv. 17–21).

Chapter 23. The Lord appeared to Paul while he was held prisoner in Jerusalem and encouraged him by telling him he would not only testify about Jesus in Jerusalem, but he would also testify in Rome (v. 11).

Chapter 24. In Caesarea, Paul gave a speech before Felix, the governor, that was inspired by the Holy Spirit in fulfillment of Luke 12:11–12 and 21:12–15 (vv. 10–21).

Chapter 25. Paul gave another speech at Caesarea to Festus, the governor who succeeded Felix, that must be viewed in the same light as the speech of chapter 24, an inspired utterance by the Holy Spirit in fulfillment of Luke 12:11–12 and 21:12–15 (vv. 8–12).

Chapter 26. When king Agrippa came to visit Paul, he retold the story again of his conversion and how the Lord had appeared to him on the Damascus road (vv. 9–16).

Chapter 27. Paul accurately predicted the destruction of the ship meant to take him to Rome (v. 10). An angel of the Lord appeared to him during the night, telling him he would not drown in the shipwreck and that God would spare the lives of all on board with him (vv. 21–26).

Chapter 28. In the final chapter, God supernaturally spoke through miracles. The first miracle occurred when a poisonous viper bit Paul's hand, but he was not hurt (vv. 3–6). This led to a series of miracles in which Paul was used to heal all of the sick on the island of Malta (vv. 7–9).

REVELATION IN THE EARLY CHURCH

The book of Acts portrays a church that lives by revelation. But what do the biblical writers mean when they speak of revelation? And why was God's revelatory activity so vital to the early church?

In the New Testament, "revelation" refers to a secret God has made known. When God "reveals" something, he is showing us something we could not know, or did not know, through natural means. For example, in the context of defending his apostleship, Paul said,

> Fourteen years later I went up again to Jerusalem, this time with Barnabas. I took Titus along also. I went *in response to a revelation* and set before them the gospel that I preach among the Gentiles (Gal. 2:1–2).

By using the term "revelation," Paul is telling us he did not go because he thought it was a good idea or because he felt pressured by others. He went because God directed him. He doesn't tell *how* the revelation came. Apparently that wasn't important for his readers to know. What was important was that they understood it was the Lord himself who had directed him. If the Lord had not given the revelation, Paul would not have known he was supposed to be in Jerusalem.

Paul was confident that God would reveal things to ordinary Christians. He wrote to the Philippians,

> Let us therefore, as many as are perfect, have this attitude; and if in anything you have a different attitude, God will *reveal* that also to you (Phil. 3:15 NASB).

In effect, Paul was telling the Philippians that he knew some of them had a different attitude about maturity than he had. However, this didn't seem to bother him. He was confident God could remove the veil from their eyes and make known to them the same truth God had revealed to him. Paul could have used logical arguments or an apostolic command to force his view on the Philippians, but instead he seems to have believed this would be an unnecessary use of his apostolic authority. He trusted the revealing ministry of God to change the Philippians' attitude. Both Paul's letters and the book of Acts demonstrate that Christians never outgrow their need for God's revelatory ministry.[3]

AGENTS OF REVELATION

The ultimate source of revelation in the early church is God the Father. He is the one who poured out the Holy Spirit (Acts

2:17ff.) and who "anointed Jesus of Nazareth with the Holy Spirit and power" (Acts 10:38). Normally, however, when God chooses to reveal something to one of his servants in the book of Acts, the agents of revelation are the Holy Spirit, Jesus, or angels.

The Holy Spirit Reveals

The Spirit may speak directly to individuals, telling them where to go and what to do (Acts 8:29; 10:19–20), or he may speak to a whole church, telling them how to begin a new missionary enterprise (Acts 13:2). The Holy Spirit can hinder or forbid a missionary team when they unwittingly begin to leave the geographical will of God (Acts 16:6–7). On other occasions the Holy Spirit may compel a person to go to a certain destination (Acts 20:22). And the Holy Spirit may warn a faithful servant ahead of time about the suffering that will accompany the fulfillment of the servant's task (Acts 20:23).

The Holy Spirit may also inspire a sermon or testimony for Jesus. When Peter was brought before the religious leaders to give an account of the healing of the lame man, he was "filled with the Holy Spirit" (Acts 4:8). The filling of the Holy Spirit is the power of God speaking through an individual.[4] On other occasions, however, it is said that believers themselves speak "through the Spirit" (Acts 11:28; 21:4). The guidance of the Holy Spirit may even become so dramatic that he supernaturally transports a believer from one place to another, as in the case of Philip (Acts 8:39). The leadership of the early church was so sensitive to the Holy Spirit they could describe his leading by saying, "It seemed good to the Holy Spirit and to us . . ." (Acts 15:28).

Jesus Reveals

Jesus appears to Stephen as he is being stoned to death (Acts 7:55) and to Paul on the Damascus road. Paul's experience was so foundational for the history of the early church that it is told three separate times in the book of Acts (9:3–6; 22:6–16; 26:9–16). The Lord also appeared to Ananias and gave him specific instructions for his ministry to Paul (Acts 9:10ff.). We don't know how many times Jesus appeared to Paul throughout his ministry, but the book of Acts does record three appearances of Jesus to Paul that occurred after his conversion. In these cases, Jesus appeared to Paul giving him directions, comfort, and encouragement (Acts 18:9–11; 22:17–21; 23:11). I began this chapter by describing the first of these appearances, which occurs in Acts 18:9–11. The other two are instructive as well.

Paul described the first appearance of the Lord to him after his conversion:

> When I returned to Jerusalem and was praying at the temple, I fell into a trance and saw the Lord speaking. "Quick!" he said to me. "Leave Jerusalem immediately, because they will not accept your testimony about me." "Lord," I replied, "these men know that I went from one synagogue to another to imprison and beat those who believe in you. And when the blood of your martyr Stephen was shed, I stood there giving my approval and guarding the clothes of those who were killing him." Then the Lord said to me, "Go; I will send you far away to the Gentiles" (Acts 22:17–21).

In this instance, the Lord spoke to Paul for three reasons. First, to give him protection through a warning, "they will not accept your testimony about me." Second, to give him direction, "Leave Jerusalem immediately . . . I will send you far away." And third, to provide Paul with a long term definition of his ministry, "I will send you far away to the Gentiles." At first, this did not seem to Paul to be the best possible plan. It made more sense to stay in Jerusalem. After all, he was well-known, no one would doubt his sincerity, and he had impeccable credentials. He was sure he would be a credible witness to other Jewish leaders. But he was wrong. In fact, if he had stayed, he would have been *dead* wrong. This episode in Paul's life is a perfect illustration of Isaiah 55:8–9:

> "For my thoughts are not your thoughts, neither are your ways my ways," declares the LORD. "As the heavens are higher than the earth, so are my ways higher than your ways and my thoughts than your thoughts."

God had a radically different *perspective* on the situation in Jerusalem than Paul did. He also had a very different *way* for Paul to minister than Paul had planned. If God had not spoken to him,

Paul would never have known God's particular thoughts and ways for him at this point in his ministry.

The third recorded instance of Jesus appearing to Paul after the Damascus road conversion took place in Jerusalem. After a violent dispute in the Sanhedrin, the Roman commander put Paul in protective custody. "The following night the Lord stood near Paul and said, 'Take courage! As you have testified about me in Jerusalem, so you must also testify in Rome'" (Acts 23:11). This proved to be an extremely timely word of encouragement from the Lord, for "the next morning the Jews formed a conspiracy and bound themselves with an oath not to eat or drink until they had killed Paul" (Acts 23:12). Paul did not have to worry about the success of their plot because the Lord had personally appeared to him, assuring him that he would carry the testimony of Christ to Rome.

There is another way in which Jesus is revealed to be a primary agent of revelation in the early history of the church. Lydia was born again when "the Lord opened her heart to respond to Paul's message" (Acts 16:14). Neither the book of Acts in particular, nor the Scriptures in general, ever credits anyone's salvation to his or her own disciplined study or pursuit of God. It is always God who takes the initiative and opens a person's heart to believe.

Angels Reveal

Angels were famous for engineering jail breaks (Acts 5:19–20; 12:7–11). They also appeared to various servants of the Lord with specific directions, as in the case of Philip (Acts 8:26) and Cornelius (Acts 10:4–6). On Paul's voyage to Rome, an angel came to him in the night and said, "Do not be afraid, Paul. You must stand trial before Caesar; and God has graciously given you the lives of all who sail with you" (27:24).

DOES THE BOOK OF ACTS REPRESENT NORMAL CHRISTIANITY?

The biblical evidence is clear: Jesus heard his Father's voice both within and outside the Scriptures. So did the apostles and the first-century Christians. The book of Acts shows what it was like to experience God in the first-century church. Remember, in every chapter, with the exception of chapter 17, Christians experience direct supernatural communication.

Through repetition, which is one of the common teaching techniques of the New Testament writers to emphasize their most important themes,[5] Luke was teaching his readers that neither they nor the early church could do without God speaking to them in all the diverse ways characteristic of the creativity of an omnipotent and omniscient God.

Why should this surprise us? Isn't this just what Jesus said would happen when he sent the Holy Spirit? He promised his disciples that the Holy Spirit would *teach* them all things, *remind* them of his words, *testify* about him, *guide* them into all truth and *show* them things to come.[6] Teaching, reminding, testifying, guiding, and showing are all normal functions of the Holy Spirit, according to Jesus. So when the Holy Spirit came, he taught Peter that the wind, fire, and tongues in the upper room were what Joel prophesied long before.[7] When Peter was confused about the events in Cornelius' house, the Holy Spirit reminded him of the words Jesus had spoken earlier, and thus guided him into truth.[8] When Peter stood before the Sanhedrin, the Holy Spirit filled him, and he testified about Jesus.[9] When Peter stood before the deceivers Ananias and Sapphira, the Holy Spirit showed him they had lied to God and would die.[10] Teaching, reminding, testifying, guiding, and showing—exactly what Jesus said the Holy Spirit would do.

And these activities were not confined to the apostles. The same things happened in the lives of Stephen, Philip, Agabus, Ananias, and other unnamed individuals in the book of Acts.[11]

Some try to dismiss the testimony of Acts by calling it a transitional book. But transition to what? A better form of Christianity? Where is this better form? Or is the transition to a type of experience where God speaks only in the Bible? That form of Christianity is not a transition forward, but rather backward, to the religion of the Pharisees who preferred the Book over the living, speaking Word of God (John 5:36–47). The transition Jesus predicted was to an age of revelation by an omniscient Spirit who would surprise God's people by teaching, reminding, testifying, guiding, and showing. And that's just what the Holy Spirit did in the first-century church.[12]

Still, the experience of some Christians leads them to conclude the Christianity of Acts is not normal Christian experience.

Okay, for a moment let's concede that the book of Acts represents abnormal Christianity. In the same way, we could also say that the apostle Paul's passionate devotion to Jesus Christ was abnormal. How many people have you met who could truthfully say with the apostle Paul, "I do all things for the sake of the Gospel" (1 Cor. 9:23 NASB)? Or "For to me, to live is Christ" (Phil. 1:21)? I've found this kind of passion to be abnormal in the church today. But wouldn't we be better off to choose the abnormal in this case?

If Acts represents abnormal Christianity when compared with the present state of the church, wouldn't we be better off to choose the abnormal experience of Acts? Isn't it a biblical principle never to be content with our experience of God, but to always want more of his presence, more of his voice, more of his power? We are to be content with our material possessions (Heb. 13:5), but we are never to be content with our present experience of God—thankful, but not content. To be content means to become Laodicean, lukewarm, complacent. And lukewarm believers are in danger of losing the conscious presence of God (Rev. 3:14–22). Wouldn't it be safer to assume that *normal* Christian experience is depicted in the book of Acts rather than in the Western church? Then, if for some reason or other we don't attain the goal, at least we can't be charged with not trying, with settling for less than what God is willing to give.

Before we close this chapter, there's a danger we need to consider. If we say that the book of Acts represents an abnormal state of Christianity, we may be unwittingly guilty of judging Scripture.[13] When we say it is abnormal, we are comparing the experience of the New Testament church in the book of Acts to *something else which we regard as normal.* Is this "something else" another scriptural history of the New Testament church? No, the book of Acts is the only inspired, inerrant account we have of the church's history. None of the histories of the church written since Acts have the same divine authority or truth. Because its ultimate Author is God, the book of Acts is a perfect witness to the kind of life the early church experienced. It is also a witness meant to teach us about life in God.

Luke's repeated stress on the creative ways in which the voice of God broke through every kind of barrier in every kind of circumstance to speak, warn, guide, deliver, inspire, comfort, predict, and judge, ought to make us careful about calling these experiences abnormal. It could be that if we're not experiencing these things, it is *our* experience of God which is abnormal, rather than the experience of the New Testament Christian.

Don't misunderstand me. I am not saying we should experience an unbroken chain of angelic visitations and audible voices. Even the apostles were forced to live with ambiguity and endure the silence of God. Sometimes God let an apostle die an "untimely" death as in the case of James, while on another occasion he sent an angel to deliver Peter from execution.[14] There will always be times when "the word of the LORD was rare; there were not many visions" (1 Sam. 3:1). Who can deny the sovereign ebb and flow between the ocean of heaven and the shores of earth? But aren't we to long for the flow rather than be content with the ebb?

If all things are possible for him who believes, and Acts shows us some of these possibilities, shouldn't we make the Christianity of Acts our goal? Better yet, why should we assume that Acts represents the apex of Christian experience? What if the Lord of history really has saved his best wine for the last days? Wouldn't you like to drink it?

I never saw a miracle, never heard God's voice outside the Bible, until the Christianity of Acts became a serious model for me. Since that turning point, I have experienced many of the same things reported in apostolic times. I know credible witnesses who have experienced more than I have. I believe Acts *does* represent normal Christianity. And anything less really is less.

The very same thing could happen to you if you gave God a chance to speak to you as he did to those in Acts. Somewhere I read that it only takes the faith of a grain of mustard seed.

5

Presbyterian Prophets?

Years ago, I was on the pastoral staff at Vineyard Christian Fellowship of Anaheim, California. One Sunday evening instead of going to our adult service, I took one of the staff prophetic ministers with me and went to spend the evening with our ten to twelve-year-old kids in their version of children's church. There were about 150 to 200 of these kids in a large room in the back of the church. When we got them all seated, I told them they could ask me any question they wanted. It could be about the Bible, or church, or what it was like to be a pastor, or anything they wanted to ask. I hadn't even thought to pray or ask God for special direction that evening. After all, they were just kids. Obviously, what they needed most was knowledge of the Bible, and I was sure I was qualified for that task. Truthfully, I felt overqualified, awesomely overqualified. How hard could it be to answer the questions of ten to twelve-year-old church kids?

The first child raised his hand. "Pastor," he said, "why is it that bad things happen to people who love God and try to follow him?"

Hmm, I thought. *Why do bad things happen to good people?* Theologians have been grappling with the problem of suffering for two thousand years, and no one has really solved its mystery. Even the book of Job never tells the ultimate reason why God permitted all Job's suffering. I mumbled some sort of answer about God not wanting robots but rather friends with freedom and dignity. It didn't impress the kids all that much. They looked a little bored.

A second hand went up. "Pastor, why did God create the devil?"

Hmm, why did God create the devil? Again, I mumbled some sort of answer about God not wanting robots but rather friends with freedom and dignity. They were less impressed than before and looked more bored. It went on like this for forty-five minutes. I had begun to think that some demon from hell had smuggled the kids a list of all the unsolved theological problems for the last twenty centuries and said, "Here kids, ask him these." I decided to retire from the theological question-answering business. I looked over at the prophetically gifted pastor I had brought in with me and said, "Has the Lord shown you anything about these kids? He sure isn't showing me much."

"Yes he has," he said. "He has shown me something about this young lady right here," with that he pointed to a young, cute twelve-year-old girl sitting in the front row, "about that young man back there," he pointed to a twelve-year-old boy sitting in the middle of the room, "and about this lady in the back," he pointed to one of the Sunday school teachers in the back of the room.

He looked at the young girl. "What's your name?" he asked.

"J-J-Julie." Julie was not so sure she wanted someone giving her a prophetic word in front of two hundred of her peers.

"Julie, while Jack was speaking I had a vision of you. It was Tuesday night. That's five nights ago. You went to your bedroom and shut the door. You were crying. You looked up to heaven and said, 'God, do you really love me? I have to know—do you really love me?' God didn't say anything to you on Tuesday night, Julie. He sent me here tonight to tell you he really loves you. *He really loves you.* He also told me to tell you that the trouble going on around you is not your fault. He didn't tell me if he is going to change the trouble, but he wants you to know you aren't the cause of it."

Then he went on to say something about the young man and something about the lady. After it was all over, I called those three people up to the front so we could talk privately. I wanted to make sure of two things—one, that there were no misunderstandings between the people and the prophetic minister, and two, that everything that had been said was true. If part of the messages given to these people was false, then we wanted to own up to it and clear up any misconceptions.

"Julie, last Tuesday night were you in your bedroom crying really hard, and did you ask God if he really loved you?" I asked.

"Yes."

"Are your parents fighting now?"

"Yes."

"Are they talking about getting a divorce?"

"Yes."

"Do you think that's your fault?"

She looked up at me, smiled, and said, "Not any more."

I walked out of church that night thinking, *Who in the world could be against this ministry? Why wouldn't anyone want the voice of the Lord to speak like this in their church?* I know what it is like to carry the guilt for something a parent did. My father "divorced" my mother by committing suicide when I was twelve years old. I know how hard it is for a twelve-year-old mind to understand something like that. I know what it is like to feel guilty for not treating my father better, especially in his last weeks. I know what it's like to grow up thinking if I had been a better son, perhaps my dad wouldn't have left us. I was thinking about my dad and my own sense of guilt when I walked out of church that night.

Then I thought about a little twelve-year-old girl in Anaheim, California, who won't be sitting in some psychiatrist's office when she is thirty years old, trying to get rid of guilt she has carried around for the last twenty years. Even if her parents divorce, she will never blame herself for it. The prophetic word of the Lord came to her and delivered her from that guilt. The prophetic word of the Lord convinced her that God really does love her. And the prophetic word of the Lord convinced about two hundred of her friends that night that the God they talk about in church really does know everything about their lives and loves them in spite of it.

THE DEBATE

Why would anyone be against this kind of ministry? Some people have never experienced the kind of positive prophetic ministry I have described with Julie. All their experience with "prophets" has been negative. Just the word "prophet" conjures up images of cult leaders and charlatans in the minds of many people today.

Others oppose the idea of modern day supernatural revelation because they think it might lead to new books being added to the Bible. They don't want to give anyone that kind of authority, and neither do I. To them, a prophet is someone like Isaiah, or Jeremiah, or the apostle Paul, who wrote inerrant Scripture. They don't see anyone today with the authority of an Old Testament prophet or a New Testament apostle. Therefore, they conclude that prophecy and prophets, along with supernatural revelation, died out with the last of the New Testament apostles. They believe the only *reliable* form of communication from God is the Bible.

Well, I had a Bible in my hand the Sunday night I walked into the room where little Julie was sitting, but my Bible didn't tell me that she was hurting, or that her soul was being crushed under guilt that was not her own. Neither did her expression or body language reveal any of the pain she felt that night. There was no sign around her that proclaimed she thought God might not love her. I didn't pray or ask for help that evening because I had confidence in my "awesome knowledge" of the Bible. I have observed over the years that when a person thinks they possess awesome knowledge of a sufficient Bible, they don't tend to ask God for many directions. They don't need to, because they have all the directions they ever need in their awesome knowledge of the Bible.

That evening God was not interested in using my awesome knowledge. Actually, he was determined not only to hide my knowledge of the Bible from the kids, but also to give them a false impression of my intelligence. After the kids had received about 45 minutes of *my* ministry, I turned to the prophet, ready to let him fail for a while. The "prophet" who came into the room with me was oblivious to the present hurts and needs of the children as well. But the difference between us was that the prophet didn't have a great confidence in his biblical knowledge, so he asked God to show him how to minister to the kids. Without consulting me, God had decided to use the prophet—but not the prophet's intelligence or knowledge of the Bible. I had a Bible; my prophetic friend had a vision.

God could have used the Bible to tell Julie he loved her. He could have used the Bible to remove her false guilt. But he didn't. He used a vision. He bypassed our plans, our intelligence, our knowledge of the Bible, and sovereignly, through a vision, filled the room with his presence and the heart of a twelve-year-old girl with his love.

I still believe my Bible is more reliable than anyone else's visions. I'll take the certainty of a text of Scripture any day over the shadowy character of a vision—if I get to choose. Unfortunately, when you serve a sovereign God, you don't always get to choose. Sometimes you have to make a few adjustments to his way of doing things. Apparently, he enjoys speaking in a variety of ways and expects us to listen to any way in which he chooses to communicate. The more of his ways that we *can* hear, the more we *will* hear.

BUT HE'S NOT A PROPHET

For some people, the most disconcerting fact about the experience with Julie is that the vision came through a young "prophet" who sometimes makes mistakes. To be fair to him though, I should mention that he is right the majority of the time. Some people mock a statement like this. They ask, "Would you trust a Bible that was only right a majority of the time?" That would depend on what the Bible claimed. If the Bible claimed absolute authority and inerrancy but was only right a majority of the time, the answer is, "No, I wouldn't trust that kind of Bible."

On the other hand, I trust teachers, pastors, evangelists, and friends who all make serious errors. None of the people I trust are right all the time. None of them claim that. Neither do any of the mature prophetic people I know. The most gifted prophetic people I know advise everyone to test their words and to make no decision solely on the authority of the prophetic words they have been given. All prophetic words outside the Bible are subject to the Bible's authority.

Some people think one missed or failed prediction makes a person a false prophet. The Bible, though, doesn't call someone a false prophet for simply missing a prediction. In the Scripture, false prophets are those who *contradict* the teaching and predictions of true prophets and attempt to lead people away from God and his Word.

My friend certainly doesn't fit into this category. Besides, the fruit of his vision about Julie was good fruit. That vision removed false guilt and produced love for God. It filled all of us with a sense of awe at God's omniscience and love. Jesus tells us in Matthew 7:15ff. that the way to discern between false and true prophets is to examine the fruit of the prophet's ministry. Bad fruit comes from a false prophet. Good fruit comes from a true one.[1]

Perhaps my friend is not a false prophet, some will concede, but all the same, you still can't call him a prophet. Why? Because he is not 100 percent accurate, and according to Deuteronomy 18:15–22, *all* Old Testament prophets were 100 percent accurate. I don't believe this is the correct interpretation of that text, nor do I believe the New Testament teaches that all New Testament prophets would be 100 percent accurate in their noncanonical prophecies; that is, in their prophecies God did not include in the completed Bible.[2] But for the time being, I'll go along with the idea that we can't call someone a prophet who is not 100 percent accurate. Then what do we call them?

Pushing aside the debate over terminology and theory, consider this fact: We do have *prophetically gifted* people in the church today. Some of the most gifted of these can regularly predict the future, tell you the secrets of your heart, receive accurate impressions and dreams, see accurate visions, and some are even used to do miracles. I don't really care what we call these people, as long as we are wise enough to see the value of their ministries and benefit from them.

Since the beginning of the New Testament church, God has given prophetically gifted ministers to each generation of believers, just as he has always given evangelists, pastors, and teachers.[3]

REFORMATION PROPHETS

There is one period and one tradition, however, in which you would expect to find no prophets. I am referring to the Protestant tradition during the time of the Reformation. One of the Reformers' principle concerns was to preserve the unique authority of the Bible. One of their great cries was *Sola Scriptura,* "the Scriptures alone." They argued against their Catholic opponents because they saw them making their tradition equal to the authority of the Scripture. The Reformers persecuted the Anabaptists because they saw them making claims to divinely inspired revelations they considered equal to the Scriptures in authority. Because the Reformers rejected the claims to miracles and prophetic inspiration in both the Catholic and the Anabaptist traditions, you would not expect to find any prophets or prophetically gifted people in the Reformed tradition during this period of conflict. This is, in fact, not the case. Let's take a look at one relatively brief time period and one relatively narrow section of Reformed history and faith. Get ready for a surprise.

George Wishart

George Wishart (c. 1513–1546) was one of the early Scottish Reformers and a mentor of John Knox. He was a powerful evangelist and teacher of the Bible. Knox regarded Wishart as a prophet. What kind of a prophet?

> He was not only singularly learned as well in godly knowledge as in all honest humane science, but also he was so clearly illuminated with the spirit of prophecy, that he saw not only things pertaining to himself, but also such things as some towns and the whole realm afterward felt, which he forespake, not in secret, but in the audience of many . . . .[4]

Wishart's Protestant doctrines, prophetic power, and popularity with the people earned him the implacable hatred of David Beaton, Cardinal and Archbishop of St. Andrews, Scotland. Cardinal Beaton hated the Reformers not so much because they threatened the doctrine of the Catholic Church, but because he viewed them as a threat to international political alliances he valued.[5]

Wishart's public lectures on the book of Romans were so well attended in Dundee that Beaton used his influence to have the local magistrate forbid Wishart to preach again in that city.[6] The magistrate, Robert Mill, delivered the charge in public at the conclusion of one of Wishart's lectures. The preacher looked toward heaven and remained silent for a while. No one moved. Then at last he said,

> "God is my witness, I never desired your trouble, but your comfort; . . . but I am sure, to reject the word of God and drive away his messengers, is not the way to save you from trouble, but to bring you into it. . . . When I am gone . . . if it be well with you for a long while, I

am not led by the Spirit of truth; but if unexpected trouble comes upon you, remember this is the cause, and turn to God by repentance, for he is merciful."[7]

Wishart then left town and went elsewhere to preach.

Four days after Wishart left Dundee, a severe plague broke out there. A month later, news of the plague reached Wishart, who was then in western Scotland. He immediately returned to Dundee to comfort the sufferers. When he arrived, he stood at the east gate and preached a sermon on Psalm 107:20, "He sent forth his word and healed them; he rescued them from the grave." At the risk of his life, Wishart stayed with the infected people, caring for them until the plague abated.

Wishart escaped two public attempts on his life through supernatural revelation. He also prophesied in 1545 that the town of Haddington would be judged with a severe plague followed by bondage to foreigners. This was fulfilled in 1548–49, when the town was destroyed by the English. The plague was so severe it hindered even the burial of the dead.

Earlier, having escaped one of Cardinal Beaton's attempts on his life, Wishart predicted the Cardinal would ultimately be successful in his quest to kill the Reformer. When that time drew near, God revealed to Wishart his impending martyrdom. This revelation saved the life of John Knox. When Wishart was leaving Haddington, Knox begged him to let him go along with him to Ormiston. Wishart declined saying, "One is sufficient for one sacrifice." At Ormiston, Cardinal Beaton had Wishart arrested, and through a series of political intrigues and an illegal trial, had him condemned to be burned at the stake for heresy.

On March 1, 1546, they came to Wishart's cell, put a rope around his neck, tied his hands behind his back, fastened sacks of gunpowder about his body, and led him to a specially built scaffold just opposite the foretower of the Cardinal's palace in St. Andrews. Rich cushions had been placed in the windows of the tower so the Cardinal and his guests might watch the spectacle in comfort. When the executioner tied him to the stake, Wishart prayed for his accusers, asking God to forgive them. The executioner was so moved by this he asked Wishart's forgiveness. To which he replied, "Come hither." When his executioner drew near, Wishart kissed his cheek, and said, "I forgive you. Do your work." The man turned and lit the fire. The gunpowder blew up, but Wishart was still alive. When the captain of the castle guard saw this, he told the dying man to be of good courage. Wishart replied, "This flame has scorched my body; yet it has not daunted my spirit." Then referring to Cardinal Beaton, he continued, "He who, from yonder place, looks upon me with such pride, shall, within a few days, lie in the same [i.e., the same castle], as ignominiously as he is now seen proudly to rest himself." These were the last words of George Wishart, the Stephen of the Scottish Reformed Church, the forerunner of revival and renewal.

On May 28, 1546, less than three months after Wishart's death, at about fifty-two years of age, Cardinal David Beaton was murdered in the very palace from which he watched the prophetic martyr's execution, fulfilling Wishart's last prophecy.

John Knox

John Knox (1514–72), the great Scottish Reformer, not only regarded Wishart as a prophet, but also thought he himself had prophetic powers. Many of the people of Scotland also believed Knox to be a prophet. No less an authority than James Melville, divinity professor at St. Andrews University, referred to him as "the prophet and apostle of our nation."[8] One of Knox's most famous prophecies is quoted by a number of his biographers. While on his deathbed, Knox asked his friends David Lindsay and James Lawson to go to the Lord of Grange, William Kirkaldy, whom Knox dearly loved. Kirkaldy was attempting to hold the castle of Edinburgh for Mary, Queen of Scots, against the English army. Knox said,

> Go, I pray you, and tell him for me, in the name of God, that unless he leave that evil course whereon he has entered, neither shall that rock [the castle of Edinburgh] afford him any help, nor the carnal wisdom of that man, whom he counteth half a god [William Maitland of Lethington, Mary's former Secretary of State]; but he shall be pulled out of that nest, and brought down over the wall with shame, and his carcass shall be hung before the sun: so God hath assured me.[9]

Lindsay and Lawson faithfully delivered the message, but Kirkaldy chose to ignore Knox's warning. On May 29, 1573,

Kirkaldy was forced to surrender the castle. The castle gate was blocked with fallen stones due to the English bombardment. Just as Knox had prophesied, Kirkaldy was lowered over the wall by a rope in shame. On the sunny afternoon of August 3, 1573, Kirkaldy was hanged at the Market Cross of Edinburgh. He was facing east, away from the sun, but before he died, his body swung around to the west, so that he was "hung before the sun," just as Knox had prophesied.[10]

John Welsh

John Welsh (c. 1570–1622) was another of the Scottish Reformers who showed remarkable prophetic powers. Samuel Rutherford (1600–1661), one of the most famous of the Scottish Reformed theologians, called Welsh "that heavenly prophetical and apostolic man of God."[11] After spending some of his early years as a prodigal, Welsh returned to the Lord and married John Knox's daughter Elizabeth.

By all accounts, Welsh was an extraordinarily godly man. It was said of him that "he reckoned the day ill-spent if he stayed not seven or eight hours in prayer."[12] When he became the pastor of the church of Ayr, it was not uncommon for him to spend the whole night in prayer at the church.[13] Many of Welsh's prophecies have been recorded, along with their fulfillment. He prophesied accurately about various individuals' prosperity, blessing, and vocation. For example, while Welsh was the pastor at Kirkcudbright, he told a wealthy young man, Robert Glendinning, that he ought to start studying the Scriptures because he would succeed Welsh in the pastoral ministry at Kirkcudbright. The man gave no indication at all that he had any interest in a pastoral career, nor was there any other evidence to lead Welsh to this conclusion, yet it came to pass.[14]

Welsh was also famous for prophesying judgments over individuals. On a number of occasions, he prophesied the loss of house and property to individuals who refused to repent. These judgments came true.[15] He was also known to have prophesied the unexpected deaths of a number of individuals, the most dramatic of which came while Welsh was being held prisoner in Edinburgh Castle before he was sent into exile.

One night at supper, he was speaking of the Lord and his Word to all who were sitting at the table. Everyone at the table was being edified by Welsh's conversation with the exception of one young man who laughed and sometimes mocked him. Welsh endured this for a while, but then abruptly stopped in the middle of his discourse. A sad look came over Welsh's face, and he told everyone at the dinner table to be silent "and observe the work of the Lord upon that mocker." Immediately, the young man sank beneath the table and died.[16]

The people in the city of Ayr regarded Welsh as a prophet. During the time the great plague was raging all over Scotland, the city of Ayr had been spared. The city magistrates set guards at each of the entrances of the city in order to protect it from being infected by any suspicious visitors. One day, two traveling cloth merchants came to the city gates, both with horses packed with reams of cloth. The guards refused to let the merchants in. They called the magistrates, who in turn called John Welsh. They asked him whether they should let the merchants in. After praying for a while, John Welsh advised the magistrates to turn the merchants away, for he feared the plague was contained in the packs of cloth on the horses. The merchants turned and went to the city of Cumnock about twenty miles away, where they were admitted there and sold their goods.

The goods were infected, just as Welsh feared. The plague broke out immediately and killed so many people there were hardly enough living left to bury the dead.[17] After Welsh was imprisoned at Edinburgh castle, the plague did break out in Ayr. The people there came to him asking for help, but he was not permitted to leave the castle. Instead, he directed them to a godly man in their town, Hugh Kennedy, who he said should pray for them, and God would hear him. Immediately after this, Hugh Kennedy led a prayer meeting in the city, and the plague began to decrease.[18]

The most famous incident in Welsh's life occurred while a godly young man, the heir of Lord Ochiltree, captain of the castle of Edinburgh, was staying at Welsh's house. He fell sick there and, after a long illness, died. Welsh had great affection for the man and was so grieved by his death that he would not leave the young man's body. After twelve hours, some friends brought a coffin and attempted to put the body into it. Welsh persuaded them to wait. He stayed with the body a full 24 hours, praying and lamenting the man's death. Again they attempted to put the body into the coffin, but he refused to let them. They came again 36 hours after the death of the young man, now angry with Welsh. He begged them to wait twelve more hours. But after 48 hours, Welsh still refused to give up the body!

At this point, Welsh's friends were beside themselves. They could not understand his strange behavior. Perhaps he thought the young man had not really died but had succumbed to some kind of epileptic fit. So the friends summoned physicians to the room in order to prove to Welsh that the young man was truly dead. With their instruments, they pinched the body of the young man in various places and even twisted a bow string about the corpse's head with great force. No nerve in the body of the corpse responded at all to these measures. The physicians pronounced him dead. One last time, Welsh persuaded both friends and physicians to step into the next room for an hour or two.

Welsh fell down on the floor beside the body and cried to God with all of his strength. The dead man opened his eyes and cried out to Welsh, "Oh sir, I am all whole, but my head and my legs." He was restored to his life and healed of his long illness. The only ill effects he suffered were in his legs where he had been pinched by the physicians and around his head where they had twisted the bow string. Later this young man became Lord Castlestuart, the Lord of a great estate in Ireland.[19]

In addition to Wishart, Knox, and Welsh, there are numerous accounts of prophetic utterances being fulfilled among the Scottish Reformers and Covenanters.[20] This was especially true of the period from 1661 to 1688, when Scottish Presbyterians were being persecuted by the Stuart regime.

Robert Bruce

Robert Bruce (1554–1631) was the leading churchman in Edinburgh in his time, and "it was largely under his influence that the Scottish Reformation found stability."[21] He was known not only for his prophetic ministry but for other supernatural experiences as well. One of his biographers, Robert Fleming, wrote in 1671 that even though he had well-authenticated accounts of many of Bruce's supernatural experiences, he had refrained from writing them down because they would seem so strange and marvelous.[22] He did say this of Bruce:

He was one that had the spirit of discerning in a great measure. He did prophetically speak of many things which afterwards came to pass, yea, which I had attested by sober, and grave Christians, who were familiar with him. Various persons distracted [insane], and of these who were passed all hope of recovery in the falling sickness [epilepsy], were brought to Mr. Bruce and after prayer by him in their behalf were fully recovered . . .[23]

Robert Bruce had a healing ministry in which the insane and epileptics were completely healed! We can only wonder about the nature of the experiences which Fleming considered too supernatural to record. During this period of time, Fleming also mentions angelic visitations, the audible voice of God, bright lights appearing in the darkness, physical manifestations of the Holy Spirit in meetings, and other things equally difficult for today's skeptics to believe.[24]

Alexander Peden

One of the most remarkable prophetic Scottish Covenanters was Alexander Peden (1626–1686). His prophetic ministry was so outstanding he was called Prophet Peden.[25] In 1682, Peden performed the wedding ceremony for the godly couple John Brown and Isabel Weir. After the ceremony, he told Isabel she had gotten a good man for her husband, but that she would not enjoy him long. He advised her to prize his company and to keep a linen burial sheet close by, for when she least expected it her husband would come to a bloody end.[26] About three years later, Peden spent the night of April 30, 1685, at the Browns' home in Priesthill. Peden left the house before dawn. As he was leaving, they heard him repeating these words to himself, "Poor woman, a fearful morning. A dark, misty morning."[27] Not long after Peden had left, John Graham of Claverhouse arrived with a group of soldiers. Graham gave John Brown an opportunity to repent of his conviction that Christ was the head of the church rather than the King of England. Brown refused. "Then go to your prayers, for you shall immediately die," replied Graham. Brown prayed, turned to his wife Isabel and said, "You see me summoned to appear, in a few minutes, before the court of heaven, as a witness in our Redeemer's cause, against the Ruler of Scotland. Are you willing that I should part from you?"

"Heartily willing," said Isabel. John took her into his arms, kissed her good-bye, then kissed his baby boy. He knelt down before his two-year-old daughter, kissed her and said, "My sweet child, give your hand to God as your guide; and be your mother's comfort." When he rose, his last words were to God: "Blessed be thou, O Holy Spirit, that speaketh more comfort to my heart than the voice of my oppressors can speak terror to my ears!" Captain Graham of Claverhouse was enraged at John Brown's godly courage. He ordered six of his soldiers to shoot him where he stood. The soldiers stood motionless, refusing the order. The furious Graham drew his own pistol and shot Brown through the head.

With a cruelty that is difficult to imagine, he turned to Isabel and asked, "What thinkest thou of thy husband now, woman?"

"I have always thought well of him," the widow replied, "but never more than now."[28]

The murder was committed between 6–7 A.M. By that time, Peden was eleven miles away. He entered his friend John Muirhead's house and asked to pray with the family. "Lord," he said, "when wilt Thou avenge Brown's blood? O, let Brown's blood be precious in Thy sight." He explained to the family what he had seen in a vision:

> Claverhouse has been at the Priesthill this morning, and has murdered John Brown. His corpse is lying at the end of his house, and his poor wife sitting weeping by his corpse, and not a soul to speak comfortably to her. This morning, after the sun-rising, I saw a strange apparition in the firmament, the appearance of a very bright, clear, shining star fall from heaven to the earth. And indeed there is a clear, shining light fallen this day, the greatest Christian that ever I conversed with.[29]

Meanwhile, back at Priesthill, Isabel had gotten up to get the linen burial sheet she had reserved since the day of her wedding for this moment. With a shattered heart, she wrapped the linen around her husband's body. And though her heart was shattered, it was not shattered with bitterness. She was not bitter over wasted days in her marriage, nor was she bitter at God, or even at the enemies of God who took her husband's life. Three years before this tragic day, the word of God had come down from heaven through an old celibate prophet and prepared her heart for this hour. Her heart was shattered, but it was shattered the way hearts are meant to be shattered, with love.

When people ask, "What use are prophets now that we have the whole Bible?" I wish Isabel were here to answer that question.

6

A Conspiracy Against
the Supernatural

Why have you not heard about the people in the preceding chapter and their supernatural experiences? Part of the reason is that most books that tell these stories have long been out of print and are difficult to find today. But there has also been a conspiracy against the supernatural by more recent writers of theology and church history.

Remember George Wishart? His contemporaries called him a prophet and recorded some of his prophecies. John Howie wrote a short biography of Wishart's life in 1775, using John Knox's writings and other sources, some of which came from people who lived at the same time as Wishart. In the 1775 edition of his book, *Scots Worthies*, Howie wrote of Wishart, "He possessed the spirit of prophecy in an extraordinary degree." In a revised and expanded edition of *Scots Worthies* published seventy-one years later in 1846, the editor changed Howie's original sentence to read, "He possessed an extraordinary degree of sagacious foresight."[1] Sagacious foresight! What's that? It means that due to Wishart's own wisdom he was able to accurately guess how some events would turn out. It means that Wishart's predictive powers did not come from God's supernatural revelation but rather from his own wisdom.

William McGavin, who supplied the notes to the 1846 edition, justified the change from "prophecy" to "sagacious foresight" by stating that the Scottish Reformers were simply mistaken about the nature of prophecy. According to McGavin's understanding of the Bible, prophecy was no longer given.[2] In other words, he felt free to actually change an original text in order to conform it to his own theology.

You may be wondering how an editor could justify changing original texts to conform them to his own beliefs. Theological bias is a powerful force. McGavin's bias caused him to look for a non-supernatural explanation of the prophetic powers of the Reformers and Covenanters. He justified his editing by *explaining away* examples of prophecy in their lives, calling prophecy just sagacious foresight. But can you really attribute Wishart's prediction of Beaton's premature death to good guessing? Remember, Wishart predicted Beaton would die in shame, in the same castle where he watched Wishart's execution, and in a few days. And less than three months later, he was murdered in that very castle. McGavin's explanation:

> This, I believe, is one of the best authenticated instances of what has been called prophecy, by any of our worthies; and yet the words themselves, supposing them to be verbatim as uttered by the dying martyr, do not necessarily imply more, than that, in a few days, the proud Cardinal should lie a corpse in his own palace; and by a few days, he might mean the remaining period of his life, which, however protracted, would appear but a few days to a man passing into eternity. It happened that, about three months thereafter, the Cardinal was murdered; and then, Wishart's words were considered prophetical of that event. I do not believe, and would by no means insinuate, that he was privy to the conspiracy; but this is more probable than that he should be endowed with the spirit of prophecy for no conceivable purpose. It could not be to confirm the truth for which he died, for that is abundantly confirmed by the testimony of Christ and his Apostles, and to look for any new confirmation of it, is to doubt the sufficiency of the Scriptures.[3]

McGavin had to change the ordinary meaning of words to explain this prophecy away. Wishart predicted three things about Beaton's death:

1. He would die in shame
2. He would die in the castle at the execution site
3. He would die in a few days

But according to McGavin, "a few days" doesn't really mean a few days, but instead "the remaining period of his life," however long that might be. In his opinion, Wishart's prediction just turned out to be a good guess that was literally fulfilled. But that's not the worst part of McGavin's explanation. He claimed he would find it easier to believe Wishart was part of a conspiracy to murder Beaton—the one way he could have known ahead of time about the cardinal's shameful death in the castle—than to believe God had spoken to this godly martyr by the spirit of prophecy. There is a conspiracy here, but not on the part of Wishart!

Why couldn't McGavin accept Beaton's death for what it was, a remarkable fulfillment of a specific prophecy? Why was it easier for him to believe that a godly martyr would be more likely to murder an opponent than to hear the voice of God? Because this way of hearing God's voice contradicted McGavin's theory of the sufficiency of the Scriptures.

The second way McGavin explained away prophetic ministry was to claim the original accounts were not true. There were so many examples of accurate predictions in Alexander Peden's life that McGavin was forced to attack the credibility of Patrick Walker, one of Peden's early biographers. He is even less convincing with this method.[4] Shortly, we will take a closer look at the issue of credibility through the eyes of well-known theologians who were closer in time or even contemporaneous with the Reformers and Covenanters.

The third reason you may not have heard about supernatural events is that modern historical writers ignore them. Historical writers have much greater access than the ordinary reader to the original accounts, which are usually not only out of print but sometimes found in select libraries, where their use is occasionally restricted. The writers who use these sources to find out what happened in the sixteenth and seventeenth centuries often ignore experiences that do not conform to their twentieth-century experience and theology. Instead, they often let their own interests dictate what they include in their accounts.

Modern historical writers are usually interested in the doctrine, godliness, and sacrifice of the Scottish Reformers rather than their supernatural experiences. When they retell the story of the Scottish Reformation, the supernatural element usually gets left out. This is not true of just the Scottish Reformation, but in the modern retelling of virtually any period of church history. For example, I have read several twentieth-century accounts of the lives of Jonathan Edwards and George Whitefield, both of whom lived in the eighteenth century. None of these accounts gave a hint about the extent of the strange physical manifestations that accompanied their ministries. Presumably, these things offended the sensibilities of the modern authors. The result of this selective writing is that ordinary modern readers remain ignorant of the supernatural elements of the lives of godly people in earlier history.

So there are at least three reasons why you may not have heard of the wonderful prophetic ministries of Christians in the past centuries. First, the original sources that describe them are difficult to obtain. Second, modern authors' own theology leads them to explain this part of history away by changing the original texts, by explaining away events, or by denying the credibility of the original sources. And finally, modern histories don't mention supernatural happenings because their authors aren't interested in them.

I talk with seminary graduates every year who say they have never heard about the miraculous incidents of the Scottish Reformers' lives, or Whitefield's or Edwards' either, until after their graduation when they began to read the original accounts. Until then, all their information came from modern writers who omitted the miraculous elements of those events.

This conspiracy against the supernatural has been going on for a long time. C. S. Lewis demonstrated fifty years ago that when a person's philosophy or theology excludes the miraculous, no miracle will ever change his or her mind.[5] They will find a method to explain away the miracle by calling it a coincidence or saying it was simply the force of nature acting in an unusual way. Or they may attribute it to latent powers within the human mind, such as sagacious foresight. They may even attack the credibility of the report, saying the event never really happened or was grossly exaggerated. Christian skeptics may point to the same phenomena in non-Christian religions, or even say the devil did the miracle or made the prediction come true. Or they may simply ignore the event as though it never happened.

But none of these explanations or techniques can make the prophetic Reformers and Covenanters of Scotland go away. Listen to the historians and theologians of that period talk about these remarkable Christians.

HISTORIANS OF THE SEVENTEENTH CENTURY

Robert Fleming

One of the early historians of this period, Robert Fleming (1630–1694), was a minister and theologian who was a contemporary of Peden. In 1669, he wrote *The Fulfilling of the Scripture*, in which he included an account of miraculous events during the Scottish Reformation. In the book, he made the bold claim that it could not be denied that, during the time of the Reformation in Scotland, God poured out a prophetic and apostolic spirit on some of his servants that did not fall short of the outpouring of his Spirit in New Testament times.[6] Why would he say such a thing? Should we trust his account?

Fleming and his contemporaries should be considered credible because they saw many of these things with their own eyes. Fleming's spiritual fathers and other witnesses had passed on accounts of miracles before his time or the events were a matter of public record.[7] Usually, these kinds of testimonies are considered as credible historical sources. They are the kinds of sources Luke used to write his account of Jesus' ministry (Luke 1:1–4).

Fleming should also be considered credible because he was not a gullible person. He did not think prophetic revelations and miracles were the usual way of the Lord. He thought the Lord had favored Scotland with miracles during the time of Reformation because of the church's extreme need for supernatural power in overcoming the darkness that had spread across his country. He criticized those who pursued miracles and those who would rather have the Spirit to work miracles than to see people saved.[8]

As for Fleming's own sincerity and character, he noted that he had been very cautious in recording these events because he judged it a "horrid" theology that would "make a lie for God."[9] He claimed not to have knowingly set down anything false and to have carefully investigated each incident. And he claimed he recorded only a few of the many miraculous stories that could be brought to light by anyone willing to make the same careful search.[10] He refused to put in his book some stories told to him by credible witnesses because he thought they were so strange people would have trouble believing them.[11]

Yet another reason to believe these stories is because the character of the people to whom miracles and prophetic utterances were attributed is beyond question. Fleming notes that the supernatural element in their ministries never contradicted the Bible. They never pressed people to believe their revelations. They were cautious, humble, and sober people,[12] many of whom suffered exile and imprisonment for their beliefs. Many were tortured and killed because they refused to give up their Presbyterian convictions. These people were neither flighty nor fraudulent.

What were Fleming's motives for writing down these stories? What use did he make of them? We might expect him to say that the prophecies and miracles proved Presbyterian doctrine, but he would have none of that. Instead, he was absolutely certain that any doctrine that required a miracle to prove it was false. For his beliefs, he appealed to a higher authority than miracles—the Bible.[13] His motive in writing down miraculous stories was to glorify God:

> We judge it a grave and a concerning duty to observe
> the wondrous works of the Lord in our times, yea, to
> make a diligent search thereafter, that we may tell our
> posterity some of the great acts of our God . . .[14]

Finally, we should remember that Fleming was imprisoned for his faith and died in exile from his beloved Scotland.[15] When all of these things are considered together, Fleming would seem to be a better authority on what was actually happening in his time than someone writing about these things two or three hundred years later, especially someone hindered with a bias against the supernatural. But Fleming was not the only credible witness to these events.

Samuel Rutherford

Samuel Rutherford (1600–1661) was one of the great church leaders and theologians of seventeenth-century Scotland. He was one of the Scottish delegates to the famous Westminster Assembly. He knew about the ministry of John Welsh and other Scottish Presbyterians who were making prophetic utterances. Rutherford saw no necessary conflict between the authority of the Bible and God giving divine revelation to certain people:

> There is a revelation of some particular men, who have foretold things to come, even since the ceasing of the Canon of the Word, as John Husse [John Hus], Wickeliefe [Wycliffe], Luther, have foretold things to come and they certainly fell out, and in our nation of Scotland, M. George Wishart foretold that Cardinall Beaton should not come out alive at the Gates of the Castle of St. Andrewes, but that he should dye a shamefull death, and he was hanged over the window that he did look out at, when he saw the man of God burnt, M. Knox prophesied of the hanging of the Lord of Grange, M. Ioh. Davidson uttered prophecies, knowne to many of the kingdome, diverse Holy and mortified preachers in England have done the like . . . [16]

Notice that Rutherford had no difficulty believing that revelation continued "even since the ceasing of the Canon." Although he was writing against the revelations of the Anabaptists, he had no difficulty accepting the prophecies and revelations of the Scottish Covenanters, as well as prophecies which came from other Reformers. The reasons he gave for accepting these prophetic revelations were:

1. They were not contradictory to the Bible
2. They came from godly people
3. The people who had these revelations did not claim that their prophecies had the same authority as Scripture
4. They required no one to obey their prophecies[17]

Men like Rutherford and Fleming were not gullible. They were theologically astute, and they were godly. And they were contemporaneous with some of the events they reported. Normally, these credentials make for credible historical witnesses.

The biographers of these Scottish Reformers do not claim their subjects were 100 percent accurate, yet their contemporaries still called them prophets and even oracles. Some today would rather say these Reformers were "prophetically gifted" in order to distinguish their authority from the Scriptures and Scripture-writing prophets. I tend to use the term "prophetically gifted" for those who are just beginning to function in the gift of prophecy, and reserve the term "prophet" for those who have an established, mature, prophetic ministry. Perhaps it doesn't matter too much what we call them as long as we make room for their ministry.

AN EXPLANATION OF PROPHETIC POWER

How did Rutherford, Fleming, and their contemporaries account for the miraculous ministries of Wishart, Knox, Peden, and the other prophets? The constant theme running through the writings of this period is "the secret of the LORD is with those who fear him" (Ps. 25:14 KJV). All these prophetic ministers were filled with the fear of the Lord. Think about John Welsh, who counted his day wasted if he spent less than eight hours a day in prayer. What kind of secrets do you think God might share with you and me if we spent one-third of every day in prayer?

Remember also that many of these saints suffered martyrdom. They traded their respectability for the anointing of the Holy Spirit and were pursued as common criminals, enemies of the Crown. None of them could have ministered long, or even survived, had they not been able to hear the voice of God. Have you ever put yourself in a place where you would fail miserably unless God spoke to you from heaven? Are you risking anything for God that requires supernatural revelation?

The Scottish Reformers and Covenanters had a great deal in common with the apostles and other first-century Christians. They shared similar godliness and faced similar persecutions. Throughout the history of the church, there were amazing reports of the supernatural when extraordinarily godly Christians were persecuted. According to the contemporary historians, godliness, persecution, and need accounted for the supernatural outpouring of the Holy Spirit during this period. The same is true today.

Several years ago, I was ministering at a conference of Chinese-speaking Christians in San Francisco. I was having lunch with eight Chinese-speaking pastors from different parts of the world. I asked the man on my left, through an interpreter, where he was from. His answer shocked me. He was from Shanghai. I never did learn the details of how he had managed to sneak out of China for our conference, but I did learn some other details that were amazing. The man had just been released from prison after serving eighteen years for preaching the Gospel in China. Now he was preaching the Gospel again.

I told the man I had read many accounts of supernatural happenings in the lives of ordinary Christians in China. I had even seen films smuggled out of China depicting some of these things. I asked him if he had personal knowledge of miracles happening in the church in China. He smiled and said that miracles were happening throughout the underground church in China. But he had seen them the most where persecution was the most intense and godly people were desperate for God's help.[18]

To illustrate this point with another example, let's take a look at the life of Corrie ten Boom, the saintly Dutch Christian whom the Nazis sent to a concentration camp for protecting Jews. Read her books *The Hiding Place* and *Tramp for the Lord*.[19] They are filled with stories of supernatural visions, prophecies, and miracles.

After she and her sister had been imprisoned, Corrie managed to get a small bottle of liquid vitamins. The miracle was, the vitamins would not run out. Corrie said:

> It scarcely seemed possible, so small a bottle, so many doses a day. Now, in addition to Betsie, a dozen others on our pier were taking it.
>
> My instinct was always to hoard it—Betsie was growing so very weak! But the others were ill as well. It was hard to say no to eyes that burned with fever, hands that shook with chill. I tried to save it for the very weakest—but even these soon numbered fifteen, twenty, twenty-five. . . .
>
> And still, every time I tilted the little bottle, a drop appeared at the tip of the glass stopper. It just couldn't be! I held it up to the light, trying to see how much was left, but the dark brown glass was too thick to see through.
>
> "There was a woman in the Bible," Betsie said, "whose oil jar was never empty." She turned to it in the Book of Kings, the story of the poor widow of Zarephath who gave Elijah a room in her home: "The jar of meal

wasted not, neither did the cruse of oil fail, according
to the word of Jehovah which he spoke by Elijah."

Well—but—wonderful things happened all through
the Bible. It was one thing to believe that such things
were possible thousands of years ago, another to have
it happen now, to us, this very day. And yet it happened this day, and the next, and the next, until an
awed little group of spectators stood around watching
the drops fall onto the daily rations of bread.[20]

The little vitamin bottle did not run out until the day someone smuggled them several huge jars of vitamins. That night the
little bottle of liquid vitamins refused to yield another drop. They
didn't need it any longer.[21]

All of the ingredients for a miracle were present in the concentration camp—godly people, persecuted for their faith, desperately asking God for help. Is it surprising that he should
answer with a miracle?

What do you think about Corrie's story? Does it give you
hope or make you feel uncomfortable? Are you thinking there
must be another explanation for those vitamins not running out?
If the latter is your first reaction, maybe you've been victimized
by a conspiracy.

When Christians from the Western world hear stories like
this, they sometimes ask, "Why don't we have more supernatural
revelation in our churches?" I think it's because the Western
church often has more in common with the Laodicean church
than with the faith of those like Corrie ten Boom. And we certainly don't look much like the Scottish Reformed Church of the
sixteenth and seventeenth centuries.

Nobody really persecutes the church in America because it
doesn't threaten anyone. And it won't until it becomes a praying
church. A study of prayer in America published in 1972 reveals
that prayer was not a significant factor in the life of the average
American pastor or seminary professor back then. When the
study was begun, most seminaries didn't even offer a course in
prayer.[22] Twenty-five years later, some seminaries have attempted
to correct this neglect. Many of them offer courses on the spiritual
life and prayer. I wonder if it's helping. I hope it is. But I fear the
emphasis might still be almost exclusively on the cultivation of

the mind rather than on the formation of the heart. The number one confession I hear from pastors all over the world and all across denominational lines is they don't have significant prayer lives, nor do they have regular quality times of meditation in the Scriptures. Why should we expect God to speak to us when we spend so little time with him?

The question is not, "Why don't we see more miracles and have more supernatural revelation in the church today?" Rather, given the apathy and the lack of godliness in the church today, the question is, "Why do we have any supernatural experiences at all in the American church?"

PROPHETIC POWER IN RECENT TIMES

I have chosen only a small period and a small part of the church from which to draw most of these examples, purposely examining a period and a tradition that would not be expected to produce these kinds of ministries. If anyone cares to search for them, the history of the church is filled with these kinds of incidences. Accurate words of knowledge and prophecies have not simply occurred in that part of church history which is regarded with suspicion by today's reigning orthodoxy. Conservative church leaders whose orthodoxy is above suspicion, and who cannot, by any stretch of the imagination, be called charismatic, have experienced and witnessed prophetic phenomena.

Take, for example, Charles Spurgeon's (1834–92) ministry, the great Baptist preacher from England. Once while giving a sermon at Exeter Hall, Spurgeon suddenly stopped in the middle of his sermon and pointed to a young man saying, "Young man, those gloves you are wearing have not been paid for. You have stolen them from your employer." Afterwards, the young man confessed to Spurgeon he had stolen the gloves, but that he would now make restitution for his sin.[23] On another occasion while he was preaching, Spurgeon said there was a man in the gallery who had a bottle of gin in his pocket. This not only startled the man in the gallery who had the gin, but it also led to his conversion.[24]

Listen to Spurgeon's own explanation of his prophetic ministry:

While preaching in the hall, on one occasion, I deliberately pointed to a man in the midst of the crowd, and said, "There is a man sitting there, who is a shoemaker; he keeps his shop open on Sundays, it was open last Sabbath morning, he took ninepence, and there was fourpence profit out of it; his soul is sold to Satan for fourpence!" A city missionary, when going his rounds, met with this man, and seeing that he was reading one of my sermons, he asked the question, "Do you know Mr. Spurgeon?" "Yes," replied the man, "I have every reason to know him, I have been to hear him; and, under his preaching, by God's grace I have become a new creature in Christ Jesus. Shall I tell you how it happened? I went to the Music Hall, and took my seat in the middle of the place; Mr. Spurgeon looked at me as if he knew me, and in his sermon he pointed to me, and told the congregation that I was a shoemaker, and that I kept my shop open on Sundays; and I did, sir. I should not have minded that; but he also said that I took ninepence the Sunday before, and that there was fourpence profit; but how he should know that, I could not tell. Then it struck me that it was God who had spoken to my soul through him, so I shut up my shop the next Sunday. At first, I was afraid to go again to hear him, lest he should tell the people more about me; but afterwards I went, and the Lord met with me, and saved my soul."[25]

Spurgeon adds this comment:

I could tell as many as a *dozen* similar cases in which I pointed at somebody in the hall without having the slightest knowledge of the person, or any idea that what I said was right, except that I believed I was moved by the Spirit to say it; and so striking has been my description, that the persons have gone away, and said to their friends, "Come, see a man that told me all things that ever I did; beyond a doubt, he must have been sent of God to my soul, or else he could not have described me so exactly." And not only so, but I have known many instances in which the thoughts of men have been revealed from the pulpit. I have sometimes seen persons nudge their neighbours with their elbow, because they had got a smart hit, and they have been heard to say, when they were going out, "The preacher told us just what we said to one another when we went in at the door."[26]

Even though our historical records are imperfect and scanty, they abound with stories like this from every period of church history. And here is another thing to consider. Most of these records deal only with the lives of the leaders of the church or with controversial figures within church history. Supernatural phenomena that have occurred in the lives of everyday ordinary Christians rarely ever get recorded. Let me give you a modern example of this from Os Guinness:

> Speaking once at Essex University, I saw sitting in the front row a strange looking girl with an odd expression on her face. Remembering an incident the previous night when a radical had tried to disrupt the lecture, I spoke on but also prayed silently that she would create no trouble. She remained quiet the whole evening but came up as soon as it was finished with a very troubled look and asked me what spell I had cast to keep her quiet. She told me she was part of a spiritist circle in the South of England and that the spirits had ordered her to travel to Essex, where she had never been before, to disrupt a series of lectures beginning that week. The curious sequel to this was that when I arrived back in Switzerland someone else in the community, far from a fanciful visionary, asked me what had happened in the Essex lectures. Praying for them one morning, she had seen a vision, as real as waking reality, of the lecture hall and the strange girl about to disrupt the meeting. Having prayed for her, she was convinced that nothing had happened, but she wondered if it was just her imagination. The presence of a Christian praying in the power of the Holy Spirit is always enough to render the occult inoperable.[27]

This kind of experience is much more common than is generally recognized. Once a week or so, someone in my church tells me a wonderful experience of being surprised by the voice of God. Robin Munzing, a marriage and family counselor in my church, was having severe abdominal pain. Her doctors suspected endometriosis. She had surgery in 1994, but the pain still continued. In December of 1994 Robin's pain became so intense she had to be helped out of a Sunday morning worship service and taken to the hospital. Over the next few months, we elders anointed her with oil and prayed for her several times. Neither prayer nor medical science took away the pain. It got worse.

In March 1995 Robin was washing dishes at the kitchen sink. She wasn't praying or meditating, but a sentence as clear as an audible voice invaded her mind. It said, "You will be pregnant in four to five months." She knew it was God speaking to her. She had heard his voice before. She was overjoyed. For four and a half years, Robin and her husband Dan, a family physician, had been trying to have a baby without any success.

Dan was just as happy as Robin when she told him about the voice at the sink. Maybe now she would be healed of the pain. But she wasn't. By May, the pain on the left side of her abdomen had become unbearable. She was convinced her left ovary was the cause of the pain, and her doctor agreed to remove it.

Knowing how much she wanted to have a baby, and knowing that the removal of her left ovary would significantly decrease her chances of getting pregnant, both Dan and the other physician asked Robin if she was sure she wanted to go on with the surgery. "God told me that I would be pregnant in four to five months [July or August]," she replied, "and God can make me pregnant with one ovary or none, if that's what he wants. He hasn't healed me, and I can't stand the pain. The ovary has to come out. God will take care of the pregnancy."

After the operation in May, the pain left. The biopsy revealed that Robin's ovary was indeed filled with endometriosis. In July, four months after God had promised her a baby, Robin "felt" a warning not to drink wine. *Maybe I'm pregnant*, she thought. *After all, this is the fourth month, and God said I would be pregnant in four to five months.* She went to a pharmacy and bought a pregnancy test. She was pregnant, just as the voice had promised.

When I asked Robin how she could be so sure it was God who had spoken to her, she told me she heard the voice before. Her brother, Ron Andrews, had two bouts with cancer. The first one involved radiation and surgery. In the second one, chemotherapy sent the cancer into remission. In January 1995,

Ron went in for his weekly blood test on Friday. Bad news. The cancer was back in the cells of his blood. He was devastated. He hated to think about another round of radiation or chemotherapy. He called Robin later that afternoon with the report. After Robin put the telephone down, a surprising voice spoke in her mind, "He will be healed this weekend." She called her brother back and told him what God had said to her. Ron is a Christian who believes God is still speaking today. He believed Robin's report of the voice and prepared to go in on Monday for another test. The physicians were baffled by the results. The second test, three days later, showed no trace of cancer in Ron's blood. He had been healed over the weekend, just as the Lord had said.

Robin told me several more stories like this. She doesn't claim to be a prophetess or a visionary, just a Christian who's trying to obey her God and fulfill her roles as wife, mother, and counselor.

There is no way to know how many times throughout the history of the church this kind of experience has been repeated among ordinary Christians. The lady in Switzerland had a real vision from God. However, had she not been acquainted with a well-known author like Os Guinness, her experience would never have become known beyond a small circle of friends. How many dreams, how many visions, how many real impressions have been given to the people of God over the centuries and gone unrecorded? How many times has God given supernatural revelation to save someone like Julie from condemnation and open her heart to feel God's love? How many more of us could be helped if the whole church learned to appreciate and welcome all of God's communications?

The Language of the Holy Spirit

7

God Speaks Through the Bible

The only person Monica loved more than her son was her God, the Lord Jesus Christ. When her son was a baby, she used to sing hymns to him while she was breast-feeding him. She dedicated him to the Lord and prayed he would be a blessing to the kingdom of God.

Monica's faith and love were well-known throughout the Christian community in her city, and when her son grew up, his brilliance was equally well-known. But so was his immorality and hostility toward God. The young man had become a rhetoric professor. He had given himself over to the full-time occupation of drunkenness, sexual immorality, and turning people away from the one, true God with his philosophical speculations. Even the most highly trained Christian intellectuals could make no headway with Monica's son.

Monica had come close to utter despair several times, but she refused to give up. She continued to labor in prayer for the salvation of her son. When her son was nineteen years old, Monica had a dream. In this dream she and her son were walking hand in hand together in heaven. She knew God was telling her through the dream that he would save her immoral son, and the dream encouraged her to intensify her prayers. A year went by. Then another year. And another. Instead of her son growing closer to God, he seemed to be growing farther away. He had gotten more intelligent, more arrogant, and more committed to evil than ever before.

A famous, respected, and wise church leader visited Monica's city to conduct some religious services there. Because Monica was so highly thought of among the Christians in her city, it was not difficult for her to obtain a private meeting with the church leader. She told him of her prayers for her son and that his condition had actually worsened. She implored him to speak with her son, but he refused. He knew any attempt on his part to persuade Monica's son to repent would only serve to harden his heart.

"How will my son ever be saved?" Monica sobbed. The wise old man looked down on Monica's tear-stained face with affection.

"Woman," he said, "it is impossible for the son of those tears to perish." The interview was over.

Monica was encouraged by those words in the same way she had been encouraged by her dream years earlier. With renewed zeal, she continued to do the only thing she could do. She prayed.

Nine years after Monica's dream, her son was sitting in a garden, still an unbeliever, when he heard an audible voice speak the words "Take it and read, take it and read . . . ." over and over in the singsong voice of a child's nursery song. At first he thought the voice must be from some children playing nearby. But there were no children, and he had never heard this child's song before. He sensed the voice was a divine command from heaven to open the Scriptures and read. Monica's son took up the Bible, and his eyes fell on Romans 13:13–14:

> Let us behave decently, as in the daytime, not in orgies
> and drunkenness, not in sexual immorality and debauch-
> ery, not in dissension and jealousy. Rather, clothe your-
> selves with the Lord Jesus Christ, and do not think about
> how to gratify the desires of the sinful nature.

The son's heart was miraculously transformed. He would no longer be known as Monica's immoral son. Instead, he would go down in history as St. Augustine—one of the greatest theologians and champions of the faith in the entire history of the church.

A few years after Augustine had been saved, Monica said to him, "My son, for my part I find no further pleasure in this life. What I am still to do or why I am here in the world, I do not know, for I have no more hope on this earth." She had been given the great desire of her heart, her son's salvation. There was nothing more she wanted in this life. Nine days later she died.[1]

THE POWER OF THE BIBLE

When Monica came close to despair, God gave her a dream to encourage her to keep praying. When she came to another low point, he gave her a prophetic word from a bishop of the church. And when the time was right in his eyes, God the Father sent his audible voice to the rebellious Augustine and opened his heart through the words of Scripture. In the fourth century God was still speaking through dreams, prophetic words, his audible voice, and the words of Holy Scripture.

You might be tempted to think the written Word of God wouldn't be necessary in the presence of dreams, prophetic words, and an audible voice. But in Augustine's case the voice was meant to lead him to a text of Scripture, Romans 13:13–14, which God illumined in such a way to lead him to a new birth in Christ. When the Bible is illumined by the Holy Spirit, its power is incredible. Its light can dispel the darkness of the most convincing satanic deception.

Many since Augustine have been surprised by the power of God's Word. Dorothy is a woman I know who was sinking into suicidal despair. She came to church on Easter Sunday hoping to find an excuse not to take her life. She listened to a sermon on Luke 24, but nothing about it gave her any hope. That night she stood in front of the mirror to say good-bye to a life filled with suffering and despair. As she prepared to commit suicide, a text of Scripture from the morning's sermon rose up in her heart—"Did not the Christ have to suffer these things and then enter his glory?" (Luke 24:26). That was it! First the suffering, then the glory. If she ended her suffering by her own hand, she might miss the glory later. If Christ suffered before he came into his glory, then so would she. She put down the pills and picked up the Bible. The voice of God not only surprised her, but it completely drowned out the demonic voice asking for her life.

Such is the power of God's written Word, and such is God's commitment to use it in our lives. The One who heard the Father's voice better than anyone said, "I tell you the truth, until heaven and earth disappear, not the smallest letter, not the least stroke of a pen, will by any means disappear from the Law until everything is accomplished" (Matt. 5:18). Anyone who ignores the Bible is inviting deception and disaster to be his intimate companions in the journey of life.

BENEFITS FROM THE BIBLE

The most common way the Holy Spirit reveals Jesus and speaks to us today is through the Bible. No one has ever said it better than the apostle Paul:

> All Scripture is God-breathed and is useful for teaching, rebuking, correcting and training in righteousness, so that the man of God may be thoroughly equipped for every good work (2 Tim. 3:16–17).

No one has ever illustrated this truth better than Jesus did on the road to Emmaus (Luke 24:13ff.). After Jesus' death, the disciples were tremendously depressed. At one time they had been confident that he was the Redeemer of Israel, but by this time they had lost that confidence (Luke 24:21). Jesus had predicted his death and resurrection on several occasions. He had told the disciples he would rise from the grave after three days (Luke 9:22; John 2:19). Now it was the third day, and the tomb was empty. They had even heard a report from the women who had visited the tomb that angels had told them Jesus was alive (Luke 24:23). Still, in spite of all of these positive indications, the disciples could not get their confidence in Jesus back.

When Jesus appeared to the two disciples as they were walking along the Emmaus road, they did not recognize him. He listened to their tale of woe up until the point where they mentioned the empty tomb. Then he said to them, "How foolish you are, and how slow of heart to believe all that the prophets have spoken! Did not the Christ have to suffer these things and then enter his glory?" (Luke 24:25–26).

At this point, you would think Jesus would simply have revealed himself to them so they could believe in his resurrection. Instead of doing that, he preached a sermon to them—"beginning with Moses and all the Prophets, he explained to them what was said in all the Scriptures concerning himself" (Luke 24:27). Here was the greatest sermon in all the world, preached by Jesus on the first resurrection morning. The theme was Jesus, the text was Moses and all the prophets, and only two people were in the audience! It went on for hours. Think of it. The greatest sermon ever preached was preached by Jesus to only two people.

Why didn't Jesus simply reveal himself to the disciples at the beginning of their walk? Why did he take them to the Scriptures? Jesus was telling us, right at the very beginning of the church's history, that the primary way he will be known is through the Scriptures. This is the primary benefit of the Bible—it reveals Jesus to us.

Guidance and the Bible

Turning to the book of Acts, we find the apostles showed the same respect as Jesus did for the Bible. We would expect them to use the Scripture to prove the basic truths of the Gospel, and they do. For example, Paul used Psalm 2:7, Isaiah 55:3, and Psalm 16:10 to prove God raised Jesus from the dead (Acts 13:32ff.).

God used the Bible to do more than teach theological truths. He used it to guide his servants in ministry. The Holy Spirit illumined Psalm 69:25 and Psalm 109:8 to show Peter that he wanted to choose another apostle to fill the vacancy left by Judas' betrayal (Acts 1:15–22).

God also used the Bible to explain circumstances and events in the life of the early church. When the Holy Spirit brought the mighty wind and the tongues of fire on the Day of Pentecost, many people thought the 120 people from the Upper Room were drunk. But God opened Peter's mind to understand that these phenomena were the beginning of a fulfillment of the ancient prophecy spoken of in Joel 2:28–32. Peter used the Joel passage to explain to the crowd the meaning of the Pentecost (Acts 2:14ff).

Obedience and the Bible

Neither Jesus nor the apostles were the least bit innovative in their attitude toward the Scriptures. The people of God, especially God's leaders, had always shared a respect for the authority and power of God's holy, written Word. When Moses passed from the scene and the leadership of God's people fell to Joshua, God gave Joshua one of the most extraordinary promises ever given to any individual. He said to him, "No one will be able to stand up against you all the days of your life. As I was with

Moses, so I will be with you; I will never leave you nor forsake you" (Josh. 1:5).

With this promise, Joshua was virtually assured a success and a protection very few world leaders have ever enjoyed. Yet Joshua was very apprehensive about trying to fill Moses' place. Three times during his commissioning service the Lord had to warn him to be "strong and courageous" (Josh. 1:6, 7, 9). After all, who could really take the place of Moses? And actually, who would want to? Moses had been given the impossible task of leading a people who had been rebellious to God throughout the tenure of his entire leadership (Deut. 9:24). Moses himself had not been permitted to go into the promised land. How would Joshua ever take them in?

The secret of Joshua's future success was not found in his leadership skills or his discipline, but in the first person singular pronoun "I." God promised, "*I* will be with you; *I* will never leave you nor forsake you." When spoken by God, there is no more powerful force on earth than this pronoun. God made a commitment to prosper Joshua. That was the divine part.

Now for the human part. Joshua had one main responsibility in order to fully enjoy the promise of God's commitment. God commanded Joshua,

> Be strong and very courageous. Be careful to obey all the law my servant Moses gave you; do not turn from it to the right or to the left, that you may be successful wherever you go. Do not let this Book of the Law depart from your mouth; meditate on it day and night, so that you may be careful to do everything written in it. Then you will be prosperous and successful (Josh. 1:7–8).

At first this command to meditate on the Scriptures day and night doesn't seem to make much sense. Joshua knew the Law better than any living Israelite. He probably acted as Moses' scribe on a number of occasions when the Scripture was actually being written. He had spent forty years serving the man of God and studying the words of God. You would think that by now he knew the Bible so well, he could relax a little bit. Why should he have to meditate on it day and night at this stage of his life?

The answer is this. There is a realm of obedience called *careful to do everything written in it* (Josh. 1:8). The only people who will ever enter that realm of obedience are those who meditate on the Law day and night. The only people who will ever have the divine success the Lord wishes to give them in this life are those who meditate day and night on his holy Word. And the greater the responsibility God gives to individuals in his kingdom, the greater their need to meditate on his Word.

Stability and the Bible

The only people who achieve real stability in their inner lives are the people who meditate day and night on the Law of the Lord. The person who does that "is like a tree planted by streams of water, which yields its fruit in season and whose leaf does not wither. Whatever he does prospers" (Ps. 1:3). The only people who are successful at resisting the lust and greed and temptations of the world are the ones who treasure the Word of God in their hearts (119:9–11). The only ones who will successfully persevere through trials are those who love the Word of God. The psalmist said, "If your law had not been my delight, I would have perished in my affliction (Ps. 119:92). The same psalmist reminds us that, "Great peace have they who love your law, and nothing can make them stumble" (Ps. 119:165). All these benefits and more are given by the Holy Spirit to the person who consistently visits the Word of God with a pure heart.

In the Old Testament, no one said it better than David in Psalm 19. He wrote,

> *The law of the LORD is perfect,*
> *reviving the soul.*
> *The statutes of the LORD are trustworthy,*
> *making wise the simple.*
> *The precepts of the LORD are right,*
> *giving joy to the heart.*
> *The commands of the LORD are radiant,*
> *giving light to the eyes.*
> *The fear of the LORD is pure,*
> *enduring forever.*
> *The ordinances of the LORD are sure*
> *and altogether righteous.*
> *They are more precious than gold,*

> *than much pure gold;*
> *they are sweeter than honey,*
>   *than honey from the comb.*
> *By them is your servant warned;*
>   *in keeping them there is great reward (vv. 7–11).*

There is no book like the Bible, and no substitute for regular daily meditation in the Scriptures. The Holy Spirit is committed to nourishing and washing our hearts by the words of the Bible.

WHEN THE BIBLE DOESN'T WORK

Although it is rare to find a Christian who will deny the importance of the Bible, it is rather common to find Christians who will say they rarely experience the power of the Scriptures to wash them, nourish them, keep them from sin, guide them, and inflame their hearts with passion for the Son of God.

For every person like Augustine who was delivered from the power of lust and born again through a text of Scripture, it seems we can find another for whom the Bible had no effect at all. Their hearts remained darkened and separated from Christ. And I've also talked to Christian men who have read the Bible yet still remain in bondage to lust. Does this mean the claim of the written Word to cleanse and keep us pure (Ps. 119:9, 11) is just religious talk?

Take the case of William Cowper (1731–1800), the hymn writer who wrote "There is a Fountain Filled with Blood." Cowper was a devout Bible-reading, Bible-believing Christian whose most famous hymn extolled the power of the blood of Christ. But in spite of all his Bible reading, he never really experienced the power of the blood that the Scriptures and his hymns so eloquently praise to free him from his tormenting thoughts. In fact, he lived most of his adult life under the power of a suicidal mania with repeated lapses of incapacitating insanity.[2]

How is it that the voice of God could come so powerfully through the Scripture to deliver my friend Dorothy from suicidal voices and fail to silence those same voices dragging one of our most famous hymn writers into the pit of madness? Why does not only the meaning but also the power of the Bible remain closed to many who desperately need it?

A Little Bit Doesn't Help

I grew up loving to play sports. I was so active physically, I never had to be concerned about my diet. Then I graduated from college, went to seminary, got married, and started a family. With all those new responsibilities, my athletic activity slowed down—and so did my metabolism. I began the battle of the bulge. Over the years, through various diets, I lost hundreds of pounds. Of course, I managed to find them again, every one of them, and a few new ones as soon as I got off the diet. Occasionally I mixed regular periods of exercise with the diets and got better results, but none that lasted.

About two years ago I threw away all the diets that promised quick fixes and started eating foods low in fat. My tastes have now changed. I actually prefer low-fat foods to the fatty stuff I used to eat. I don't go on diets any more, and I never go hungry. I have found a lifestyle I can live with day in and day out.

I also started an exercise program with a good friend of mine. Benny and I meet at a local gym three to five times a week to work out with weights and do some aerobic activity. The result of all this is that I'm in better physical condition now than when I was in high school or college.

When I first started a low-fat diet and exercise program, I didn't notice much change in my physical appearance or in my health. Actually, it was about three months before I noticed any significant difference. After nine months though, the difference was dramatic.

I learned a very important lesson through all this. One workout doesn't change you, and diets you can't live with day after day aren't going to help you either. It is the repeated workouts over a period of months, even years, that dramatically change you.

The same is true with the Bible. A little Bible reading won't really change you. It is the daily meditation, month after month, year after year, that changes you. Reading the Bible is very much like eating food.[3] Food is fuel for the body, but without exercise, it can't be used to build up and repair the body. In the same way, the Bible is fuel for the soul, but without exercise, the soul will shrink into a weakened state, just as our muscles do without exercise.

The first step to spiritual health is taking in the right fuel day after day. The second step is using the fuel to make right, often hard, choices every day. Over several years, obeying the Bible, not simply reading it, produces Christ-like character. Quick fixes don't exist in the spiritual realm any more than they do in the natural realm.

Attitude Matters

Any coach will tell you that the right diet and exercise are essential for optimum performance. But a *good* coach knows you can have both diet and exercise and still lose if the players don't have the right attitude. Listen to the story of Matt Biondi:

> Americans who follow swimming had high hopes for Matt Biondi, a member of the U.S. Olympic Team in 1988. Some sportswriters were touting Biondi as likely to match Mark Spitz's 1972 feat of taking seven gold medals. But Biondi finished a heartbreaking third in his first event, the 200-meter freestyle. In his next event, the 100-meter butterfly, Biondi was inched out for the gold by another swimmer who made a greater effort in the last meter.
>
> Sportscasters speculated that the defeats would dispirit Biondi in his successive events. But Biondi rebounded from defeat and took a gold medal in his next five events. One viewer who was not surprised by Biondi's comeback was Martin Seligman, a psychologist at the University of Pennsylvania, who had tested Biondi for optimism earlier that year. In an experiment done with Seligman, the swimming coach told Biondi during a special event meant to showcase Biondi's best performance that he had a worse time than was actually the case. Despite the downbeat feedback, when Biondi was asked to rest and try again, his performance—actually already very good—was even better. But when other team members who were given a false bad time—and whose test scores showed they were pessimistic—tried again, they did even worse the second time.[4]

Biondi's confident attitude made the difference between a good swimmer and a champion.

Attitude is critical in the world of athletics. It's even more critical when we talk about reading the Bible. The words of God will never benefit us unless we believe them (Heb. 3:7–19). If my friend Dorothy had not believed the words of Luke 24:26, those words could never have turned her away from her suicidal course. Reading and attempting to obey the Bible without having confidence in God's words robs the Bible of its power.

Not only do we need to have faith and confidence in the Bible, we need to read it for the right reasons. C. S. Lewis wrote that we when come to the Scripture it's not a "question of learning a subject but of steeping ourselves in a Personality."[5] In other words, our primary purpose for meditating on the Bible should be to meet Christ, to hear his voice, and to see him more clearly that we might love him more passionately. Scripture reading is meant to aid in the process of "forming Christ within us" (Gal. 4:19).

The wrong attitude can make Bible reading worthless or even harmful. Here is where I've gone astray so often and why so much of my Bible reading at times has not really helped me. It wasn't that I didn't have confidence in the written Word of God, but I also had a misplaced confidence, which canceled out many of the benefits of my Scripture meditation.

Confidence in Our Intelligence and Discipline

I used to think if a person understood the principles of biblical interpretation, had a working knowledge of the original languages, and was disciplined enough to spend some serious time studying the Bible, that person could achieve a fair degree of accuracy in understanding and applying the Scriptures. In short, in order to get the benefits of the Bible, I put my emphasis on the role of intelligence and discipline. I was mistaken in my emphasis. As far as I know, the Bible does not put any emphasis at all on the intelligence of its readers as the key to its interpretation.

To be sure, discipline is important if we want the written word to find a home in our hearts, for "blessed is the man . . . [whose] delight is in the law of the LORD, and on his law he meditates day and night" (Ps. 1:1–2; cf. 119:9, 11). But you can have both intelligence and discipline and still not have the Scriptures "work" for you.

One day Jesus himself looked at men who spent the majority of their days studying Holy Scripture—in fact, they were the
best interpreters of the day—and he said to them:

> You have never heard his [my Father's] voice nor seen
> his form, nor does his word dwell in you, for you do not
> believe the one he sent. You diligently study the Scrip-
> tures because you think that by them you possess eter-
> nal life. These are the Scriptures that testify about me,
> yet you refuse to come to me to have life (John 5:37–40).

Neither the intelligence nor the discipline of the Pharisees
unlocked the power of the Bible in their lives. The message of the
Bible must be *spiritually* discerned. The apostle Paul claimed that
apostolic doctrine did not come "in words taught us by human
wisdom but in words taught by the Spirit, expressing spiritual
truths in spiritual words" (1 Cor. 2:13). These words cannot be
understood by mere human intelligence, but must be "spiritually
discerned" (1 Cor. 2:14). And attitudes of carnality, pride, or divi-
siveness cause us to lose the ability to discern the "meat" of the
Word (1 Cor. 3:1–4).

One of the reasons there is so little meditation on the Scriptures in the church today is because teachers have unwittingly
taught their hearers to put emphasis on their own intelligence and
discipline when studying the Scriptures. For many Christians this
is intimidating, because they feel they have neither their teachers'
discipline nor intelligence. Discouraged, they give up on their own
times of meditation and settle for second-hand exposure to the
Word of God through their teachers. Even those who do give
themselves to a disciplined study of the Scripture, find that, in the
end, it becomes a dry and unsatisfying religious duty. The Bible
has become dull for them because the Spirit of God will not open
their eyes to see wonderful things in the Bible while they are
depending on their own intelligence and discipline.

Confidence in Tradition

If brilliance and discipline are not the keys to understanding
Scripture, neither is tradition. The apostle Peter was absolutely
convinced he knew which foods were clean and unclean. He had
read Leviticus 11:1–23 and Deuteronomy 14:3–20, which divided

foods into clean (i.e., foods the Israelites were allowed to eat) and unclean (i.e., foods the Israelites were not allowed to eat). One day during a discussion with Peter and the other disciples, Jesus, in effect, declared "all foods clean" (Mark 7:19). This declaration went right over Peter's head.

Years later, Peter was on a roof praying, and fell into a trance. He saw a large sheet being let down from heaven. The sheet contained all kinds of unclean animals. Peter heard a voice saying,

"Get up, Peter. Kill and eat."

"Surely not, Lord!" Peter replied. "I have never eaten anything impure or unclean."

The voice spoke to him a second time, "Do not call anything impure that God has made clean."

This happened three times, and immediately the sheet was taken back to heaven (Acts 10:13–16).

Even though the Lord himself told Peter to eat unclean animals, Peter refused because it went against his tradition and his interpretation of Scripture. The Lord had to repeat this vision three times in order to get Peter's attention.

Of course, the ultimate meaning of this vision goes beyond clean and unclean foods. It has to do with the opening of the church to the Gentiles, people Jewish believers regarded unclean and unacceptable for membership in the church. Jewish believers would not eat with the Gentiles because they ate unclean foods. This was all backed up by a very traditional interpretation of Scripture. God eventually changed Peter's interpretation and practice, but he had to repeat the vision three times in order to get Peter to begin to question his own prejudices. If the apostle Peter required that kind of direct challenge by the Spirit of God to correct his understanding of the Bible, how much more do we?

Some might argue that this kind of correction is no longer necessary today because we have the whole Bible, whereas Peter had only the Old Testament at the time of this vision. But on this very point, Peter *did* have New Testament revelation. He had been there when the Lord declared all foods clean (Mark 7:19), yet the Lord's declaration had not been enough to correct his erroneous interpretation.

Confidence in Our Ability to Apply the Bible

So far, I've been speaking only of interpretation, but the area of application is just as serious. Whenever we speak about hearing God, we are always dealing with three areas: first, the revelation itself; second, the interpretation of the revelation; and third, the application of the interpretation. The Bible is always true because God, who can't lie (Heb. 6:18), is its Author (2 Tim. 3:16; 2 Peter 1:19–21). But someone's interpretation may not be true, and even if their interpretation is true, their application may be wrong. We need the Holy Spirit to speak to us about both the interpretation and the application.

The Old Testament unambiguously states that the penalty for murder is death (Gen. 9:6; Num. 35:16). The penalty for adultery is also death (Lev. 20:10). David committed both murder and adultery (2 Sam. 11). David should die, right? That's what any scribe or professional interpreter of the Bible would have said. The revelation (the Bible) is easy to interpret at this point: murderers and adulterers are to be executed. Yet, Nathan the prophet said God was not going *to apply* the law in the usual manner. Instead, he was going to forgive David (2 Sam. 12:13). In this case, God's will went against the normal application of the Bible. Furthermore, the application could only be known by listening to the One who wrote the Bible. And this time, God chose to reveal his application through the prophet rather than the scribe. Let's consider a less dramatic example from the New Testament.

Every Bible-believing parent has read the command, "Fathers, do not exasperate your children . . ." (Eph. 6:4). The command is true because it comes from the Bible. The interpretation is not difficult. Parents are not to provoke or exasperate their children, because this will encourage rebellion against God as well as against the parents. So far so good. Now for the hardest part: the application.

I have been counseling Christian parents for twenty-five years. During that time, I have observed that parents who consistently provoke their children with condemning words or lack of praise, with harsh or inflexible discipline, or with unrealistic expectations, often don't have a clue they are provoking their children. They can quote Ephesians 6:4 from memory, but are totally blind to the fact that they are not obeying it. They can't see they are actually encouraging their children to rebel.

Sometimes when I try to tell parents they are provoking their children, they get defensive. They feel insulted instead of helped. Occasionally, even when they mentally accept my diagnosis, they go back home and do the same thing all over again. Why? Not because they don't know what the Scriptures say about provoking their children, but because they are not allowing the Holy Spirit to show them how to apply the Scripture. We need the illumination of the Holy Spirit in the process of application just as much as we do in the process of interpretation. The right interpretation applied incorrectly will never help us. In fact, it may even be destructive to those we love.[6]

Think about the complexities of the application of Ephesians 6:4. First of all, parents are people who have deceitful hearts (Jer. 17:9). Who really understands the human heart? Only God (Jer. 17:10). Often, we don't understand our own motives. Though we may not suffer from total blindness, none of us have perfect vision when it comes to assessing ourselves. The apostle Paul said:

> My conscience is clear, but that does not make me innocent. It is the Lord who judges me. Therefore judge nothing before the appointed time; wait till the Lord comes. He will bring to light what is hidden in darkness and will expose the motives of men's hearts. At that time each will receive his praise from God (1 Cor. 4:4–5).

What is true of the hearts of parents is also true of the children. A child's deceit is even compounded by foolishness, for "folly is bound up in the heart of a child" (Prov. 22:15).

In addition to the problem of the human heart, the application of Ephesians 6:4 can be influenced by complexities of family relationships and individual differences between children. No two children are alike, let alone two families. What angers one child may be needed by another. What works in your friend's family may prove to be a disaster in yours. A form of discipline that worked when a child was ten years of age may provoke rebellion at fourteen. If we're left to our own wisdom in trying to apply the Scripture, it's not very encouraging.

Thankfully, however, there is another option, one we will consider in the next chapter. If we have the right attitude, there is

Someone who is willing to guide us both in the interpretation and application of the Bible.

TREASURING THE BIBLE

In order to experience the power of the Scriptures, our attitude and desire to obey them is crucial. Yet the main reason the Bible is ineffective in the lives of so many Christians is that they simply don't read it. Make up your mind to set aside a regular time every day to meditate in the Scriptures, so you can hear the voice of God and see the glory of the Lord Jesus. When you do, you will find that the voice of the Son of God is indescribably sweet, and the face of the Lord Jesus, indescribably lovely (Song 2:14).

Anyone who wants to hear God's voice on a regular basis will have to become intimately acquainted with the written Word of God.[7] I have been treasuring the Word of God in my heart for over thirty years, and I don't regret a moment of the time I have spent reading, meditating, and memorizing the words of Scripture. If I could turn back time and do those thirty years over again, I would spend even more time meditating in the Bible and less time reading other Christian books.

Many times the Holy Spirit has brought the words of Scripture to my mind, not only to guide me, but also to save me from disasters. He has used the words of Scripture to guide me in serving others, to keep me from hurting them, and to increase my love for his Son and his people.

I remember a time at the conclusion of one of our services when I was listening to an older woman pray for a younger woman. The older woman was one of about a hundred people from our ministry team praying for many people that night. I was standing far enough away not to be obtrusive, but I could hear everything the older woman and the younger woman were saying. The older woman was trying to convince the younger woman that the Lord had given her a revelation about the younger woman's character. The younger woman kept saying that the revelation wasn't true. This offended the older woman, who continued to force this "revelation" on the younger woman. It wasn't a good situation, and the lady on our ministry team was violating one of our basic rules of etiquette: no private revelation is ever to be forced on another person.

I decided to correct the lady, but I waited until the encounter was over to minimize the embarrassment of the correction. Just before I started to walk toward her, I prayed and asked the Lord if I had his permission to rebuke this lady. With my very next step, the words of Isaiah 42:3 came ringing into my mind, "A bruised reed he will not break, and a smoldering wick he will not snuff out." This was a prophecy about the coming of Jesus that I had memorized and treasured in my heart some twenty years earlier, and now the Holy Spirit was speaking to me through these words.

I realized that the Lord saw this woman as a "bruised reed" and a "smoldering wick." All it would take was one rebuke from her pastor to break her and snuff her out. A few seconds earlier I had felt irritated by this woman, but now I saw her through the Lord's eyes, and I felt his compassion for her. The Lord was telling me that this was not the day to rebuke her, that he would handle her correction in another way, at another time. Twenty years earlier, when I was sitting at a desk and memorizing Isaiah 42:1–4, I had no idea God would ever use those verses to turn my irritation into compassion.

This was a time when the Bible really worked for me. All the right ingredients were there—consistent meditation, the desire to obey, and confidence in God's Word. But something else was there too, a key for the release of God's power that I haven't yet mentioned. Before we come to that key, we need to consider another way—a much maligned way—in which God speaks to us.

8

God Speaks Through Experience

Do you remember the story about the religious fanatic trapped on the roof of his house during a flood? A rescue team came by in a boat while he was sitting on the edge of his roof, and invited him to get in. "No thank you," he said, "God is going to deliver me." Night came, and the waters rose. The man climbed to the top of his chimney. A helicopter searching for survivors hovered over his chimney and shined the spotlight on him. "Take the rope ladder," yelled one of his rescuers. "No thank you. God is going to deliver me," came the resolute reply. As the helicopter left, the man fell off the chimney, was swept away in the flood waters, and drowned. When he came into heaven, he complained to the Lord that he had not kept his promise to "save the needy from death" (Ps. 72:13). "What do you mean?" replied the Lord. "I sent you a boat and a helicopter."

I used to be like that man. I believed my circumstances or experiences had nothing to do with hearing God's voice. As far as I was concerned, God spoke in the Bible, not in my circumstances. I loved to say that I lived by the Bible, not by experience. In fact, terms like "experience" and "feelings" had become almost dirty words in my vocabulary. Only shallow, lazy, biblically ignorant people paid any attention to feelings or experience. Mature Christians lived by the Bible, and that was that.

Somehow I managed to miss the fact that the Bible teaches us that God often speaks to us in our experiences, that is, through the events and circumstances of our lives. God may use an illness, a tragedy, or some other kind of trial to get our attention and bring correction to us. "God whispers to us in our pleasures, speaks in our conscience, but shouts in our pains: it is His megaphone to rouse a deaf world," wrote C. S. Lewis.[1] In fact, every trial in life can become an occasion for God to speak to us.

THE HOLY SPIRIT SPEAKS TO US THROUGH OUR TRIALS

Sometimes a trial may come on us because of our sin or neglect of something important to God. For example, in 520 B.C. the people of Israel were under a divine curse because they had stopped the rebuilding of the temple. They weren't lazy. They were working hard building nice houses for themselves. At first things went well for them. God didn't seem to mind that they were ignoring his house. But then their circumstances changed. They came to the point where the harder they worked, the less they had to show for it (Hag. 1:5–11). Twice, God commanded the people through the prophet Haggai to "give careful thought to your ways" (Hag. 1:5, 7). He was speaking to the Israelites through their situation. Their circumstances were telling them they were under a divine judgment, but they weren't listening.

In Bible times it was common for God to speak to his people through the daily events of their lives. Sometimes they were sensitive to this form of the Spirit's language, other times they refused to listen, prolonging the judgment. Finally, God would send a prophet like Haggai to interpret their experience for them.

During the time of Malachi, many of God's people were experiencing economic disaster. Pests were devouring their crops, and their investments were failing. These severe conditions were a message from God to the people. They had been neglecting their obligation to tithe, so God withdrew his protection from their economic endeavors (Mal. 3:6–12).

The prophet Joel observed a severe invasion of locusts. Joel saw God saying two things to the people through the locusts. First, he saw the locust invasion as the judgment of God on a drunken, pleasure-seeking people who had turned away from God (Joel 1:5). He called the leaders of the people to repent (Joel 1:13–14). Second, he saw an even more terrifying message in the locust invasion. He saw the locusts representing an army and the cataclysmic judgments of the last days (Joel 2:1ff.).

Haggai, Malachi, and Joel teach us an important principle: God may speak to us through unpleasant circumstances. Some Christians never ask God about their unpleasant circumstances. Assuming that negative events are just simply a part of life, some of us grit our teeth and face our trials with a stoic resolve. As a result, some of us never learn what God wants to teach us in hard times.

Others of us seem to assume that every negative circumstance, every obstacle in our path, is a result of Satan's personal opposition to our endeavors. This assumption can keep us from hearing God. If God has permitted a trial to lead us to repentance or to refine us, and we assume it is only Satan hindering us, we will never seek the repentance nor the change God wants to bring us. Many trials in our lives are prolonged because we fail to hear what God is saying to us in the trial.

THE HOLY SPIRIT SPEAKS TO US THROUGH COMMON EVENTS

Sometimes God may speak to us through circumstances or events that have nothing to do with trials or suffering. Jeremiah observed a potter at work, and he heard God say to him that just as a potter can shape the clay in any way he chooses, so God could do whatever he pleased with the nation of Israel (Jer. 18:1–6). On another occasion, when Samuel turned to leave Saul, Saul grabbed Samuel's robe and tore it. Samuel told Saul that this action was a message from God. The LORD had torn the kingdom from Saul's hand and had given it to another who would be a better servant (1 Sam. 15:27–28). When we find our attention being drawn to a specific circumstance or event, we should become alert to the possibility that God may be speaking to us through it.

HELP FROM ANOINTED OBSERVERS

A wise person possesses the skill of being able to hear God speak through the events of everyday life. The men who wrote the wisdom literature of the Old Testament (e.g., books like Proverbs, Ecclesiastes, and Job) were "anointed observers" of human experience. They saw God speaking in the common events of daily life, and they formulated their observations into principles of life, or proverbs. For example, when a wise father wanted to teach his son how to stay out of sexual immorality, he began like this, "I saw among the simple, I noticed among the young men, a youth who lacked judgment" (Prov. 7:7). He then described to his son the process by which the young man fell into sin and what it cost him. The father was an "anointed observer." He began by telling what he "saw" and "noticed." From his experience he was able to discern a pattern of satanic temptation and warn his own children.

Psalm 37 is one of the "wisdom psalms." David wrote, "I was young and now I am old, yet I have never seen the righteous forsaken or their children begging bread" (Ps. 37:25). An anointed observer of experience, David, now an old man, realized that his repeated observation of God always feeding the truly righteous was, in fact, a divine principle. As a result of the Holy Spirit speaking to him again and again through his experience, that principle finally became recorded as Scripture.

WINDOWS OF THE SOUL

But you say, "I'm not a David or a Scripture-writing wise man. I'm just an ordinary Christian who has difficulty understanding the plain words of the Bible, let alone seeing God's hand in the fabric of everyday life." Perhaps no one has ever taught you how to look at the fabric of life. God provides us with encounters daily that serve as windows for our souls to catch a glimpse of eternity and hear his voice. Remember Elizabeth Barrett Browning's famous lines?

> *Earth's crammed with heaven,*
> *And every common bush afire with God;*
> *But only he who sees takes off his shoes;*
> *The rest sit round it and pluck blackberries.*

Although the voice of God runs through all experiences, most of us have diligently trained ourselves to ignore his voice and get on with the business of life.

My favorite author, Ken Gire, has written a book called *Windows of the Soul*[2] that teaches us how to listen to the voice of God in the experiences of our every day humdrum lives. His thesis is, "Everywhere we look, there are pictures that are not really pictures but windows."[3] God can be seen and heard through these windows.

You don't have to be a David or a writer of Proverbs to hear God, but you do have to always be looking and listening, for his voice will break through when you least expect it. The voice may come to you while staring at a van Gogh painting or while watching a little boy with cerebral palsy play roller hockey on a Sunday afternoon. With the grace of a poet and the passion of a prophet, Gire describes how God spoke to him in two such divergent experiences. For anyone who would like to learn more about hearing God in the common events of day-to-day living, *Windows of the Soul* is a must-read.

THE HOLY SPIRIT SPEAKS TO US THROUGH MIRACLES

Miracles are special events that always point beyond themselves to something greater. For this very reason, they are called *signs*. When Jesus turned the water into wine at the wedding feast in Canaan of Galilee, he was revealing that he was Lord over the processes of nature (John 2:11). Many people also see in this miracle Jesus' ability to transform our tasteless, shallow lives into lives filled with meaning and purpose. Some even see it as being a message about the last days, namely that God has saved the best wine for the very last. Miracles also speak to us of the character of God, of his power, compassion, and mercy.[4]

THE HOLY SPIRIT CORRECTS WRONG INTERPRETATIONS AND BAD ATTITUDES THROUGH EXPERIENCE

The apostles were able to discern the Lord's voice in the daily events of their lives, so they did not hesitate to use their experience as evidence of God's voice. One of the most controversial events in the early life of the New Testament church was the salvation of Cornelius, his family, and friends, who were Gentiles. Because Jewish believers had an enormous prejudice against the Gentiles, Acts 10 records this story as an important turning point in the history of the church.

In Acts 11, Peter faced the difficult task of proving to the Jewish Christians that the Gentiles' salvation was real. Their hostility toward the Gentiles was so great that at the beginning of his explanation the Jewish believers attacked Peter. They "criticized him and said, 'You went into the house of uncircumcised men and ate with them'" (Acts 11:2–3). God had just opened the doors of heaven to the Gentile world, and the Jewish believers were upset that Peter ate with Gentiles!

You would expect Peter to begin his proof in the face of that kind of hostile prejudice with the Scriptures, right? But that's not what he did. He began by appealing to his *experience*. First, he said that he had been praying when he fell into a trance and saw a vision (Acts 11:5). Second, he related the content of the vision and the voice that he heard, as well as his initial refusal to obey the voice (vv. 5–10). Third, he appealed to the Holy Spirit's command to go with the three visitors to Cornelius' house (vv. 11–12). Fourth, he told them of Cornelius' report of the angel that had been sent to him (vv. 13–14). Fifth, he described how the Holy Spirit fell on the Gentiles in the same way he had fallen on them at Pentecost (v. 15). Finally, Peter appealed to the words of Jesus, who had promised they would be baptized with the Holy Spirit (v. 16). Peter concluded, "So if God gave them the same gift as he gave us ... who was I to think that I could oppose God?" (v. 17). Peter's clinching argument was that the Gentiles at Cornelius' house shared the same experience as the Jewish believers had at Pentecost. This appeal to a *shared experience* won the Jewish Christians over (v. 18).

Later, the issue of whether or not the Gentile Christians were required to keep the Law threatened to divide the church. Acts 15 records three steps the apostles and elders took to resolve this issue.

First, Peter appealed to the events at Cornelius' home where God "*showed* that he accepted them by giving the Holy Spirit to them, just as he did to us" (v. 8). Peter reasoned from this experience that the Gentiles did not have to keep the Law (vv. 9–11). Second, Barnabas and Paul told the group "about the miraculous signs and wonders God had done among the Gentiles through them" (v. 12), a report of experience. And third, James cited Amos 9:11–12, which prophesied that Gentiles would bear the name of God (Acts 15:13–18). James argued that the Scripture *agreed* with Peter's experience. The apostles "married" experience and Scripture to convince the elders of the church to follow the right course of action. They heard God speak in both experience and in the Bible, and they used their experience to prove a point or demonstrate that a work was truly divine.

In both cases, God used experience to correct wrong interpretations of the Bible and bad attitudes toward people. In Acts 10 he corrected Peter, in Acts 11 he used Peter's report of his experience to correct the Jewish Christians in Jerusalem, and in Acts 15 he used Peter's report along with the experience of Paul and Barnabas.

The Problem With Our Fear of Experience

The apostles do not share the modern Christian's fear of experience. Paul explicitly stated that Jesus had called him to be a witness "of what you have seen and heard" and of "what I will show you" (Acts 22:15; 26:16). John began his first letter by claiming to write about what "we have heard," what "we have seen with our eyes," and what "our hands have touched" (1 John 1:1). Apparently the apostles thought their appeal to experience strengthened their credibility rather than weakened it. They never seemed to think much of doctrine that was *not* supported by their experience.

But some Bible-believing Christians become nervous when they hear talk about God speaking through the events of everyday life. They concede it happened to the apostles, but they feel it doesn't happen to them. Some think God only speaks reliably through the Bible. Others are certain God can only speak reliably to them in their daily experience if that experience is interpreted by the Bible.

Strictly speaking, the Bible doesn't interpret their experiences. It is *their knowledge of the Bible* that interprets experiences. Knowledge of the Bible acts as a filter through which the events of their daily lives must pass before they can discern if God is speaking in these events. This works well in situations where interpretations and applications of the Bible are accurate. When a young woman asks her pastor about marrying her non-Christian boyfriend, for example, she may have the testimony of her feelings and perhaps even the testimony of experience from friends who have done the same, and everything worked out fine for them. But the pastor must tell the hopeful bride-to-be that her feelings and the experience of her friends in this situation contradict the Word of God (2 Cor. 6:14; 1 Cor. 7:39). If she ignores the light God has given for her path, she will wander off the path (Ps. 119:105).

Bad Filters

As I pointed out in the last chapter, there are cases where our interpretation and application can be wrong. In these situations, our feelings and our experience will pass through a faulty filter. An improperly working filter can hurt us in two ways: It may let poison through, or it may keep out the antidote that would neutralize the poison already in our souls. In the latter case, our wrong interpretation of the Bible may actually lead us to ignore something God is saying to us through our experience. We may be using the shield of faith against the sword of the Spirit! Our faith in wrong interpretations can keep the real Word of God from piercing our hearts.

And there is another problem. What would you think about having surgery from a physician who correctly diagnosed your diseased heart (interpretation) and knew the right surgical procedure to correct it (application), but had never performed such a surgery (experience)? What about the cases where we have right interpretations and applications of the truth but no experience of it? This is called "theoretical knowledge." Most people don't find knowledge helpful when it is divorced from experience. Theoretical knowledge might get someone a college professorship, but it won't normally help them in real life—romance, marriage, raising a family, relating to friends. Knowledge untested by experience is incomplete and can be just as poor a filter as wrong knowledge.

How We Get Bad Filters

Often the key to fixing something is discovering how it got broken. When analyzing bad filters, it's important to realize that bad interpretations and applications may be due to flaws in our *rules* of interpretation. Theologians refer to these rules of interpretation as hermeneutics. Violate the rules of an athletic contest, and you're disqualified. Violate sound hermeneutical procedures, and you'll probably get a bad interpretation. But hermeneutics are only part of the answer, and sometimes they are not the answer at all. Sometimes people using the same set of rules with the same consistency come up with mutually exclusive interpretations.[5]

Another thing to consider is that bad interpretations can be produced by the unseen, unfelt influence of our culture. Or by hidden things in our heart such as fear, arrogance, and anger—things even more undetectable than our cultural influences.

And some wrong interpretations and applications arise because of our failure to listen to God's corrective voice in our experience. This leads us back to the problem of theoretical knowledge. None of us likes to be accused of having only theoretical knowledge, but many of us do, at least in some areas. A pastor I know made the upsetting discovery that much of the theology he was teaching his congregation was irrelevant to their daily lives. He was teaching them all the things he studied in seminary—as though everyone in his congregation was called to be a pastor or seminary professor. When he realized his mistake, he adopted a new teaching policy. He would teach theology only on a need-to-know basis. He was finished with handing out merely theoretical knowledge.

Finally, there is another way we acquire more theoretical than experiential knowledge of the Bible. When we make the goal of our lives to know the Bible, we exalt knowledge over experience. When we think the key to life is how much of the Bible we know, it becomes more important to us to know than to experience. The truths of Scripture can only be fully known through experience.

We don't experience the biblical truth of humility by reading about it and acquiring a theoretical knowledge of humility. We actually experience humility when we do what the Son of God did as he voluntarily gave up his high position and took on the form of a servant (Phil. 2:5–11). The Christian who makes acquiring knowledge of the Bible the key to life *will be more concerned to give a good explanation of humility than to actually participate in it.* Paul warned us about this danger when he said, "Knowledge puffs up, but love builds up" (1 Cor. 8:1).

No one learns skills very well from just reading or listening to lectures. When I was in my early twenties, I took up the sport of snow skiing. I took lessons from a very good ski instructor and spent a lot of time skiing. One of my academic friends from another state also took up the sport a bit later. When I unexpectedly ran into my friend at a ski resort in Colorado, we began to discuss skiing. I had been skiing for four years. It was his first year. I was amazed at his technical knowledge of the sport. He knew everything about the latest boots, skis, and bindings. He could cite several professional skiers' opinions on equipment and technique. I had been skiing four times longer than he, but he seemed to know four times more about the sport than I.

It wasn't until we stopped talking about the sport and went out to the mountain to ski that I discovered he was an awful skier! He couldn't keep up for even one run down the mountain. He was on the beginner slopes, while I was on the more advanced trails. He may have known more about skiing than I did, but I had more experience actually skiing, and at that point in our lives I could ski circles around him. Who had you rather have teach you how to ski, someone who has exhaustive technical knowledge of the sport but can't ski well, or someone who can actually ski?

Obviously, no one would take skiing lessons from a person who couldn't ski. But the same absurdity often goes undetected or is considered normal in the church when dealing with knowledge versus experience. I hear young people all over the world complaining that the church is irrelevant and powerless. But no one is more relevant or powerful than Jesus. *He* never bores anyone. Could it be that we churchgoers have gotten so numb to spiritual realities that we are content to preach biblical truths without experiencing them? Are we teaching truths that we either won't or can't practice?

Unbelievers continually mock Christians for our hypocrisy and our harsh public treatment of one another. But isn't harshness the inevitable result of exalting doctrine over behavior? If the church became more concerned to experience the life of Jesus, we might stop hurting each other and stop boring unbelievers.

THE KEY TO LIFE AND THE ANSWER TO OUR FEAR IS A PERSON

Right about now some of you probably feel as if I've led you into an existential sea of subjectivity and stolen your life preserver, the Bible. You're wondering what will protect us from deception if we throw out the Bible. I'm not advocating throwing out the Bible. In my opinion, the Scriptures are the inerrant and infallible Word of God. I have nothing but praise for them.

The problem is not with the Bible. The problem is in depending on our knowledge and interpretation of the Scripture. The Pharisees gave a lot of their time to Bible study, but their real confidence was in *their interpretation* of the Bible, not in God himself. That's why they were powerless.

Our biblical interpretations don't give us power. Only a Person can do that. But that Person requires us to put our confidence in him, not in our knowledge, before he gives us power. This explains why sometimes there is such a gulf between what we preach and the reality of our daily experience. Why is it that on Sunday morning we confidently proclaim that "the peace of God, which transcends all understanding, will guard your hearts and your minds in Christ Jesus" (Phil. 4:7), but on Monday we fill the psychiatrists' offices and stand in line for Prozac like the rest of the world?[6] We may have more in common with the Pharisees than we realize.

THE SPIRIT OF TRUTH

When Jesus came to the Pharisees in the everyday events of their lives, they used their interpretations of the Bible to reject Jesus (John 5:39). Why? Because his way of doing things contradicted their expectations and their interpretations, and ultimately because their hearts were evil.

Contrast the Pharisees with Peter on the rooftop in Joppa in Acts 10. He had an experience—he fell into a trance, saw a vision, and heard a voice—an experience that contradicted one of his most basic interpretations of Scripture. However, Peter allowed his experience to correct his interpretation of the Bible.

Of course, it wasn't really his experience that was correcting him, it *was the Spirit of Truth speaking to him through his experience.* It would have been easy for Peter to act like the Pharisees. He could have reasoned that the trance, vision, and voice were from the devil, since this message contradicted an interpretation of the Bible practically all Christians at the time held to be true. Even later, when the Holy Spirit told him to go with the three visitors who had told him the story of the angelic visitation to Cornelius,

Peter could have reasoned all of this was an elaborate demonic trap, the purpose of which was to introduce heresy into the church and weaken its practice.

What made Peter different from the Pharisees? Peter had received the Spirit of Truth; the Pharisees had not. For approximately three and a half years Jesus had been physically present with the apostles as their teacher, counselor, and protector. After he ascended to heaven, Jesus sent the Holy Spirit to do what he had done for the apostles during those years when they enjoyed his physical presence. Now the Holy Spirit had become their counselor (John 14:16). Jesus called this counselor the Spirit of Truth because he would perform the following five ministries:

1. He "will teach you all things" (John 14:26)
2. He "will remind you of everything I have said to you" (John 14:26)
3. He "will testify about me" (John 15:26)
4. He "will guide you into all truth" (John 16:13)
5. He "will tell you what is yet to come" (John 16:13)

Peter had an infinite advantage over the Pharisees because he had an infinite Person to *teach, remind, testify, guide,* and *tell* him the truth about the past, present, and future! The Pharisees had only *their* interpretation of the Bible. Which would you choose?

In the last chapter, I told you that there was more to releasing the meaning and power of the Bible than our consistent meditation and desire to obey it. The key that unlocks the power of the Scriptures is a Person. The Old Testament writers knew this. They put their confidence in God's ability to teach them the Bible, not in their ability to interpret it. "Open my eyes that I may see wonderful things in your law," prayed the psalmist (Ps. 119:18). Many times throughout this psalm the writer asked the LORD to teach him the Word, or to give him understanding of the Word, or to help him follow the Word.[7] He knew he would never understand or follow the Word apart from the teaching and empowering ministry of the Spirit of God.

The New Testament authors felt the same way. Paul told Timothy, "Reflect on what I am saying, *for the Lord will give you insight into all this*" (2 Tim. 2:7). The first condition for understanding and applying Scripture is to reflect, consider, and meditate on the Scripture. The second and indispensable condition is to come before God in humility, acknowledging our foolishness and ask him for wisdom to understand and apply the Scriptures. Those who ask for wisdom in this way will never be turned down (Prov. 2:1–10; James 1:5–8).

The apostles had learned by experience how much they needed the Holy Spirit to help them understand Scripture. Even after traveling with Jesus for three and a half years, listening to his teaching and accepting his rebukes, they still failed to understand that he was fulfilling Scripture right before their eyes. When Jesus rode into Jerusalem on a donkey at his triumphal entry, he was fulfilling Zechariah 9:9, "Rejoice greatly, O Daughter of Zion! . . . See, your king comes to you, righteous and having salvation, gentle and riding on a donkey . . ."

All the apostles were with Jesus on that day, and they heard the crowds calling him the King of Israel and shouting messianic texts of Scripture in praise of Jesus (John 12:13–14). But the apostle John said, "At first his disciples did not understand all this. Only after Jesus was glorified did they realize that these things had been written about him and that they had done these things to him" (John 12:16). Their own knowledge of the Bible was not sufficient to guarantee that they would understand the scriptural prophecies. They needed a Person to explain the Word to them. This is why the apostles never put their confidence in *their* ability to interpret the Bible or their experience. Instead they trusted the Spirit of Truth to interpret the Bible and their experience.

We don't have to be nervous about God speaking to us through the daily events of our lives if the ministry of the Spirit of Truth operates within us. He spoke both in the Bible and in the circumstances of the New Testament believers. They welcomed his communications however they came. When the New Testament leaders had critical decisions to make regarding the life of the church, they listened to God in their experience and in the Scriptures because they knew that their Counselor, the Holy Spirit, was committed to using both their experience and the Scriptures to guide them into all truth.

Their Counselor was so present in the apostles' experience that they felt comfortable expressing his "opinion" at the conclusion of the Jerusalem council. They wrote, "It seemed good to the Holy Spirit and to us not to burden you . . . ." (Acts 15:28). How strange that phrase sounds to some of us today: "It seemed good to the Holy Spirit and to us." Is the Holy Spirit any less near to us than the church of the first century? Is he any less communicative?

Please don't misunderstand me. I am not saying that we should make our experience a higher standard of truth than Scripture. Nor am I saying that experience and Scripture are equal standards of authority for us (see the example above about the woman who wanted to marry a non-Christian). The words of Scripture must remain our only absolute standard. But I am saying that the Holy Spirit often speaks through our experiences in ways consistent with Scripture, and even in ways that may challenge us to correct our wrong interpretations of Scripture. People who say the Holy Spirit never speaks through experience have failed to give enough weight to the way he did this again and again in the Bible itself.

THE DISCIPLINE OF AWARENESS

Give yourself to the discipline of awareness and you will begin to hear the voice of God in the most mundane experiences. Ken Gire, the author I mentioned earlier, felt God leading him to write a book on the life of Christ, which he titled *Intimate Moments With the Savior*.[8] When the idea for the book first came to him, he glanced at the bookshelves of his library. Listen to Ken tell his story:

> Wondering where to start, I began looking over my shelves of theological books. It was there I made an unsettling discovery. I had more books on Greek grammar than I did on the life of Christ.
>
> It was incriminating to realize that He who had given so much occupied so small a shelf in my life. In the quiet courtroom of my heart, I was suddenly the defendant, suddenly the one put on the witness stand and called to give an account of my life. The questions were indicting.
>
> What had I been doing in seminary? Had I been learning how to live my life, or had I simply been learning how to use my gift?
>
> What had I been pursuing those four years? A Savior, or simply a skill?

If the truth, the whole truth, and nothing but the truth were known, what verdict would be handed down to us, to you and to me, about what we've been pursuing for so much of our lives, and why?

Had I been reading the Bible the way van Gogh's sister read books, "to borrow therefrom the force to stimulate my activity?"

Had I read it, searching for principles, to make my life in some way more successful?

Had I read it, searching for promises, to make my life in some way more safe?

Had I read it, searching for proof texts, to give certainty to my own faith or make it more defensible to others?

Had I read it, searching for preaching material, because that was my job?

Had I read it, searching for power, for whatever reason?

Or had I read it, as van Gogh had read his books, searching for the man who wrote it?[9]

That experience led Gire to receive one of God's greatest mercies, a revelation of the spiritual poverty of his own heart and his inadequacy for divine service. It was a great mercy, for with the revelation of the poverty came a purifying hunger for more of God. "From that point on," Gire says, "my view of the Scriptures changed. I realized then that the Scriptures revealed a person who was searching for me, reaching out to me. A person who wanted not simply a personal relationship with me, but an intimate one. Now when I read the Scriptures, I read searching."[10] Who would have ever thought that a simple glance at some bookshelves could have led to a profound experience with the voice of God, melting pride and coldness in the secret recesses of the heart?

The other day I was running on a treadmill and listening through headphones to a portable CD player. I wish I could say it was Beethoven or Bach I was listening to. It wasn't even contemporary Christian music; it was plain ol' country western. A love song came on, and the voice of God came through the words of the ballad. How did I know it was God? Because a sharp, clean edge of conviction slit an opening in my heart. I had been insensitive and ungrateful to the woman I love. Leesa never said anything.

Maybe she didn't notice it, or maybe she chose to ignore it. I was certainly oblivious to it—until the song came on. When it did, the lyrics laid bare my sin in such a specific way that it not only shamed me but humbled me to repent.

Still not sure it was God speaking to me? Scripture says it was, for the Holy Spirit is the only Person powerful enough to break through the darkness of the human heart with a conviction of sin which leads to repentance (John 16:8). If you're wondering of what particular sin I repented, keep wondering—I'm not telling. All I can tell you is this. The words may have been from Nashville, but the message was from heaven. And it was a message for me. A message that moved me to bring my life in harmony not only with the Word of God . . . but also with my wife.

9

God Speaks Through Supernatural Means

Early in his ministry, Francis Schaeffer faced a minor crisis. He and his young family needed temporary housing during a transition time, but had very little money. They needed a "minor miracle" from the Lord. While Francis was praying about this, he said to God, "Where can we live, Lord? Please show us." Immediately, in response to his question, he heard an audible voice. It wasn't a voice inside of his mind. It didn't come from another human. He was alone. The voice simply said, "Uncle Harrison's house."

Although the answer was perfectly clear—it *was* an audible voice—it made no sense. Uncle Harrison had never given the Schaeffer family anything, and they thought it would be very unlikely he would offer his house for them to live in. Yet the voice that spoke to Francis was so startling and direct he felt he had to obey it. He wrote his uncle, asking him what he planned to do with his house for the next year. He was astonished when his uncle replied that he planned to live with his brother for the next year and would like to offer his house free of rent to Francis and his family for a year. Francis Schaeffer claims that this was the second time God had spoken to him in an audible voice.[1]

Francis and Edith Schaeffer are two of the most credible Christian writers and leaders of the twentieth century. There is no doubt in my mind that his report of the audible voice is true. But why did God choose to speak to him in an audible voice? Why didn't God just give him an *impression* about his uncle's house? The Holy Spirit could have used a dream or vision to communicate the same idea. Why does he choose to speak to one person through a dream and to another person in an audible voice?

THE AUDIBLE VOICE

Ancient Israel lived in a world of impersonal gods. It was common for the Israelite people to worship the creation, the sun, the stars, and the moon, as well as idols. When God formed the people of Israel into a nation by making them a unified people, giving them a constitution and a land of their own, he spoke to them—to the whole nation—in an audible voice. Because they heard God speak in an audible voice, the Israelites realized they served a personal God who was over all the creation, not part of it (Deut. 4:15–20), and that their God was unique among all the pagan deities (v. 35). Because they *heard* the voice, they knew that *they* were unique among all the peoples of the earth (v. 33).

Hearing the audible voice was not a pleasant experience—it terrified the Israelites. But God wanted to terrify them in order to instill a godly fear in them that would keep them from sinning (Ex. 20:18–20; Deut. 4:36; 5:23–29).

This brings us to an important point about the audible voice: *The clearer the revelation, the harder the task*. God gave the Israelites the ten commandments with the clarity of an audible voice because keeping the commands of a holy God would be the most difficult task that the nation of Israel would ever face. When God speaks in an audible voice, you can be sure the powers of hell will rise up to challenge that voice. When God speaks to you most clearly, it usually means you are going to go through such a difficult experience that later you will need to be absolutely certain that God had spoken to you. In fact, the clarity of the voice may be the main thing that gives you the power to endure the subsequent testing.

Some people seem to think that it was normal for all the Old Testament prophets to hear God's audible voice. However, the normal mode of communication for prophets was dreams, visions, riddles, and the like. When Miriam and Aaron challenged the authority of their little brother Moses, for example, God came down in a pillar of cloud and said to them, "When a prophet of the

LORD is among you, I reveal myself to him in visions, I speak to him in dreams. But this is not true of my servant Moses; he is faithful in all my house. With him I speak face to face, clearly and not in riddles; he sees the form of the LORD. Why then were you not afraid to speak against my servant Moses?" (Num. 12:6–8). God made it very clear that he only spoke *regularly* in the audible voice to people he was raising to a prominent place of leadership (Ex. 19:9).

In the New Testament the audible voice becomes a Person, the Lord Jesus Christ. Yet the Father still speaks audibly to Jesus from heaven. God spoke audibly to his Son at his baptism (Matt. 3:17), at the transfiguration (Matt. 17:5), and just before the cross (John 12:27–33).

Others heard the audible voice as well. God spoke to Paul on the Damascus road while he was yet an enemy of Christ (Acts 9:1–9). His traveling companions heard the voice but did not understand it (Acts 9:7; 22:9). Ananias heard the voice in a vision telling him to go minister to Paul (Acts 9:10–16). Peter heard the voice in a trance; it prepared him to understand the inclusion of the Gentiles into the church (Acts 10:9–16). John heard the voice when he was in the Spirit on the Lord's Day, and so began the unfolding of the revelation of the last days (Rev. 1:10ff.).

Common threads run through all these experiences. First, the audible voice comes at a turning point in the lives of the saints and in the history of the church—the beginning of Jesus' ministry, just before he died on the cross, at the conversion of the apostle to the Gentiles, at the conversion of the first Gentile, and at the revelation of the last days. Second, the voice comes when the divine ministry about to be performed is extraordinarily difficult to accept or believe, or when the task about to be undertaken is so hard that it will require the clarity and assurance of an audible voice in order to endure and complete the task. Would the Israelites have accepted the Law without the audible voice? Would Ananias have gone to the greatest persecutor of the church to minister to him without the assurance of an audible voice? Perhaps he would have, but the mercy of God didn't require him to do so.

That factor, the mercy of God, is the third thread binding these experiences together. Each time God speaks audibly, his mercy is displayed, and his Son is honored. The audible voice at the baptism, transfiguration, and before the cross of Jesus were all acts of mercy, as were the conversion of Paul and the Gentiles, and the revelation to John of the last days.

Does God still speak in an audible voice? Let me ask you, does he still assign impossible tasks? Are there still dramatic turning points left in the history of the church and the individual lives of those saints who make up the history of the church? Is God still showing mercy to weak people?

Yes, he still speaks in an audible voice. I myself have never heard it, but I know people who have. They choose not to talk about their experience in public, so I won't mention their names. It is still the rarest way that God speaks, and I would be highly suspicious of anyone who claimed the audible voice was part of their daily experience or who tried to use an alleged experience of the audible voice to enhance their authority or to control others.

Finally, Luke adds a feature about the audible voice that the other gospel writers leave out. He wrote that when the audible voice came to Jesus at his baptism, Jesus was praying (Luke 3:21). When the voice came at his transfiguration, Jesus also was praying (Luke 9:28–29). When Paul heard the audible voice in the temple during a trance experience (Acts 22:17–21), again he was praying, and so was Peter when he heard the voice (Acts 10:9–16). Perhaps it is the people most intensely interested in communicating with God who receive the privilege of hearing him audibly.

Francis Schaeffer was praying when he heard the mercy of the audible voice. It was a turning point in their lives, and later Edith would say the clarity of that voice helped them through one of their most difficult years.[2]

THE VOICE AUDIBLE TO YOU ALONE

When Samuel was just a young boy his mother Hannah entrusted him to the care of the priest Eli. Samuel slept in the house of the Lord in a room close to where Eli slept. One night after Samuel had gone to bed he heard a voice call out, "Samuel! Samuel!" The voice was so loud he assumed Eli was calling him from the next room. When Samuel went into Eli's room, Eli said, "I did not call; go back and lie down." This same experience was repeated twice more. Finally, Eli understood what was happening. He remembered the time when he used to hear that voice, though he no longer heard it. He told Samuel that the next time he heard the voice to say, "Speak, LORD, for your servant is listening." When the Lord called Samuel the fourth time, he answered as Eli had instructed him. Then the Lord delivered a full message to Samuel about the coming judgment on the house of Eli.[3]

This story teaches us that God can speak in a voice audible to you alone. The voice that called Samuel was so loud Samuel thought it must be coming from Eli in the next room; however, Eli heard nothing at all. Samuel had heard an audible voice with his human ears that no one else could hear.

An interesting aspect of this story is that the Word of the Lord came to a very young boy. I have talked to a number of prophetically gifted people who began to have supernatural experiences at a very early age. In the last days this will become a very common experience according to the prophet Joel. He foresaw a time when "your sons and daughters will prophesy" (Joel 2:28; Acts 2:17).

Another interesting feature of this story is that it shows us it's possible to have a supernatural encounter with the voice of God and not recognize it. The writer said that Samuel did not recognize the voice of the Lord because "the word of the LORD had not yet been revealed to him" (1 Sam. 3:7). At this point Eli's instruction was very helpful to Samuel. We can benefit from another's experience in learning how to recognize the supernatural voice of the Lord.

THE INTERNAL AUDIBLE VOICE

Often in the Old Testament, the king or the elders of the people would go to a prophet to hear a specific word from the Lord. One day the elders of Israel sat down in front of Ezekiel, wanting a prophetic word from the Lord. While they were sitting in front of Ezekiel, the Scripture says,

> Then the word of the LORD came to me: "Son of man, these men have set up idols in their hearts and put wicked stumbling blocks before their faces. Should I let them inquire of me at all? Therefore speak to them and tell them, 'This is what the Sovereign LORD says: . . . .'" (Ezek. 14:2–4).

While the elders were sitting down in front of him, Ezekiel said, "The word of the LORD came to me." What was Ezekiel actually experiencing? It certainly wasn't an audible voice, because the elders could not hear it. It is also doubtful Ezekiel heard this voice in an audible way with his ears. Most likely, God was speaking to him internally. The words of God were forming complete sentences in his mind, and his heart was feeling the emotions of God. This was not some sort of mechanical dictation. God was speaking to Ezekiel, but he was doing it in such a way as to use Ezekiel's own thoughts and language.

While the actual *spoken* words reflected Ezekiel's own personality and style of language, Ezekiel was conscious that these thoughts were different from his own thoughts. They had an authority that went beyond his authority. That's why he said, "Then the word of the LORD came to me." When God speaks to us in complete sentences in our minds, even though the vocabulary may be our own, the voice comes with an authority that causes us to recognize those sentences as coming from God.[4]

This explains why there are so many different styles of writing within the Scriptures. When God spoke "internally" to the writers of Holy Scripture, he used their own personalities and language styles in which to communicate his truth. This happened in the Old Testament, as we have seen with Ezekiel, as well as in the New Testament. When the apostle Paul had finished giving instructions on the controversial subject of the gifts of the Spirit, he knew that some members of the Corinthian church might disagree with him. He wrote them, "If anybody thinks he is a prophet or spiritually gifted, let him acknowledge that what I am writing to you is *the Lord's command*"(1 Cor. 14:37). Paul was conscious of the fact that when he wrote 1 Corinthians, he was not just writing advice, but Scripture—the very thoughts of God. Yet these thoughts were expressed in a style very different from that of the apostle John, or the apostle Peter, or the prophets of the Old Testament like Isaiah and Jeremiah.

A few years ago I was counseling a mother of a young, sixteen-year-old boy. This mother knew her son had a significant calling of the Lord on his life for ministry. Just as Monica had prayed for Augustine, so this mother had prayed for her son even while he was in her womb. But by his sixteenth year, the boy was rebelling against the Lord and breaking his mother's heart.

One day while she was driving in the car, she poured out her heart to the Lord, weeping. She reminded him of the prophetic words that had been given over her son and of the personal promises and assurances God had spoken to her heart about him. Then a voice "went off" in her mind. "My time is wise," said the voice. Just four words, "My time is wise."

The mother recognized this voice as the voice of the Lord. She didn't make it up. It wasn't her thought. She had been thinking just the opposite. She had been complaining about God's timing. She had been thinking that it was time for her son to submit to the Lord and begin to show the fruit of the Holy Spirit. Yet that sentence, those four little words—"My time is wise"—came with such an authority that it dispelled the mother's anguish and brought great comfort to her. It was as though the Lord said to her, "You don't really see the whole picture. I see your son's life from beginning to end. I know the plans I have for him, and these plans will not be thwarted. I am going to use everything in his life, even his rebellious experiences, to mold him into a profitable servant. Trust me, my time is wise."

Just like the dream Monica had about her son Augustine, these words remained with the mother and gave her a new diligence and hope to labor in prayer for her son. Don't be surprised if God should speak to you in the same way while you are pouring out your heart to him in prayer.

How often can we expect God to speak to us through an internal "audible" voice? People who are more prophetically gifted than I am may have this experience much more often, but I have only heard him speak to me in complete sentences like this perhaps fifteen or twenty times over the last ten years. Each time it has occurred, however, it has been significant and life-changing.[5]

THE VOICE OF ANGELS

Twenty-five years ago the church didn't seem very interested in the contemporary ministry of angels. They were talked about only as a matter of historical interest or academic study. Few Christians seemed to think angels had a significant role in the practical ministry of the church. Today all that has changed. Stories of "angelic encounters" abound. Recently, both Christian and secular presses have published incredible stories of contemporary angelic visitations.[6]

This renewed interest in the ministry of angels is a welcome turn of events, for it agrees with the New Testament teaching on angels. The author of Hebrews warned his readers not to "forget to entertain strangers, for by so doing some people have entertained angels without knowing it" (Heb. 13:2). In other words, at that time, angelic visitations were still a live option. According to the author of Hebrews, if you failed to show hospitality to a stranger, you might just miss out on the blessing of an angelic ministry.

The same author wrote that angels are "ministering spirits sent to serve those who will inherit salvation" (Heb. 1:14). Since angels are the servants of Christians, it shouldn't surprise us that from time to time God would allow us to see them so that we might thank him for his profound supernatural care. This was certainly the case during the life of Jesus. The ministry of angels was prominent at his birth, his temptation, his resurrection, and his ascension.[7] If the Son of God could benefit from angelic ministry, how much more can we?

In addition, many people believe that all of us have guardian angels. They refer to the Scripture where Jesus said, "See that you do not look down on one of these little ones. For I tell you that their angels in heaven always see the face of my Father in heaven" (Matt. 18:10).

Angels function not only as servants and guardians, they also function as agents of supernatural divine revelation. In the early church, angels were famous for engineering jail breaks (Acts 5:19; 12:7ff.). They also brought supernatural guidance and revelation to God's servants. Philip was directed by an angel to bring the Gospel to the Ethiopian eunuch (Acts 8:26). Cornelius, the first Gentile convert, was visited by an angel prior to his conversion with instructions for what he should do (Acts 10:3ff.). When Paul and all of his sailing companions were in danger of losing their lives at sea, God sent an angel who brought prophetic revelation to save them (Acts 27:23–26). And the greatest prophetic book, the book of Revelation, was communicated to John through an angel (Rev. 1:1).

Finally, angels serve as avengers of the saints and executioners of God's enemies (Acts 12:23). As you can see, the Scripture assigns angels a prominent role in the life of the church.

Many people do not report encounters with angels for fear of what others might think. Early in my ministry a lady in my church told me the following story. Neither the lady nor my church were charismatic. Actually, our church had definite prejudices against the gifts of the Spirit. The woman had never told anyone this story for fear of being thought crazy.

She had been driving on the interstate in our city when she became so ill she was afraid she might pass out and lose control of the car. Then she saw a handsome young man dressed in a black leather jacket hitchhiking along the side of the road. She pulled off the road and picked him up. "Please sir," she said, "I'm so sick. If you could just drive me to the west side of town where my doctor's office is located, I'll make sure you get a ride to anywhere you want to go." The young man agreed, and drove her to her doctor's office. He helped her out of the car and into the doctor's office, where a nurse took her immediately into one of the examination rooms. A few minutes later the woman realized she had forgotten to thank the young man and make arrangements for him to get another ride. She walked back into the lobby and asked the receptionist where the young man had gone. The receptionist said, "What young man?"

"The young man who practically carried me in here," the lady answered.

"No one carried you in here! You came in here by yourself and put your keys here on the counter." The lady thought she was truly sick! She imagined the whole thing had been a hallucination.

A year or so later, she was shopping at one of the large malls during the Christmas season and came out late at night, just as the stores were closing. She had parked her car in an underground garage adjacent to one of the stores in the very last space in the far corner. Directly in front of her car and along the passenger side was a cement wall. The space next to the driver's side was empty.

When she entered the garage and began to walk toward her car, the garage was empty. Then she heard footsteps coming out of the dark on her right. She glanced in that direction and saw a man walking toward her. She quickened her pace. The man quickened his pace. She began to run, and so did her attacker. As she ran, she fumbled in her purse for her keys. When she got to the door of her car, she realized she wouldn't have time to open the door before the man reached her. She turned to face her attacker. As she did, she saw him stop about thirty feet from her with a terrified look in his eyes. Abruptly, he turned around and ran out of the garage. The woman turned back to her car, and there standing between the cement wall and her car was the young man she had picked up a year or so before on the freeway when she was sick. He was dressed in the same black leather jacket and was smiling at her. She glanced over her shoulder to make sure her attacker had gone, and when she turned back to the young man to thank him, he had vanished. She walked all around the car, searching for him. There was no door in the cement wall. He was not under the car. He had simply vanished. Then she knew. She had been visited by an angel. Once again, he had saved her life.

And then there's Gene Stallings, head coach of the University of Alabama's football team. Stallings has had an impressive coaching career—head coach at Texas A&M, assistant coach of the Dallas Cowboys during the Tom Landry era, and head coach of the Phoenix Cardinals. His most significant encounter, however, has not come on the playing field, but rather in the bedroom of his young son Johnny.

Johnny was born with Down's syndrome. Unless you've been through the experience of having a child with Down's, you can't imagine the trauma and confusion that comes with having to deal with the many problems these kids face. One night when Johnny was very small, Coach Stallings heard a noise coming from his son's bedroom.

> I immediately went to check on him. When I opened the door, I discovered not one, but two baby boys sitting in Johnny's crib. They were playing a game known only to them and squealing with laughter. The other baby turned toward me, looked into my eyes with a piercing glance, then suddenly disappeared.
>
> To this day I believe with all my heart that God allowed me to see Johnny's guardian angel momentarily in order to encourage me for the years that lay ahead.

Ever since that time, Gene Stallings has had a tremendous ministry of comfort and encouragement to families who have Down's syndrome babies.

You can find these kinds of stories documented throughout the history of the church. Today there seems to be a significant increase in the reports of angelic encounters. This may be due to the fact that it's becoming more acceptable to talk about angels in the church today, or it may be because angelic encounters are actually increasing. Jesus taught that angels would have a prominent role at the end of the age (Matt. 13:39ff.; 24:31; 25:31). So did the apostle Paul (2 Thess. 1:7). The book of Revelation, which was written about the last days, mentions angels approximately eighty times!

One thing is clear: Whether or not we are nearing the end of the age and the stage is being set for the return of the Lord Jesus, we ought "not forget to entertain strangers, for by doing so some people have entertained angels without knowing it."

THE CONCEALING OF THE SUPERNATURAL VOICE

We have been considering the most overtly supernatural ways in which God speaks to his children—an audible voice, a voice audible to you alone, an internal audible voice, and the voice of angels. You would think it would be impossible to misunderstand any of these voices, but this is not so. Some have failed to recognize angels (Heb. 13:2). Samuel thought the voice of God came from Eli.

The most instructive example of all comes from the life of Jesus. Just before Jesus' crucifixion, God spoke audibly once more to his Son in the presence of witnesses. Jesus was speaking to a crowd:

> "Now my heart is troubled, and what shall I say? 'Father, save me from this hour'? No, it was for this very reason I came to this hour. Father, glorify your name!" Then a voice came from heaven, "I have glorified it, and will glorify it again." The crowd that was there and heard it said it had thundered; others said an angel had spoken to him. Jesus said, "This voice was for your benefit, not mine. Now is the time for judgment on this world; now the prince of this world will be driven out. But I, when I am lifted up from the earth, will draw all men to myself." He said this to show the kind of death he was going to die (John 12:27–33).

The voice brought honor to Jesus. He prayed, and his Father answered audibly in public before a crowd. How many people can claim that kind of experience?

Jesus specifically said that the real purpose of that voice was not for his sake but for the benefit of the people there. Remember the principle, "the clearer the revelation, the more difficult the task"? Jesus was about to die on a cross, a form of capital punishment reserved for the dregs of society. How difficult it would be for anyone to believe he was the Messiah! So God spoke audibly to him—with a crowd as witnesses—to show that the honor of God rested on Jesus, that he was set apart in divine favor from all men. This was the mercy of God. The voice was clear and audible. God did not stutter. He spoke audibly so that the people might believe in Jesus as the Son of God when everything was about to indicate otherwise.

John records the strangest thing. He says some people there did not understand the audible voice of God. In fact, some heard no voice at all. They simply said to the ones who did hear, "You're wrong, it only thundered." God was speaking distinctly, audibly, and for their own good, and all they heard was thunder! How different from his audible voice at Mount Sinai.

With the coming of the Son of God, the audible voice changed tones. Now the audible voice could be understood only if certain conditions were met. Why did some hear the voice and others hear only thunder? The answer to this mystery is the key to understanding the language of the Holy Spirit, whether he chooses to speak to you with the clarity of an audible voice, or in the precise language of the Scriptures, or in the ambiguities of a mysterious dream. The key that unlocks the meaning of the Spirit's language is the same no matter the form in which his language comes to you. Before we try to use that key, we need to consider other forms of the voice of God.

Who knows? One day, Jesus may decide to grant *you* the mercy of hearing his voice audibly. If he does, would you recognize that voice? Or would you hear only a little thunder?

10

God Speaks Through Natural Means

During my first pastorate, I came to church early one Sunday morning filled with enthusiasm for the sermon I was about to preach. The sermon was on the meaning of the Lord's Supper. I was sure it was going to be a glorious experience for the whole church. In those days it was our custom to have the deacons administrate the serving of communion. We always had the Lord's Supper before the sermon, but tod.., ' 'ecided we would have it after my wonderful message. That way, the Lord's Supper would be much more meaningful to all the congregation, who would have just had the benefit of receiving my profound wisdom on the subject.

I found the deacon in charge of the Lord's Supper just before the service was to begin, and I told him about my plan to have the Lord's Supper after the message. He explained to me that my plan wouldn't work because all the other deacons were expecting to serve the Lord's Supper before the message. I asked him to notify them again and change his plans, being careful to explain how much more the people would get out of the Lord's Supper if they could take it after my sermon. He very carefully explained back to me that this was just not possible.

Things escalated. We began to raise our voices. Before long we had clenched our fists. There we were, on a Sunday morning, standing squared-off and red-faced in the church office, about to come to physical blows over the order of the Lord's Supper. Mercifully, two elders heard us, ran into the room, and got between us.

They were able to quiet us down, and we gave each other the customary, perfunctory apologies and shook hands, but I was furious with that deacon. Oh, by the way, we did have the Lord's Supper after the sermon. I saw to that. But the sermon wasn't so glorious and neither was the Lord's Supper afterwards. I don't think I have ever preached a sermon on the love and sacrifice of Christ with as much hate in my heart as I did on that Sunday morning.

By Sunday afternoon I was on the verge of being consumed by rage against this deacon. Of course, I didn't identify it as rage. I thought I was feeling righteous indignation and concern for the spiritual health of the church. This man was clearly no longer qualified to be a deacon. Anyone with a temper like that was capable of doing great damage if he were left in a position of leadership. Somehow it escaped my notice that *my* temper could be just as harmful. I convinced myself that I must act quickly and decisively . . . for the sake of the church.

I conceived a plan in my mind for having this deacon removed. To be honest, I didn't just want him removed from the office, I wanted him to leave the church. I knew I had to be very careful in my subsequent actions to appear forgiving, so I formulated a plan for his dismissal that concealed my vindictiveness.

On Tuesday morning I was driving from Fort Worth to Dallas on Interstate 30 to teach my seminary class on the book of Psalms. One part of my lecture that day was to be about the meaning of the Hebrew word for "love." I was in a good mood, and my anger had subsided, since I now had what I thought was a fool-proof plan. I put one of my favorite worship tapes in the cassette player and began listening to a beautiful tenor voice singing the Psalms.

Halfway between the two cities, Interstate 30 faded from my view, and I saw the sanctuary of our church. The vision was so real. It seemed I was in the sanctuary standing at the back of the balcony looking down toward the altar. The worship music I had been listening to in the car was now permeating the sanctuary. The church was empty of people but filled with the presence of God. Then I noticed one man on his knees before the altar at the front of the sanctuary. His face was turned to heaven. Tears were rolling down the sides of his cheeks. There was a golden glow coming off his face. It was obvious that he loved God and that he was worshiping God. It was also obvious that God loved him very much. Then the man's face turned slightly so I could recognize him. It was the "dangerous deacon"!

God was showing me a picture of the heart of the man I had been hating since last Sunday. Tears rolled down my cheeks. I felt so ashamed. How could I hate someone that God loved so much? How could I plot the demise of someone who loved and worshiped my God so much? Then the vision faded, and Interstate 30 came back. When I came out of the vision, my cheeks were still wet. Although I had said nothing to God, my heart had already repented. I thanked God for showing me my brother's heart and the sinfulness of my own. I couldn't wait to get home to seek reconciliation. Now I was ready to do more than give a perfunctory, hollow apology. Because of that vision, we were reconciled.

It may seem odd that God did not use a text of Scripture to convict me of my sin. There is, of course, an abundance of texts dealing with the subject of loving your brother, and after all, I *was* a seminary professor. But sometimes, knowing the Bible can be a hindrance to repentance. Not only can Bible knowledge be a source of pride, but we can also use knowledge of the Bible to justify sin. This was true of me. I had already amassed a number of Scriptures to justify my hateful plan of action. Sometimes the hardened heart of a professional interpreter of the Bible is tougher to penetrate than armor plating. My anger had allowed my heart to "be hardened by sin's deceitfulness" (Heb. 3:13), and I was using my knowledge of the Bible to harden it even more. So God penetrated my heart with a vision of the very man's heart I wanted to hurt.

A vision led me to repentance and saved me from sin. It is as simple as that. If visions can do that, I want to have visions, and I want to be able to understand them. Visions are a part of the language the Holy Spirit regularly speaks.[1]

There is saving power in the language of the Holy Spirit. The more of his language we understand, the more of his saving power we will experience. If we really want to be saved from our sinful and hurtful ways, we must diligently learn how to hear the voice of God in the Bible, in our circumstances, in visions, in impressions, and in the other ways in which he speaks.

DREAMS, VISIONS, AND TRANCES

Dreams consist of images—accompanied by thoughts and emotions—we "see" while we are asleep. The images may tell a coherent story or seem to make no sense at all. Visions are dreams we have while we are awake,[2] and trances are a visionary state that occurs while we are awake. People in trances have a profound loss of consciousness of their surroundings, as well as a loss of bodily functions. In a vision or trance we also may hear an audible voice.[3]

During Bible times it was common for God to speak to people through dreams, visions, and trances. The absence of dreams and visions was usually a sign of God's judgment during a time of apostasy (Lam. 2:7; Mic. 3:6–7; 1 Sam. 3:1). In the Old Testament, dreams and visions were mainly for prophets. They were the normal way God spoke to prophetic people: "When a prophet of the LORD is among you, I reveal myself to him in visions, I speak to him in dreams" (Num. 12:6).

But with the New Testament coming of the Holy Spirit, dreams, visions, and other prophetic experiences *become the normal experience* for the whole church (Acts 2:17–18). Later we will explore the nature of these visionary experiences more fully. For now I simply want to make the point that they are common ways for God to speak to his children.

Even though dreams are a scriptural means of divine communication, some remain skeptical of their value. Listen to Ken Gire tell how God removed his skepticism. It is one of the most tender and moving accounts I have ever read about God's intimate love for us.

> No communication is as intimate I think as a dream whispered to our soul in the middle of the night. I didn't always think that, though. Mainly because most of the dreams I've had over the years have bubbled up from the fears or desires cauldroned within my subconscious. You know, the ones where you're in class and suddenly realize you've got nothing on but your underwear. Or you're in bed and a robber's hiding in your closet and you're screaming to your parents down the hall except no words are coming out and the robber's coming to get you and despite your efforts to jump out of bed and run your body is a sack of concrete and he's coming closer and you can't even pull the covers over your head and you scream louder but still no words are coming out. Those kinds of dreams.
>
> I used to put people who talked about God speaking to them in dreams in the same category as palm readers.

At best, I thought them suspect. At worst, downright spooky. And if I ever got cornered by one at a party or somewhere, I'd gulp down my drink and go darting for the nearest punchbowl. I used to think that way about a person who dreamed.

Until that person was my wife.

The dream she had was set in a huge gymnasium. Windows lined the top of the thirty-foot walls, letting in diffused rays of sunlight. She was sitting on the floor with a young man she didn't recognize but somehow felt she knew. The two of them were watching a ballet where hundreds of beautiful dancers in soft gowns were dancing. It was the most wonderful dance she had ever seen. Though her body wasn't moving, everything inside her was caught up in the dance and she felt part of it, one with it, and it filled her senses so fully she felt she would never tire of it.

The young man stood up and walked to the center of the gym. As he did, the ballerinas all bowed before him and floated on their toes to the far walls. Then he made an announcement: "Now I want *her* to dance."

Judy realized he was talking about her.

She got up and walked to where he was standing. Once by his side, she realized she was wearing grubby-looking workout clothes with torn leggings. But her concern was only momentary. When the young man left the center of the floor and sat down to watch, she began to dance. She swung her leg up high, turning her body in the opposite direction as she did, and then danced to the end of the gym. Each time she reached one end, she swung her foot high in the air, pivoted on the other foot, turned and danced to the other end.

Then, as quickly as she started dancing, she stopped and sat down beside the young man. He walked to the center of the gym and addressed the ballerinas: "See how beautifully she dances. She has had no training, yet see how she dances. I love her dance."

As little Judy left the gym floor, the ballerinas resumed their places, and the ballet continued. The young man took her aside and showed her a photo album filled with pictures of a beautiful house. The rooms were lavish and the furnishing exquisite. As she marveled over them, he said: "This is my home. I want you to make your home there and dance for me."

When Judy woke from the dream, she couldn't understand it. It was so vivid in her memory, yet so vague in its meaning. She knew God had spoken in the past to people through dreams. Both Old and New Testaments were full of such accounts. But did He still? She didn't know.

She got dressed and took the kids to school with little thought of the dream. After she finished her morning routine, though, she was driving home, and the dream came back to her. Vividly came back to her. As she was watching herself dance, her thoughts were interrupted by memories she had long since forgotten. Memories of when she was a young girl.

During her growing-up years when it was her turn to do dishes, Judy would dawdle at the sink. She would dip a dish into the soapy water, blow a bubble, think about something a minute, wash the dish, play with the water, think about something else, rinse the dish. And sometimes this would go on all evening until the dishes were done.

But when no one was around, young Judy would leave the dishes and dance back and forth from the kitchen to the living room. Each time she would come to the end of the room, she would swing one foot high in the air, pivot on the other foot, turn, and dance to the other end.

When that memory came back to her, a flood of tears came with it, tears for the little girl who carried so much sadness within her, never letting it come to the surface, never telling anyone her dreams or her heartaches.

Then suddenly it dawned on her.

The young man in the dream. It was Jesus. He had been there, watching her dance in that living room during

those painful years of growing up. He knew her longing to be a ballerina. He knew she had no training.
Knew she had to drop out of college to go to work.
Knew the feelings of inadequacy she held so fragilely
within her. Feeling that she was nobody special, that
her life didn't matter, that other people could teach the
Bible but not her, that good things happened to other
people but not to her, that other people had interesting
lives but not her.

Yet Jesus wanted *her*. Out of all the ballerinas, he picked
her to dance for him, picked *her* to come to his house. It
didn't make any difference that she didn't have any
training or that she didn't have the lovely outfits the
other ballerinas had. She had the heart of a ballerina.
And she loved to dance. Those were the things that
mattered.

Judy called me at work to tell me about the dream, not
knowing how I would react but needing to tell me
because it was such a beautiful dream and had touched
her so deeply.

"So," I said, after she finished, "are you saying you
want ballet lessons?"

"It's not about ballet," she said. "It's His way of telling
me that He was there. Back then, when I was younger.
He saw me. Nobody else saw me, but *He* saw me. I
think, I don't know, but I think the dream was about
Him being pleased with me and about His delight in
my worship of Him, and I think He's inviting me into
a more intimate relationship with Him."

I tried not to sound skeptical, for even over the phone
I could tell how much the dream had meant to her, the
emotion in her voice kept breaking the surface. After I
hung up, I thought about it a few minutes. It was all so
foreign to me. And yet there was no one in the world I
respected more than Judy, no one whose heart I trusted
more. She was not one to exaggerate or one who was
prone to extremes. And she was not emotional. Yet she
couldn't talk about the dream without tears.

I remember praying before I left work for God to help me understand. If indeed this was His voice, I didn't want to squelch it. If it wasn't, I didn't want to encourage it. I was driving home with these thoughts when I stopped at a Salvation Army Thrift Store, where I usually stopped once or twice a week, looking for used books. As I looked, my eye caught the spine of a slender book, titled, *A Dream So Real*. I remember thinking, *Odd coincidence*. I pulled the book off the shelf, and it fell open to a picture of a little girl on one page and a poem on the other. The little girl had her leg raised, as if trying to dance. And the poem? "Dream Dancer."

Was this the answer? So soon? Was God meeting me in a thrift store and telling me, yes, it's true, yes, it was me, it was my voice? I bought the book and brought it home, told Judy what I had prayed when I got off the phone, and I read her the poem. Again, she wept. Especially at the stanza which read:

> *Step then*
> *from the staid and somber line.*
> *Move out in dancing*
> *into dreams so daring;*
> *without them you will settle for the road*
> *that wanders by and winds to nowhere.*

For three days Judy cried, the emotions at times seeping to the surface, at other times surging with irrepressible force. After those three days, the tears were gone. And miraculously, so were the hurts from her past. Just like that. And they haven't come back.

Do you see what God was doing?

He paged through my wife's dog-eared dictionary of childhood memories, picked out an image that was dear to her, and one night bent down and whispered it in her ear. That image touched her in places where words alone couldn't reach. And with that touch, brought healing.

Look deeper into that picture. Do you see the window?

Do you see the ways of God revealed in the way He speaks? He didn't require Judy to go to seminary and learn Hebrew, the language through which He first spoke to His people. Instead, He learned hers.

He learned the language of her heart, which He had been studying since she was a girl. And it's a different language than He . . . uses when speaking to you and to me. Can you see how incredible that is?[4]

The people in the Bible knew how powerful a dream from God could be. Maybe Judy Gire's dream will help some of us in the forgetful church recover the art of hearing God in our dreams.

SENTENCE FRAGMENTS AND SINGLE WORDS

Sometimes the Lord may speak to us by invading our minds with only part of a sentence or just a single word that we may not even understand at the time. When this happens, the fragment or the single word that appears suddenly in our mind does not seem to come from within our mind. Although we recognize it in our mind, it comes rather like an invasion. It gets our attention precisely because we recognize its "foreign" character, or sometimes because it seems to make no sense at all.

Once I found myself in a very awkward situation and did not know what to do. I felt God was calling me to confront a group of leaders. Several reliable witnesses had told me about strife and deceit going on within this group. At first I dismissed the idea of confrontation. I thought it would be arrogant of me to confront a group of leaders when I hadn't even been invited to their meeting. I also wondered if the impression had really come from God. I could see how easily it might have come out of some "macho" desire in my own heart. I wanted to be obedient to God, but I didn't want to hurt someone through my own arrogance and impure desires.

My wife was with me at the time, so I told her about the dilemma. She didn't have a clear opinion about what I ought to do, so I knelt down beside the bed in our hotel room and said, "Lord, if this impression really is from you, if you really want me to confront these leaders, then you will have to give me a sign, or else I can't go."

Within ten seconds the telephone rang. A friend of ours who had been staying in the same hotel said, "Jack, I don't know what this means but I was praying a few minutes ago. I wasn't even praying for you or Leesa, but while I was praying, this particular chapter of Scripture came into my mind. I don't even know what's in this chapter, but I am sure God spoke it to me. I had an impression I was supposed to call you and say it's for you."

The chapter my friend gave me had to do with prophetic confrontation. Just three months earlier, in a private session, a prophetic person had spoken that chapter over me, saying, "You will be doing the things in this chapter." I told no one, not even my wife, about that experience or that chapter of Scripture. I just hid it in my heart. Now I had asked for a sign, and God had given me an unmistakable one. He did it by speaking just two simple words—the name of a scriptural book and the number of a chapter. My friend had no idea what this meant or what was in the chapter, but she knew God had clearly spoken it.

Today I find these kinds of experiences are not that uncommon in my life when I place myself in situations where I need to hear from God. Sometimes in conferences or in a church service, when I look at a person, I will "hear" a single word or a couple of words about them. God speaks to us like this whenever we need to hear from him. If we don't think we need to hear from him, or if we think our knowledge of the Bible is sufficient or that our ministry skills will get us through, then we probably won't hear him speak like this.

IMPRESSIONS

Frequently the Holy Spirit speaks through impressions. By *impression* I am referring to the Holy Spirit's influence on our feelings, our physical senses, or our minds. This differs from the complete sentences or even the single words the Holy Spirit forms in our minds. Impressions lack the precision of sentences or single words. Supernatural revelatory impressions are similar to intuition in that they both communicate direct knowledge without any rational evidence or logical inference to support that knowledge. Impressions from the Holy Spirit are *different* than intuition in respect to their origin. A divine impression comes to us from the Holy Spirit, while intuition arises from within our human spirit.

Some people use a technique called "cold-reading" to give the appearance they are receiving a supernatural impression about a person. For example, a "prophet" notices pet hair on a lady's dress and says to her, "The Lord shows me that you love animals." Then he may continue to observe her appearance or body language for other clues, phrasing statements in such a way that the lady's response gives him additional information. If the lady is a little gullible, or is desperate to believe God is speaking to her through this "prophet," she can be easily deceived. Professional gamblers are highly skilled at reading signs given by demeanor and body language. They call these signs "tells" because they "tell" them something about the person they are observing.

An impression from the Holy Spirit is totally different than cold-reading or observing a "tell." Impressions are not necessarily connected with our observations or logical inferences. Sometimes an impression from the Holy Spirit will communicate knowledge that is opposite of what our minds believe or our senses are telling us.

Paul Cain, a leading prophetic minister in the American church, was in a well-known celebrity's home. The woman looked as though she were in perfect health, but Paul had an impression that something was wrong with her gall bladder. When he told her about the impression, she replied that he must be mistaken, she had never felt better. Shortly afterward she had gall bladder surgery. This knowledge did not come from Paul Cain's powers of observation or any logical deduction within his mind. It was a simple impression from the Holy Spirit that contradicted his natural senses.

This sort of thing happens to me frequently when I am teaching or preaching. Recently I was speaking to about 1,200 people at a conference in a suburb of Karlsruhe, Germany. While looking over the audience, I found myself staring at a small section on my left that seated about fifty people. I had an impression that someone in that section was contemplating suicide. I pointed my finger at the section and said, "Someone in this section is thinking of taking your life. Would you come forward so we can pray for you?" A lady in a white dress got up and came forward. I was not even conscious of the fact that when I pointed to the section I was pointing directly at her.

Impressions like these can happen any time—you don't have to be preaching a sermon or speaking at a conference. Years ago, a young woman named Kristy Greer had just started coming to a church Leesa and I were helping to start. We had only talked to Kristy and her husband Carl a couple of times when she called and asked if she could come to our home to talk with us about a book she was reading. When she walked through the door, she smiled and seemed to be in a light-hearted mood. However, suddenly I "knew" two things about her—one, she was about to start crying; and two, she wasn't a Christian and was about to be born again. Before she walked through the door, I had assumed she was a Christian and her demeanor when she arrived gave no clue that she was near tears.

After a few minutes of polite conversation, I asked her, "Why do you feel like crying?"

"I don't know," she replied, "It's the strangest thing. I've felt like crying ever since I walked into your home. How did you know?"

"The Lord is showing me something about you."

"Do you *know* why I feel like crying?"

"Yes, I do. You're about to be born again," I said.

"What do you mean by born again?" As Leesa and I talked with her, Kristy *was* born again, right there in our living room. Without those impressions from the Lord, I wouldn't even have thought to talk to her about her salvation.

Over the years I have come to rely on divine impressions for guidance in our everyday affairs and for directions in ministry. For me, these impressions have grown more frequent and specific, even to the point of knowing someone's name without ever having met them and knowing a condition that God wants to heal or touch. I have observed the same thing happening to many other Christians who

1. believe that God will speak to them through impressions;
2. want these impressions to serve God and his people;
3. pray regularly for God to speak to them;
4. and act on the impressions when they come, even at the risk of looking foolish in front of others.

Hearing God through impressions is a very biblical aspect of the language of the Holy Spirit. Nehemiah told how God led him by an impression: "So my *God put it into my heart* to assemble the nobles, the officials and the common people for registration by families" (Neh. 7:5). It was not an audible voice Nehemiah heard, but rather an influence he felt in his heart to register the people. He was able to discern that this impression on his heart had come from God, not from himself.

Sometimes an impression can lead to a miracle. While Paul was preaching in Lystra, there was a man in the audience who had been lame since birth. As he was looking at the man, he "*saw* that he had faith to be healed" (Acts 14:9). Paul commanded the man to stand up, and he was instantly healed. How do you "see" faith on someone? Of course you can't literally *see* faith. In this context, the word "see" means that Paul had a spiritual perception or impression about the man.[5] Through an impression, God gave Paul direct knowledge of this man's heart.

Another way of describing an impression may be found in the story of the paralytic who was lowered through the roof in front of Jesus. When Jesus told the man that his sins were forgiven, "some teachers of the law were sitting there, thinking to themselves, 'Why does this fellow talk like that? He's blaspheming! Who can forgive sins but God alone?'" (Mark 2:6–7). They hadn't said a word out loud, but in their hearts they were furious with Jesus. Mark wrote this story as though he were an eyewitness at the scene. He said, "Immediately Jesus *knew in his spirit* that this was what they were thinking in their hearts . . . ." (Mark 2:8). Often divine impressions are just like that, an immediate knowing in our spirit. It is a form of knowledge that does not come to us through logical reasoning or personal observation. Suddenly we just know that we know.

I believe God speaks to us through impressions all the time, but that many Christians have trained themselves to ignore their impressions. We associate them with feelings, and we've been taught that feelings are bad, or at best unreliable. People who are logical and analytical are strong. People who pay attention to feelings are weak. The rationalism of Western tradition has long been offended by knowledge that bypasses the mind. Our proud minds tell us that everything worth knowing must pass through our intellects. Sometimes God has to remove our confidence in our intelligence before he can talk with us.

God created us with feelings, a mind, and a body. He can and does speak to us through all three of these avenues, and all three can be the source of blessings or curses to us depending on how we use them. If we listen to our feelings, minds, or bodies and follow their promptings in contradiction to God's commands, they will become instruments of rebellion. But if we learn to discern the voice of God in our feelings, minds, and bodies, we will become better servants of Christ.

HUMAN MESSENGERS

It hardly needs to be said that God can speak to us through human messengers. All Christians have become accustomed to hearing the voice of God through teachers, preachers, and prophetic ministers. This doesn't mean, of course, that everything teachers, preachers, and prophetic ministers say is from God. Paul told us to evaluate prophetic messages (1 Cor. 14:29). Teachers "know in part" and prophets "prophesy in part" (1 Cor. 13:9). None of us is infallible.

You don't have to be a professional minister to be used by God in a special way. My friend Peter Lord says that he frequently travels hundreds of miles and pays a lot of money to attend a Christian conference in order to learn a truth that his wife could have told him if he had just stayed home and listened! God will frequently speak to us through our family, friends, and even acquaintances—if only we have the ears to hear.

The other day I was having dinner with a successful and well-known pastor. He was telling me his story. His first pastorate was a church of only sixty people. He is now the senior pastor of a church which serves about twelve thousand. From sixty to twelve thousand. That's quite a range of experience! He told me that his worst time in ministry had been when his first church was growing from sixty to three hundred. He was the only staff member. It was as if he lived in a glass house. Everyone knew what he was doing, and he was always doing something that offended someone. At one point, even his best friend turned against him. He received far more criticism from the three hundred than his present church of twelve thousand!

During that sixty-to-three-hundred transition, this pastor's number one personal problem was bitterness. He found himself preaching sermons out of anger, beating up his little flock Sunday after Sunday. Finally, one Sunday morning he came with another fiery message condemning his enemies in the congregation. As he approached the pulpit, a voice went off in his head, "One more time and you're out." He slid his prepared notes under the pulpit and gave a spontaneous message about God's love for them—for all of them. He told me that experience taught him to fear bitterness more than anything else in his ministry. It also changed him dramatically.

I had just met this minister. He knew nothing about my own church situation. For the last ten years I had been associated with very large churches, and only recently had I become the pastor of a small church of about three hundred. Every word he spoke about his bitterness was like a surgical knife peeling layers of hardness from my heart. I was doing the very same thing he had done. I had almost no joy speaking in my own church because of the strife going on, and I was talking down to the people. This pastor was speaking prophetically to me without even knowing it! God was illumining his words, and they were convicting me of my sin. Someone else listening might have only heard a man's success story, but I heard the Spirit of God say to me, "One more time, and you're out." And not caring to find out exactly what he meant by "out," I repented.

In these last four chapters I have attempted to summarize the various ways in which the Holy Spirit speaks. My summary hasn't been exhaustive. I didn't mention burning bushes, fleeces, or any number of other supernatural revelatory phenomena found in the biblical record. I have confined my discussion to that part of the language of the Holy Spirit that seems most common in the Scriptures, or to those aspects that either I have personally experienced or that someone I know to be a credible witness has experienced.

Unless we know how God speaks, we will never understand his voice. But knowing how God speaks doesn't guarantee he will speak to us or if he does that we will recognize his voice. How do we know if an impression is from him? How can we encourage prophetic ministry to grow in our church? What are the dangers we must avoid to keep the devil from seducing us with his voice? How do we interpret dreams from God? How much authority are we to give "prophetic" words from others? These are the kinds of questions I will attempt to answer in the next section of the book.

Learning the Language of the Holy Spirit

11

Learning the Language
of the Holy Spirit

I was taking an archery lesson the other day from the current Montana state champion. After watching me shoot a few arrows, he made some corrections in my form. "You need to learn what a good shot *feels* like," Tim said to me. He positioned me ten feet in front of the target and had me draw the arrow back and close my eyes. "Release the arrow when you want," he said. He didn't care where the arrow hit on the target. The purpose of the exercise was to learn what the proper form feels like when the shot is released. If the release is not smooth and fluid, the arrow will never consistently hit the bull's eye.

With eyes closed, I shot the first arrow. "Shoot another," said Tim. I did, and he said nothing. I shot a third arrow, and he said, "Now that was a good shot." He said nothing when I shot the fourth, fifth, and sixth arrows. On the seventh he said, again, "Now that was a good shot." I felt a little proud. Then I released the eighth arrow. I looked to my teacher for approval. Instead, he asked me, "Was that a good shot?" I wanted to say yes. But I hesitated when I realized I was standing in front of the state champ who already knew if it was a good shot. While I hesitated, he asked again, "Was that a good shot?" Then, looking straight into my eyes with the sternness of an Old Testament prophet, he said, "Don't ever lie to yourself. If you don't tell yourself the truth first, you'll never become a good shot. You'll never progress beyond the novice level. You've got to become your *first* and *best* critic if you want to achieve excellence with the bow. And don't think you can become a good shot by simply shooting a lot of arrows. If you don't realistically assess each shot, you'll just end up repeating the same mistakes."

A spiritual analogy gripped my heart, and for a moment I forgot about my archery lesson. Some of us in the church never progress spiritually, because we lie to ourselves and to each other. We tell ourselves that we have a New Testament church and that we're New Testament Christians when neither our church life nor our personal lives resemble very much of anything in the New Testament. We don't grow automatically with the passage of time. Some of us have been Christians a long time, but instead of progressing beyond the novice level we've ended up repeating the same mistakes, one spiritual arrow after another. We have not only become content with a Christian experience far below that of the New Testament, we have even developed theologies to justify our inferior experience. Without a realistic New Testament assessment of our spiritual experience, we will never progress in the kingdom of God.

Growth begins when we realize our spiritual poverty and powerlessness. There was a time in my life when I felt my church experience was so superior to everyone else's that I couldn't even begin to make a realistic assessment of my walk with God or my church's experience of the Holy Spirit's power. But in his mercy God showed me how bad my spiritual form was. And he did it like Tim did, by drawing me close to the target and having me close my eyes to my old prejudices in order to feel what the form of a New Testament church is like. Here's how it happened.

HOW TO SPLIT A CHURCH

I was pastoring a church I had helped to start years before. There were two other pastors on the staff and four elders. We had begun to pray for the sick in our church services and had moved to a more contemporary form of worship. Some in the church were overjoyed at this change, others were a little nervous. Nobody was really against praying for the sick or against a more contemporary form of worship, but there were some who were worried we might be moving in to a full-blown "charismatic" experience. Before long, battle lines were drawn and sides were taken. The pastors and elders were equally divided. Half wanted to pursue the gifts of the Holy Spirit. The other half wanted to put on the brakes. Both sides could quote Scripture to support their position. But none of the quotes caused anyone to change their position. They just reinforced each side's own prejudices. The conflict escalated when we began judging one another's motives. Then we attacked one another's character. It seemed so easy to call someone a liar on the other side. It was turning into a mess.

One day we pastors and elders were sitting around a table discussing our conflict. It finally dawned on us—we were headed for a church split. None of us had ever taken a course in church-splitting, but we all seemed to know instinctively how to get the job done. We really didn't want to split the church—some of us were best friends when this conflict had started. Some of us had histories together that stretched back twenty years. I had been there at the birth of their babies. They had been there at the birth of mine. These were my best friends. I had planned on serving with them in that church until the Lord came back.

We all felt that way about each other in the deepest part of our hearts. We weren't just people going to church together. We were friends who together had started a church with a common vision. And now we were being torn apart.

As we looked into each other's faces, we acknowledged that we were about to be torn apart, and we asked each other how we could prevent it. Finally, someone said, "I know, let's pray." I thought, *You mean, it's come to that? Are we really that bad off?* Until this point I think I had argued, intimidated, manipulated, quoted Scripture, and done just about everything else except seriously ask God his opinion on our conflict. I hadn't asked his opinion because I was sure that I was right.

Now that I am so many years removed from this conflict I can see that I caused a large part of it by my arrogant, self-righteous behavior. But at the time I was blind to my own sin in the conflict. All I could see was what was wrong with everyone else. The idea to pray seemed like a good thing to me because God might show the other side how wrong they were! I was so naive in those days. I didn't know how dangerous it was to pray or what this prayer meeting would lead to.

PRAYER MEETINGS CAN BE DANGEROUS

After some discussion, we all decided that the three pastors should go away for a day to pray, then the elders would join them, and we would all spend the next day in prayer. This was to be a prayer meeting I would remember the rest of my life.

On the first morning we were sitting by a stream under a tree on a beautiful ranch. After we had prayed for about an hour, one of the pastors pleaded, "Oh God, don't let this conflict escalate so that our church gets wiped off the face of the map." At the very second he prayed that prayer, a voice went off inside my mind, *What would be so bad about that?*

What a horrible question to ask! I knew the question had come from God, and it offended me. I thought it was rude. Then I realized that an omniscient Being doesn't ask a question to obtain information. When God said to Adam in the garden, "Where are you?" he wasn't asking for directions. This question was meant for me. What *would* be so bad about our church being wiped off the face of the map? I couldn't wait for the other two pastors to finish praying so I could ask them.

As soon as the prayer time ended, I asked, "What would be so bad about our church being wiped off the face of the map?" They stared at me in disbelief. How could I be so dumb and calloused?

"Well, it would hurt a lot of people," responded one of the pastors.

"I'm sure it would," I responded. "But eventually they would find another church to go to, and they would get over the hurt. What I'm really asking is, What would the kingdom of God lose in our city if our church didn't exist anymore?"

We all thought about that for a minute. What was important in the kingdom of God? What things happened in the New Testament when the kingdom of God came?

We all agreed that evangelism was an important aspect of the work of the kingdom. At that time, our church had anywhere from four hundred to five hundred people attending on Sundays. We asked ourselves how many people had been led to Christ through the ministry of our church in the last eighteen months. We could only come up with four names, and the leadership of the church had led none of these people to Christ. It was almost as if they had accidentally fallen into the kingdom of God and ended up in our church. We concluded that if our church didn't exist, there would be no great loss of evangelism in our city.

Then we asked ourselves how many people had been physically healed through the ministry of our church in the past eighteen months. After all, healing was important in the New Testament. It was certainly a sign of the coming of the kingdom. The Lord commanded the elders of the church to pray for the sick so that he could heal them (James 5:14–16). Although we had begun to pray for the sick in our church, at this point we couldn't count very many people who had been healed through our prayers. We concluded that the healing ministry of the Holy Spirit would suffer no great loss in our city if our church no longer existed.

Then we asked ourselves how many people no longer had to take antidepressants or no longer visit the psychiatrist's office on a regular basis because of the ministry of our church. We couldn't count anyone here. We could, however, count a few who had *started* taking antidepressants.

We couldn't count any failing marriages we had saved. But we could count some we had lost.

Next came addictions to drugs, alcohol, and sex. From our private counseling sessions we all knew people in our church who were struggling with these sins, but none of us could point to one person who had been conclusively delivered from one of these sins.

We also realized that if our church ceased to exist there would be no missionary who would be forced to come home from the mission field, nor would there be any significant loss in the social care programs for the poor in our own city.

We were forced to conclude that without the existence of our church the kingdom of God in our city would suffer no appreciable loss in evangelism, in the healing of bodies, spirits, emotions, marriages, in the care of the poor, or in the support of missionaries in other lands.

We looked at each other and said, "Well, what *do* we do?" One of us answered, "We're the best Bible teachers in the city." At the time we believed that was true. We didn't realize how arrogant that belief was, nor how stupid it was to make that claim. We didn't even know all the Bible teachers in that city. How could we claim we were the best of all the Bible teachers?

But even though we believed we were the best, we realized something was dreadfully wrong with our ministry. What were we teaching the people? We weren't teaching them how to evangelize. We weren't teaching them how to get people's bodies, souls, or spirits healed. We weren't teaching them how to get delivered from addictions or how to care for the poor. We weren't teaching them how to get vitally involved with foreign missions. Even though we may have had some token support of some of these ministries, our contribution was so insignificant that it made virtually no impact in the kingdom of God. So what were we teaching the Bible for?

I looked at the other two pastors. "You know, I wouldn't even go to this church if they didn't pay me." The other two pastors said, "Now that you mention it, neither would we. We don't like this church either." The irony of all this was that I had been the main catalyst in starting the church. I had made the church just like I wanted it—a Bible-teaching station—and now I didn't like it at all and neither did the other pastors.

The elders arrived later that night. "Has the Lord spoken to you?" they asked.

"Yes he has," we said.

"What did he say?"

"Well, he showed us that we wouldn't even go to this church if you didn't pay us!"

"What! What have you three guys been doing?" the elders asked.

"Praying."

It can be dangerous to pray. Sometimes the Lord may lead you to a realistic assessment of the effectiveness of your ministry. On that particular morning, sitting by that stream under the tree, I realized that the church I had built had more in common with a country club than it did with the church of the New Testament.[1] I had helped create a church that was significantly different from the church of the New Testament. We three pastors had lost our joy in the ministry. We were now attending that church out of an obligation to duty and because we were drawing a paycheck. Not very good reasons to go to church.

GOING TO CHURCH TODAY

Why do *you* go to church? Remember the point I made above—you're never going to grow without an honest assessment of your practice and your motives. What drives you to be there Sunday after Sunday? Some people go to church out of a sense of duty. Some go because it's the thing to do on Sunday morning—their family has always gone to church. Some go to church because they've found it's a good place to do business. It helps their image in the community. Some people go to church because they like the feeling they get when the sun comes through the stained glass windows onto the robed minister who leads them in the same formal liturgies week after week. These are the people who often comment how "beautiful" the service was on a particular Sunday. Some people go because their friends go, and the church has become the center of their social life. Some people go to be entertained. Some go to be enlightened. Some go to hear a great speaker. Some go to learn the Bible. Some go to please their mate. Others go to find a mate. Still others go to get *away* from a mate. Having been a pastor for more than twenty years, I have learned there are as many reasons why people go to church today as there are people.

GOING TO CHURCH IN NEW TESTAMENT TIMES

It was much more difficult to go to church in New Testament times. It could cost you your property, your family, even your life. It's still that way in some places in the world today, but not in America. So why did they go? Why did they take the risk?

First, they came to hear Jesus and be healed by him (Luke 5:15; 6:18). I used to come to learn the Bible, and later, to teach the Bible. I even called my church a "Bible church." How different from the beginning, when people came to meet a Person.

Second, they came to worship God together. Of course, it is possible to worship God alone and anywhere. But there is a spiritual dynamic that occurs when the people of God come together corporately to express their unrestrained affection for God. To put it simply, we enter into the presence of God when we sincerely and exuberantly sing him our thanks and praise (Ps. 100:1–5). God's presence was so manifest during corporate worship that New Testament Christians risked their lives just to be part of that experience.

Third, they came together to be equipped to do the work of the ministry. Paul said,

> It was he who gave some to be apostles, some to be prophets, some to be evangelists, and some to be pastors and teachers, to prepare God's people for works of service, so that the body of Christ may be built up until we all reach unity in the faith and in the knowledge of the Son of God and become mature, attaining to the whole measure of the fullness of Christ (Eph. 4:11–13).

The Lord never sent apostles, prophets, evangelists, pastors, and teachers simply to do the work of the ministry. Their primary responsibility was *to prepare God's people for works of service*. This is the main way the body of Christ is built up. The body of Christ will be anemic and unable to fulfill the Great Commission as long as only a few people are doing the work of the ministry. This New Testament pattern for ministry was set by Jesus. If anyone was ever capable of doing all the ministry alone, it was the Lord Jesus. But instead, he trained twelve apostles, who in turn trained others to do the work of the ministry.

Fourth, people came to church to be strengthened, that is, built up in Christ. At the conclusion of Paul's' controversial discussion about the gifts of the Spirit and their use in the church he wrote, "What then shall we say, brothers? When you come together, everyone has a hymn, or a word of instruction, a revelation, a tongue or an interpretation. All of these must be done for the strengthening of the church" (1 Cor. 14:26).

Was this strengthening meant to occur through the ministry of one person? Absolutely not. Paul said that *everyone* was to bring something to church with them that would contribute to the edification of others present. What could you bring? Paul's list only has five things in it: a hymn, a word of instruction, a revelation, a tongue, or an interpretation. I'm sure this list was not meant to be exhaustive but rather a simple representation of the kinds of things we could bring to church to build up our brothers and sisters in Christ. The New Testament church service was never meant to be a one-man show.

If you lived in the New Testament times, you prepared your heart to come to church, you prepared your heart to worship, you came expecting to be equipped for ministry, and you asked God to give you a gift to bring with you so that you might be used to strengthen someone else. This was the New Testament way of going to church.

The New Testament church was not only the dwelling place for the presence of God, it was also a learning center for the language of the Holy Spirit. People not only worshiped God in church, but they were equipped to *hear* him, and after hearing God, they were able to give something to someone that would build them up.

The question God asked me that day as I sat by the stream forever changed my view of church life. I decided that from that day on I was going to go to church like Paul recommended. I made up my mind that I was going to find a group of people who felt the same way I did. We would come together to meet Jesus, to hear him and be healed by him, to worship him, to be equipped for ministry, and to bring gifts to build one another up.

LEARNING THE LANGUAGE OF THE HOLY SPIRIT

There was just one obstacle to being a part of a church like the one I just described—I couldn't hear the voice of God. About the only thing I could do from the list in 1 Corinthians 14:26 was bring a word of instruction. I had been trained to teach the Bible, but I didn't have a clue about bringing a revelation, a tongue, or an interpretation. Nor did I understand how the other supernatural gifts functioned—gifts like words of wisdom, words of knowledge, the gift of faith, the gift of healing or miracles, or the gift of distinguishing spirits, and so on (1 Cor. 12:8–10). I had no understanding of dreams or visions. All of these things were important in the New Testament church. Without them, no church—however good the music or gifted the speaker—can really claim to be a New Testament church.

The only part of the language of the Holy Spirit I could understand was the written text of the Bible. And now I was wondering how much of my understanding was simply traditional interpretations passed down over the years through various teachers and how much really came from the illumination of the Holy Spirit.

In beginning the process of learning the language of the Holy Spirit, I felt like a little child trying to learn the language of his parents. I did have three things going for me. First, I had an acute sense of my spiritual poverty. I now believed that I could not hear the voice of God very well. Second, I had come to believe God was still speaking in all the ways that he spoke in the Bible. And third, I knew I needed God to speak to me in more personal ways if I was ever going to experience the kind of church life described in the New Testament.

Learning When You Are Young

I found out that the process of learning the language of the Holy Spirit is similar to the process of learning any foreign language.

In 1984 I took a sabbatical from my teaching duties at seminary and moved with my family to southern Germany for a year. When we moved there, I could read academic German very, very slowly, but I could not speak conversational German. I entered a formal school to learn conversational German. My goal was to learn to think in German so I would be able to read academic German more rapidly.

Our children were three, five, and seven when we moved to a small village in the Black Forest of Germany. We put the children in a German-speaking school. They had no prior instruction in German—or formal training in English for that matter—while I had had a great deal of linguistic training, had studied a number of languages, and was going through a very rigorous formal training in the German language.

At the end of the year my children spoke German so well they actually sounded like Germans—they had virtually no American accent. But even though I spoke German well enough to carry on conversations and go any place in the country I wanted, I had a horrible accent! Every German I conversed with recognized me as an American even though I was speaking German. I knew much more German grammar and vocabulary than my children, but they actually spoke the language better. This illustrates what language teachers all over the world have always known: the best time to learn a language is when you are very young. Why is this?

First of all, my children were highly motivated. The highest value in their young lives was to play with other children. In order to play with the other kids, my children *had* to learn German; it was a means to their chief goal. The motivation factor is just as important in learning the language of the Holy Spirit. I became convinced that I would never experience the fullness of the New Testament ministry of the Holy Spirit unless I learned to hear the Holy Spirit speak in the variety of ways he spoke in the New Testament.

A second factor that helps young people learn a new language is that their native speech patterns are not nearly so ingrained in them as in their parents. For example, the word order in a typical German sentence can be dramatically different from the word order of a typical English sentence. To an English speaker it seems that the verbs, subjects, and direct objects are completely out of order in the German sentence. Years of speaking English have taught us where the verb is supposed to be in a sentence and where the subject is supposed to be. My three, five, and seven-year-old children were not sophisticated enough to notice there was a difference in the word order. In our home, where we spoke English, verbs simply followed the subjects closely. On the playground, where the kids were speaking German, the verb might not come until the very last word in the sentence. Both ways seemed natural depending on the environment in which they found themselves.

In the same way, those of us who for years have believed that the only way God speaks to us is through the Bible or through sermons from the Bible, have the most difficult time learning the language of dreams or impressions. It seems unnatural to us that God would speak in any way except the Bible.

A third factor that enables children to learn a foreign language faster than adults is that their young vocal cords have not yet hardened like those of an adult. Our kids' vocal cords were still so flexible that it was easy for them to make the guttural sounds and vowel distinctions of German that are lacking in English. Likewise, when learning the language of the Holy Spirit, there is a point at which some of us become so hardened by our doctrines and traditions that it makes it difficult for us to hear God in any way except the way in which we have always heard him.

Trial and Error

You simply cannot learn a language apart from trial and error. When a group of missionaries goes to a foreign land, the first thing they do is enter into a rigorous study of the language.

The interesting thing is that it is often not the most academically skilled of the missionaries who learn the language first or best. Often, the academically-oriented missionary prefers to spend long hours studying a grammar book. He or she wants to make sure they learn the grammar perfectly so they will not make any mistakes when they speak. On the other hand, the missionaries less inclined toward academics are the ones who volunteer to go buy the groceries and run errands. They make their grammatical mistakes right in front of native speakers as they try to speak the new language, usually getting on-the-spot correction!

The same is true with learning the language of the Holy Spirit. Only those who are willing to try and fail will ever become proficient at understanding which impressions come from God and which arise merely from their own soul. This is one of the reasons my children learned to speak the German language better than I did. I spent more time studying, while they spent more time practicing. I threw myself into learning, while they threw themselves into living. I learned through the sequestered safety of a book, while they learned through trial and error.

One of my most prophetically gifted friends, Rick Joyner, the president of Morning Star Publications, is currently leading a "School of the Spirit" which meets on Friday nights in Charlotte, North Carolina. People regularly drive a hundred miles in order to come to this meeting because they are learning how to hear God's voice in new and effective ways. Rick told me that the trial and error methodology had given them some humorous moments as well as some humiliating failures. Then he made this very interesting observation, "You know, we are learning as much from our failures as our successes."

At this point I can hear one of my objectors saying, "Trial and error is okay when you are learning a language, but it's a much more serious matter when you are telling someone that God told you something." I heartily agree. It is a very serious thing to tell anyone, "God said . . ." But all Christians do that. Every time we quote the Bible and interpret it or apply it to someone else, we are telling them that God said something. And our interpretation or application may not be what God has said at all. It may just be *our* interpretation or *our* application. Or even if we are correct, our timing may be off. We may be quick to speak when God would prefer we be quick to hear. No matter what our doctrinal position is, there is always the temptation to use our faith to control or direct the lives of other people. There is always the temptation to hear God for other people instead of hearing him for ourselves.

The Embarrassment Factor

"Folly is bound up in the heart of a child" (Prov. 22:15). Parents know the truth of this famous text only too well. But a child's foolishness can have a positive effect when it comes to learning a language. Because of their foolishness, children are natural risk-takers. They will try anything because they are not afraid to fail or to look foolish. When my children began to speak German, they made many grammatical errors. But they weren't embarrassed by them. They were so uninhibited, compared to me. I was so afraid to look foolish that I actually *avoided* conversations in German, the very thing I needed to do to learn conversational German!

The fear of failure and embarrassment, which is a manifestation of insecurity, self-consciousness, or in the worst case, pride, is one of the great hindrances to learning the language of the Holy Spirit. You can't learn a natural language or the language of the Holy Spirit apart from trial and error. And unfortunately, errors make us look foolish. Even worse, they make us *feel* foolish. No one likes to feel foolish. Yet God chose the foolish and despised things of the world to shame the wise and the proud (1 Cor. 1:26–29). Anyone who becomes skilled at hearing God's voice will have paid the price of appearing and feeling foolish many times.

A Safe Environment for Caterpillars

Sitting under the tree on the ranch with the other two pastors, I decided to become like a little child and suffer whatever embarrassment was necessary in order to learn to hear the Holy Spirit speak. I'm glad that at the time I had no concept of the embarrassment and humiliation that lay ahead. I found a group of people who were willing to risk a little humiliation, and we began meeting on Wednesday nights, about forty of us. Our main goals were to worship God, hear God, get equipped for ministry, and edify one another. None of us were charismatics. Most of us had been anti-charismatics. We would worship God for thirty to forty minutes, singing hymns and contemporary choruses. Then one of us would do a little teaching. And after that, we would bow our heads and ask God to speak to us.

In worshiping this way, we were trying to experience 1 Corinthians 14:26. We hoped God would give us a revelation, a word of knowledge, a word of wisdom, a tongue, an interpretation, a healing, a teaching, or anything else that might edify some of those present. And it actually started happening. People began to get genuine revelations. God healed some people. Other people became saved. Christians were growing closer to God. In a few weeks the forty turned into one hundred, and our little meeting kept growing.

Before long, word got out that there was power at our Wednesday night meeting, and then some people came to the meeting to investigate rather than participate. One night some of my seminary students came late and sat in the back row. They had heard that their professor was involved in some strange charismatic meetings. They wanted to see for themselves. I seemed so normal and dull in the classroom they found it difficult to believe that I was participating in wild worship services.

Everything went fine until we came to the part where we waited for God to speak. After waiting in silence for a few minutes, I asked the group if anyone thought the Lord might have spoken to them. The wackiest lady in the whole group raised her hand. "Oh no," I thought, "Please, God, anybody but her." I don't mean to be rude by calling this lady "wacky," but every group, every church, has some people that are just, well, they're just wacky. When anything new comes along, it seems they're the first ones to try it. They've got nothing to lose. No one ever asks them out to lunch. They're just politely tolerated by the rest of us. (Maybe that's why God has such mercy on them and usually heals and speaks to them first.) However, I felt no mercy when this lady raised her hand, only dread. It was impossible to ignore her. She was the only one raising a hand.

"Yes," I said.

"I just had a vision," she said. Vision? Did she have to use *that* word? Alarm began to show on the faces of the seminary students.

"What was the *picture* you saw?" I asked.

"Well, in the *vision* I saw a purple caterpillar crawling in the gutter. He ate four small pebbles and then vomited them up. What does that vision mean, Jack?"

What does that mean? My first thought was, *It means you're wacky, lady!* My second thought was, *It means God hates me! I must have done something really bad today to bring this on.* The seminary students were rolling their eyes at one another, scoffing at the "vision." For a minute I was tempted to think that the caterpillar was the seminary and the students were the pebbles. I kind of wished they would be vomited up or at least out of the meeting. Then I noticed a strange dichotomy in the meeting.

On the one hand, the students, through their expressions and body language, were imploring me to tell the group that this was definitely not a real vision. I could almost hear them say, "Don't let these people be deceived." On the other hand, the rest of the group seemed filled with tension. They weren't deceived. None of them thought the vision was from the Lord. They were waiting to see how badly the lady was going to be punished for saying something so wacky.

I looked at the students. I looked at the people. I looked at the wacky lady. "You know, the Lord is not giving me an interpretation of what you saw. Let's wait a few minutes to see if anyone gets an interpretation, and then we'll come back to your vision," I said. The students looked exasperated. The looks on their faces said, "Our professor really has gone strange. He's treating that story as if it's a real vision." Actually, I didn't think it was. I was just treating the lady like a real person. But the interesting thing was that the rest of the people relaxed. All over the room people began to raise their hands to "try out" their impressions or visions. They knew they're weren't going to be punished for failing. It is so much easier to learn the language of the Holy Spirit when you have a safe and loving environment.

Being Where the Language Is Spoken

I told you that I had studied German for several years while living in America, reading grammars and memorizing vocabulary, and later reading German books. Then I went to Germany and lived in a small German village where most of the people only spoke German. In just a few months I had learned more of the language than all of my previous years of study in America. I found that being where people speak German is the best way to learn German.

In the same way, being around people who speak and understand the language of the Holy Spirit is an invaluable aid in learning to interpret visions, dreams, impressions, and the Bible as well. Just as some people are more gifted at learning human languages, there are those who are more gifted at hearing God's voice in its various forms. For example, Joseph and Daniel were gifted in the interpretation of dreams. The apostle Paul was extraordinarily gifted to interpret the Bible and to understand revelatory phenomena outside the Bible. The church at Antioch was a place where the language of the Holy Spirit was spoken and understood (Acts 13:2). Those who find themselves in these kinds of environments usually progress more rapidly in the Holy Spirit's language than those in places where his language is not spoken at all, or spoken in only one dialect.

The Bible Is the Menu

Normally, one of the first things you learn when studying a foreign language is the menu of that country. Ordering food is a basic necessity of life. In much the same way, the Bible is the menu of the Holy Spirit and the explanation of his language. The Bible not only tells the various ways in which the Holy Spirit will speak to us, it also tells us the very things we must eat if we are to live. And it warns us of spiritual poisons. No one who purposely avoids the Bible is ever going to hear God reliably and consistently.

There are people, however, who devote themselves diligently to Bible study and are still spiritually malnourished. This frequently happens in environments where people make Bible study an end in itself. They are like people who study a menu with great precision and can tell you every detail about it: when it was first written, how it has changed over the years, how each dish is prepared, how it ought to be served, which food should come first—even why the chef has organized the menu in its present order. Perhaps they even went to schools whose major goal was to explain menus. When they graduated, the ones who were the best at explaining menus were able to build the biggest "menu clubs" where many people meet regularly just to hear a new and inspiring explanation of the menu. Yet no one grows strong from an explanation of the menu or even from first-hand study of a menu. Only those who order from the menu and eat grow strong. Don't mistake the menu for the meal.

Jesus Christ is the Bread from heaven. If our Bible study does not lead us to experience Jesus Christ, then it is leading us to spiritual malnutrition. The Bible is the menu meant to lead us to experience God in every facet of our lives. If we make Bible study our goal, we will end up just like the Pharisees who searched the Scriptures diligently but never came to Christ (John 5:39–40). They studied the menu regularly and religiously. But they never ordered. Never tasted. And that was both the irony and the tragedy. So close to the menu, yet so far from the meal.

The Time Factor

No one learns a language instantly. Languages are acquired over time through constant use. The same is true of the language of the Holy Spirit. Those who become skilled at hearing God's voice are those who have consistently trained themselves to listen for him to speak (cf. Heb. 5:14). If we keep our hearts open to God's correction, develop the habit of frequently asking him his opinion on matters, and then listen for his answers, then over time we will become skilled at hearing his voice. Be patient. Give yourself time.

If you really desire to learn the language of the Holy Spirit, your desire is a sign that the mercy of God has come to rest on you. He put that desire into your heart, and his mercy will remain on you through all the trials of learning the Spirit's language. C. S. Lewis once said that if only the will to walk is there, God is pleased even with our stumbles.[2] If that is true, then perhaps if only the will to hear is there, he is pleased even with our errors.

12

Facilitating Prophetic Ministry

Several years ago Paul Cain and I were in a conference hosted by Metro Vineyard Christian Fellowship of Kansas City. Paul had given a message and afterward had given prophetic words to six individuals in the audience. Then he looked directly at me and said, "Jack, would you stand up please?"

As I rose to my feet, Paul said, "I had a vision of your mother this afternoon. Her name is Wanda Jean. I saw her standing on a cliff looking for her missing jewel. That must mean your father's name is Jewel Clifford. Then I saw your father. When I saw him, he was in heaven, face-to-face with the Lord Jesus. The Lord showed me that sometime before your father had died, like Abraham, he believed in the Lord, and the Lord counted it to him for righteousness."

I was absolutely stunned. No one knew my mother's real name. She hated the name Wanda. She would only use the name Jean. It was one of our best kept family secrets. Likewise, my dad never went by the name Jewel Clifford. Everyone called him Jack. I had never told Paul that my parents' names were Jean and Jack, let alone that their birth names were Wanda Jean and Jewel Clifford. I knew that the only way he could have gotten those names was by supernatural revelation from the Lord.[1] Anyone could have told me they had seen my father in heaven, but only the Lord could have told me the real names of my parents in such a way that it would confirm the supernatural revelation about my father's presence in heaven.

My father committed suicide when I was twelve years old. Five years later I became a Christian. After that time, I used to wonder about my father, whether he was in heaven or hell. Over and over again, I would try to evaluate all the evidence. On the negative side, we hadn't been a churchgoing family, and my father had taken his own life. On the positive side, my dad had owned a Bible and read it, and I had also heard him pray aloud to the Lord more than once. Some days, after I weighed all of the negative evidence together, I would be convinced my dad was in hell. Other days, after weighing all the positive evidence, I would believe he was in heaven. It went back and forth like this for several years until finally I just put it out of my mind. Now, not too long after I had turned forty, the very age at which my dad took his life, the Lord in his mercy revealed to me that my father was in heaven.

The next day I picked up Paul at his hotel to take him to a pastor's luncheon. I asked him why the Lord chose this time to give me this revelation about my father. Not only had I not been asking the Lord about my father, but years ago I had put the whole subject out of my mind. As far as I knew, it didn't trouble me any longer. I wanted to know if the Lord had shown Paul why he had given me this revelation.

Paul told me that after I had become a Christian, the question of my father's eternal destiny troubled me more than I realized. He said that not long after my conversion, a root of bitterness grew up in my heart over my father's death and over the possibility that he might spend eternity in hell. He said that root of bitterness had caused a harshness in my behavior toward others. The revelation was meant to help remove that harshness.

The removal of harshness *was* something I had been praying about. I had been asking the Lord to give me his love and gentleness for his people. Today I'm not as gentle as I would like to be, but neither am I as harsh as I used to be. I know that the prophetic word from the Holy Spirit regarding my father's eternal destiny has been a significant factor in softening my heart.

Prophetic ministry like this won't just happen in your church. Like preaching and teaching it has to be cultivated and properly administered. The following are some descriptions and guidelines I have found to be helpful in facilitating prophetic ministry, both from the Scripture and from experience.

WHAT IS A PROPHET?

A Prophet Discerns the Future

Isaiah referred to the prophets as the "eyes" of Israel (Isa. 29:10). Through the Holy Spirit, the prophets can "see" things regularly that others don't regularly see.[2] The greatest of all prophets is, of course, is Christ, who during his earthly ministry did not judge by what his eyes saw or his ears heard. Instead, he judged with the discernment of the Holy Spirit (Isa. 11:2–4).

Prophets can see the future. They can predict future judgments and future blessings. They can describe ahead of time the rise and fall of nations. They can also do practical things, like telling where your lost donkey can be found (1 Sam. 9:20). And they can tell you the secrets of your heart, so that when they announce God's future plans for you, you will believe them (9:19; 10:1–9).

A Prophet Discerns the Present

Prophets are also skilled at discerning the present priorities of the Lord. Sometimes this is referred to as "forthtelling." A common form of forthtelling is when prophets speak against present sins. I suppose anyone in any society can find plenty of sin to complain about—social reformers have always had plenty of sins to crusade against. What makes a true prophet unique is that he or she is moved by the Lord to speak out against a condition that the Lord wants to change at that given time.

Just as there are hundreds of things wrong with any given society, there are hundreds of things wrong with any of our individual lives. Normally, the Lord does not correct all of these things at once. If he showed you or me all of our sin and immaturity at once, it would probably crush us, and we would give up all hope of ever changing. Often, the Lord shows his prophets what he is *presently* interested in changing.

Forthtelling does not always mean the announcing of our sins. The apostle Paul commands us to find out what is pleasing to the Lord (Eph. 5:10). Sometimes the Lord will show a prophet God's present priorities or plans for our lives. A few years ago I had a dream in which I wrote a book that the Lord used for a specific purpose. At the time, I was busy in a conference ministry and also in pastoral ministry, and I had not planned to devote any serious time to writing for another few years. I was not sure if I should interpret the dream literally. Shortly after the dream, Paul Cain called me and told me that he had had a vision of me that afternoon. His interpretation of his vision was that the Lord intended for me to make writing a greater priority in my schedule. Paul knew nothing about my dream. Even with my dream and Paul's vision, however, I still could not find the time to begin writing. Soon, everything in our lives changed so that I could begin my book. When the changes came, we weren't upset because we knew why they were coming. My dream and Paul's prophetic vision had shown us that the Lord was changing his priorities for our lives.

CAN EVERYONE PROPHESY?

In the Old Testament there were relatively few prophets and seldom did anyone other than a prophet prophesy. In the New Testament the coming of the Spirit changed all that. Peter claimed that the day of Pentecost was the beginning of the fulfillment of Joel 2:28–32. Listen to the words spoken by the prophet Joel:

> In the last days, God says, I will pour out my Spirit on all people. Your sons and daughters will prophesy, your young men will see visions, your old men will dream dreams. Even on my servants, both men and women, I will pour out my Spirit in those days, and they will prophesy (Acts 2:16–18).

With the coming of the Spirit there is a sense in which every Christian is to be prophetic. There will be prophecies, dreams, and visions in the church without distinction in regard to gender, age, or economic position. Everyone in the New Testament may at one time or another prophesy, dream, or have a vision. Everyone in the New Testament may evangelize and may teach. This doesn't mean, however, that everyone in the New Testament will be a prophet, evangelist, or teacher. But those who consistently do these activities and do them well may be said to be prophets, teachers, or evangelists.

Not everyone who has a ministry of prophecy is going to be prominent in this ministry. Gifts vary in their intensity, and ministries vary in their levels of authority. Paul spoke of this when he wrote, "We have different gifts, *according to the grace given us*. If a man's gift is prophesying, let him use it *in proportion to his faith*" (Rom. 12:6). Jesus taught the same thing in the parable of the talents, where God gives some five talents, others two, and others one (Matt. 25:14–30). Some evangelists have international ministries, while other evangelists' ministries are confined to a single Sunday school class year after year. The same is true with prophetic ministries.

WHY NOT JUDGE THE PACKAGE?

Our churches will never have effective teaching ministries unless we recognize who the effective teachers are. This is also true with prophetic ministry. We'll never be able to recognize prophets if we make the mistake of judging prophetic ministry by the package in which it comes. Some prophets can come in very ordinary packages—like a carpenter's son who did nothing noteworthy in public until he was thirty years old. Other prophets may not be so ordinary. They may be poor public speakers, uneducated, and may even be a little weird. They can be depressive (Jeremiah), have bad attitudes (Jonah), be subject to mood swings (Elijah), mystical (Ezekiel), have a tendency to go naked for long periods of time (Isaiah), marry a prostitute (Hosea), talk to donkeys (Balaam), travel by marine mammal (Jonah again), lie in order to get out of trouble (Abraham), be a vegetarian (Daniel), wear unusual clothes (John the Baptist), get mad at God and refuse to answer him (Jonah again), argue with God (Habakkuk), or have peculiar eating habits (John the Baptist again). In short, don't judge the prophet by the package. If you do, you may miss out on the blessings of prophetic ministry.

Besides coming in sometimes peculiar packages, prophets may have some peculiar methods of ministry. On some occasions a prophet may need to hear music before he can minister prophetically (Elisha, 2 Kings 3:15ff.). I know some prophetic people who don't see things until they shake your hand or lay hands on you to pray for you. Some prophets may use strange symbolism. Elisha told King Jehoash to strike the ground with some arrows. Jehoash struck the ground three times and stopped. Elisha was angry with Jehoash and said, "You should have struck the ground five or six times; then you would have defeated Aram and completely destroyed it. But now you will defeat it only three times" (2 Kings 13:19). How was Jehoash supposed to have discerned the meaning of Elisha's symbolism? Or how about the linen belt that Jeremiah buried and then later retrieved when it was ruined? It was meant as a symbol of Israel's and Judah's ruin (Jer. 13:1–11). The religious people, however, just thought Jeremiah was being eccentric and negative. Even these kinds of symbolic actions were mild in comparison with Isaiah's three-year period of nakedness (Isa. 20:2–3) or Hosea marrying a practicing prostitute (Hos. 1:2).

Jesus said we are to evaluate prophetic ministry by the fruit it produces (Matt. 7:15ff.). The important questions to be asked about the ministry of prophetic persons are questions like the following:

1. Are they honoring Christ and bringing glory to him, or are they bringing attention to themselves?
2. Are they walking in humility, and does their ministry produce humility?
3. Does their ministry produce the fruit of the Holy Spirit?
4. Are their words accurate and do their predictions come true?
5. Does their teaching fall in line with the Scripture?

Notice on the last question that I asked if their teaching falls in line with the Scripture, not with your doctrine or interpretation of the Scripture. I am assuming that anyone we let minister in our church would believe in the fundamentals of the faith even though they may not necessarily agree with our interpretations of debatable areas. The frequent cry, "That's unscriptural," often indicates nothing more than disagreement with someone's interpretation of a minor area of doctrine.

HOW MUCH AUTHORITY DO NEW TESTAMENT PROPHETS HAVE?

A friend of mine was going to a well-known charismatic church back in the 1970s. When he was nineteen years old, he broke up with the young woman that he had been dating. He had decided the relationship wasn't going anywhere, and he didn't want to pursue it any further. He knew he didn't love this woman and that they weren't right for each other. A "prophet" in the church told the young couple they had made a serious mistake, and that God wanted them to be married. They didn't love each other, but neither did they want to disobey the Lord. They got married. If there was ever a couple that shouldn't have gotten married, it was this couple. Without going into the details, I will tell you that my friend gave it his best shot, but in the end his wife divorced him.

In some circles of the charismatic movement in the 1970s it was not uncommon for prophets to arrange marriages like this. Does God give that kind of authority to prophets? Not only does he *not* give that authority to New Testament prophets, he doesn't even give it to New Testament apostles. The Bible does indicate that believers are to marry believers (1 Cor. 7:39; 2 Cor. 6:14–15), but neither New Testament prophets nor apostles tell you which believer to marry. They didn't have the authority to tell people whether or not to have children, or how many children to have. They didn't have authority to tell believers where to live, work, or what their vocation should be. They could not command your conscience (1 Cor. 8:7ff.). They could encourage you to give money (1 Cor. 16:2; 2 Cor. 9:6–15), but they could not tell you how much money to give (2 Cor. 9:7) or bring you under church discipline if you didn't give money.[3]

Who's in Charge?

In the Old Testament, God gave kings authority to rule the nations of Israel and Judah. Prophets were a wonderful blessing to godly kings and a thorn in the flesh to evil kings. Some prophets were very powerful and had a great deal of influence. But the government of the nations was given by God to the kings, not to the prophets.

In the New Testament, the government of the local church was given to the elders of that church, not to itinerant prophets, nor to the prophets within that church. Paul wrote, "The elders who *direct the affairs* of the church are worthy of double honor, especially those whose work is preaching and teaching (1 Tim. 5:17).

There are two groups in the church that continually cause problems for the leadership of the church. One group is the prophetic people. Because they frequently have visions, dreams, and unusual impressions, they may have a tendency to think they know more than the leadership of the church. Some get offended when the leadership doesn't listen to them. They assume they know better what the Lord wants for the church.

The other group that frequently causes difficulty is the intercessors. Intercessors are people whose primary ministry is to pray. They spend long hours in prayer—frequently more than anyone else in the church. Sometimes this makes them feel more spiritual than the leadership, and they resent not having a significant say in the affairs of the church. Both of these groups, the prophets and the intercessors, are required by God to submit to the elders.

Also, there are a number of people functioning as itinerant prophets who aren't submitted to any local authority. Frequently they come in the back door of a church through friends in that church or through people in that church whom they met at a conference. These itinerant prophets tell aggrandizing stories about themselves and magnify their ministries. They demonstrate some prophetic gifting, though never to the degree of the stories they tell about themselves. Frequently they seek donations to their "ministry" or loans that they never pay back. Paul described these people as "the kind who worm their way into homes and gain control over weak-willed women, who are loaded down with sins and are swayed by all kinds of evil desires" (2 Tim. 3:6). I never understood what Paul meant by this text until I saw some itinerant prophets in action. I have actually seen them do what Paul described here.

Churches in transition that are just learning about the gifts of the Spirit are easy prey for these kinds of "ministers." Sometimes the elders of a church in transition feel like they have been arrogant and aloof in their prior ministry. Now they want to be "open to whatever God is doing." In their desire to embrace humility they can actually be naive with regard to some of these itinerant prophets. Church leadership should never allow ministers of any sort, prophets or teachers, to minister in their church unless they are submitted to the authority of a local church and genuinely accountable to its leadership. Home group leaders should not give authority or a place of ministry to people who are not themselves genuinely under authority. Make calls and check references before allowing unknown people to serve in your church. This rule is not meant to quench the Holy Spirit or promote legalism, but rather to protect the church from predators. An itinerant minister who refuses to be submitted to spiritual authority is always filled with spiritual pride. Loss of accountability inevitably leads to a fall, a fall which will hurt and possibly corrupt those involved with the proud prophet.

I would make one exception to the above rule. It is difficult for heads of mission boards and parachurch organizations who travel all the time to be submitted to the authority of a local church because they are always speaking in other churches or on the mission field. While these kinds of leaders may not be submitted to the authority of a local church, they are under the authority of strong boards. Their organizations are regularly audited, and their lives are under constant scrutiny.

Usurping the Role of the Holy Spirit or Confirming God's Leading?

New Testament prophets never used prophetic authority to control someone's life. Instead, the New Testament prophets edified, exhorted, consoled, encouraged, and strengthened believers (Acts 15:32; 1 Cor. 14:3). Sometimes a prophet can do this by telling you something about your future.

Once a prophetic person told me that I was going to go through a time of sifting. "Bad sifting?" I asked.

"Let's put it this way," he said, "you will feel like you have been hit by a freight train when it is over." Then he accurately predicted the week the sifting would start.

Was that supposed to be edifying? Well, yes it was. He also told me that if I would endure the sifting with grace and humility, the Lord would reward me. When the freight train hit, I hung on to that last promise, and it came true.

A prophet can also edify or encourage you by telling you something about your present life. Like the prophet who told me the very prayer that I had prayed that morning in private. Then he said this, "The Lord said to tell you that this prayer is from him and that he is going to grant it. He wants to encourage you to keep praying along these lines." That word was given to me years ago, and the Lord has still not answered the prayer I have prayed almost every day since then. But that prophetic word has provided me with the encouragement I need to persevere in prayer. Actually, the Lord has given me a number of prophetic confirmations in addition to the one I just mentioned that this dream in my heart really is from him.

Although there are many ways in which prophetic ministry can be edifying, the prophetic ministry is never meant to replace the Holy Spirit in our walk with God. Nor can prophetic ministry ever remove our accountability before the Lord.

During the reign of King Jeroboam, the Lord sent a prophet to Bethel with a message of judgment (1 Kings 13:1ff.). God commanded the prophet not to eat, or drink, or return to Judah by the same way he came to Bethel (1 Kings 13:9). After he delivered the word of judgment and was on his way back to Judah, an old prophet came out to meet him and said, "I too am a prophet, as you are. And an angel said to me by the word of the Lord: 'bring him back with you to your house so that he may eat bread and drink water'" (1 Kings 13:18). The younger prophet listened to the old prophet and went into his house to eat, but the old prophet had lied to him. As a punishment for the younger prophet's disobedience, a lion killed him on his way back to Judah. This story demonstrates how God holds each one of us accountable to hear his voice for ourselves and to obey it. He will never let us blame a prophetic minister for our failed marriages, our financial misfortunes, or our other bad decisions. He holds us accountable to obey the light he gives us, not the light he gives someone else.

Can prophetic people ever help us with decisions about marriage, children, work, or money? Yes, I believe they can speak words that *support, confirm,* or *clarify* a leading God has already given to us. Or they may cause us to pray about something we hadn't even considered. God may respond to our prayers with new guidance. Note, however, that these kinds of prophetic words should never be delivered in a controlling or authoritative way. Once a prophetic minister came to our church and said to a young mother, "Thus says the Lord, you are going to have another baby about this time next year." She didn't look happy. Afterwards she came to me and said, "I've got four children now, and they are driving me crazy. Do I have to have another one? Will I be displeasing the Lord if I don't try to get pregnant again?"

"Absolutely not," I told her.

This prophet had overstepped his bounds. He was attempting to make a decision for this young mother that could only be made by her and her husband. The one place I think it *is* acceptable to prophesy the birth of a baby is in the case of a barren couple. I have seen Paul Cain and other prophetic ministers do this on a number of occasions and bring great blessing to the couple and the congregation.

WHO SHOULD MINISTER IN PUBLIC SETTINGS?

When we come together, all of us should be prepared to use our gifts to bless other people. This doesn't necessarily mean that we will use those gifts in front of the whole body—having a spiritual gift doesn't give someone the right to speak in public gatherings. Some people's gifting is most appropriately used one-on-one or in front of small groups. It is possible that their gifting may grow in intensity and later bring them in front of larger groups, but the level of gifting ought to always be appropriate for the setting in which the gifting is to be used.

Some very skilled prophetic ministers are also very skilled at teaching the Bible. However, many who are exceedingly skilled in prophetic ministry have little or no skill in teaching the Bible. Yet they are often asked to teach the Bible before they minister prophetically. This usually bores everyone and confuses some. Most people in those kinds of meetings simply want the prophetic minister to finish the teaching so they can get to the "real ministry." Unless the prophet is gifted in the teaching of the Bible, we shouldn't require him or her to teach the Bible.

There is another thing I have also found unprofitable in prophetic ministry. When a person's prophetic gift makes it appropriate for them to speak in large public gatherings, they shouldn't give long uninterpreted visions. That is equivalent to a teacher spending a long time introducing a theological problem and then failing to give an appropriate solution to that problem. This simply perplexes most of the people and edifies none.

When a prophet feels he or she has a directive word for the whole body, that word should be given first to the leadership of the body. Then, with the leadership's permission and blessing, that word may be shared with the body.

HOW IS PROPHETIC CREDIBILITY AND AUTHORITY ESTABLISHED?

Christians who seek prominence in the kingdom of God are wasting their time. Everyone in the kingdom is equally significant to God, but not all will be equally prominent in his service. It is God who raises up leaders and who removes leaders. He gave Moses, Joshua, Solomon and others prominence, credibility, and authority in the eyes of the people.[4] He also wanted the people to have confidence in prophets—not just in any prophets, but in *his* prophets, the ones that he himself had raised up and sent to the people (2 Chron. 20:20). Because it is God's job to raise up leaders and prophets, we usually get into trouble when we try to raise ourselves up before the people. Diotrephes loved prominence and tried to gain it on his own. But his plan backfired, and for two thousand years his name has been covered with shame (3 John 9–10).

Credibility and authority begins with the calling of the Lord Jesus. The twelve got to be apostles because the Lord "called to him those he wanted" (Mark 3:13). The same goes for elders (Acts 20:28) and for prophets (1 Cor. 14:28–29; Eph. 4:11). In God's house you can't be something you're not called to be. So we must learn to function within our calling.

God will determine our prominence in the church. He will supply to each servant the credibility and authority necessary to fulfill the level of their calling. Prophetic people begin to gain credibility and authority when they obey their calling and submit to the level of their calling, or to put it in the apostle Paul's words, when a prophet prophesies "in proportion to his faith" and "according to the grace given" him. Most evangelists, prophets, and teachers will minister all their lives in a single church and maybe even to a single age group, a children's Sunday school, for example. A few will be called to translocal ministry. For instance, in the New Testament we think of prophets like Agabus, Judas, and Silas, who had authority to minister translocally in different churches. And very few will be raised up to an international ministry like that of Billy Graham.

Prophetic credibility and authority is also gained by submission to the leadership of one's local church. If God should give a prophetic person a ministry outside their own church, then in each church where they minister they must be submitted to the authority of that church as well as to the authority of their own church.

Do not forget that there is a difference between prophetic gifting and prophetic authority. It is possible for someone to be very gifted prophetically, but not have much authority in their local church or outside their church. Prophetic people who exhibit the character of the Lord Jesus and consistently give accurate predictions and helpful guidance gain authority and stature in the eyes of the church.

There are even some prophetic people who have gained such authority in the secular world that the Lord has been able to send them to leaders of nations today. There are prophetic people whom contemporary world leaders have sought out for help. The prophetic people I know who have attained this level of credibility and authority sought neither of these. Instead they have spent their lives seeking the face of God, who has given them the level of gifting and authority necessary for the tasks to which he has called them.

WHAT IS YOUR CALLING?

Perhaps the best way to facilitate any ministry, not just the ministry of prophecy, is for us to know our own callings. The church is the body of Christ, and he has assigned each of us a function within his body. Some of us are "eyes," others are "hands," and so on. What are you?

My friend I mentioned earlier, Rick Joyner, regularly takes a survey of the audiences where he speaks. He asks them if they know their calling in the body of Christ. He tells me about ten percent of the audiences claim to know their calling. Then he asks the ten percent if they're walking in their calling. And only ten percent of that group generally claims that they are. If this were an accurate survey of the whole church, it would mean only one percent of the church is actually functioning within the role Jesus has assigned to them.

What would happen to your physical body if only one percent was functioning properly? Would you be happy to have fifty percent functioning properly? Most of us want our physical bodies to operate with one-hundred-percent efficiency. How do you think Jesus feels about his body?

Some of us can't function efficiently because we don't know what part of the body we are. Others of us know what part we are, but we don't think other parts are necessary. Perhaps none of us can walk fully in our callings until we believe in the necessity of all callings. For only then will we have the humility to fulfill our role.

Whether you have a prophetic calling or not, remember that Paul told the church to facilitate prophetic ministry (2 Cor. 14:1), and Isaiah called prophets the eyes of the body (Isa. 29:10). And who wouldn't want eyes?

13

"God Told Me to Tell You ..."

Here is a story I have heard repeated all too often. A prophetic person in the church gets a "revelation" that the church is not supposed to take up an offering. Instead, the church should put several boxes at the back of the auditorium so that people can give on their way out. If the church follows this advice, God will honor them with an increased budget. The prophet tells this revelation to the pastor, who thanks him and says that the leadership will pray about this word.

Next Sunday the prophet watches very carefully to see if his revelation is obeyed. There is no announcement about a new offering policy, and they take up the morning offering just as they have always done. He can't believe it. The leadership of the church has defied the word of the living God! That night, while sleeping, he has a dream. He sees the church on fire and people running out like human torches. The judgment of God has come!

In the days that follow, the prophet warns all of his friends that the leadership of the church has defied the word of the living God, and now judgment has been decreed on the church. More negative revelations follow, which the prophet also shares in order to warn the true believers. The leadership hears about these revelations, which they take to be slander. Before long, sides are chosen and there is a split. Or a sizable number of people pull out. Or the pastor leaves.

Several years later, after things have calmed down, a young man walks into the pastor's study. He says, "Pastor, I had a dream about the church last night."

Oh no, not again, thinks the pastor. He wonders if he could just kill the young man and somehow convince God that he found him dead. That's how he feels about prophetic ministry now.

I may be exaggerating a little bit, but not by much. I know pastors who have been so badly burned by prophetic ministry that they don't want anything to do with it. How can these kinds of hurtful scenarios be avoided? How should prophets give words to people? Or for that matter, how should anybody share what they think God has told them?

GIVING PROPHETIC WORDS

Get Permission from God to Speak

Let's assume that the Lord *does* give you a true revelation about a church or about someone you know. Perhaps it came through your meditation in Scripture, or in a dream, or a vision, or an impression. The first rule is: Don't assume that just because you received a revelation that you have permission to share it. Sometimes God grants revelations that his servants are not permitted to share (Dan. 8:26; 12:4; 2 Cor. 12:4), or he reveals his secret plans to his servants the prophets (Amos 3:7 NASB; Jer. 33:3ff.), but expects them to keep these revelations secret until he grants them permission to speak them publicly. Whether you are a prophet or not, "the LORD confides in those who fear him" (Ps. 25:14). In other words, he reveals his secrets to those who will keep his confidence. He doesn't share his deepest secrets with blabbermouths.

There is a divine timing for the release of every genuine revelation from God. A wise person is not content with simply getting a revelation. They know that "a word aptly spoken is like apples of gold in settings of silver" (Prov. 25:11). When we speak a true revelation from God at the wrong time, we are acting as the fool whose "reckless words pierce like a sword" (Prov. 12:18).

Distinguish Between Revelation, Interpretation, and Application

The second rule regarding revelation is: Learn to distinguish between the revelation, its interpretation, and its application. It is possible for a person to receive an accurate revelation, but give it a wrong interpretation and therefore a wrong application. A pastor told me about a very gifted prophetic minister in his church. They were attending a conference together, and the prophetic minister was giving people messages at the end of the service. As the prophet looked at a man in the back of the room, he saw a dollar sign over his head. There was a black cloud over the dollar sign. It seemed obvious to the prophet that this meant there was sin in the man's finances. He asked the man to stand up and then said to him, "The Lord shows me that there is sin in your finances. He is giving you time to repent and make things right. You can escape his judgment if you will act now."

After the service was over, the man who had received the public rebuke came forward with his pastor to talk to the prophet and the prophet's pastor. The man denied that there was any sin at all in his finances. He served as an elder in his church and had a reputation for impeccable financial integrity. The man owned his own company and had been very generous with his church and other charitable causes. His pastor bore witness to this, and they very graciously told the prophet that he had made a mistake. Even the prophet was convinced by their sincerity. However, he knew that he had not made up that vision. He was sure that it had come from the Lord.

Some weeks later, one of that elder's employees was caught embezzling from the company. He had apparently been embezzling for quite some time. So the revelation had been true after all. The interpretation of it, though, was wrong. The prophet assumed he knew the meaning of the vision, when he *should* have prayed and asked the Lord what it meant. And the application— calling out the man and embarrassing him publicly—was horrendous. He never should have rebuked the man publicly. Even if he thought the vision referred to the man's sin, he should have gone to him privately (Matt. 18:15–17).

Before going to anyone with a revelation you think is from God, make sure you have the correct interpretation and the right application. Insofar as is possible, when telling a person something you think the Lord has given you for them, you ought to make sure to differentiate between the revelation, its interpretation, and its application. This is especially true with dreams and visions.

The same is true with our use of the Bible. In my opinion, the Bible is the inerrant, infallible, revelation of God. But I must be careful to distinguish between what the Bible *says* and what *I say* the Bible says (interpretation). I must be even more careful to distinguish between what I say you ought to do based on what the Bible says (application). The Bible will always be true, but my interpretations—however well-researched—and my applications—however well-meaning—may contain a mixture of truth and error. The same is true with a genuine revelation from God in the form of a dream, vision, or impression. If the revelation is from God, it has to be true, for God cannot lie (Heb. 6:18). But *my* interpretation and application of that impression may contain a mixture of truth and error.

Give Prophetic Words with Humility

This leads me to the third rule in the giving of prophetic words: Always give prophetic words with humility. The most skillful prophetic people I know avoid phrases like "Thus says the Lord ..." and "The Lord showed me that you are supposed to...." These kinds of phrases imply a very high level of clarity and authority, a clarity and authority that God is not giving to very many people today. Most of us would do much better introducing our prophetic messages with, "I think the Lord might be indicating ..." or "I feel impressed to ..." or something like that.

Some people feel they are cheating God out of his glory if they don't attribute the revelation to him in a direct way by saying something like, "The Lord showed me ..." It is good to want to give credit to God for something you think he revealed to you. You just need to find a tactful, nonmanipulative way to do so. Anytime you find yourself using the Lord's name in order to enhance your authority, you are misusing the Lord's name, and in the end, you will undermine your credibility.

Leave the Results to God

The fourth rule is: Once you have delivered the prophetic message, your job is over—except to pray. If your advice is not taken, you shouldn't feel rejected or unesteemed. Nor should you feel that those who refuse your advice are in the grip of evil or are hard-hearted. In time, everything may work out just fine. Or it may be that you will see it wasn't the Lord speaking to you at all, or that you had significantly misunderstood what he was saying. Perhaps you were just one in a series of confirmations to help a friend change courses. At any rate, it is not up to you to make someone obey a message from the Lord. Ultimately, that is between them and him.

Pray for Those to Whom You Prophesy

On a number of occasions the Lord has supernaturally shown me sin in a person's life. The story about Robert at the beginning of this book is just one of those occasions. On a number of occasions both my wife and I have "seen" sexual sins, marital discord, and other things well-concealed from public inspection. Sometimes we have seen personal calamities before they have actually happened to people. Other times we have seen child abuse or suicidal thoughts struggling for control of a person's mind with absolutely no indication of any of these things in the natural realm. What do you do when you have impressions like these?

Most of the time, if you share a negative impression or dream with someone other than the person who is in the dream, you are sinning. If the impression is true, your report to the third party is the sin of gossip. If the impression is false, it is slander. On rare occasions, you may be justified in talking to a third party first in order to get some discernment or help, but most of the time negative impressions should never be shared with anyone except the person about whom you had the impression. And then, you should only share a negative impression if you have permission from the Lord. Often the Lord will deny permission to share a negative impression because he has a better way of handling the situation.

Why did the Lord give you an impression if you aren't to share it? In order to prompt you to pray for the person. I believe that the majority of dreams, impressions, and visions we receive are meant to lead us to pray and not to do anything else. The greatest prophetic people I know see and hear far more from the Lord than they ever speak. They are men and women who spend a great deal of their time in prayer. It is more important to them to be intimate with the Lord than it is to be prominent in ministry. They would rather go down in the history of the church as spiritual parents than spellbinding prophets.

A young woman came to me and confessed that she was in a lesbian relationship with a woman with whom she was living. I advised her to get out of the living arrangement, even though it wasn't economically feasible. And, of course, I told her she should stop her physical relationship with the woman immediately. The next time I saw her for a counseling appointment, I asked her if she had found another place to live. She hadn't, but she intended to move soon. I asked her if she had stopped the physical relationship with the woman. She assured me it was completely over. I had an immediate impression that she was lying. I started to confront her, but when I asked the Lord for permission, I felt he was saying no. I started to confront the woman anyway, but I felt more strongly that the Lord was saying no. I obeyed the impression, even though it didn't make sense to me. The rest of the counseling time seemed wasted, and I thought the woman was no better off when she left my office.

The next day when I returned to my office from lunch, the woman was standing outside my door, crying. She asked if she could see me for just a minute. When we got inside the office, she confessed that she had lied to me the day before. She still had a physical relationship with this woman. She told me that for the last twenty-four hours she had been miserable under the conviction of the Holy Spirit. She felt horrible for her sin, and she felt horrible for lying to me. She was ready to do whatever it took to get out of that relationship and get clean before the Lord. I could have probably wrung a confession out of her in my office the day before, but the Lord had already decided to put her in the hands of the Holy Spirit for the next twenty-four hours. Today this woman is serving the Lord and is free of her former bondage. Which way do you think was more effective? My way or God's?

Give Negative Messages with Tact and Gentleness

If the Lord does give you permission to deliver a negative word, you ought to do it in the most tactful, gentle, and humble way possible. Our goal is not to be awesome in ministry, but to lighten another's burdens through our love (Gal. 6:1–2). Instead

of telling a person, "Your pride is going to split the church," say
something like, "I think there is a trap being set for you. Some
people in the church are not going to listen to you, and you will
feel wounded by them. You may be tempted to be impatient
with them, and if you give in to that impatience, it could have
disastrous results." Remember, "a gentle answer turns away
wrath" (Prov. 15:1) and "a gentle tongue can break a bone"
(Prov. 25:15).

JUDGING PROPHETIC WORDS

Problems with "Open" Meetings

In large churches today there are many practical problems
involved in letting people speak extemporaneously. I sometimes
speak in large churches which allow an "open time" for anyone
to address the congregation. Many times there are visitors present
who are unknown to the pastoral staff or others in the church.
Some of these visitors have been forbidden to speak in their own
churches because what they say is usually not profitable or
because they have refused to submit to the authority structure in
their church. Sometimes people with a history of mental problems will use this time to speak out. Occasionally members of the
congregation will speak and, while there is nothing wrong with
what they say, it is just not profitable. Another common practice
is for an angry person to get up and deliver a condemning
"prophecy" in King James English—"Yea I say unto thee . . . Have
I not told thee . . . etc."

I would have to say that most of the time in large public services I haven't found "prophecy" from the congregation to be all
that profitable. Usually, general words are given with little conviction or power from the Holy Spirit.

Who Judges?

In a conference I attended several years ago one of the
prophets got up and said that God was not going to do anything
for seven years. Then the main speaker came to the platform and
announced that the title of his message was, "Suddenly, Immediately, Quickly." Needless to say, the speaker didn't have a great

deal of appreciation for that prophetic message being given just before he came to the pulpit.

It was probably situations like these that gave rise to the need for judging prophetic words. Paul told the Corinthians, "Two or three prophets should speak, and the others should weigh carefully what is said" (1 Cor. 14:29).

Prophetic words are to be judged or carefully weighed. Who does the judging? Paul said, "*the others* should weigh carefully what was said." Who are "the others?" Some argue that "the others" that should judge are the other prophets. Some think Paul has the elders of the church in view, and some think he means all who hear the prophets.[1] While there is no universal agreement about who is to do the judging, elders are ultimately responsible for what goes on in the church. Many wish Paul had been more specific about the details of evaluating prophetic words, but apparently the Lord intended to give the church a great deal of freedom in how they applied Paul's directives, both in 1 Corinthians 14:26 and in 14:29. Each church is responsible to hear from God how he wants them to evaluate prophecies.

The Role of Discernment

Suppose someone stands up in a congregation on Sunday morning and delivers a prophetic message to the whole church. The first thing I do is ask whether or not the word is *scriptural*. I rarely ever hear a prophetic word given in church that actually contradicts the Scripture. Most prophetic words given in the church can find some analogy in the Scripture, if not direct scriptural support. But it is not enough to simply ask if the word is scriptural. What if someone stands up and says, "The Lord wants our church to start a food ministry to the poor." It is certainly scriptural to care for the poor (Gal. 2:10), so the word is scriptural in that sense. It is also a *directive* word. In this case, it is the elders who must weigh this word and decide if and how it is to be implemented.

What if someone gives a *predictive* word such as, "In two years the Lord is going to bring revival to our church"? If the person who gives a word like this has established a good track record in his or her predictions, then we will automatically begin to take the word more seriously. If it is a stranger who gives a word like this, or someone who habitually gets things wrong, then we will tend not to take it so seriously. The problem with these tendencies is that the credible person could be wrong, and the stranger could be right. Ultimately, predictive and directive words can be judged by the leadership of the church only through the discernment of the Holy Spirit.

One aspect of discernment is the ability to judge not by what our eyes see, or our ears hear, but with righteousness through the Holy Spirit (Isa. 11:2–4). The Holy Spirit can show us whether or not predictions will come true. But this is not the highest level of discernment that he has to offer the church. The Spirit of Truth is given to the church to show the church, especially its leadership, what promotes the love, testimony, and glory of Jesus.[2] If the leadership of the church would follow resolutely after these three things—the love of Jesus, the testimony of Jesus, and the glory of Jesus—it would be very difficult for them to be deceived.

The reason so many of us in leadership have so little discernment is because we are continually judging by what our eyes see and our ears hear. If we don't like its outward appearance, or it doesn't agree with our prejudices or interpretations of debatable doctrines, we reject the message. This is why it is so important not to judge the package in which the prophetic word comes. This is why it is so important to ask the Lord for discernment and hold our prejudices in abeyance. When the church begins to diligently pursue discernment, the judging of prophetic words won't be so difficult.

There are several methods by which a church can judge prophetic words. In some churches, if a person thinks they have a prophetic word for the whole church, then they have to come to one of the pastors or elders prior to the service and tell the church leader first. If the leader agrees, then they can give that word at the microphone during the service. Some churches follow this same procedure, only it is the elder or the pastor who gives the word at the microphone. In other churches they let people speak extemporaneously from the floor, then a designated person among the leadership of the church responds immediately to the prophetic word, saying whether or not they think it is authentic. In still other churches no response at all is made to an extemporaneous prophetic word, unless the word is doctrinally incorrect or is "off the wall" in some other way. The leaders in these churches feel that most of the time people will recognize a true prophetic word.

The Role of Small Groups

As I said earlier, it seems to me most of the general prophetic ministry given from the congregation during worship services is not really all that helpful. In a large church we wouldn't normally invite someone to preach the Sunday morning sermon who is just learning how to preach. Normally, we would insist that whoever preaches or teaches on Sunday morning have a level of gifting appropriate to the size and nature of the meeting. The problem with allowing anyone to prophesy on Sunday morning is that a person may have a prophetic gift and calling to minister effectively to individuals, but not to the collective gathering of the church. For the most part we seem to be able to figure out who has the gifting, calling, and authority to *teach* in large public gatherings. Why can't we use the discernment of the Lord to find those who have the same gifting, calling, and authority to *speak prophetically* in large public gatherings?

In my opinion, the ideal place for allowing all present to speak is in home groups that meet during the week. Home groups, or cell groups, or whatever you want to call them, are the best place to learn to minister with spiritual gifts and also to receive ministry. These smaller meetings during the week can offer a nonthreatening atmosphere conducive to taking risks. People have to risk failing and looking foolish if they are going to discover their gifts and how to use them effectively—freedom to fail is an essential part of learning anything. Harsh correction, or mocking people who make mistakes, will cause them to stop trying to learn. Done in public, these kinds of responses will not only stop the beginner, but will discourage everyone present from risking anything. In home groups of fifteen to thirty people it is much easier to risk, especially when we have the security of feeling loved by others in our group.

There are some people in home groups who monopolize the time or continually try to function in an area where they are not gifted. What do you do with these "habitual offenders?" Here is what I do. I let the mistakes go uncorrected for the first few times. I look to see if there is any improvement in their behavior or sensitivity. If there is not, I go to that person privately and gently. I had to do this with a lady in one of our first home groups who was continually giving inane "messages from God." After letting her disrupt the group in a small way for three or four weeks, I went to her privately. I asked her how she felt when she gave "a word" at our home group. She said she felt foolish most of the time because the words never seemed to mean anything to the people. On the other hand, she felt she would be disobeying God if she didn't follow these promptings.

I asked how things were going in the rest of her life. They weren't going too well at home or at work. I asked if she would like for me and my wife, and perhaps a couple of other people, to meet with her for the next six or seven weeks privately. We would pray with her and for her in order to see if the Lord wouldn't ease some of the turmoil in her life. She was delighted. I also asked her if she would mind not giving any more words in our home group during the next six or seven weeks, since the words hadn't been profitable thus far. I knew it was possible that she might become programmed for failure and frustration if she continued to follow these promptings. I assured her that this was just a temporary thing. It was meant to help her and not restrict her. She didn't mind at all complying with these instructions. Before too long she came to see that she didn't really have a prophetic gifting. Her gifting was in the area of helps and she became one of the most valuable servants in our whole home group.

This was one of those good situations where everything worked out fine. What happens, though, if the person doesn't respond to correction and continues disrupting the group? Then forbid them to speak in the group. If the person doesn't respond to the prohibition to speak publicly, they will have to be rebuked in public. If they do not respond to public rebuke, then they will have to be denied the privilege of coming to the meeting.

OBEYING GOD'S "NO"

If I could have given you only one line of advice in regard to giving and receiving prophetic words, it would have been the first rule of this chapter—get permission from God before you speak. I have seen more blessing come from obeying this principle and more harm come from disregarding it than from all the other principles given in this chapter. Yet, often this is the hardest rule to obey. Sometimes when we are certain that we should speak, God will deny us permission without giving us a reason at the time. The following incident taught me the value of obeying God's "no" even when it made no sense and seemed to go against biblical principles.

A young, single mother I had not met before came into my office for counseling. She and a man she was dating were serving as Sunday school teachers in our elementary Sunday school. She had come in to talk about a problem with her children, but while she was talking, I had the distinct impression she was sleeping with the man she was dating. That weekend my wife and I happened to sit right behind this couple in the Sunday evening service. I leaned over and quietly asked Leesa to pray about this couple to see if God would show her anything about them. They were completely unknown to her. Leesa didn't see a vision or hear an audible voice, but she had a rather distinct feeling or a knowing quite apart from any rational process about this couple. At the end of the service, Leesa said to me, "I don't think that couple is married, but I think they are sleeping together. The man seems to have a lot of religious pride." That was enough for me. I decided to ask them to come into my office for a counseling appointment.

Now, I know the New Testament does not normally permit us to accuse people of sin based on our impressions. There must be evidence beyond our impressions. So I had no intention of accusing them. I just wanted to talk to them and gently suggest that I might be able to help with any problems in their relationship. I wanted to give them an opportunity to confess and repent of sin, if they really were sleeping together.

Before I called the couple, I prayed, "Lord, do I have your permission to invite them into my office to give them an opportunity to repent if they are indeed sleeping together?" I don't usually get instantaneous answers to my prayers, but this time I got a very clear instantaneous "No!" What do I mean by "a very clear instantaneous 'No'?" It was not audible or visual. It was an overwhelming feeling or inarticulate sense that if I tried to bring this couple in for a counseling appointment, I would be displeasing the Lord.

This feeling wasn't based on reason or knowledge of the Bible. My reason and biblical understanding told me to do just the opposite. That's why this surprised me—I felt more than ever

I was right about the sin of this couple. I said, "But Lord, they are teachers in our Sunday school department." Then the thought came to me that the Lord could tell me other things about our Sunday school department that would shock me even more, and that I had better leave this matter to him. It didn't seem right to me, but as well as I knew how to hear the Lord's voice, I was certain that he was telling me not to explore the matter any further.

About six to eight weeks later, in a Sunday evening service, John Wimber, the senior pastor, was preaching on sexual immorality. There were about two thousand people present that night, many of whom were visiting from other churches. At the conclusion of his message, John said, "There are a number of you here tonight who are in bondage to sexual immorality." Then he began to list different forms of sexual immorality. Some people were surprised at his frankness. They were shocked at what he did next. John said, "I believe that the Lord is opening a window of grace for you tonight who are in bondage to sexual immorality. If you will come forward and publicly confess your sin, and let others pray for you, I believe God will break the power of that evil bondage over many of you."

I thought perhaps John would call out some other problems, like depression, or physical illnesses, and invite those people to come down as well at the same time with the first group. That would afford a little anonymity for those who were in the grip of sexual immorality, and it wouldn't be so embarrassing for them to come down to the front of the church. But John didn't do this. He just stood on the platform and waited for people to respond.

I felt John was right. I felt there were a lot of people in that evening service with sexual sin, but I didn't expect more than five or six people to have the courage to suffer the public humiliation of walking down the aisle to the front of the church to confess their sin. I closed my eyes and began to pray for people to respond to the invitation. I heard chairs move, lots of chairs, followed by lots of footsteps. Instead of five or six people, approximately two hundred people came down to the front of the church to be prayed for. Many of those people were from other churches. They felt the freedom to publicly confess their sin because they weren't known in our church.

There were so many people coming down to the altar that there was not enough space at the front of the church to contain them. They began to back up into the aisles of the church. Leesa and I were sitting in seats next to the aisle about eight rows back from the front of the church. When Wimber gave the invitation, we stood and prayed with our eyes closed. I could hear people standing, kneeling, and crying in the aisle beside me and even behind me. When I opened my eyes and looked down in the aisle to my right, who do you think I saw? That's right—the young couple we had sat behind eight weeks earlier who we felt the Lord had told us were committing sexual immorality. Leesa and I slipped out of our chairs and knelt down with them.

"Could we help you?" I asked.

"I am so ashamed," said the man. "We have been sleeping together and we are not married. We want to get married, but we are not married yet, and I know it is not right for us to sleep together." Then he added, "I am so filled with pride." We began to pray for them and help them with the process of restoration.

God and I had two different ways of handling this case of sexual immorality. I wanted to confront immediately. He wanted to wait. Wasn't it much better for the couple to come forward in a public way like that and confess their sin? Wasn't that much better than a pastor dragging a confession out of them?

If our ministries are to reach their full potential we must have the revelatory guidance of the Holy Spirit. We must be able to hear God say a simple no or yes. What do you think would happen to our ministries if we learned, really learned, to place our confidence in the Holy Spirit's ability to lead, not in our ability to follow? If we learned not to judge by what our eyes see (Isa. 11:2–4), nor be bound by our traditions (Matt. 15:3)?

14

Prophetic Pitfalls

A prophetic person I know made a stunning prediction about a turn of events in the international money market. His prediction, given before a public audience, seemed impossible, but it came true within the specific time limit he had predicted. Several years later he made another stunning prophecy about our national economy that also came true within the specified time of his prophecy. These two remarkable successes led him to make a whole series of economic prophecies for the following year. One of my friends who is an exceptionally astute businessman acquired a tape of this "prophetic economic forecast." He was highly skeptical of it. At the end of the year he compared every specific economic prediction with what had actually happened in the economy. Virtually every "prophecy" was wrong! If anyone with money had invested it according to the predictions on the tape, they would have lost all their money.

The irony of this is that the person who made the economic predictions has a genuine prophetic gifting. What went wrong? He fell into a very common trap. Depending on our gifting and calling, all Christians are susceptible to specialized traps. There are traps designed for evangelists, other traps designed for pastors, yet others for teachers, and so on. I call the traps designed for prophets "prophetic pitfalls." In this chapter, I'd like to discuss some of these prophetic pitfalls.

PROPHESYING OUT OF JEALOUSY AND ANGER

Never trust a negative impression about someone with whom you are angry or jealous. Jealousy and anger cannot only obscure your ability to receive revelation from the Lord, but they can also open you up to demonic revelation. Saul knew what it was like to feel the Holy Spirit come upon him in prophetic power (1 Sam. 10:10). He also knew what it was like for the Spirit of God to empower him for heroic action (1 Sam. 11:6ff.). Later in his life, Saul's jealousy of David drove him to rage (1 Sam. 18:6–9). This is what happened to him during one of those periods of jealousy and anger:

> The next day an evil spirit from God came forcefully upon Saul. He was prophesying in his house, while David was playing the harp, as he usually did. Saul had a spear in his hand and he hurled it saying to himself, "I'll pin David to the wall." But David eluded him twice (1 Sam. 18:10–11).[1]

One of the most instructive things about this passage is the phrase used to describe the evil spirit—it "came forcefully." This is exactly the same phrase in Hebrew that is used of the Holy Spirit coming on Saul in 1 Samuel 10:10 and 11:6. Another remarkable thing about this story is when the evil spirit came on him, Saul began to "prophesy." This is the same word for prophesying used in 1 Samuel 10:10. I think the biblical author is telling us that when the evil spirit came on him and gave him demonic prophecy, Saul mistook it for the power and inspiration of God. His jealousy and anger caused him to mistake the power of an evil spirit for the power of the Holy Spirit. Jealousy and anger can lead us into great deception. Never trust your negative thoughts and impressions about people with whom you are angry or jealous.

THE "REJECTED PROPHET SYNDROME"

Prophetic people are especially susceptible to rejection. This rejection can lead to bitterness, negativism, and self-pity—all things that make prophetic people useless for the ministry of the Holy Spirit. The greater the prophetic gifting, the greater the rejection that can attack them. Even the great prophet Elijah hid himself in a cave and was ready to give up his prophetic calling when "the word of the LORD came to him: 'What are you doing here, Elijah?'" (1 Kings 19:9). Notice the bitterness and self-pity in Elijah's reply: "I have been very zealous for the LORD God Almighty. The Israelites have rejected your covenant, broken down your altars, and put your prophets to death with the sword. I am the only one left, and now they are trying to kill me too" (1 Kings 19:10).

But Elijah was wrong. The Lord told him that there were seven thousand more people in Israel who had not bowed down to Baal, even though Elijah felt like he was the only one.

Good prophets have never been liked. They have always been rejected by orthodox religious leadership. Jesus said, "Blessed are you when people insult you, persecute you and falsely say all kinds of evil against you because of me. Rejoice and be glad, because great is your reward in heaven, for in the same way they persecuted the prophets who were before you" (Matt. 5:11–12).

The greater the prophetic calling, the greater the *religious* persecution that will come against that prophetic ministry. Who persecuted the prophets? The leaders of Israel. Stephen was speaking to the Bible scholars of his day when he said, "You always resist the Holy Spirit! Was there ever a prophet your fathers did not persecute? They even killed those who predicted the coming of the Righteous One" (Acts 7:51–52).

The bottom line is that very often good prophets will be rejected and bad prophets will be accepted. Prophetic people must learn to deal with rejection. And the church needs to learn to pray for her leaders instead of preying on them.[2]

THE DESIRE TO PLEASE PEOPLE

The apostle Paul said, "If I were still trying to please men, I would not be a servant of Christ" (Gal. 1:10). People-pleasing is a killer for all ministry, not just for prophetic ministry. Sometimes churchgoing people can be the meanest, most demanding folks in the world. When someone not only thinks he's right, but is also sure that God is on his side, look out! In that person's mind, by opposing them you are opposing God, and they will not hesitate to launch a holy crusade against you. I think it was Pascal who said, "Men never do evil so completely and cheerfully as when they do it from religious conviction." It's much easier to try to please these rebellious folks than to resist them, to flatter them instead of tell them the truth.

In the Old Testament, false visions and flattery go hand in hand (Ezek. 12:24). When prophetic people give in to the pressure of telling people what they want to hear, they end up prophesying out of their own imaginations (Ezek. 13:2). The desire to please people leads a prophet, or any other leader, to ignore sin and give vain comfort (Lam. 2:14; Ezek. 13:15–16; Zech. 10:2). In the worst case, this desire to please can open the door for a demonic spirit to speak through a prophet (1 Kings 22:6–28).

Churchgoing people can actually encourage false prophecy. People accept and like false prophets because the false prophets say things people want to hear. False prophets don't challenge the religious establishment or commonly accepted hypocritical religious practices, nor do they criticize contemporary doctrinal prejudices. Instead, they bless the establishment and status quo. Jesus said, "Woe to you when all men speak well of you, for that is how their fathers treated the false prophets" (Luke 6:26). All of us, but especially prophetic people, must come to the point where we live for God's approval not man's.

THE DESIRE TO BE AWESOME

Another trap into which I commonly see prophetic people fall is the desire to be awesome in ministry, to be "a prophet to the nations." This is exactly opposite of the true Spirit of prophecy. An angel told John, "The testimony of Jesus is the spirit of prophecy" (Rev. 19:10). Prophecy is meant to testify to the awesomeness of Jesus, not to the prophetic ministry. The greatest prophets want people to behold the glory of Jesus. They care little about how they are viewed. John the Baptist was one of the greatest of all prophets because he said, and *meant*, "He must become greater; I must become less" (John 3:30). People who feel like John the Baptist can be entrusted with great revelations.

When I first met Paul Cain, I asked him questions about the healing revival that went on in the early 1950s in America. He told me some wonderful stories about healing and prophetic ministry. He told me the names of some famous healing evangelists and how God had used them in miraculous ways. Then he told me several stories without mentioning the names of the healing evangelists involved. He said, "There was a woman in one meeting who was called out and told by revelation that she had colon cancer but that the Lord was going to heal her that very night. And the Lord did heal her." Then, "There was a man in a meeting who had been estranged from his son and had been praying for reconciliation a long time. He was called out and told by revelation that although he and his son hadn't spoken for a number of years that within twenty-four hours his son would call him, and they would be wondrously reconciled, and it happened."

Finally I asked him, "Who called these people out and said these things to them, Paul? Was it you?"

"Well, yes it was."

"Why didn't you just say, 'I called a woman out and told her ...'? It is not good style to use the passive voice, 'A woman was called out ...,' when you could use the active voice, 'I called a woman out ...'"

"Well, Jack," Paul answered, "it may be better style to use the active voice, but the Lord don't like it none too good, if you understand what I mean." Paul was mocking my "grammatical expertise" because he knew from personal experience that the Lord would prefer for us to develop ways of telling stories in which the Lord receives the glory and not us.

RATIONALIZING MISTAKES

Still another trap prophetic people fall into is rationalizing their mistakes or simply refusing to admit they made one. I don't know any prophetic people today who are 100 percent accurate. All the prophetic people I know make mistakes just like evangelists, teachers, pastors, or other Christians leaders. Sometimes they mistake their own impressions for one of the Lord's impressions. (This doesn't happen that often in the most gifted and mature prophetic people, but it can happen.) More commonly, they make mistakes in interpreting and applying impressions the Lord gives them.

Sometimes a prophetic person has a hard time admitting a mistake because he or she thinks it would ruin their credibility. Usually just the opposite happens. Rationalizing or failing to admit our mistakes is what usually ruins credibility. People trust people who say they were wrong. They can't trust those who *won't* admit they were wrong. The person who won't admit he was wrong frequently causes trouble for everyone.

THE "GEHAZI" MINISTRY

After Naaman was healed of leprosy through Elisha's ministry, he was so grateful that he attempted to give Elisha a gift, but Elisha refused (2 Kings 5:15–16). Elisha's servant, Gehazi, couldn't believe what a golden opportunity Elisha had passed up, so he followed Naaman and told him that Elisha had changed his mind. Naaman gladly gave the gifts to Gehazi who, in turn, hid them. As a reward for his deception, the Lord gave Gehazi Naaman's leprosy and made him leave Elisha's presence. God has not raised up the prophetic ministry to become a successful financial enterprise.

Materialism and money have always been a problem in prophetic ministry. Micah complained in his day, "This is what the LORD says: 'As for the prophets who lead my people astray, if one feeds them, they proclaim 'peace'; if he does not, they prepare to wage war against him'" (Mic. 3:5). When prophets succumb to the temptation to give good prophecies to those who treat them well and bad prophecies to those who don't show them special deference, then the Lord may cease speaking to any of his prophetic people. Micah went on to proclaim:

> Therefore night will come over you, without visions, and darkness, without divination. The sun will set for the prophets, and the day will go dark for them. The seers will be ashamed and the diviners disgraced. They will all cover their faces because there is no answer from God (Mic. 3:6–7).

Prophets aren't the only ones who can be corrupted by money. Micah also complained that Jerusalem's "leaders judge for a bribe, her priests teach for a price" (3:11). Even New Testament church leaders were tempted to show special consideration to the wealthy (James 2:1ff.). But the prophetic ministry is especially vulnerable to this sin. If a person has a real prophetic gifting, it is not difficult to manipulate people into giving money. It is also easy to gravitate toward serving people who can benefit you and to avoid people of low estate. Paul Cain refers to this as the "Gehazi ministry."

MAKING ECONOMIC PREDICTIONS

I think it is a good idea for prophetic people to avoid all financial predictions and leave the stock market, bond market, and real estate market to the experts in those areas. There are at least two reasons for avoiding these kinds of predictions. First, it cheapens prophetic ministry. God is raising up the prophetic ministry to exalt Christ, not to enrich church members. Second, too often these predictions will be wrong, since the Holy Spirit is against using spiritual gifts for personal financial gain.

Ask God yourself how to invest and spend your money, but don't prophesy to others what they should do with theirs. You will probably be wrong.

PROPHETIC GOSSIP AND SLANDER

Remember what I said in the last chapter about praying for people when you see something negative about them? If you tell a negative vision or impression to someone other than the person who was the subject of your revelation, you are most likely committing a sin. If the vision is true, the sin is gossip. If the vision is false, the sin is slander.

I have seen significant trouble caused by prophetic people who have revealed the sins of others and prophesied judgments on churches without ever going to the original people. Often this comes from a prophet being hurt or rejected by these people. Jesus gave us a way of minimizing this kind of damage:

> If your brother sins against you, go and show him his fault, just between the two of you. If he listens to you, you have won your brother over. But if he will not listen, take one or two others along, so that "every matter may be established by the testimony of two or three witnesses." If he refuses to listen to them, tell it to the church; and if he refuses to listen even to the church, treat him as you would a pagan or a tax collector (Matt. 18:15–17).

When we are wronged, we are obligated first to go to the person who hurt us and try to win that person. Until we do that, we can't talk to others about that person, prophesy against them, or go over their head to their leadership. Jesus didn't leave any loopholes here. He didn't say, "You don't have to go to the person if he is more intelligent than you, can out argue you, won't listen to you anyway, or is mean." He did not leave us a single excuse for not going first to the person we think has sinned against us.

People who are wise and righteous in their own eyes often feel they are special exceptions to Matthew 18:15–17. Others think they have a special revelation that allows them to violate Jesus' peacekeeping principles. Still others imagine that their enemies are such a danger within the church that God will make a special ruling in their case. Some even use a little theological sophistry to extricate themselves from their obligation to go to their brother first. I have heard cult-busters and heresy-hunters say that their targets are not brothers, or that Matthew 18:15–17 doesn't apply in their case because their target has hurt the church, not them personally. These people claim to be acting out of love for the church, but they really aren't at all.

Most of the time, people who flagrantly disobey a clear commandment, offering the shoddiest theological excuse for their disobedience, are acting out of religious pride. Let someone attack the *heresy-hunter's* ministry, and the first words out of his mouth will be, "They didn't even come to me to find out if these things were really true!" Which one of us really thinks it's okay for someone to write or say negative things about us without coming to us first? When we do this, we're exalting our discernment over that of the Lord Jesus. We're acting as though we have found better peacekeeping principles than the ones he gave us. Maybe that's why we have so much strife in our churches.

CALLING OUT SINS PUBLICLY

While we are on the subject of areas to avoid, what about calling out sins in public? Some prophetic people feel that this is an appropriate thing to do. They remind us that Old Testament prophets did this. And in the New Testament, Peter called out Ananias' and Sapphira's sin, and Paul called out Elymas' sin and sometimes named people's sins in his epistles. Certainly there are times when it is appropriate to make someone's sin public. For instance, elders who are sinning are to be publicly rebuked (1 Tim. 5:20). And when someone is disciplined by the church, it has to be done in public (1 Cor. 5:1ff.). However, in the New Testament, public exposure of a believer's sins is reserved for extreme cases. The normal procedure is to go to a brother or sister privately and attempt to win them before there is ever a public exposure (Matt. 18:15–17; Gal. 6:1–2). Normally, you may never accuse someone of sin based on a private revelation. In the case of an elder, the church is not even allowed to entertain an accusation against the elder unless it is brought by two or three witnesses who have firm evidence (1 Tim. 5:19).

I'm not saying that a prophetic minister should never name people and their sins publicly. On rare occasions God may lead a person to do this. But few prophets I know have the maturity, credibility, and ability to hear God's voice well enough to do this. The majority of cases I have seen where this has been tried have been disasters.

If you think God is showing you the sins of others while you are in a public meeting, you can express this in a way that gives people an option of making a confession. For example, recently I was speaking to an audience of committed Christians, many of whom were leaders and pastors. At the conclusion of the meeting I had an impression that a number of people in the audience were addicted to both prescription drugs and alcohol. My attention was drawn to a small section in the back of the room. I said, "I think the Lord will help some people today who are struggling with an addiction to prescription drugs and alcohol. If you'll stand up where you are, we'll pray for you now." Then I pointed to the section in the back and said, "There is someone in this section who needs help." Immediately a man stood up, and then people in every section began to stand.

I have seen this kind of thing happen often. I think this is an appropriate way of publicly naming sins. It gives a person the opportunity to choose to make a public confession. It also does this in a way that says to him or her, "We want to help you, not embarrass you." People frequently write and say they repented and were delivered of sins in meetings like this.

Let me give you a word of caution. The church is filled with sins. In my travels I have found virtually every sin that is in the world to be also present in the church. Anyone can stand up before a Christian audience and say, "The Lord shows me that some of you are committing the sin of ... ," and accurately name sins present in the audience. But if the Lord is not really leading someone to name those sins, not much good will come of that "ministry," and, in fact, significant harm may follow. Naming sins takes no gift at all. The key is knowing what particular sins the Lord wants named—and when, where, and how he wants to deal with them. He gives grace to deal with these things when he is leading. We usually get frustrated and cause frustration when *we* are leading.

Remember, the goal is not to appear as an awesome prophet. The goal is to please God and help his people. Often the best help we can give a brother or sister in sin is to deal with their sin in private, and keep it private before and after they've repented.

THE "GOD-TOLD-ME" TRAP

I was once in a meeting of about three thousand people at the Vineyard Christian Fellowship of Anaheim, California, when a man came up on the platform uninvited. John Wimber was playing the keyboards during the worship service. The man, whom none of us knew, walked directly toward John. Two ushers who were also large ex-football players ran to the platform to restrain the man. John waved the bouncers—I mean ushers— away. The would-be prophet stopped directly in front of John and told him to get down on his knees. John kept his seat at the keyboards and very calmly looked into the man's eyes and said, "No." The assailant prophet then delivered a totally irrelevant "prophecy" and vanished into the night.

This incident illustrates an important principle for Christian ministry: Once permission or encouragement is given for any spiritual activity, the natural human tendency will be to abuse that permission. A significant portion of the New Testament was written to correct various abuses of legitimate spiritual gifts and legitimate ministry.

At one time or another I have allowed my flesh—my carnal nature—to abuse and misuse virtually every spiritual ministry. Abuse and misuse are native to our human hearts. Anywhere people believe God still speaks to his children, you will find them abusing his voice. Christians can do these sort of things with their prophecies or with their interpretations of the Bible. They will give directional "words" to others that they do not have the authority to give. They will give corrective "words," rebukes, and condemnations without divine permission. In each case, they are abusing the voice of God.

For some this comes out of a desire to control others. They never recognize it as a desire to control, however; they see it as a desire to make things right, to bring situations and people into conformity with God's will. Others misuse the voice of God out of anger. Prefacing a mean statement with "God says" or "the Bible says" seems to legitimize their anger. Part of growing up spiritually is learning how to recognize these things in ourselves and repent of them. Then, perhaps, we can learn how to correct them with love in others.

The story about the would-be prophet commanding Wimber to kneel illustrates a dilemma we all face when we believe God gives us messages for other people. That man sincerely believed he had a word from God for John. His dilemma was, "Do I obey this prompting from God or give in to the fear of doing something potentially very embarrassing?" It's a dilemma we all face. Or we may experience the dilemma in a different form. We may think God has spoken to us, but we're not quite certain. What if we give the message, and it turns out to be wrong? We could end up misleading or hurting someone because we failed to hear God correctly. So sometimes it's the fear of being wrong, as well as the fear of man, that conflicts with our desire to obey what we think God has shown us.

How do we escape this "God-told-me" trap? One way is to simply deny that God speaks at all except in the Bible. This position certainly tidies up things a bit. Not that people can't abuse the Bible. They do, but it only leaves them one thing to abuse instead of many. No messy dreams or subjective visions to deal with if the Bible is the only way in which God speaks. The problem with this sanitized approach is that it does not resemble divine communication within the Bible. The only group in the Bible that seems to confine the voice of God to the Bible is a group that never heard his voice (John 5:37).

In addition to not being biblical, this sanitized method of escape leads to sterility. Ken Gire explains it in the following way:

It could be argued, though, that to open the possibility of God's speaking through other means than the clear teaching of Scripture is to let in all sorts of confusion. After all, a window lets in pollen along with the breeze, flies along with the sunshine, the cackle of crows along with the cooing of doves.

If that were your argument, I would have to agree.

But if we want fresh air, we have to be willing to live with a few flies.

Of course, we can shut out the flies and the pollen and the cackle of crows. And if a clean and quiet house is what's most important to us, perhaps that is what we should do. But if we do, we also shut out so much of the warmth, so much of the fragrance, so many of the sweet songs that may be calling us.[3]

I've had the life without confusion. I've lived in the house with the closed windows. Not a speck of dust anywhere. Everything in its proper place. But my soul withered in that environment, so I started looking for another way to escape the "God-told-me" trap. For a while, I was searching for a door of escape, a door to walk through and then shut behind me so that the embarrassing possibilities of mishearing God's voice were shut out. What I've found is a path, not a door. A path of love and humility.

The more we love God, the more we will risk for him, even to the point of public humiliation. Also, the more we love God, the better we will hear his voice. And as our love for God increases, our love for his people will increase. The more we love God's people, the harder it will be for us to rebuke them in a manner which takes away their hope. That kind of rebuke is condemnation, and the greatest lovers don't condemn. Instead, love will lead us to use prophetic words for the New Testament goals of "strengthening, encouragement, and comfort" (1 Cor. 14:3). And when our words are not consistent with these three goals, love and humility will lead us not to speak.

When we are walking on the path of humility, we will be open to the possibility that we might be wrong. On that path, we are much easier to correct. Humility is the pathway to intimacy with God, for he dwells with the humble (Isa. 57:15). That means humble people will hear God's voice better. God is the only one who really knows our hearts (Jer. 17:10). When we embrace humility, we will be able to hear the voice of God exposing unconscious motivations of anger, the desire to control, and the desire to appear awesome—motivations that lie in the darkest part of our hearts and spread a pollution through our speech which our natural minds cannot detect.

This is all well and good, you may say, but it doesn't guarantee I won't fall into the "God-told-me" trap, humiliating myself and hurting others. No, the path of love and humility doesn't offer a guarantee against mistakes, even serious mistakes—unless you are perfect in love and humility. So far, only one Person has managed that feat, and he *did* hear God perfectly. But if you and I are waiting to risk until we find a guarantee that we'll never mishear the voice of God, then we're like a man waiting for all the water to flow by before he crosses a river.

I wish there were a way of embracing the prophetic ministry of the Holy Spirit without having to deal with prophetic pitfalls. Those traps are real, and they hurt. But doesn't everything worth having, hurt? Think about love. Does anything hurt worse than love? Has anything been abused more than love? Yet who wants to live without love? The same God who told us to pursue love (1 Cor. 13) also told us to pursue the prophetic ministry of the Holy Spirit (1 Cor. 14). Perhaps he doesn't share our concern to avoid pain. Perhaps he lets the prophetic ministry remain imperfect so he can be the answer to our pain.

15

Dreams and Visions

Did you know that the inventor of the modern sewing machine, Elias Howe, credited his invention to a dream? Or that Niels Bohr, a Nobel Prize winner, claimed he had seen the structure of the atom in a dream?[1] Modern readers might find this surprising, but it would have been rather normal in the ancient world. For example, the Philistine King Abimelech thought Sarah was only Abraham's sister, so he took her for his wife. Then God came to Abimelech in a dream and said, "You are as good as dead because of the woman you have taken; she is a married woman" (Gen. 20:3). The amazing thing about this experience is that when the king awoke the next morning, he immediately called for Abraham and gave Sarah back—he instantly obeyed his dream. In Bible times, people knew God spoke frequently through dreams, so they took them seriously.

But dreams and visions have fallen on hard times in the highly rationalistic western world of today. Well-known preachers mock dreams and visions, warning their followers to have nothing to do with them. Others think that dreams are a valid form of divine communication just for those who are immature in their faith. The mature presumably need only the Bible for God to speak to them.

At one time in my life I knew there were dreams and visions in the Bible, but I thought that God only used them to communicate when he didn't have a clear text of Scripture at hand. If what God wanted to say to a person had already been written in the Scripture then, according to my theology, he would never have given them a dream or vision. He would have simply brought the Scripture text to their mind. Why would he use an "inferior" means to communicate when he had the Bible at hand? This position sounds logical, but it actually contradicts the teaching of Scripture.

One of the most famous dreams in the Scripture is the dream God gave Joseph when Joseph had made up his mind to divorce Mary because he thought she was carrying another man's baby. An angel of the Lord appeared to Joseph in the dream and told him that Mary's child was not the result of an immoral act with another man. The child had been conceived by the Holy Spirit. This child was to be named Jesus, for he would save the people from their sins (Matt. 1:21–22). The startling thing for me about this dream is that it was unnecessary. God did not have to use this dream to communicate the truth to Joseph about the virgin conception of Jesus. God could have simply brought Isaiah 7:14 to Joseph's mind: "The virgin will be with child and will give birth to a son, and will call him Emmanuel."

The name Jesus is the Greek equivalent of the Hebrew Old Testament name Joshua. The name Joshua comes from a Hebrew verb which means "to save." God could have used any number of biblical texts to suggest to Joseph that he ought to name his son Joshua, or Jesus. He chose, though, to use a dream. According to the theory above, God should have chosen the Scripture.

After Jesus was born, how did God protect his Son from Herod's murderous wrath? He gave Joseph another dream in which he told him to take the child and his mother to Egypt (Matt. 2:13). He risked the safety of his Son on something as "flimsy" as a dream. But the dream wasn't really necessary. God had a perfectly good scriptural text for communicating the same thing to Joseph. He could have used Hosea 11:1, "Out of Egypt I called my son." God could have simply brought this passage to Joseph's mind rather than giving him the dream.[2]

We find the same phenomenon happening in the book of Acts. When Paul went to Corinth, he was apparently worried that he would be attacked there and possibly even killed. God came to him in a vision of the night and promised him that no one would harm him and that he had many people in the city of

Corinth (Acts 18:9–11). Now why did God give Paul a vision to communicate this? There were many perfectly good Old Testament texts he could have brought to Paul's mind in order to communicate the same truth. For example, he could have led Paul to Isaiah 54:17: "No weapon forged against you will prevail, and you will refute every tongue that accuses you." The completed Old Testament rendered this vision unnecessary, yet God still chose to give the vision.

Apparently God didn't share my view of dreams and visions. Actually, according to the Bible, dreams and visions are the *normal* language of the Holy Spirit when God speaks to his prophets. Numbers 12:6 says, "When a prophet of the LORD is among you, I reveal myself to him in visions, I speak to him in dreams."[3] Joel promised that one day dreams and visions would be common among the people of God, saying, "And afterward, I will pour out my Spirit on all people. Your sons and daughters will *prophesy*, your old men will *dream dreams*, your young men will *see visions*. Even on my servants, both men and women, I will pour out my Spirit in those days" (Joel 2:28–29). The apostle Peter claimed that the coming of the Spirit on Pentecost began the fulfillment of Joel's prophesy (Acts 2:16ff.).

Dreams have always been an important means of divine communication. The book of Job answers the complaint against God, "Why do you complain to him that he answers none of man's words?" (Job 33:13) in the following way:

> For God does speak—now one way, now another—
> though man may not perceive it. In a dream, in a
> vision of the night, when deep sleep falls on men as
> they slumber in their beds, he may speak in their ears
> and terrify them with warnings, to turn man from
> wrongdoing and keep him from pride, to preserve his
> soul from the pit, his life from perishing by the sword
> (Job 33:14–18).

According to the Bible, the problem is not with God. God does speak, but we often are simply not "tuned in." He gives us dreams to warn us, but we ignore them. If we are ever going to hear all that God wants to say to us, we must adjust to his ways of speaking. And one of his favorite ways of speaking is through dreams.

THE PURPOSES OF DREAMS

God may use a dream to warn, encourage, or guide us. He may visit us in a dream to commune with us or to reveal the future to us. Or he may use a dream to command us. He even uses dreams to speak to unbelievers.

Warning

The book of Job has already told us that God frequently uses dreams to warn us (Job 33:16–18). Dreams can warn us of events that are decreed by God, that is, events that are surely going to happen. Pharaoh had the same dream in two different forms. First, he saw seven fat cattle being eaten by seven skinny cattle, and then seven fat heads of grain being eaten by seven skinny heads of grain. Joseph said to Pharaoh, "The reason the dream was given to Pharaoh in two forms is that the matter has been firmly decided by God, and God will do it soon" (Gen. 41:32). The dream meant that after seven prosperous years a seven-year famine was coming. Apparently, it would have been useless to ask God to withhold the famine. He had already decreed it. The dream was meant as a warning so that the people could prepare for the famine ahead of time.[4]

Other dreams warn us of *potential* events that can be averted by our prayers or our repentance. Nebuchadnezzar had a dream about a man whose mind was changed into that of an animal (Dan. 4:16). Daniel told Nebuchadnezzar that the dream referred to the king himself. The disaster could possibly have been averted, for Daniel said to Nebuchadnezzar, "Renounce your sins by doing what is right, and your wickedness by being kind to the oppressed. It may be that then your prosperity will continue" (v. 27). God gave Nebuchadnezzar one year in which to repent of his pride and arrogance, but when he failed to repent, God brought on him the disaster warned about in the dream (v. 28ff.).

It has been my experience that most of the negative dreams we have are those which warn us of sins or calamities that can be averted by prayer or repentance. In 1988, many prophetic people were having dreams of John Wimber's death. In their dreams they would see things like a coffin with a date above it. Almost all of these prophetic people thought that God was revealing to them the time of John's death. Actually, these were warning dreams meant to encourage people to pray that God would heal John's heart condition and extend his life. John did not die when the dreams said he would. Instead, his heart condition was turned around by careful attention to his diet and regular exercise. These people weren't false prophets, nor were their dreams false dreams. The dreams were merely warning dreams misunderstood by those who had them.

Encouragement

When Paul first came to Corinth he went to the synagogue every Sabbath, preaching the Gospel. Eventually he was forced to leave the synagogue. Paul's Jewish enemies had hounded him in almost every city he had visited. Once before, some of the Jews from Antioch had come to Lystra and managed to get a crowd so worked up that they stoned Paul and left him for dead. Now the same process was starting at Corinth. Some key synagogue leaders had become believers in Christ, and Paul knew it wouldn't take too long for his enemies to retaliate. Would he be stoned again?

It was in this context that "one night the Lord spoke to Paul in a vision: 'Do not be afraid; keep on speaking, do not be silent. For I am with you, and no one is going to attack and harm you, because I have many people in this city'" (Acts 18:9–10). This vision brought great comfort and encouragement to Paul. I am sure Paul would have stayed in the city until God told him to leave, even if it meant he would be stoned again. But how kind it was of the Lord to take those worries out of Paul's mind by giving him this vision. I find it is common for the Lord to give comfort and encouragement through dreams and visions.

Guidance

On Paul's second missionary journey, God gave him a vision in the night "of a man of Macedonia standing and begging him, 'Come over to Macedonia and help us'" (Acts 16:9). On this particular occasion, a vision was God's means of guiding Paul to the place where the Lord wanted him to minister.

Years ago I was about to make a major commitment to join someone on a ministry project. The commitment was going to cost me a lot of time, money, and energy, but both Leesa and I felt it was the right thing to do. Then she had a dream revealing some very negative characteristics of the person to whom we were about to make the commitment. To make matters worse, a couple of nights later I had a similar dream. I didn't like either one of the dreams. I sincerely liked the person who was asking us for the commitment. I decided that my dream probably just came out of my own emotions and was due to the influence of Leesa's dream. As for her dream, I decided to ignore it.

Just before it was time to finalize our commitment, I was walking into a store, complaining silently to the Lord about Leesa's dream. Opening the door, I said to the Lord, "I just can't see those negative traits about this person." Just like that, a voice in my mind said, "Why do you think I gave you the dream?"

How could I have been so stupid! The reason God had given us the dreams was because we were blinded to this person's negative character traits. That's what dreams do. They show us things we can't see with our natural eyes. We refused to make the commitment. About two months later, things were publicly revealed about this person that made us very thankful that our names were not connected together in ministry, and that our time, energy, and money had not been wasted.

Intimacy and Communion

On a number of occasions in the Scripture God appears to his servants in dreams and visions. These appearances may involve instructions, guidance, comfort, or other kinds of directions. What sets them apart from other dreams is that the Lord himself actually appears and speaks to his servants. There is a level of intimacy and communion with God that transcends other less personal dreams and visions.

One of the classic examples of this kind of a dream is what happened to Solomon when the Lord appeared to him in a dream at Gibeon. During this dream, Solomon and the Lord carried on an extended conversation (1 Kings 3:5–15). Many people have told me of an experience similar to this where a "faceless" man appears to them in a dream. I believe the faceless man frequently represents the Holy Spirit, whose primary task is to point us to the face of Jesus Christ. Think about your own dreams. Can you recall a significant dream in which a kind person whose face you couldn't see was giving you important directions or protection? It was very likely the Holy Spirit.

Revealing the Future

God can use dreams to reveal the immediate future or even the events of the last days. When Joseph was a young man, he was given two dreams about the immediate future that indicated that one day he would be elevated to a position of leadership (Gen. 37:5ff.). Both Daniel and John were given dreams and visions that related not only to the course of world history in their time but also stretched down into the events of the last days.

Commands

Sometimes the Lord will use dreams to give direct commands. In a dream he said to Jacob, "Now leave this land at once and go back to your native land" (Gen. 31:13). When Laban wanted to harm Jacob, God came to Laban in a dream and said, "Be careful not to say anything to Jacob, either good or bad" (Gen. 31:24). I have already mentioned the fact that God used dreams to command Joseph to take Mary as his wife (Matt. 1:20–21) and to escape to Egypt (2:13). He also used dreams to command Joseph to return to Israel (2:19 20).

Speaking to Unbelievers

Many Christians feel that God does not speak to unbelievers. Yet the Bible is witness to the fact that he does. In the Old Testament he spoke to unbelievers through the prophets, but he also spoke to them in more direct ways. It was not at all uncommon for God to speak to rulers through dreams. He spoke this way to Abimelech (Gen. 20:3–7), to Pharaoh (Gen. 41:1–7), and to Nebuchadnezzar (Dan. 2:1ff.; 4:9ff.). He also spoke in dreams to those who weren't rulers, for example, the Midianite soldier in Judges 7:13. In the New Testament God spoke to Pilate's wife in a dream, but when she told her husband the dream, he ignored her warning (Matt. 27:19). In the New Testament God also spoke to the

Magi, who were probably pagan astrologers, in a dream, warning them not to return to Herod (Matt. 2:12).

God still speaks to unbelievers in dreams. Outside the church there is an increasing interest in dreams and their practical value.[5] The topic of dreams is going to come up more and more in our conversations with unbelievers, especially those who have been influenced by the New Age. Undoubtedly, some of these dreams will have a satanic origin or arise out of emotional conflicts, but some of them may actually represent the Lord speaking to people. Whatever their cause, they can be used as an effective evangelistic tool if we will listen sympathetically to find a point of contact between us and our unbelieving friends.

INTERPRETING DREAMS

Recording Dreams

You can't interpret dreams if you don't remember them. Dreams are fleeting and easily forgotten (Job 20:8). That's why Daniel "wrote down the substance of his dream" (Dan. 7:1). If God regularly speaks to you in dreams, then it is a good idea for you to keep a tablet or a recorder near your bed. If you dream every night, you obviously can't record all of your dreams. You will have to be selective and record the ones you think are most meaningful.

The most important time for remembering a dream is in that state just before you wake up, where you are not quite awake, but no longer sleeping. When you first become conscious that you are waking up, train yourself to review your dreams. Most people who don't record their dreams forget them within five to ten minutes and can't get them back. Some people have told me that they find it helpful not to wake up with an alarm. An alarm can be so jarring to some people that it causes them to lose the recall of their dreams.

If you wake up in the middle of the night at the conclusion of the dream, do not go back to sleep before you record it. The fact that you woke up most likely means that the dream is important. I have awoken in the middle of the night at the conclusion of the most vivid dream, and thought that I would never forget it because it was so vividly impressed upon my mind. Then I went back to sleep and promptly forgot the dream. All I could remember in the morning was that I had an important dream during the night. I couldn't recall a single detail.

Symbolism

Don't let the symbolism of your dreams intimidate you. Symbolism often makes a dream difficult to interpret, just as the symbolic visions of the prophets were and are difficult to interpret. Frequently, however, the most symbolic dreams are also the most meaningful dreams. One benefit of symbolism in our dreams is that it causes us to depend on God for the illumination of the dream. Symbols also let us know that we didn't make up the dream. Dreaming in symbols we don't normally use and can't understand is a sign that the dreams are not coming out of some conscious opinion that we hold.

There are no mechanical formulas for interpreting symbols in dreams, although there are some things that seem to function as universal symbols. After listening to people's dreams for a number of years, I have found that clean, moving water often symbolizes the power of the Holy Spirit. Cars sometimes symbolize a particular ministry. Trains may symbolize movements or denominations. And I have already noted that a faceless man may represent the Holy Spirit. Yet even with these common symbols, we must remember that symbols, by their very nature, have layers of meanings. They can mean different things in different contexts. I find it common for God to give a "dream vocabulary" to those who dream regularly. For example, a baby might appear in your dreams as a recurring symbol of some ministry the Lord has given you. To someone else the baby might function as a symbol of immaturity.

How do we discern these things? We interpret dreams the same way we interpret the Bible: contextually with the illumination of the Holy Spirit. Both Joseph and Daniel were very careful to say that the interpretation of dreams belongs to God.[6] All of the rules for the interpretation of symbols in the Bible are also valid for interpreting symbols in dreams. However, without the illumination of the Holy Spirit, the greatest literary genius in the world will fail to produce a beneficial interpretation of either a dream or a biblical text. If we are willing to patiently meditate on our dreams, taking time to write down the ones we think are more meaningful, and pray about their meaning, sooner or later God will unlock the mysteries of our dreams to us.

Another benefit of symbolism in dreams is that it often reveals the perspective of God. For example, when the pagan king Nebuchadnezzar dreamed about world empires, he saw the successive empires in terms of a beautiful statue. However, when Daniel dreamed about these same empires, he saw them in terms of beasts. Nebuchadnezzar's dream represents the world's view of human empires, while Daniel's represents the divine perspective.

Remember to pay attention to details that either fascinate you or stand out in some way in your dream. The details themselves don't have to be fascinating, but the fact that you remember them and that they seem to have captured your attention, means that these details are significant for the dream's interpretation. To cite an instance, in a dream you may be in a parking lot and have your attention drawn to the white lines which outline the individual parking spaces. You may notice that the lines are perfectly white and straight. In the dream you find yourself staring at these lines. In this case, the lines will be significant for the interpretation and application of the dream. Also be careful to remember your feelings in the dream. The way you felt about a certain event or person can be a significant clue to the meaning of the dream.

Literalism

Some dreams are literal and require little interpretation. Still, understanding the time to which the dream refers and its application can be very difficult. Even when the interpretation of the dream is obvious, God still has to lead us in the application and the timing of the dream. Most dreams are not literal, however, and their interpretation is just as difficult to understand as their timing and application. I find that the most common error in the interpretation of dreams is to interpret the dreams too literally.

I once made the mistake of giving a public lecture on dreams. Since then, people have been bringing their dreams to me for an interpretation. I have learned that it is very common for women to have dreams about being raped. This kind of dream frightens a woman and she often wonders if she should take extra precautions against this violent crime. I have never found any of these dreams to be literal. Usually they represent some sort of spiritual robbery.

Years ago, a pastor's wife came to me with an upsetting dream. She dreamed she was being raped by men who had tied her hands behind her back. They were also strangling her with a string of her own pearls. She was terrified by the dream and asked me if I thought it was literal. I didn't think it was literal, but I had no context in which to interpret the dream. I asked her what was going on in her life. She said that she and her husband were serving as pastors in a relatively large church with multiple staff members. Some of the staff members had begun to say both untrue and unkind things about her husband. One of the pastors in particular was leading what was obviously an attempt to discredit this pastor and get them to leave the church. I still couldn't connect the dream with the woman's present circumstances, but I was sure it wasn't literal. My assurances weren't particularly comforting to this woman.

Later that day, I told Paul Cain the dream. He asked me about the circumstances and then gave me the interpretation. He said the rape represented what the other pastors were doing to this couple. They were trying to take away not only the reputation of this couple, but the ministry that God had given them in the church. I asked him what it meant that the woman had her hands tied behind her back. He said the staff was doing this behind their back and giving them no chance to face their accusers. Consequently, they had no way to defend themselves against the charges. What about the pearls? Paul said that the pearls represented the woman's husband, her most precious possession. Their attack on her husband's integrity was "choking" the life out of her. I thanked Paul for the interpretation and said that I was going to call the woman back. Then Paul said, "Jack, tell her this dream represents the way God feels about what is being done to them. The slander and gossip, the underhanded attempt to remove them from ministry, is like a vicious rape in the eyes of the Lord. Tell her that if she and her husband won't fight back and can keep their heart free of bitterness and accusation, the Lord will let them emerge from this victoriously."

When I told the pastor's wife what Paul had said, she was tremendously encouraged. What some people might have interpreted as a nightmare was actually meant as a divine comfort for this couple. Paul's interpretation gave them the courage and determination to forgive their detractors and not fight back. In the end, it all happened just as Paul said it would.

This particular experience illustrates another valuable feature of symbolism in dreams. Visions and dreams often impact our emotions in ways that sermons or printed words do not. God sometimes uses dreams to "terrify" us (Job 7:14; 33:16). There are occasions when only terror will turn us away from sin or traps leading us into sin. After some of his visions and dreams, Daniel's emotions were so shaken that all his strength left him and he even became ill.[7] Sometimes a dream can have a greater effect on us than a thousand words.

THE MISUSE OF DREAMS

Dreams are not given in order to enhance our stature in the church or give us control over others. Some things the Lord shares with us are meant to be kept to ourselves. Sometimes dreams are meant to teach us how to pray about a situation or how to pray for certain people. The fact that we have had a dream does not mean we have permission to share it with others, even though they may have appeared in the dream. Other times God may give us a dream that indicates he is going to do something wonderful for us. This makes us feel special, and we may want to tell other people about the dream so that they too can see how special we are to God. In reality, God may have given us the dream because we are about to go through an excruciatingly difficult time, and we will need all the encouragement we can get from him in order to make it through this time. By telling the dream to others, we may be giving in to pride and increasing the difficulty of the trial.

This was what happened to Joseph. He had two dreams that indicated God was going to promote him to a high level of leadership. Then he unwisely told the dream to his brothers, who already hated him because of the favoritism shown to him by their father (Gen. 37:5). Instead of working in Joseph's favor, the telling of the dream actually increased the pain in his life. God worked it all out in the end for everyone's benefit, but Joseph was still unwise to tell the dream.

INTERPRETERS OF DREAMS

Although it is not expressly called a gift in the Scripture, God does gift certain individuals with the ability to interpret dreams. This was true both of Joseph and Daniel.[8] It was said of Daniel that he "could understand visions and dreams of all kinds" (Dan. 1:17). I have found people today who are very gifted with the interpretation of dreams and visions. On some occasions I have even seen them tell the dream and its interpretation just as Daniel did for Nebuchadnezzar's first dream (Dan. 2:1ff.).

AN UNFORGETTABLE LESSON

In February 1988, God gave me an unforgettable lesson on the importance of dreams. It was 11:00 P.M., and the children were asleep. Leesa and I were reading in our family room. "I have been afraid to tell you this," she said, "because I didn't want to worry you unnecessarily. For the last six months I think God has been telling me that Alese is going to die." I was stunned. Why would God take our seven-year-old daughter? By this time, I had developed profound respect for my wife's ability to hear the voice of the Lord. This time, however, I wanted to believe that she was wrong. Would the Lord tell someone ahead of time that their loved one was about to die prematurely, or was this some sort of demonic deception sent to worry us? How were we to decide?

For the last year Leesa had been having specific and accurate prophetic dreams about people and events. We decided to pray that night and ask God to give her a dream that would tell us whether or not Alese was in any real danger. When I prayed for the dream, I asked the Lord to protect Leesa from any demonic deception or from any influence that might arise out of her own emotions and fears. When she woke up the next morning, Leesa related to me the dream she had during the night.

In the dream, Leesa found herself lying in the middle of a huge athletic stadium filled with thousands of people. She was lying in the center of the field with a long spear thrust through her heart. People were filing by, looking at her, amazed that she was still alive. As she looked up to the end of the spear, she saw a cross on it. Both of us were convinced that the dream meant that just as Mary's heart was pierced with a sword through her

Son's death on the cross, so God was going to take our little Alese from us.

At once I walked into my closet and shut the door and got on my knees. I began to cry and plead with God not to take our youngest child. Then I became angry with the Lord, asking him why he would treat me this way. In the midst of my anger I remembered that he too had lost a child, but it didn't make any difference to me. Somehow the comparison didn't seem fair. He got his Son back after three days through the resurrection. If he took Alese, how long would it be before I would see her again?

I don't know how long I went on like this, but I know when I came out, my eyes were swollen and I was in despair. I decided to fast and ask God to change his mind. Shortly after the dream, a prophetic person came to our church. He prayed over our two boys, Craig and Scott, and said some wonderful things about them. Then he and his wife sat down before Alese and started to prophesy over her. He began to say, "The Lord is going to—" he stopped in mid-sentence and said, "We need to pray for the safety of your daughter." Later, he took me aside and said that the devil wanted to kill her. The devil wanted to kill her? All this time we had been thinking that the *Lord* was going to take her from us. When we told the prophetic minister about the dream, he said that the dream was a warning dream and that we should pray for Alese every day by laying hands on her and asking the Lord to protect her.

We gathered the children together and told them that the devil wanted to attack us. This meant that we would need to be more careful than we usually were about where we went and with whom we talked. We let them know we were going to be a little more restrictive with their privileges than was our normal custom. We assured them we would make it through this time just fine if we were careful and prayed every day for God's protection. Every morning we laid hands on our daughter Alese and asked God to protect her, to surround her with the power of the Holy Spirit, and to send angels with her wherever she went. We did the same thing each night before we went to bed.

One Sunday, shortly after we began to do this, I had just finished preaching a sermon at our church. Our friends Doc and Nancy Fletcher had brought Doc's mother, Joy Fletcher, to our church that day. Joy was a Southern Baptist who lived in West Texas and was visiting our church for the first time. After the service, she came up to shake my hand. After shaking hands, I attempted to withdraw my hand, but she held on to it firmly. We were just exchanging small talk, so I couldn't figure out why she wouldn't let go of my hand. After what seemed like a long time, I finally managed to get my hand back and swiftly put it into my pocket. Joy left with her son, Doc, and I began to talk to other people.

Thirty-five minutes later, when everyone had left the church, Doc and his mother came back. Doc's eyes were red. He had been crying. His mother was somber. He said to me, "Sometimes my mother has visions of people. These visions almost always come true. Four times she has seen a person's death ahead of time. Each time the vision of death has come true. The first time it happened to us was when she saw the death of my nine-year-old brother two weeks before he died. Mom, tell him what you saw."

Joy looked at me and said, "Sometimes when I touch people, I see visions about them. While I was shaking your hand, I saw a brick home that had a driveway running down the side and turning behind the house. Along the driveway was a white iron fence. Then I saw a little girl with long, light brown hair who looked to be about seven or eight years old. She was in the driveway playing, when a man walked up to her and . . . ." Her voice trailed off.

"Did the man come to hurt her?" I asked.

"Yes."

"Was he going to kill her?"

"I think that was his plan."

I thanked them for coming back and telling us the vision. Now we had three independent confirmations that the devil intended to kill our daughter Alese—my wife's dream, the prophetic minister's impression, and the vision that Joy had. Out of the mouth of two or three witnesses an event is confirmed. We knew for sure that God was warning us so that our daughter might be spared. We not only continued praying for her, but also we informed the whole church of the satanic attack on our daughter's life and how we had learned about it. We asked our church to pray for us each day until the attack had lifted. Sometime after Easter that spring, we felt like our daughter was out of danger. The attack was over. To this day, my wife and I are convinced that Alese was spared through the warning dream so graciously given to us by our heavenly Father.

Pay attention to your dreams. God might use one to save you or your loved one from disaster. I wonder how much love and mercy we may have missed over the years because we dismissed a dream God sent to warn us. "For God does speak—now one way, now another—though man may not perceive it. In a dream, in a vision of the night . . ." (Job 33:14).

Why Doesn't God
Speak to Me Like That?

16

God Knows the Proud from Afar

After reading the last few chapters, you might be tempted to ask, "Why doesn't God ever speak to me like that?" It's a question I hear all the time. The answer may be as simple as James 4:2, "You do not have, because you do not ask God." Anyone who sincerely asks will eventually hear the voice of God (James 1:5–8). For most people, though, God has already spoken to them. The Bible claims, "For God does speak—now one way, now another—though man may not perceive it" (Job 33:14).

Perhaps God has spoken to some of you repeatedly, but you didn't recognize his voice because no one's ever told you the various ways in which he speaks. Or you may know about those ways, but no one has ever given you practical instruction in how to understand things like dreams and impressions. For some of you, fear has obscured the divine voice—either fear that he might not speak at all or fear of what he would say if you stopped to listen. I know others who don't hear the voice of God because they think too little of themselves. "Why would God want to speak to someone like me?" they ask. Everyone knows the answer: "Because you're his blood-bought child. And if he loved you enough to die for you, don't you think he loves you enough to talk to you?" This is good theology, and perfectly logical, but it's not the kind of answer that usually helps someone who asks such a question.

When you stop to think about it, it's *not* logical for God to love us. It doesn't make any sense at all. God's love is a love "that surpasses knowledge" and can only be known through divine revelation (Eph. 3:18–19). It wasn't an argument that captured the hardened hearts of prostitutes in first-century Palestine. It was the affection they felt coming from the heart of Jesus to their hearts. Somehow they knew he delighted in them, but not for the reasons other men delighted in them. So if you find yourself thinking that you're not important enough for God to speak to you, follow Paul's example and pray to feel the affection of God resting on your heart (Eph. 3:14–19).

PRIDE

Those obstacles listed above are relatively easy to overcome compared with the obstacle I am about to introduce. The most powerful hindrance I know to hearing God's voice is thinking too much of ourselves. It's possible to commit this sin in two ways. The first way is to be like the person who said, "I may not be much, but I'm all I ever think about." This is not so much the sin of pride as that of self-centeredness or selfishness. A very selfish person may also have low self-esteem. The other way to commit this sin is far more deafening. It is holding too high an opinion of oneself. The Scripture calls this pride, and says that God "opposes" proud people (1 Peter 5:5).

One of the things that makes pride the most dangerous of all sins is that it is the hardest of all to detect. Jonathan Edwards said that pride "lies lowest of all in the foundation of the whole building of sin, and is the most secret, deceitful, and unsearchable in its ways of working.... It is ready to mix with everything."[1] The Pharisees, who were the most proud people in the New Testament, gave no indication they were even remotely conscious of this sin. I regularly see pride in other Christians, but I seldom see it in myself. What I call pride in them, I call in myself "a concern for the truth," or "the desire to get things right."

C. S. Lewis gave us perhaps the best test for detecting pride when he said, "The more we have it ourselves, the more we dislike it in others."[2] Even with this test, I have come to despair of detecting pride in my own life. I think it is probable that pride can never be *detected*, only *revealed*.

But what exactly is pride? The next few sections deal with various aspects of pride.

A Superior Attitude

Pride is more insidious than simply thinking too much of ourselves. Pride is both a desire and an attitude. It is, above all, the desire for self-exaltation. This is why pride places us in an unholy competition. Everyone, even God, is our rival because God is interested in exalting no one but his Son. Isaiah gave us a picture of pride when he prophesied the downfall of the king of Babylon:

> How you have fallen from heaven, O morning star, son of the dawn! You have been cast down to the earth, you who once laid low the nations! You said in your heart, "I will ascend to heaven; I will raise my throne above the stars of God; I will sit enthroned on the mount of assembly, on the utmost heights of the sacred mountain. I will ascend above the tops of the clouds; I will make myself like the Most High" (Isa. 14:12–14).

The king of Babylon felt in his heart that he was intrinsically superior to the rest of humanity. This attitude of superiority led him to want to be exalted like God. He was determined to rise above the stars (angels) of God. The attitude of superiority and the desire for self-exaltation strengthen and encourage one another.

A Desire to Dominate

Another element of pride is the desire to dominate. By the time I was in my early thirties, I honestly believed I had lost the desire for athletic competition. I saw myself as having risen above the immature urge to prove myself athletically. I am sure this had nothing to do with the fact that my athletic skills were on the wane by then. Rather, I attributed the demise of the competitive spirit to my growing Christian maturity.

I had all but stopped playing competitive sports when one of my friends who was also a pastor invited me to join him for a game of racquetball. Although I hadn't played racquetball for quite a while, I was sure my friend would offer me no serious challenge. I had always regarded myself as athletically superior to him. I lost the game. I couldn't believe it. How could *he* beat *me*? I quickly challenged my friend to another game. I was sure that my loss had been a mere fluke. I didn't want to simply win the next game, I wanted to win it decisively. I wanted to humiliate my friend in such a way that he would be convinced of my superior athletic ability. When he won the second game, I was furious. I began to despise his athletic ability. How could someone with so little ability beat me? Before the afternoon was over, we had played a total of five games. He won every one of them. My rage grew with each defeat. In the end he refused my request for a sixth game. If he hadn't, I would probably still be on the racquetball court today, trying to win.

You know the sad thing about this story? My opponent had been one of my best friends since the ninth grade. We had become Christians at the same time. We had been in ministry together since college and had even gone to the same seminary. At the time of our racquetball game we were pastoring the same church. There was hardly anyone's company I enjoyed more. I was as close to him as to my own brother. And yet when we left the racquetball court, I was so enraged that I would not even speak to him. My pride had been deeply wounded. My belief in my athletic superiority had been seriously challenged, and my desire to dominate had been completely frustrated.

Blind Hatred

Pride is the worst of all sins because it separates us from one another and God more quickly and thoroughly than any other sin. C. S. Lewis wrote, "A proud man is always looking down on things and people: and, of course, as long as you are looking down, you cannot see something that is above you."[3] An alcoholic or a sexually immoral person can see the damage wrought by his sin. Both the alcoholic and the sexual addict may even have periods of sobriety where they look up to God and ask for help. But the truly proud person can't see his pride or the damage it has done to others. Pride permanently intoxicates. As long as there is one rival left, pride can never be quenched. It will strive to bring that rival into submission.

Pride's attitude of superiority and desire to dominate, feed one another. Satan's attitude of superiority led him to despise other creatures. What he despised he wanted to dominate, and what he dominated he despised all the more. That's why pride, in its purest form, is implacable hatred. When pride was fully

formed in Satan, he lost the power to love. You can't love someone and despise them at the same time. The truly proud man
enjoys his rival's loss as much as his own victory. On the racquetball court that day, I needed my friend to lose as much as I
needed to win. I wanted it proved that I was clearly superior.

Pride is anti-God because it strikes at the very heart of his
character—love, and at the very heart of his program—the exaltation of his Son. That explains why God hates pride with a purer
hatred than we can imagine. He says that the "proud in heart is
an abomination" to him (Prov. 16:5 NASB). An abomination is
something that repulses. For example, the ancient practice of sac-
rificing children to idols repulses any normal person. God calls
child sacrifice an abomination (Deut. 12:31)—the same word he
uses to describe pride. Pride is an abomination that repulses him.

RELIGIOUS PRIDE

The worst form of pride is religious pride. It might seem
impossible to be religious and proud at the same time. After all,
the essence of religion is bowing in humility before a God against
whom we cannot possibly compete, a God who is infinitely superior in every way to those who worship him. Yet Jesus gave a very
clear illustration of how the religious become proud:

> To some who were confident of their own righteous-
> ness and looked down on everybody else, Jesus told
> this parable: "Two men went up to the temple to pray,
> one a Pharisee and the other a tax collector. The Phar-
> isee stood up and prayed about himself: 'God, I thank
> you that I am not like other men—robbers, evildoers,
> adulterers—or even like this tax collector. I fast twice a
> week and give a tenth of all I get.' But the tax collector
> stood at a distance. He would not even look up to
> heaven, but beat his breast and said, 'God, have mercy
> on me, a sinner.' I tell you that this man, rather than the
> other, went home justified before God. For everyone
> who exalts himself will be humbled, and he who hum-
> bles himself will be exalted" (Luke 18:9–14).

The Pharisee stood before God and rejoiced in his commitment to God rather than rejoicing in God. He even credited God

with making him superior to other men. A religiously proud person not only thinks he is superior to other people, but he is also sure that God shares his opinion. The spiritually proud person uses God to help him look down on others.

Christian commitment and Christian works can lead us into pride. So can knowledge. During the Feast of Tabernacles the chief priests and Pharisees sent temple guards to arrest Jesus, but they returned empty-handed. When the chief priests and the Pharisees asked the guards why they hadn't brought Jesus back, they said, "No one ever spoke the way this man does" (John 7:46). The Pharisees were furious. They asked the guards, "You mean he has deceived you also? ... Has any of the rulers or of the Pharisees believed in him? No! But this mob that knows nothing of the law— there is a curse on them" (John 7:47–49). The Pharisees' superior knowledge of the Bible led them to look down on the rest of the worshiping community as nothing more than an ignorant, cursed rabble. They assumed their own commitment and knowledge had made them superior in God's eyes to all other worshipers.

And here's the really nasty thing about religious pride, it leads us to despise the people that God loves.

Have you ever seen a prodigal come home to a Pharisee? Religious pride turns away the very people that God is calling home.

Taking God's Place

So religious pride is not only the *attitude* of thinking we are superior to other people, but also the *belief* that God thinks we are superior. I also said that pride is the desire for self-exaltation and domination. How does that work on a religious level? Surely no Christian would ever follow in the footsteps of the king of Babylon who said, "I will make myself like the Most High" (Isa. 14:14)? Surely no Christian would ever desire to take God's place! Let me try to answer these questions by reminding you of a passage that initially won't seem to have any relevance to the topic at hand. Paul warned the Corinthians:

> Don't you know that you yourselves are God's temple and that God's Spirit lives in you? If anyone destroys God's temple, God will destroy him; for God's temple

is sacred, and you are that temple. Do not deceive yourselves. If any one of you thinks he is wise by the standards of this age, he should become a "fool" so that he
may become wise (1 Cor. 3:16–18).

Frequently people use this passage as a warning to take care
of their physical bodies since they are the temple of the Holy
Spirit. We are to take care of our physical bodies, but Paul is not
speaking of our physical bodies in this chapter. Paul was address-
ing the Corinthians corporately, not as individuals. He was
reminding them that they, as the church of Christ, were also the
temple of the Holy Spirit. Corinth had many temples, but there
was only one temple in Corinth where the Spirit of the Living
God dwelled. That temple was the church of Christ in Corinth.[4]

How could someone "destroy" the church at Corinth? In an
absolute or literal sense, no one can destroy the church of the living God. The gates of hell will not prevail against it. There are,
though, many examples of local churches being "destroyed"
through various means. In fact, the word translated "destroy"
could be used for the destruction of a house, financial ruin, or
ruining or corrupting someone morally.[5] God was warning the
Corinthian Christians that if anyone sought to ruin his temple in
Corinth, God would ruin him.

Who would risk doing such a thing to God's church? In the
immediate context there is only one possibility. It is the people
who think they are "wise" (v. 18). People who think they are wise,
people who are proud of their knowledge, do more damage to the
church than anyone outside the church. They are the ones who
always know what is wrong with everyone else and how to get
them "fixed." The truly proud in the church use their knowledge,
their commitment, and their zeal to control other people. They feel
it is their right to control others because they are wiser and more
committed than anyone else in the church. They usurp God's
place, giving directions to people only God has a right to give.

My first year in seminary I began to study the Bible an hour
every day. I studied a different biblical book each month. No matter whether I had a test or a paper due, I faithfully kept my commitment. I would not turn on the television set nor read a
newspaper until I had finished my hour of Scripture meditation.
During this time I was also leading a large college fellowship and

Bible study group. I told them that they should also study the
Bible an hour a day. I even told them what method they should
use to study. After a few weeks, one of the young women in the
group told me she had tried to study the Word an hour a day, but
she just couldn't do it. She felt guilty and thought she was disap-
pointing God. She asked me what to do. I thought about it for a
few minutes. I could say something to her that would be comforting, or I could tell her the truth. The truth might hurt her
short-term, but in the end it would be the best for her. I decided
to tell her the truth.

I said to her, "You *should* feel guilty. You are sinning, and
when people sin, they feel guilty. If you can't give God at least an
hour of your day, you can't be very serious about your relationship with him. You find time to do everything else you want to
do. Why can't you give God just an hour of your time every
day?" She was devastated by my comments. She was only a
freshman in college, and I was a first-year seminary student. She
looked up to me as a spiritual leader, but I wasn't a spiritual
leader on that day. I had become like one of the teachers of the
law of whom Jesus said, "They tie up heavy loads and put them
on men's shoulders, but they themselves are not willing to lift a
finger to move them" (Matt. 23:4). I had put a load on her that
God was not putting on her. When she cried out for help to carry
the load, I made it worse by increasing her guilt. I knew more of
the Bible and theology than all of those college students. I was
sure I was superior to them. I was sure God thought I was superior. I was sure God was speaking through me to them. I knew
that he wanted them all to study the Bible at least an hour a day.

Without realizing it, I had taken the place of God in their
lives. What gave me the right to tell them God wanted them to
study the Bible an hour a day? Why an hour? Why not two or
three or four or ten hours a day? Some of those kids didn't read
anything an hour a day. It was completely unrealistic of me to
expect them to *begin* reading the Bible that long. How long should
they have prayed every day? I didn't give them any advice there.
I hadn't had that much experience with prayer. Reading the Bible
was what was important to me, so I took what was important to
me and forced it on them. This is what a controlling person does.
Their actions are nothing more than pride's desire to dominate,
expressed in religious terms.

Religious Pride Deafens

When someone tried to rebuke me for the harshness and control birthed in me through spiritual pride, I thought they were weak or sentimental. In my own eyes I wasn't spiritually proud, I was committed. Most of the rebukes I received meant nothing to me. Looking back on those days, I now see how little respect for the authority or for the opinions of others I had. I don't think I was very much influenced by what people thought of me in those days. I told myself that this was because I was only concerned about God's approval. The approval of man meant nothing to me. In retrospect, I see that the approval of man meant nothing to me because I thought myself wiser than most men. Why should I care what those beneath me thought? When you look down on so many people, it is easy not to feel guilty when you hurt them. And the religiously proud are constantly hurting people.

What does all this have to do with hearing God's voice? Of all people, the proud have the most difficulty hearing God's voice. They seldom seriously ask God's opinion because they are convinced they already know what God thinks. There is also a divine hindrance. God is repulsed by pride, and you don't normally talk to someone who repulses you. One of the most frightening statements in the Bible is contained in Psalm 138:6: "Though the LORD is on high, he looks upon the lowly, but the proud he knows from afar." In other words, God is intimate with the humble, but distant with the proud.

On one occasion the disciples told Jesus they were worried he had offended the Pharisees. They thought he had been a little careless in his treatment of the religious leaders. But he said to them, "Let them alone; they are blind guides of the blind. And if a blind man guides a blind man, both will fall into a pit" (Matt. 15:14 NASB). This doesn't seem to be a very kind thing for Jesus to say. After all, hadn't he said that he came specifically to open the eyes of the blind (Luke 4:18)? Yet if we look at his words carefully, it is not the fact that the Pharisees are blind that causes Jesus to reject them. It is the fact that they are blind *guides*. It is one thing to be blind and groping for the truth, and quite another thing to put yourself in the position of being a guide who has found the truth but who in reality is blind. Religious pride blinds the eyes and stops the ears like no other sin. Neither her bad theology nor her immorality could keep Jesus from stopping and extending his hand to the Samaritan woman at the well (John 4). Not even a woman taken in the very act of adultery could repulse or embarrass him (John 8). But he was content to leave the Pharisees with all of their prejudices and blindness intact.

Have you ever noticed how frequently the Lord refuses to violate our prejudices? "The man who thinks he knows something" (1 Cor. 8:2) is usually left in his ignorance. This was an ancient warning. Seven hundred years before Paul had written this warning to the Corinthians, Isaiah had said, "Woe to those who are wise in their own eyes and clever in their own sight" (Isa. 5:21).

Perhaps the most chilling words ever uttered came from the Son of God when he said, "Let them alone." Is there a worse fate than to be "let alone" by the Savior of the world? The ultimate torment of hell is not the intensity of its flames but the absence of God's presence. The proud drive away the presence of God. When we embrace religious pride, God lets us alone, and we rarely hear his voice.

EXPRESSIONS OF RELIGIOUS PRIDE

I doubt that very many readers will disagree with what I've just written. In fact, you may have thought of several people in your social circle to whom you would like to send these pages. But I wonder if you thought these pages applied to you? If you're being honest with yourself, it was probably easier for you to see how this discussion applied to the pride of others than to your own pride. I want to discuss various manifestations of religious pride. Perhaps some detailed examples will help us to see our own pride a little more clearly.

The Message-A-Minute Christian

Some people seldom discern the voice of the Lord accurately because they are proud of their ability to hear God's voice. Have you ever met a Christian who thinks he or she has a "hot-line to heaven"? These people act as though they are always engaged in an uninterrupted, authoritative, ongoing conversation with God. They receive a sermon from God every second. They come off as ultra-spiritual, and though they would never say it out loud, they operate on the assumption that every single impression they have is from God. They leave no room for the frailty of their flesh. They attribute everything in their life either to God or to the devil, with no room left for the human element. *They* never seem to make any decisions. They don't have to, because God is telling them what to do at every turn of their lives.

A while back on a Sunday I bumped into one of these people at lunch. She had skipped church that morning. "Hi pastor," she said, "I wanted to come to church this morning, but God told me to stay home, although he said it was okay for me to go out to lunch. He also gave me a message for you. You need to make sure you preach what he wants you to preach and not preach just what the people want to hear." We talked for a little while longer, and she mentioned several other things that God had also told her in the last few days. I walked away from her thinking, "Either she is deceived, or she has an intimacy with God even the apostle Paul would envy." And that's the problem with people like this. They claim an intimacy with God that surpasses anything that the apostles experienced, or that the teaching of the Bible leads us to expect.

The psalmists did not experience an uninterrupted stream of messages from God. Even they frequently had to endure periods of God's silence.[6] The prophets of the Old Testament could not produce prophecies on demand. For example, during a period of civil unrest and confusion, the army officers and people asked Jeremiah to find out from God whether they should stay in Palestine or go down to Egypt to escape the wrath of the Babylonian king (Jer. 42:1–3). Jeremiah prayed, but it was not until ten days later that the word of the Lord came to him (Jer. 42:7ff.). Nor did the New Testament apostles live with the kind of divine clarity that some in the church claim to have today. The apostle Paul said that it was common for him to be "perplexed, but not in despair" (2 Cor. 4:8). He also said that "we know in part and we prophesy in part" (1 Cor. 13:9). There were times when even the apostles were forced to embrace a degree of ambiguity when they would have preferred more specific directions from God.

There is another problem with those who claim to be in constant touch with God. Their lives give no evidence of their claims. They show no real supernatural fruit in their "prophetic" ministry. Instead, dissension and confusion seem to follow them wherever they go. In the worst cases, they are using alleged conversations with God in order to control people and enhance their authority. Rather than enhancing their authority, they ruin their credibility and bring their prophetic ministry into disrepute. Generally, these kinds of people do not stay in one church for a long period of time. After losing their credibility they quickly move on to a church where new people will hopefully value "their prophetic ministry."

I have seen people like this change. The leadership of the church must give them gentle but firm and consistent correction. If they feel loved and affirmed, they may endure the correction. Often their hyperspirituality is an attempt to compensate for wounds of the past. Having a hotline to heaven makes them feel significant and gives them a tool to deal with all the rejections of the past and the present. If the church leadership can become a channel of Christ's healing mercy and love for those wounds and rejections, I've found that message-a-minute Christians will often repent of their spiritual pride and become profitable servants in the church.

Pride in Tradition

A tradition is a belief or custom handed down to us by the previous generation or by those in our own generation who have authority over us. Some people don't hear the voice of God very well because they have overwhelming confidence in their religious traditions. They are so pleased with the guidance they receive from their tradition, they don't really feel a need for God's voice. Moreover, they are sure God agrees with their traditions and would never speak anything contrary to their beliefs or practices.

Most people in Bible-believing congregations seem convinced that they don't have traditions. Instead, they have *convictions* that stem from correct interpretations of the Bible and *practices* that originate from correct applications of the Bible. In their eyes it is always the other people, those outside their particular Christian group—the ones who aren't as biblical—who have traditions. Ironically, people who think they are the most biblical are usually the ones most deceived about the power of their religious traditions.

The Holy Spirit frequently opposes some of our accepted traditions. If we can't recognize the voice of the Holy Spirit when this happens, then we are in for some serious conflict. Much of the conflict between Jesus and religious leaders of the first century was caused by the leaders' inability to perceive that it was the voice of God challenging their traditions. For example, they were offended with Jesus because neither he nor his disciples washed their hands before they ate (Mark 7:5). This tradition of washing had nothing to do with getting rid of germs. It was based on an interpretation of the ritual purity laws in the Old Testament. The Pharisees never learned to appreciate the distinction between this tradition and the Bible itself. On a practical level they gave their traditions the same—actually greater—authority than the Bible. Therefore, when Jesus neglected one of their traditions, they were sure that he was disobeying the Word of God.

In reality, just the opposite was true. Listen to another example. Even though the Bible commanded them to honor their parents, the Pharisees had devised a system whereby a greedy son could escape his responsibility to help his needy parents. All the son had to do was claim that the money he had available for their relief had already been dedicated to God through a religious vow. Through an ingenious loophole, however, he didn't actually have to give the money to God (Mark 7:10–12). Jesus rebuked the religious leaders for this, saying, "Thus you nullify the word of God by your tradition that you have handed down. And you do many things like that" (Mark 7:13).

What a stinging rebuke! The power of the Pharisees' tradition was so great it kept them from hearing not only the written Word of God but also the living Word! How arrogant and foolish we are today who think we are above doing the same thing.

Blind adherence to tradition gives some of us control and makes all of us feel secure. But this kind of control and security comes at a great price. It produces a religious people who have a relationship not to God but to a religious system. A religious system gives a great deal of false comfort. For one, it's much more predictable than the God of Scripture. It certainly is safer. After all, God might tell you to go to Nineveh, as he told Jonah, to leave Sodom, as he told Lot, or to sacrifice your favorite son, as he told Abraham. A religious system would never speak that specifically.

The second thing blind adherence to religious tradition accomplishes is that it encourages us to depend on a procedure rather than a Person. One of the keys for hearing God's voice is dependence, but tradition can easily take away our need to depend on God by supplying us with a ready-made method to achieve our religious goals.

I would be willing to bet a sizable sum that you have agreed with most of what I've written in these last few paragraphs regarding the potential danger of religious traditions. I'd also bet that as you've been reading these paragraphs, you've been thinking that they apply to someone other than yourself. That's the problem with adherence to religious traditions: We don't recognize it in ourselves. We all have religious traditions, but we don't think any of them could be hindrances to hearing God. We easily dismiss the warnings of Jesus to the Pharisees as having no relevance to us because the Pharisees weren't Christians and we are. But Christians can become just as pharisaical. Why do you think the Holy Spirit led Matthew, Mark, Luke, and John to write so much about the Pharisees in the New Testament, a book meant for Christians?

Paul was concerned that the New Testament church might succumb to the same pharisaical temptation to substitute tradition for God. He warned the Colossians, "See to it that no one takes you captive through hollow and deceptive philosophy, which depends on *human tradition* and the basic principles of this world rather than on Christ" (Col. 2:8). Tradition enters the church and takes people captive so that they stop depending on Christ and hearing his voice. Aren't we being foolish if we think we are above Paul's warning?

It only takes a few years to establish a tradition. Any denomination or local church that's been around longer than that will have a number of traditions, some of which will be set in concrete. Woe to the naive newcomer who dares to question, let alone violate one of these traditions. Dudley Hall, a close friend with whom I frequently minister in conference settings, was attending a deacons' meeting in a Baptist church shortly after he graduated from seminary. Someone was arguing for a change in the worship service because the change seemed demanded by the Bible. One of the deacons jumped to his feet and cried out, "I don't care what the Bible says—It ain't Baptist, and we ain't doin' it!" I appreciate that man's honesty. Most of us won't *say*, "We don't care what the Bible says," but we *act* that way when we choose one of our traditions over the Bible or refuse God's leading because it contradicts our tradition. For instance, anyone who lays down a blanket prohibition against speaking in tongues is exalting their tradition over the clear teaching of the Bible which says, "Do not forbid speaking in tongues" (1 Cor. 14:39).

Please don't misunderstand the Baptist example above. I have a great love and respect for that denomination. Every denomination and Christian group has similar attitudes about their own traditions. Recently, I made the mistake of asking a Presbyterian minister if a certain Presbyterian tradition was really biblical. He replied that the tradition was in the Presbyterian Book of Order, and that if I couldn't follow the Book of Order, I had no business being a Presbyterian! Clearly for him, Presbyterian traditions were above being questioned, even by the Bible. So much for the Reformed motto that Reformed churches are always reforming—not when you can't even question a tradition without being invited to leave. These examples could be multiplied *ad nauseum* from any Christian group.

Not all tradition is bad. Some is neutral. Some is even good. Paul commended the Thessalonians to hold to the traditions "we passed on to you, whether by word of mouth or by letter" (2 Thess. 2:15; see also 1 Cor. 11:2; 2 Thess. 3:6). These were good traditions based on apostolic authority, and in some cases, enshrined in Scripture. Yet we would be wise to remember that even the Scriptures can be misused when held in an arrogant, cold heart. A growing Christian is not concerned with just what is true or even with truth, but ultimately with the Truth, the Lord Jesus (John 14:6), and how he would have us use truth.

All this brings us back to the need to hear God's voice. But probably more often than not, a naive commitment to tradition often drowns his voice in a sea of confidence in human methods and rules. Jesus rebuked the Pharisees with the words of Isaiah the prophet: "These people honor me with their lips, but their hearts are far from me. They worship me in vain; their teachings are but rules taught by men (Mark 7:6–7; Isa. 29:13). According to Jesus, tradition can keep our hearts from God while giving us the illusion that he is pleased with our service. It can make our worship a vanity.

We can use tradition to justify disobeying God as we resist new works of the Holy Spirit in our generation. Anyone who wants to hear the voice of the Holy Spirit would do well to pay attention to Jesus' warning. Pride in our ability to hear God's voice or pride in our traditions can overpower the still, small voice of the Holy Spirit.

Long ago Thomas Erskine said, "Those who make religion their God will not have God for their religion."[7] This is the penalty for religious pride.

17

Confessions of a Bible Deist

Augustine had an entire book of confessions. Perhaps you will indulge me for just a single chapter of my own. Here is my confession: Somewhere along the way in my academic study of the Bible, I became a Bible deist. You probably studied deism in one of your high school history classes. The framers of the Constitution of the United States were mostly deists. They believed in a religion of morality based on natural reason, not on divine revelation. They believed in God, but they didn't think he interfered with the natural laws governing the universe. He created the world, and then left it alone—like someone who wound up a giant clock, and then left it to run down on its own. A Bible deist has a lot in common with the natural deist.

They both worship the wrong thing. The deists of the eighteenth century worshiped human reason. The Bible deists of today worship the Bible. Bible deists have great difficulty separating Christ and the Bible. Unconsciously in their minds the Bible and Christ merge into one entity. Christ cannot speak or be known apart from the Bible. At one time, Christ did speak apart from the Bible. He used to speak in an audible voice to people on their way to Damascus, give dreams, appear in dreams, give visions, give impressions, and do miracles through his servants. However, the Bible deist believes the only one who does these things today is the devil. In fact, the devil can do all the things Christ used to do. The devil can speak in an audible voice, give dreams and visions, even appear to people and do miracles. Jesus

251

doesn't do these things any more. He used miracles and divine revelation in the first century to wind up the church like a big clock, and then left it alone with only the Bible. The Bible is supposed to keep the clock ticking correctly. That's why a Bible deist reads a passage like Isaiah 28:29:

> All this also comes from the LORD Almighty, wonderful
> in counsel and magnificent in wisdom ...

and in his or her mind, translates it into something like this:

> All this also comes from the Bible, which is wonderful
> in counsel and magnificent in wisdom.

Bible deists have a tendency to substitute the Bible for God. They actually deify the Bible. Bible deists read John 10:27 like this: "My sheep listen to the Bible; I know them, and they follow the Bible." They hear Jesus say, "If I go away, I will send you a perfect book" (John 16:7). What God used to do in the first century is now done by the Bible. If the Bible can't do what God used to do—heal, give dreams, visions—then the Bible deist maintains that these things are no longer being done, and that we don't need them anyway.

Bible deists preach and teach the Bible rather than Christ. They do not understand how it is possible to preach the Bible without preaching Christ. Their highest goal is the impartation of biblical knowledge. Their highest value is being "biblical." Actually, they use the adjectives "biblical" and "scriptural" more often than the proper noun "Jesus" in their everyday speech.

THE SUFFICIENCY OF SCRIPTURE OR OF ONE'S INTERPRETATION?

The Bible deist talks a lot about the sufficiency of Scripture. For him the sufficiency of Scripture means that the Bible is the *only* way God speaks to us today. He loves to repeat slogans like "The Bible is all I need to hear from God" and "What the Bible says is what we should say, and where the Bible is silent we should be silent." Although the Bible deist loudly proclaims the sufficiency of Scripture, in reality, he is proclaiming the sufficiency of *his own interpretation* of the Scripture. Bible deists aren't alone in this error. When many people say they have confidence in the Bible, what they really mean is they have confidence in their ability to interpret the Word, in their own particular understanding of the Bible, in their own theological system. Nobody says this out loud, for fear of being labeled arrogant. But they demonstrate it when they refuse to fellowship with those who baptize differently, or with those who have a different view of the gifts of the Spirit, or with those who hold a different view of the end times. Many Christians agree on the fundamentals of the faith, but are so confident that in the debatable areas their interpretation is the correct one that they separate themselves from those who differ with them.

The Bible deist is especially guilty of this because he conceives of the Bible and his interpretation as one organic whole. After all, the Bible deist has consistently applied grammatical, historical exegesis to the text. Above all, he has a good theological framework, and his interpretations are consistent with his theological framework. He stands squarely in a tradition that is hundreds of years old and has many illustrious names within it. With that tradition behind him, plus his own personal skills and abilities, he is sure he is right. Oh, there are times, when he can admit to the possibility of being wrong—for humility's sake, or better, for the *appearance* of humility. Otherwise, he might give some people the impression that he thinks he is infallible. But in his heart of hearts he knows there is only the minutest possibility he might be wrong in any of his individual interpretations.

So it is extremely difficult for Bible deists to concede that they themselves might be *presently* holding an erroneous interpretation. They refer to their opponents' interpretations as "taken out of context," or as a failure to apply consistent hermeneutical principles. Or, in some cases, where they have little respect for their opponents, they chalk up their opponents' views to just plain sloppy thinking. In those rare cases where they have to admit that their opponent has out-argued them, it wasn't because their opponent had truth on his side. No, their opponent was a skillful debater—actually, he was downright tricky. In one case, a theologian I knew was asked why other knowledgeable interpreters of the Bible held a different eschatological position from his own. "Sin," came the terse but earnest reply.

The Bible deist is so confident in the sufficiency of his interpretation that it is difficult for him to be corrected by experience.

He usually has negative comments about subjective things like feelings and experience. He doesn't realize it, but it is more important to him to know the Bible than to experience its truth. This is the inevitable result of exalting the mind over the heart, and knowledge over experience. It also explains how someone full of biblical knowledge may be able to give a better explanation of humility than an elderly lady in his church—but *possess* so little humility when compared to her. Haven't we all witnessed this tragic disparity?

WHAT PRODUCES A BIBLE DEIST?

If you asked me why I held these kinds of positions, I would have told you the Bible clearly taught them, and I followed the Bible, not experience or tradition. But I had another motive for being a Bible deist and resisting subjective revelatory experiences. I wanted to preserve the unique authority of the Bible. I was afraid that if any form of divine communication other than the Bible were allowed, we would weaken the Bible's authority and eventually be led away from the Lord.

I thought it was possible we could be taken over by emotional instability and guided by ever-changing feelings. Authority would then be transferred from the objective standard of the Bible to the subjective state of the individual and there would be no universal standard to which we could appeal. Unity would be diminished in the body of Christ, and we would end up as in the period of Judges where "everyone did what was right in his own eyes" (Judg. 21:25 NASB). I thought there was virtually nothing to gain from allowing subjective revelatory experiences, and everything to lose. Nothing to gain, because these experiences could not add anything to the Bible, and the Bible already supplied everything we needed. And everything to lose, because all I had to do was look at the Corinthians and the chaos caused by tongues in order to see what could be lost by allowing these things. It wasn't worth the risk.

During the days of my Bible deism, I thought the above were my only reasons for my views of the role of the Bible. Looking back ten years later, I can see there were more powerful forces at work in the unconscious realms of my heart. I could easily blame my Bible deism on my teachers and the traditions I unquestioningly swallowed from them. I could blame it on a very closed system of education which punished deviations with expulsions. But I was never the kind of person who was afraid to deviate or to question. The truth is, Bible deism appealed to a serious weakness in my heart. The weakness was a fear of being hurt. I didn't like emotions because they caused me to lose control, and if I lost control, I became vulnerable. And vulnerable people get hurt. I had been hurt a lot. Although I didn't know it back then, I blamed some of those hurts on God.

Now I know that I attributed the deepest wounds of my heart to the hand of the Lord. He could have prevented the wounds, but he didn't. Where was his sovereignty when I needed it? Why did some of my most desperate prayers fall from my lips to the ground unanswered? My heart was filled with fear of God—not the biblical fear of God, but a fear of intimacy with him. I wanted a personal relationship with God, but I didn't want an intimate one. An intimate relationship would give him total control, and a voice out of some dark unexplored region of my heart told me that his control would bring me pain again, more pain than I could bear.

So I decided that my primary relationship would be to a book, not to a Person. It's so much easier to relate to a system of interpretive rules and a set of traditions than to a Person. With Bible deism, I could be in control. My principal task in life was to study the Bible and to cultivate the intellect. I didn't need my emotions for this task, just discipline and willpower. No emotions meant no loss of control. And that meant no more hurt.

If I had a question, I could ask the Bible. I didn't have to risk asking a God who might give me a painful answer. Besides, God and the Bible were practically the same. What he didn't say in the Bible, he left up to me. I found the things I liked in the Bible and ignored the rest. So all in all, it was a safe, comfortable system. And for me, it was also becoming a lifeless system.

I had tasted life in my early Christian years, and I never would have embraced Bible deism just because of the hurt in my life. The hurt was the open door, but it was my pride that welcomed Bible deism through the door and gave it a home in my heart. For much of my Christian life, I've thought myself wiser than most Christians. Since I thought myself wiser than others, it was only natural that I should be in control of them. If God only spoke through the Bible, then the one who knew the Bible the best would be the one who heard God's voice the best. Therefore, the person who heard God the best, would know best what everyone else should believe and do. This system fit in perfectly with the proud state of my heart. In Bible deism, I found a wonderful tool to keep myself from being hurt and to give me control over my life and the lives of others. The fact that I had an intellectually-oriented personality—I loved to study—helped me to be an even more effective Bible deist.

By now you've probably figured out that Bible deism is not so much a theology as it is a system that caters to a personality type. It's a system that religiously proud, hurt, intellectual people find hard to pass up. It offers us a justification for our pride without having to repent of it, an anesthetic for our pain without having to endure the surgery to heal it, and an outlet for our intellectual pursuit without having to submit our minds to a God whose ways and thoughts are not our ways and thoughts. To put it very simply, I had the kind of personality that made me much more comfortable relating to a book than to a Person.

When the principal thing in your life becomes the study of the Bible, you have become a Bible deist. But usually a practicing Bible deist does not recognize that they are a Bible deist. Whenever people accused me of being a Bible deist, I assumed that they were just lazy and didn't want to make a careful study of the Bible. They just weren't disciplined enough to learn Hebrew, Aramaic, Greek, and whatever other discipline was necessary to hear God speak. They weren't interested in things like the *Sitz im Leben* of a biblical text. They probably wouldn't even recognize a *Sitz im Leben* if they sat on one. I assumed these lazy detractors were just part of the cursed rabble that didn't know the law (John 7:49).

(Incidentally, I have just given you a test to determine whether or not you are a Bible deist. If you have grown angrier as you have read the last few pages, then you probably are a Bible deist. If you are still trying to figure out what a *Sitz im Leben* is, then read on. I think you will enjoy the rest of this chapter.)

These were my reasons, conscious and unconscious, for being a Bible deist, and wanting nothing to do with dreams, visions, impressions, or audible voices. There may have been even worse reasons than these, but if you want those kinds of confessions perhaps you ought to read Augustine after all. But before you pick up a copy of his *Confessions*, let's go on to a disconcerting thought about the Bible and authority.

THE BEST INTERPRETER

One of the most serious flaws of Bible deism is the confidence the Bible deist places in his abilities to interpret the Bible. He assumes that the greater his knowledge of the Bible, the more accurate his interpretations are. This follows logically from a hermeneutical axiom the Bible deist often quotes: The Bible is the key to its own interpretation. In other words, the Bible interprets the Bible the best. Wrong! It takes more than the Bible to interpret the Bible.

The *Author* of the Bible is the best interpreter of the Bible. In fact, he is the *only* reliable interpreter.

And if the Spirit's illumination is the key to interpreting the Bible, isn't the Bible deist's confidence in his own interpretive abilities arrogant and foolhardy? How does one persuade God to illumine the Bible? Does God give illumination to the ones who know Hebrew and Greek the best? To the ones who read and memorize Scripture the most? *What if the condition of one's heart is more important for understanding the Bible than the abilities of one's mind?* Is it possible that the illumination of the Holy Spirit to understand Scripture might be given on a basis other than education or mental abilities?

AN OMNISCIENT BEING IS NOT IMPRESSED WITH INTELLIGENCE

What kind of people does God speak to? Who is the best at interpreting the Bible? Who is the best at interpreting dreams, prophetic utterances, and other forms of God's revelation? Actually, all of these questions are one and the same: "What makes a person skillful at understanding God's revelation?" Whether the revelation comes in the form of the written statements of the Bible, in a contemporary prophetic utterance, in a dream, or in a vision, the answer is the same. There is one key that unlocks the meaning of all divine revelation.

The Bible deist believes the best interpreters of God's revelation are those who have the best interpretive methods, are the most knowledgeable in the original biblical languages and the historical backgrounds of the biblical period. In short, the best interpreters of God's word are the people who are the most intelligent and disciplined. It seems much of our current religious education operates on the lost beatitude: Blessed are the smart, woe to the dumb.

After all, where would God be if he didn't have any smart people to witness to smart unbelievers? What if God was left with just a handful of businessmen or blue-collar workers, say, people who fished for a living—whose only qualification for ministry was that they loved God and wanted to be with Jesus? Where do you think God would be if he fell into that predicament?

Christian scholarship is not nearly as important as Christian scholars have led us to believe. The American church is easily deceived in this matter, for the Western world worships intelligence and education. As far as I know, neither the Bible in general, nor Christ and his apostles in particular, ever commend intelligence as having any significant role in understanding God or his Word. Quite the contrary. If anything, the Bible is rather hard on human intelligence. When the seventy-two came back from their preaching mission, they heard Jesus pray, "I praise you, Father, Lord of heaven and earth, because you have hidden these things from the wise and learned, and revealed them to little children. Yes, Father, for this was your good pleasure" (Luke 10:21).

Jesus praised God for hiding some things. What were these "hidden things"? They were the secrets of the kingdom, secrets about authority, power, spirits, and heaven. From whom did God hide these secrets? From the wise and learned, that is, from the intelligent and educated. The real secrets of the kingdom can never be penetrated by human intelligence or education. Later, Jesus gave his disciples the sternest warning: "I tell you the truth, unless you change and become like little children, you will never enter the kingdom of heaven. Therefore, whoever humbles himself like this child is the greatest in the kingdom of heaven" (Matt. 18:2–4).

🐟 We do not progress in the kingdom of the Lord Jesus Christ by intellectual prowess. We progress by becoming like children. Remember how you felt when you were just three or four years old? Remember how much you needed your mother and father? Remember how you didn't think you knew very much, but that was okay, because Mom and Dad knew everything? God shares his secrets with the ones who manage to recover that childlike humility and trust. The problem is that we want to be smart grown-ups rather than dependent kids.

A WISDOM NOT DISCOVERED BY THE MIND

This spurning of human intelligence on the part of Jesus was not simply a tactic he adopted for the period of his own earthly ministry. He intended it to last for the duration of the church. Therefore, Paul wrote the Corinthians that not many of them were wise, influential, or of noble birth. Why? Because God had chosen the foolish things of the world to shame the wise, and the weak things to shame the strong, and the despised things to nullify the things esteemed in men's eyes (1 Cor. 1:26–30). An intelligent person might take some comfort in the fact that Paul said, "not many of you" are wise. There were, obviously, some intelligent people in the first-century church, the apostle Paul being one of them. But Paul's point is that intelligence doesn't count for very much in God's economy.

Still some might argue that God chose the apostle Paul because he was intelligent, even brilliant. Indeed, he had received some of the best theological training in his day (Acts 22:3). Apparently God thought that he needed at least one brilliant and theologically educated apostle in order to accomplish his purposes in the first-century church. But according to Paul's own explanation, neither his intelligence nor his education had any influence on God calling him as an apostle. Actually, it almost seemed that God chose him *in spite of* these qualities, and then had to retrain him. Listen to Paul's inspired explanation of his calling:

> Here is a trustworthy saying that deserves full acceptance: Christ Jesus came into the world to save sinners—of whom I am the worst. But for that very reason I was shown mercy so that in me, the worst of sinners, Christ Jesus might display his unlimited patience as an example for those who would believe on him and receive eternal life (1 Tim. 1:15–16).

Paul was not chosen for his intelligence—an omniscient Being can't be all that impressed with our intelligence—but because God wanted to give the world a dramatic example of his mercy and unlimited patience. Paul's life is not a tribute to the achievements of intelligence and education, but rather an enduring monument to the power of God's limitless mercy and patience.

Paul adopted the view of the Lord Jesus. He wrote:

> No, we speak of God's secret wisdom, a wisdom that has been hidden and that God destined for our glory before time began. None of the rulers of this age understood it, for if they had, they would not have crucified the Lord of glory. However, as it is written: "No eye has seen, no ear has heard, no mind has conceived what God has prepared for those who love him"—but God has revealed it to us by his Spirit (1 Cor. 2:7–10).

You would think that the most educated of all the apostles would place a high value on his education. But Paul didn't. The reason is simple. The wisdom in which Paul was interested could not be found in or with the intellect of man. It was a secret wisdom that God had hidden. It cannot be penetrated by the human eye, ear, or mind. It could only be revealed by God through his Spirit.

But someone might object, "That wisdom has now been revealed in the Bible. Now we have that wisdom because we have the Bible." But remember, the leading Bible scholars of Paul's day had the Old Testament. They had wonderful prophecies about the coming of the Messiah, and they could quote these prophecies effortlessly. In this sense, they possessed the wisdom of God, but when the Messiah came, they failed to recognize him. Why? Because none of God's revelation, not even the Bible, can be significantly understood apart from the revealing ministry of the Holy Spirit.

A BIBLE NOT UNDERSTOOD BY THE DISCIPLINED

Again and again the words of Jesus to the best biblical scholars of his day keep ringing in my ears. These people studied the Bible more than 99 percent of the people in the church today will ever study the Bible. They had more of the Bible memorized than 99 percent of the people in the church today will ever have memorized. Yet Jesus said to them:

> And the Father who sent me has himself testified concerning me. *You have never heard his voice nor seen his*

form, nor does his word dwell in you, for you do not believe the one he sent. You diligently study the Scriptures because you think that by them you possess eternal life. These are the Scriptures that testify about me, yet you refuse to come to me to have life (John 5:37–40).

You may think that since these words were directed to unbelieving Pharisees, they have no relevance to us Christians. After all, we're believers and followers of Jesus. So were the twelve disciples, with one exception. Jesus told them they had a greater privilege than the rest of the population. He said, "The knowledge of the secrets of the kingdom of God has been given to you, but to others I speak in parables ..." (Luke 8:10). Then, while they were on the way to Jerusalem for the last time, he said, "Listen carefully to what I am about to tell you: The Son of Man is going to be betrayed into the hands of men" (Luke 9:44). But they had no idea what he meant (v. 45), even though he had previously warned them he would be killed (v. 22). Luke said that the meaning of Jesus' words had been hidden from the apostles (v. 45). If something that plain could be hidden from Christ's closest followers, don't you think other important things could be hidden from us, things that can not be discovered with our minds?

And even though the disciples were believers, Jesus still had to warn them against being influenced by the teaching of the Pharisees and Sadducees (Matt. 16:5–12).

In principle, we acknowledge that we would never have become Christians apart from the supernatural revelatory ministry of the Holy Spirit. But now that we are "in," we seem to think that we progress through intelligence rather than through the revelatory ministry of the Holy Spirit. We seem to think that the Bible can be understood through patient, disciplined, academic study. We presume that because Paul wrote about divine mysteries and because we can read, therefore we can understand these mysteries. It is true that the Holy Spirit does enter into our lives the moment we become Christians (Eph. 1:13), but that does not guarantee he will automatically illumine the Word of God for us.

A VOICE NOT HEARD WITH THE EARS

If you are not yet convinced that intelligence plays a limited role in the understanding of God's voice, consider an incident in the life of Jesus that conclusively proves this very point. You would think that if God spoke in an audible voice, it would be crystal clear and that all would understand it. But remember the text I quoted before where Jesus prayed, "'Father, glorify your name!' Then a voice came from heaven, 'I have glorified it, and will glorify it again'" (John 12:28).

Even though the voice was clear and audible, only some heard him! Why could some not hear his voice? Was it due to their low IQ, poor interpretive skills, or inferior knowledge of biblical backgrounds? Revelation can't get any clearer than an audible voice. If someone fails to understand the audible voice of God, it demonstrates that the key for understanding God does not lie in human intelligence. The key must lie somewhere else.

The key that unlocks the meaning of Scripture is not held by institutions of higher learning. It is found in the hand of Jesus Christ. The privilege of receiving it from his hand does not go to the intelligent. It does not go to the educated. It does not go to the powerful and the influential. The key is given on an altogether different basis.

The best interpreter of any literary work is usually its author. Many authors, however, refuse to comment on their works once they have been published, leaving readers and critics to find in them whatever they please. Is God that kind of Author? On the one hand, it may seem so. He was perfectly willing to let his Book become nothing more than dead letters to many of the best biblical scholars of Jesus' day (John 5:37–40). They never heard his voice in the Bible, and he let them use his Book to argue against Jesus, his Son and their Savior. He has let others of us within the church use the Bible for destructive purposes (2 Peter 3:16). But for some people, he personally enters into the "interpretive process" and explains the meaning and application of his Word.

THE TEACHER OF THE HEART

Remember the story of the two disciples on the road to Emmaus (Luke 24:13–35)? When Jesus began walking along with the two disciples, they were prevented from recognizing him. They even told "this stranger" how sad they were about the recent death of their master, Jesus. At that point he rebuked them, saying, "How foolish you are, and how *slow of heart* to believe all that the prophets have spoken! Did not the Christ have to suffer these things and then enter his glory?" (vv. 25–26).

Jesus was not accusing them of stupidity. Their foolishness was not attributed to their defective intellects. Nor was the problem with the clarity of the Scriptures. According to Jesus, the Scriptures very clearly taught that the Messiah would have to suffer before he could enter into his glory. The problem was not with the condition of their IQ, but with the condition of their *hearts*.

After the rebuke, "beginning with Moses and all the Prophets, he explained to them what was said in all the Scriptures concerning himself" (Luke 24:27). This was not just a sermon to the two disciples. It was also a personal message from Jesus to his whole church. He was telling us that the greatest preacher in the church is, and always will be, Jesus himself. He is the preeminent preacher and teacher of the Word of God. He has not relinquished that position to anyone else, nor will he. He can't be impeached, and he'll never resign. Wherever the Word is preached or taught in power, it is because the Lord Jesus Christ is there speaking through a human voice and supernaturally revealing himself.

Jesus was telling us something else very important about the Bible as well. Luke says that Jesus *"explained* to them what was said in all the Scriptures concerning himself" (v. 27). Although the Bible was clear, the two disciples could not understand it until Jesus explained it to them. The word "explained" is the word in Greek used for translating a foreign language. It is also used for the spiritual gift of interpreting the gift of tongues.[1] In other words, *at critical points in our lives*, when we most need to understand and apply the Scripture, it will be like a foreign language to us unless the Lord himself explains its relevance to us. To be sure, we can construct theological systems and teach some accurate doctrine without his help, but if we really want to meet him in the Scripture and understand his ways at the decisive moments of our lives, he must personally explain it to us.

At the conclusion of that wonderful sermon, Jesus sat down to dinner with these two disciples. During dinner, "their eyes were *opened* and they recognized him, and he disappeared from their sight. They asked each other, 'Were not our hearts burning within us while he talked with us on the road and *opened* the Scriptures to us?'" (vv. 31–32). God supernaturally "opened" the disciples' eyes to recognize Jesus. He wasn't making dumb people smart. He was letting these two disciples see who the Lord Jesus really was. The word translated "opened" is also used by Luke in Acts 16:14 when the Lord supernaturally opened Lydia's heart to respond to Paul's preaching.

Unless the Lord Jesus opens our eyes, we will never really see him. The disciples used the same word whenever they said that Jesus *"opened* the Scriptures to us." Unless Jesus opens the Scriptures, we will miss much of their truth. We can read and memorize the Bible without Jesus. We can teach the Bible without him. But our hearts will never burn with passion until he becomes our teacher and enters into the interpretive process with us.[2]

Long ago, William Law wrote,

> Without the present illumination of the Holy Spirit, the Word of God must remain a dead letter to every man, no matter how intelligent or how well-educated he may be . . . it is just as essential for the Holy Spirit to reveal the truth of Scripture to the reader today as it was necessary for him to inspire the writers thereof in their day. . . . Therefore, to say that because we now have all the writings of Scripture complete we no longer need the miraculous inspiration of the Spirit among men as in former days, is a degree of blindness as great as any that can be charged upon the Scribes and Pharisees. Nor can we possibly escape their same errors; for in denying the present inspiration of the Holy Spirit, we have made Scripture the province of the letter-learned scribe.[3]

If what Law said is true, then you may want to ask, "Of what value *are* intelligence and theological education in understanding the Scriptures?"

Let me try to answer that question by drawing your attention to Paul's advice to the young minister Timothy. He wrote to Timothy:

> Have nothing to do with godless myths and old wives' tales; rather, train yourself to be godly. For physical training is of some value, but godliness has value for all

things, holding promise for both the present life and the life to come (1 Tim. 4:7–8).

Paul told Timothy there was a lot of unprofitable philosophical and theological speculation going on in his day. Instead of paying attention to that, he was to "train" himself to be godly. Paul was using an athletic metaphor. Just as athletes disciplined their bodies for the rigorous training that took place in the first-century gymnasiums, so Timothy was to take the same pains and use the same discipline to train himself in godliness. Certainly physical fitness has "some value," but it can't come close to competing with the value of godliness. That's what I would say about education and intelligence. They have "some value," but they can't come close to competing with godly character.

Education and intelligence have their roles to play in God's kingdom. But their roles are limited. We can be extraordinarily educated and intelligent and still be "slow of heart." It is the heart that is the key to understanding God and his Word.

If the heart is the key, then the heart should get the most attention. But what we usually do in the church and in our theological schools is to assume that the heart is right, and then strive after the cultivation of the intellect. The process should be reversed. First, we should strive after a pure heart, and then with the time we have left over, we should pursue education—being careful throughout the whole process that the heart is never neglected for one second (Prov. 4:23; Matt. 5:8; Mark 7:6–7).

Please don't misunderstand my comments about education and intelligence. I am grateful for the theological education I was privileged to receive. I love both the criticism and stimulation that my educated friends give me. What I am criticizing is the widespread tendency to exalt education and intelligence over the formation of the heart.

Someone who has been called by the Lord to give themselves to the task of theological education can be a great blessing to the church if they cultivate a Christlike character above all else. But of all callings, I think the professional theologian's is the most spiritually dangerous. Knowledge can be so seductive. The more we know, the easier it is to feel superior to others. Our hearts are more fragile than we realize.

And pursuing Bible knowledge with a weak heart may further weaken the heart. If our Bible knowledge grows faster than our love, we will become arrogant (1 Cor. 8:1). And arrogant Christians do more damage in the body of Christ than all the enemies of Christ put together. Let me illustrate this as we take up the subject of authority.

WHOSE AUTHORITY?

In the days of my Bible deism, I easily saw what a serious thing it was to say to a person, "Thus says the Lord, you should do thus and so." It was easy to see how subjective revelation could be influenced by prejudices and desires. It was easy to see how visions and impressions could be given the authority of the Bible and then misused. What I *didn't* see in those days was how easily *all* revelation can be misused. Even the Bible can be significantly misused to one's own detriment or to the detriment of others. But this is not a sufficient excuse for discarding the Bible.

One winter morning my Hebrew syntax class managed to derail me from discussing the finer points of infinitives and got me on to the subject of divorce and remarriage. Students can be so sneaky. A student who had finished about a year and a half of his four-year program confidently asserted that there could be no biblical remarriage under any circumstances after a divorce. He was absolutely certain that this was what the Bible taught.

I said to him, "Suppose you have a twenty-three-year-old woman in your church. She married when she was seventeen. She has three small children. Her husband divorced her because he was having an affair. He has now married the woman with whom he had the affair, so there is no question of him and his first wife being reconciled. She is now left alone, a single parent with three small children. She asks your advice. What would you say to her?"

"First of all you never interpret the Word by experience. You let the Word interpret your experience," said the student.

I replied that I wasn't even making an interpretation. I just wanted to know what he would tell the woman. Furthermore, I informed him that this was not a hypothetical situation. I was counseling very real people in two different but very tragic divorce cases.

"Well, I would tell her that the Word of God says that she has to remain single the rest of her life."

"Do you realize what you have just said to her?" I asked the student. "You have just told her that she will have to raise three small children on her own. You have just told her that in a few years, when her sexual desires reach their strongest level of intensity, that she will have no legitimate way of satisfying them. You have just told her that if she remarries she will be an adulteress in God's eyes. Do you realize that?"

"There you go again, citing experience to me," he replied. "You can't let experience determine how you interpret the Bible."

"No, I am not interpreting the Bible by experience. I haven't even begun to interpret the Bible yet. I just want to know if you are clear about what you are asking that woman to suffer. I just want to know if you realize the kind of life to which you have condemned her."

"I didn't condemn her to any kind of life. God is the one who says she has to remain single, and he'll give her the grace to do so."

I thought that was a pretty good answer, considering the position he had taken. Now we were ready to do a little interpretation. I asked him if he had considered the meaning of several important words in Paul's statements about divorce and remarriage in 1 Corinthians 7:8ff. He hadn't considered the meaning of those words and didn't understand why they might be significant. As the discussion progressed, it was clear his understanding of the divorce and remarriage texts was shallow. Yet based on this shallow understanding, he was prepared to say to that young woman, "*God says* you must raise your children by yourself. *God says* you can never find friendship and sexual pleasure with another man, even though it is not your fault that your husband committed adultery and left you for another woman."

In my opinion, this was a horrible abuse of the Bible. At least it was an abuse as far as the student's level of competence and biblical understanding went. He had no right to put that kind of burden on the young woman. Any time we say, "The Bible says ...," we run the risk of usurping God's authority if our interpretation or application of the Bible is wrong. Instead of the authority being located in something as subjective as a dream or a vision, we have simply transferred that authority to our own interpretation, which may be every bit as subjective as anyone else's dream or vision. Throwing out all subjective means of revelation does not protect divine authority, nor does it protect us from subjectivity or emotional instability. There are plenty of subjective, emotionally unstable, Bible deists running around loose in the church today.

SWORD OF THE SPIRIT OR BLUDGEON OF THE BULLY?

The student I just described thought of himself as a very stable person. He wasn't stable. He was hard. He had bought into Bible deism's first principle, that knowledge of the Bible is the highest value. This caused him to approach the Bible as a "subject" to be mastered. When someone thinks they have mastered the Bible, or mastered it relative to others in their circle, they inevitably become corrupted through the pride of knowledge. Remember, "knowledge puffs up" (1 Cor. 8:1). That's when the Bible, as C. S. Lewis observed, "can take on a cancerous life of its own and work against the thing for whose sake it existed."[4] Instead of operating as the sword of the Spirit, the Bible in the hands of the Bible deist becomes the bludgeon of the bully. They use the authority gained by their superior knowledge of the Bible to bully the less knowledgeable. C. S. Lewis has not been the only one to warn us about the danger of becoming an "expert" in the Bible. Long ago, Jesus said, "Woe to you experts in the law, because you have taken away the key to knowledge. You yourselves have not entered, and you have hindered those who were entering" (Luke 11:52).

Owning a sufficient and inerrant Bible doesn't guarantee we will get any help at all from the Bible. An inerrant Bible does not reveal the voice of God unless it is interpreted and applied correctly. An inerrant Bible can even be put to destructive use in the wrong hands. Some have used the Scriptures to hurt people and to bring about their own destruction (2 Peter 3:16). I know. I have used the Bible to hurt others and justify my own sin.

People who have a passion to know the Bible are capable of doing a great deal of harm to the church. Knowledge of the Bible leads to pride if it is not mixed with something else (1 Cor. 8:2). And unchecked pride in any form will lead to destruction (Prov. 16:18; 29:23).

In my enthusiasm to protect the authority of the Bible, I had committed the blunder that John Fletcher warned the church about so long ago: "embracing one error under the plausible pretense of avoiding another."[5] By trying to protect the Bible, I had thrown out all the other ways by which God might have spoken to me and even corrected me. I had even thrown out the key of which Jesus spoke, the key to understanding and applying the Bible.

To paraphrase Thomas Erskine, I had made the Bible my god, and therefore, did not often hear the God of the Bible.

18

Unbelief Through Theology

After his ministry had begun Jesus went back to Nazareth, his hometown (Mark 6:1–6). He taught in the synagogue and many were amazed, but some were offended with him. They said, "Isn't this the carpenter? Isn't this Mary's son . . . ?" Before he had come to Nazareth, Jesus had cast out many demons, healed many sick people—even the insane, blind, mute, paralyzed, and lepers—stopped a raging sea with a simple rebuke, and raised the dead. Now the wonder-working Son of God had come to bless those in his hometown, but "he did not do many miracles there because of their lack of faith" (Matt. 13:58). Here was the Son of God standing in their midst with the power to heal them, and they saw only a carpenter—just Mary's boy. So most of them went away unhealed and unaware that God had just spoken to them.

The Nazareth episode is a warning to religious people about the power of unbelief. Unbelief can stop our ears from hearing the voice of God and limit our experience of his power. It can enter our hearts in many ways, through ritualism, fear, even through theology. Theological unbelief is probably the most difficult to overcome. Very few people under the spell of theological skepticism are ever surprised by the voice of God. It does happen once in a while. Paul got the shock of his life on the road to Damascus. The voice of Jesus put him face first in the dirt. But most of us aren't like Paul, or like Moses standing before the burning bush. The majority of us are more like the citizens of Nazareth, standing not before a burning bush but before something or someone familiar and easy to reject. And yet, God usually requires us to believe in the voice and power of the carpenter before we get surprised by the Son of God.

The people from Jesus' hometown were amazed at his teaching. They even acknowledged that Jesus did miracles, yet they refused to believe in him. Why? Perhaps they thought his claims were too grandiose, or maybe they couldn't accept someone as their Messiah with whom they had been so familiar. Possibly their theology had led them to expect a more majestic Messiah. I know that for a long time my theology kept me from believing in the voice of God.

I only expected God to speak through the Bible, so that's the only way I heard his voice. If his voice came to me in any other way, I ignored it. After all, dreams, visions, and impressions couldn't be important now that we had the Bible. I embraced a theology that justified my unbelief in all forms of divine communication other than the Bible.

GOD'S MORAL WILL

When I couldn't find a single text of Scripture that said God spoke only through the Bible or that the Bible would replace the need for miracles and other supernatural revelation, I was forced to find a complicated set of theological propositions to defend my unbelief. Here's the system I used.

I argued that God was concerned primarily with our obedience to his commands, his revealed will in Scripture. He offered us guidance for our moral lives, not for the nonmoral matters in our lives. Our heavenly Father wanted to lead us to love our neighbor rather than to lead us to find a parking place at the mall. After all, what is more important: loving our neighbor or getting a good place to park? And if we obeyed his moral will, did it really matter where we parked? Or even what house or city we lived in?

God's moral will was revealed in the Bible. Until we obeyed the Bible perfectly, why should we be looking for any other guidance? Furthermore, the Bible taught that we didn't have to worry about nonmoral matters. Hadn't Jesus told us not to concern ourselves with things like food or clothes, but simply to seek his kingdom and righteousness, and all the nonmoral things would be added to us (Matt. 6:25–34)? Hadn't God told us that we were free to do whatever we wanted in nonmoral matters? For example, if an unbeliever invited you to dinner and *you wanted to go*, then you should go (1 Cor. 10:27). God didn't say, "Seek my will. Pray about it."

To me, the book of Ruth was the great illustration of how God guided us. In that book there was no miracle, prophet, king, priest, or overt supernatural guidance of any sort, yet God by his unseen hand produced good out of both tragedy and evil by bringing Ruth and Boaz together. The story of Ruth was like a great symphony in which both beautiful and discordant notes were brought together into wonderful harmony. But God, who was both the composer and the conductor, never came on the stage. He remained hidden in the background. Ruth and Boaz didn't need supernatural guidance. All they had to do was obey God's revealed will. The story of Ruth taught that God cares for us and guides us even though we may not be aware of his benevolent goodness at the time. Theologians refer to this as the providence of God. It is certainly scriptural as well as comforting.

In my opinion, there was something wrong with some people's view that God gave guidance in nonmoral matters. It forced us to believe in two kinds of revelation. On the one hand, there was one universal revelation of God's moral will for the whole church, which revealed what was necessary for salvation and sanctification. This revelation was found in the Bible. On the other hand, there had to be another kind of revelation, a "localized" or "privatized" track of revelation for our personal lives. I couldn't find this "privatized" form of revelation in the Bible, and we didn't need it anyway. We were just to obey the Bible, and God would take care of the rest.

Although this view may offer some comfort, there are so many difficulties with it that I now wonder how I could have ever seriously argued for it. First, it divides God's will into two categories, moral versus nonmoral. It also divides life into moral and nonmoral. The moral life is under God's control, while the nonmoral life is under our control. This kind of thinking encourages us to divide our life into compartments—our religious life, our family life, our work life, our recreational life, our hobbies, and so on. Is this really a biblical view of life? Where do you find a nonmoral life of Jesus? Where does the apostle Paul acknowledge an area of life that is nonmoral, under our control and not God's control? Where does the Bible divide our lives into separate compartments? Doesn't it teach that every area of our lives is to be given over to God and come under his guidance?

> And whatever you do, whether in word or deed, do it all in the name of the Lord Jesus, giving thanks to God the Father through him. . . . Whatever you do, work at it with all your heart, as working for the Lord, not for men (Col. 3:17, 23).

Does the phrase "whatever you do" refer only to those decisions we regard as moral decisions? Or do you think it might have reference to *everything* in our lives?

The second problem with the view that God speaks to us only through the Bible is that it leaves God with nothing to say about large areas of our lives. If he is only concerned about us obeying the commands of the Bible, then presumably he doesn't have much to say about what our vocations are, where we live, where we work, and so on, as long as we're moral. Doesn't this make some forms of prayer irrelevant? If the only reliable form of guidance is the Bible, why should we ask God to lead us in choosing a vocation or a city in which to live? Suppose your company is going to transfer you to another city, and they give you a choice between three cities. Why should you pray for guidance if God speaks only through the Bible and only about moral commands? On my former view of guidance, if you asked God, "Which city should I go to?," logically, he could have only two responses.

He could respond like this, "Hmm, three choices—well, my child, I don't really care what you do. It is half a dozen of one or six of the other. Just move wherever you want and be careful to obey me wherever you live, and everything will work out just fine. I don't really have an opinion in this matter." Somehow a reply like that doesn't seem consistent with the character of an omniscient Being.

The second logical response to your prayer would have gone something like this, "My child, I do care where you move, and I do know where you should move, but I am not going to tell you. After the Bible was written, I stopped talking to my children about things that weren't in the Bible. I only want you to hear my voice in my Book. If you obey my Book, I will make sure you get in the right place. I just can't tell you ahead of time where it is going to be. For the time being, read my Book and leave the details to me. When you get to your *final* home, we will talk in a different way, but for now read the Book."

A third problem with this view is that things we regard as "nonmoral decisions" may have a drastic effect on our moral lives. That Lot chose to dwell near Sodom, and finally in Sodom, had disastrous consequences for his moral life. He wound up in a cave, overcome by a drunken stupor, committing incest with his daughters. Life in Sodom had taken a toll on this righteous man. Wouldn't he have been better off to have asked God's opinion and waited for a little guidance? Where we work and live may have much more to do with our moral lives than we can foresee.

EXPLAINING AWAY THE BIBLE

But the greatest problem with my former point of view is that it is not even remotely close to the experience of the people of the Bible. God did speak to them apart from the Scripture. He warned, encouraged, and gave specific geographical leading to his people. In order to support my old view, I had to find a way to *explain away* all the biblical examples of God's regular special revelation and guidance for his children. Here's how I did it.

It's Not Normal

If someone brought up the specific way in which Abraham's servant was guided by God to choose Rebekah to be Isaac's wife (Gen. 24), I said it wasn't the normal way in which wives were chosen in the Bible. I gave the same excuse for the angel who spoke to Philip, telling him to leave Samaria and go to the desert road that leads to Gaza (Acts 8:26). I also insisted that if you used these stories as examples of God's *normal* guiding that you would have to expect all the details of the stories to be repeated today. If you weren't willing to expect angels and supernatural fleeces to help you make your personal decisions, then you should not use these stories as examples of God's normal leading or speaking.

Only for Special People

It was harder to explain away an example from the book of Acts or the New Testament Epistles that didn't have something as supernatural as an angel in it. For instance, Paul claimed that fourteen years after his conversion he went up to Jerusalem "in response to a revelation" (Gal. 2:2). Paul claimed that God gave him "nonmoral" guidance in this case. There were far too many instances of this kind of guidance in Acts and the Epistles for me to argue that they weren't normal. I had to admit that it was normal for God to speak like this—*but only to the apostles.* Almost all the examples people hurled at me were from the lives of the apostles, especially from Paul's life. Since we weren't apostles, we shouldn't expect God to speak to us like he spoke to the apostles. By holding up the shield of the apostles, I managed to deflect most of the thrusts from my theological opponents.

Only For Unique Situations

But my opponents were not so easily discouraged. In desperation they searched the New Testament until they came up with some examples of nonapostolic people hearing God's voice just like the apostles did. They used examples where God spoke very specifically about nonmoral matters. For example, Agabus, a prophet, not an apostle, accurately predicted a famine that "spread over the entire Roman world" (Acts 11:28). This prophecy was particularly embarrassing. It concerned food, or better, the lack of food. It was one of the topics about which I said God didn't speak. Remember, I had used Matthew 6:33, "Seek first his kingdom ..." to say that God didn't give us revelations about things like food and clothing, that is, about our personal lives. Here was a non-apostle getting revelation about a famine, a revelation that led to a relief fund being sent by the Christians in Antioch to those in Judea. How could I discard examples like these? It wasn't easy. My opponents were now shooting bullets that the shield of the apostles couldn't stop. I needed a bulletproof vest to survive this attack.

I found that if I looked hard enough I could always find a bulletproof vest in some kind of theological principle or historical necessity that would help me argue that these examples were also unique. In the case of the famine which Agabus predicted, I said the revelation was necessary in order to cement the relationship of the Antiochian and Judean Christians. In other words, this prophecy was not really about a famine or saving the lives of God's people. It was really about the unity of the body of Christ. It just had the appearance of being a localized, nonmoral, revelatory word. God spoke prophetically in this instance to bring about unity in the body of Christ, and unity is a moral matter.

Even this was not a sufficient explanation for some of the die-hard mystics in my church. One of them even called my explanation of the Agabus prophecy "totally unique." He also had the nerve to suggest that my explanation was irrelevant. "Even if the famine prophecy by Agabus really is about unity, why wouldn't God give prophetic words today to bring about unity in local churches?" asked the mystic. So now they were bringing out their big guns, the sixteen-inch cannons. I hated that simplistic way of reading the Bible, that "if-he-did-it-then-why-wouldn't-he-do-it-now?" mentality. If only my mystical opponents had gotten a little theological education, they would have known you can't read the Bible like that. I was also beginning to have hard feelings toward Agabus.

My bulletproof vest of historical necessity couldn't protect me against cannon shells. How could I argue that the modern church was no longer faced with "historical necessities" that required answers from the voice of God? After all, had the nature of man changed so dramatically after the apostles left the scene that men no longer needed prophecies about famines? Had history changed so dramatically that there would be no more famines? Or had God changed after the apostles' departure so that he was no longer interested in warning us about coming disasters? I needed a fortress or else I was going down before these kinds of biblical examples. At this point, I discovered the very fortress I needed. It was impenetrable!

Only During the Period of the Open Canon

"You have to understand that these kinds of revelations were given before the Bible was completed. Neither Agabus nor the others had all the completed Bible, which tells us how important unity really is," I replied. That was the clincher. In these arguments, the phrase I dearly loved was, "that happened during *the period of the open canon.*" The word "canon" means the list of books that belong in the Bible. The canon was "open" while the New Testament writings were being added to it. Somehow everything was different in this period. It was supernatural, perhaps too supernatural. It was also too subjective. But that was only because it was "the period of the open canon." What a great phrase! I could demolish any argument with it. Any example could be explained away by that profound phrase. Let God speak as often as he wanted during the period of the open canon. Let him speak to nonapostles, even to absolute dummies, or better yet, even *through* dumb animals. None of these examples was relevant because they all came from the period of the open canon. Now, however, we had the *period of the Bible*. And the Bible had replaced all other forms of God's communication. There weren't two tracks of revelation—only one, the Bible. So let my opponent use any biblical example from Genesis to Revelation. It didn't matter if the example had the force of an atomic bomb, I had found a theological fortress that could withstand the blast. "Sorry," I would say, "your example comes from the time before the Bible was completed. You can't use it now that we are in the period of the completed Bible."

Let me summarize my method for refuting the evidence of biblical examples of God's personal speaking and direct guidance. First, I would say that the example was not normally the way God spoke or guided. Second, when my opponents found examples of divine revelation that were normal, I would say that he only spoke that way to special people and that they were not one of those people. Third, if they found an example of God speaking to someone who wasn't so special or unique, I claimed the historical situation was unique. Finally, no matter what example they used, I could always claim that they had taken their example from the period of the open canon, and this made their example invalid.

Perhaps by now you've come to appreciate the brilliant character of my methodology. No matter what example you brought to me from the Bible I could discount its contemporary relevance. It never occurred to me that these four arguments actually eliminated the use of *all* biblical examples in theological discussion. *Every* biblical example must be drawn from the period of the open canon.

This way of arguing actually meant, "I have made up my mind on this matter and I will not allow any verse from the Bible to challenge or correct my position."

Apply these arguments to an area other than the supernatural and you can see how inadequate they are. For example, what if you wanted to exhort people in your church to follow Paul's example of doing all things for the sake of the Gospel (1 Cor. 9:23)? Sorry, you can't use that example. Paul was an apostle. Only apostles do all things for the sake of the Gospel. Besides, your example comes from the period of the open canon. We have the Bible now. We study all things for the sake of the Gospel. The kind of godliness Paul was talking about in 1 Corinthians 9:23 was only for apostles, and only for the period of the open canon.

In reality, the argument from the period of the open canon is simply modern theological nonsense. It was invented to *explain away* biblical examples that contradict the contemporary scarcity of biblical experience. There is no biblical text or legitimate biblical argument that says that once we have a completed Bible we no longer need to hear God's voice apart from the Bible. Think about the utter foolishness of this argument. It actually leads us *away* from the Bible! If I can't use biblical examples of hearing God, what examples am I supposed to use? Shall I go to the modern church for my examples? To the modern seminary classroom? Shall I let a theologian or preacher who has never heard the voice of God apart from their study of the Bible be my example of how to hear God? Would today's preacher be a better model than Jesus, the apostles, Agabus, Ananias, or some of the other New Testament characters? Do I really want to go outside the Bible for my primary examples of how to hear God? Shall I let someone who has never witnessed a miracle or been used in a healing be my guide in the miraculous? Shall we take swimming lessons from someone who has never swum?

There is another theological argument we have yet to consider which makes it difficult for some people to hear the voice of God. In reality, it is a powerful fear thinly disguised as a theological argument.

THE FEAR OF THE COLLAPSE OF DIVINE AUTHORITY

Some argue that all revelation from God has the same authority, whether the revelation is in the Bible or outside the Bible. I have argued throughout this book that the revelation in the Bible is unique in authority. During the period when the Bible was being written there was a significant amount of revelation that never made it into the Bible. We have only a small percentage of the words spoken by Jesus, yet everything he spoke was revelatory (John 12:49–50; cf. 5:19). Doubtless the apostles spoke many revelatory words that never made it into the Bible, and even some of their letters to the churches were not preserved.[1] Prophecy through ordinary believers was also flourishing among the New Testament churches, but little, if any, of this revelation made it into the completed Bible. Why did some revelation make it into the canon, while the vast majority of revelatory words did not?

The answer is that God chose the words of the Bible to have unique authority over all the church (2 Tim. 3:16–17). Obviously, the lost revelatory words do not have authority over the church. They're lost to the church. But the revelation in the Bible expresses God's rule for all people, everywhere, at all times. Even while the Bible was being written, it had authority over current noncanonical revelation.

For example, Paul wrote,

> If anybody thinks he is a prophet or spiritually gifted, let him acknowledge that what I am writing to you is the Lord's command. If he ignores this, he himself will be ignored (1 Cor. 14:37–38).

Paul knew he was writing Scripture that had authority over any noncanonical revelation.

He also knew some people would mistake their own thoughts and words for true revelation, even possibly contradicting biblical revelation. The safe thing to do in these cases would have been to forbid all noncanonical revelation, to simply deny God could or would speak apart from the Bible. Instead Paul opted for the opposite solution. Right after his warning about extra-biblical revelation, he wrote:

> Therefore, my brothers, be eager to prophesy, and do not forbid speaking in tongues (1 Cor. 14:39).

He actually encouraged Christians to use the two most controversial, abused, and "dangerous" gifts. The very gifts that could compromise the unique authority of the Bible, according to some modern authors.

Though Paul was concerned about the abuse of extra-biblical revelation, he didn't forbid it. Why? Because it was needed for the health of the church, and because there were guards to prevent its abuse. Private revelation had to first pass through the gate of the unique authority of the Bible. Nothing that contradicted the Scripture could be recognized as valid revelation. So when some "prophets" came to the church at Thessalonica with a false prophecy, allegedly from the apostles, saying that the day of the Lord had already come, Paul told the church there not to be alarmed by the prophecy because it contradicted previous apostolic teaching that would later become Scripture (2 Thess. 2:1–12). The prophecy also contradicted the teaching of Jesus (Matt. 24:1–35). New Testament Christians simply judged all words which claimed to be revelatory by the standard of the written Word.

This doesn't mean, though, that private revelation that doesn't contradict the Bible is automatically true. The Spirit of Truth has been given to lead us into all truth, if we have ears to hear (John 16:13). When Agabus predicted imprisonment for Paul, the apostle's friends applied the prophecy by pleading with him not to go to Jerusalem (Acts 21:10–12). The prophecy and the application did not contradict Scripture, but Paul ignored his friends' pleas and went to Jerusalem. Why? Because the Holy Spirit had already shown him he was to go (Acts 20:22–23).

Some would still object that we can't use these kinds of examples in Paul's life because the revelation given to Paul had the same authority as Scripture and, therefore, he wasn't free to disobey it. They claim it's just like Scripture, "the very words of God." Let's take Acts 16:6–10 as a test case for this claim.

A Test Case

Paul and his companions set out for Asia Minor to preach the Gospel there, but were forbidden by the Holy Spirit to do so. A vision led Paul to Macedonia to preach the Gospel there instead. According to Fowler White, practical leading like this has no relevance for the Holy Spirit's leading of Christians today because the directions given to Paul were God's "own words, always expressing accurately what he intended to communicate and invariably invested with absolute authority."[2] In other words, if you or I claim to hear God speak today through a vision or a dream, according to White we are claiming our revelation is on a par with Scripture. Of course, no one really claims this, at least no one I know. But White thinks if revelation is from God, it must all have the same authority as the Bible. Is this really true?

The vision given to Paul that led him to Macedonia was certainly from God. Once Paul and his companions concluded that the vision meant they were to preach the Gospel in Macedonia, they certainly had to obey the vision. This was also revelation apart from Scripture. It was a personal direction for Paul and his ministry team. God allowed these personal directions to become part of the biblical revelation. Why? Obviously, they are not authoritative directions for all believers to go to Macedonia to preach the Gospel. So why did the Holy Spirit direct Luke to include this story in the book of Acts? According to Paul, when this story became Scripture, it had to be "useful for teaching, rebuking, correcting, and training in righteousness" (2 Tim. 3:16).

If we take the position that God does not speak apart from Scripture, we are left with no purpose for this story. If God doesn't *guide* through visions anymore (Acts 16:9), if he does not *speak* by the Holy Spirit any more (Acts 16:6, 7), what relevance could the story possibly have today? None, unless we spiritualize it and try to draw a few general theological axioms from it regarding God's providential guidance. But the story is not about the unseen guidance of providence. It is about specific directions from the Holy Spirit for ministry purposes. If we interpret the story the same way we would other narrative literature—as we would the story of the widow who put her two coins in the treasury (Luke 21:1–4) for instance—then it becomes an example *teaching* us how God guides in ministry situations and *training* us in righteousness as we observe how Paul gave up his own ministry plans to follow those of the Holy Spirit. It also serves as a *rebuke* and a *correction* to those who believe God doesn't speak apart from Scripture.

Misunderstanding Genuine Revelation

Another problem White and those in his theological camp have with God speaking through the same means that he used in Scripture is the lack of a guarantee that we will understand the guidance offered through those means. White wonders "how these words 'freshly spoken from heaven' can be so necessary and strategic to God's highest purposes for their lives when their Father does nothing to ensure that they will ever actually hear those words."[3] How can a dream or vision be valuable when God "does nothing to ensure" the understanding[4] of such revelation?

But where do we find a guarantee that God will automatically "ensure" the hearing and understanding of the Bible or any of his revelation? Peter said some of Paul's writings were difficult to understand (2 Peter 3:16). And Peter was an apostle! Remember, there were some who only heard thunder when the audible voice spoke to Jesus, even though the voice came for their sakes (John 12:27–30). The audible voice was still revelation, even though God did not ensure all would understand it. And what about the Corinthian Christians, who had difficulty understanding such a simple text as the greeting from Paul's letter to them, "Paul, an apostle of Christ by the will of God . . ." (2 Cor. 1:1)? Paul had to spend a good portion of that letter defending his apostleship to a church that was accepting false apostles in his place (2 Cor. 10:1–12:21). And Paul was their spiritual father (1 Cor. 4:15)! God does speak true words to us in Scripture, but it takes more than the ability to read to understand those words. The key to understanding any of God's revelation lies in his sovereign will first, and second, in the condition of our hearts.

White accuses Wayne Grudem and myself of believing in fallible, practical guidance.[5] If he means we believe it is possible to misunderstand true revelation or misapply it, resulting in faulty guidance, then he has stated our position accurately. If he means we believe that God may give fallible revelation, then he has misunderstood us. It is impossible for God to lie (Heb. 6:18). He could never give fallible revelation. It is not impossible, though, for us to misunderstand infallible revelation. And through such a faulty understanding we may draw fallible guidance from the Bible, a dream, or any other form of true revelation.

The Authority of Divine Personal Guidance

White and his theological circle hold the Bible in high regard and want to protect its authority. For this, I commend them. But the position they've taken doesn't really protect the authority of the Bible or solve the problem of authority in personal leading from God.

White believes:

> God guides and directs his people by His Spirit in the application of His written word through promptings, impressions, insights and the like. All of these experiences are, however, carefully distinguished from the Spirit's work of revelation. Hence, though the Spirit's illumination and guidance may sometimes focus on phenomena such as promptings or impressions, those phenomena are not specifically interpreted as involving the biblical ministry-gifts of revelation, such as prophecy and tongues or their correlates (e.g., visions, dreams, auditions).[6]

In other words, God's *practical leading* is "carefully distinguished" from God's work of revelation in prophecy, tongues, visions, dreams, and auditions.

There are two striking things about White's statements here. First, he doesn't offer a single text of Scripture to support his assertion that God's *practical leading* is carefully distinguished from the Spirit's work of *revelation*. Instead of Scripture he cites a quote from John Murray, which itself contains not a single citation from the Bible. White is simply *asserting* a distinction that not only can not be supported by Scripture, but, in fact, contradicts the Bible. In reference to his Jerusalem visit, Paul claimed,

> I went in response to a *revelation* and set before them the gospel that I preach among the Gentiles ... (Gal. 2:2).

Is this not specific, practical, geographical leading? Didn't it come from a revelation of the Holy Spirit? Apparently, Paul didn't see the distinction between the leading of the Holy Spirit and revelation that some modern Christians do.

The second striking thing is White's assertion "that God guides and directs His people by His Spirit in the application of His written word through promptings, impressions, insights, and the like." How does White know God guides through promptings, impressions, insights, and the like? He can't use the Bible to prove this assertion. He has already said that the examples of guidance in the Bible are "the very words of God," that is, equal to the authority of the Bible. And White does not believe that this kind of guidance is available to you and me. It passed away with the closing of the canon. Does White offer a single text of Scripture that says God will "prompt" a Christian as a means of guidance? No, he doesn't. In fact, the word "prompt" never appears in Scripture with God as the subject. White is asking us to believe in a form of guidance that can't even be found in the Bible!

So we're back to our original question, How does White know that God guides us through promptings? Does White want to become our model for divine guidance? Do his assertions have more authority than the examples of the Bible? Remember, he's forbidden us to use the examples of the Bible as examples of how God guides today. Also remember that I told you the kinds of arguments used by White actually lead us away from the Bible. And that is exactly what White is doing when he doesn't offer a single text of Scripture to support the vague experiential form of guidance he sets forth. And it doesn't stop there.

He tells us nothing about the nature of this guidance. How much authority does a prompting from God have? Are we free to disobey this prompting if God is guiding us through it? What kind of authority does a divine prompting have in relation to the Bible? Someone might ask, "If it is really God prompting, how can it have less authority than the Bible?" White doesn't answer any of these questions, and thus leaves himself open to his own charge—how can the guidance of the Spirit "through promptings, impressions, insights, and the like" have any value for Christians "when their Father does nothing to ensure that they will ever actually hear those" promptings?

Once you admit there is any form of divine guidance apart from the Bible, you will have to face the authority question. And it doesn't make any difference how you refer to divine guidance. Call it God's internal leading, a spiritual prompting, or whatever. If it's from God to you, aren't you obligated to obey it? Does it have the same authority as Scripture? No, because Scripture has absolute authority over all believers, everywhere, at all times. Divine personal guidance has authority only over the person to whom it is given. And personal guidance is never given to us to control someone else.

By denying that God speaks today except in the Bible, White has merely sidestepped, not solved, the problem of authority in

God's personal communications to us. He admits that

> ... if the Bible does indeed teach the church to hear
> God's voice both through its pages and apart from
> them in words "freshly spoken from heaven," then the
> contributors to this present volume and those who
> agree with them are at least guilty of quenching the
> Spirit, if not of outright refusal to hear the very voice of
> God. We, of all people, are especially in need of fanning
> into flame those gifts of the Spirit through which God
> would speak to His church today (cf. 2 Tim. 1:6).[7]

This is the part of his article with which I find myself in most
agreement.[8]

The Validity of New Testament Experience

If the biblical examples of the miraculous and hearing God's
voice aren't valid for today, then this needs to be proved by clear
biblical statements, not by vague biblically unsupported theological axioms. To my knowledge, this has not been done. How
could it? Where would we find a New Testament text that teaches
New Testament experience is no longer valid?

How would a completed Bible make the New Testament
Christians' varied ways of hearing God obsolete? They could
hear God in dreams and visions without compromising the
authority of the Bible. Why can't we? Actually, aren't we in a better position to evaluate dreams and visions, since we *do* have the
completed Bible? And besides, much of the revelation given in
the New Testament is often not the kind of information that
could be deduced from the completed Bible. For example, God
gave directions for specific ministries (Acts 8:26ff.; 9:10–19; 10:1–
23; 13:2), warnings (20:22, 23; 21:10–11) and encouragement in
specific situations (18:9–10; 27:23–26). Certainly the New Testament gives us principles, and God may use specific passages to
speak to us about directions for our lives, but the New Testament does not tell us specifically where to preach the Gospel,
where not to, and so on. Instead the Holy Spirit had to tell Paul
where and where not to preach the Gospel (16:6–10). And he
had to tell me too, or I wouldn't have gone where he wanted me

to preach. I certainly would never have deduced it from reading the New Testament.

A "DREAM" HOME

I want to tell you how God recently guided Leesa and me to pastor a church in Whitefish, Montana, and to purchase a home. While we were on the staff of the Vineyard Christian Fellowship in Anaheim, California, Leesa began to have a series of dreams. When we moved back to Texas, the dreams continued. In the first set of dreams she and I were ministering with Presbyterians. She had four or five dreams like this from 1989–93. We didn't think they were literal. We didn't understand them, but we wrote them down. During the same period, she also had three or four dreams that we were living in Whitefish, Montana. We had vacationed there once in the summer of 1980 and knew two friends who lived there, but we certainly had no intention of moving to a small Montana town sixty miles from the Canadian border. So we couldn't figure out this series of dreams either, but we wrote them down.

Leesa's last dream about Whitefish was in August, 1993. Two months later, the First Presbyterian Church of Whitefish called me to see if I would be interested in pastoring their church. They had been without a pastor for eighteen months. Some members of the pastor nominating committee had read my book *Surprised by the Power of the Spirit*, and wanted to move in that direction of ministry. I thanked them for their interest and declined their offer. Then I remembered Leesa's dreams—Whitefish and Presbyterians! Perhaps the dreams *were* meant to be taken literally. I recanted my decision and said that we would pray about it. The dreams led to prayers. The prayers led to desires. The desires led to fleeces. The fleeces came true. We were on our way to Whitefish and to the Presbyterians.

We knew Whitefish was the city where we were supposed to live, but where in the city? And should we rent, or should we buy? Ownership of a house can be a major blessing or an unmitigated disaster. We know. We've experienced both. We've also discovered that owning things can tie you down. So a few years ago, we stopped taking it for granted that we would always own a home. In fact, we had rented for the last six years.

But now what, rent or buy? We prayed. No answer. We prayed more. Then Leesa dreamed we were sitting in a newly built house. We walked through the kitchen to the living room. The tile on the kitchen floor had a little shade of pink in it. As we talked with the builder, he seemed to have a genuine interest in us and in our ministry. Everything about the house was perfect except for one little corner of the roof, which was not yet completed. We interpreted the dream to mean three things. God was leading us to buy a house. The unfinished corner of the roof meant that it wouldn't be perfect for our immediate needs, but it could be made to fit them. And the builder's personal interest in us would serve as a confirming sign of which house we were to buy.

Encouraged by the dream, we went to Whitefish expecting to find our *dream* house without delay. We couldn't find a thing. Every home that met our needs didn't meet our budget. You probably know how frustrating that experience is. We came back to Texas wondering if we had interpreted Leesa's dream correctly.

About a month later I asked Paul Cain if the Lord had shown him anything about our home in Montana. "Yes he has," Paul replied. "I had a dream that you were living in a house either down the road or across the road from a lady named Laura. She's a single lady, or if she's married, she is not living with her husband now."

A few weeks later our realtor, Phyllis, called, "I think I may have found the perfect house for you. You might even be able to afford it." Besides being a great realtor, Phyllis is also a realist. She sent us a video of the house. The video looked good, but who wants to buy a house based on a video? But we knew we had more than a video. We also had a dream given to us from the Lord through Paul Cain as well as Leesa's dream. I called Phyllis back, "Send me a map of the development, and the names of all the homeowners across the road or down the road."

I'm sure this was the strangest request she had ever had, but Phyllis was understanding. She knew how weird preachers could be. Guess what? Right down the road from the prospective house, a lady was living without a husband. Her name was Laura.

We told Phyllis we'd take the house. When she protested that we hadn't actually seen it yet, I told her that it didn't matter. The house was meant to be ours. We made an offer. It turned out to be the only house we'd ever bought without actually walking through it first.

Not only did the house reflect Leesa's and Paul Cain's dreams, Leesa's dream of the details of the house and its builder, Dave, came literally true. The kitchen tile was exactly the color she had seen in the dream, and Dave's concern for us made the whole transaction go much more smoothly than it should have. Thanks to the Lord's guidance, we really have a *dream* house, if you know what I mean.

I can just hear someone saying, "So you think God's more interested in getting you into your dream house, than he is making you Christ-like?" No, I'm sure that he's much more interested in forming Christ in me (Gal. 4:19) than providing me with a nice home. I too am more interested in becoming like Jesus than owning a home. In fact, I'm more interested, much more interested, in my children becoming like Jesus than I am in providing them with homes or college educations. You probably feel the same way about your kids.

But still, wouldn't you help your children purchase a home if it were in your power? Why would you think it strange for God to help his children with their homes? Wouldn't you warn your children of traps if you knew about them beforehand? How do you feel about your kids' trials? Their professions? Their service to God? If you had information that would help them in these experiences, wouldn't you share it with them? Why should we expect less of our heavenly Father than we do of our earthly parents?

When put like that, God's detailed guidance sounds reasonable. Many of you may have wonderful stories of God's loving guidance. But guiding through a prophet and prophetic dreams? That seems scary. It can be risky. It can be disastrous. It can also be wonderful. But whatever else it is, I know it's biblical.

19

Unbelief Through Magic and Fear

Moving to Whitefish has reinforced my belief that the two greatest sources of joy in life are God and friends. When I look back over my life, the times I've been happiest were the times I was closest to God and had close friends I loved very much. Every time I've tried to find a greater happiness in something else—a career, a possession, a hobby—I've been disappointed. God made my heart that way, and he made your heart that way too. Real joy only comes through an intimate love relationship with God and friends. And in that order. First God, then friends. If the order is reversed, then the friends become idols—something we use instead of love—and the joy is lost.

Jesus summed it up so simply:

> "Love the Lord your God with all your heart and with all your soul and with all your mind." This is the first and greatest commandment. And the second is like it: "Love your neighbor as yourself." All the Law and the Prophets hang on these two commandments (Matt. 22:37–40).

God's specific guidance of our family to Whitefish has been a fresh revelation of his love for us and an encouragement to love him more. We've also made new friends who are so easy to love and who love us.

But we've also experienced some pain in this move. And pain is the major problem with Jesus' summation of the whole

law into the two commands to love God and love your neighbor.
Love hurts. It hurts more than anything. Any country-western
song will tell you that. Actually, the pain of love is a major theme
of all music, poetry, literature, and art. It's also a major theme of
the Bible. Just look what love did to Jesus. It led him to humiliation. It led him to a cross and to the cry, "My God, my God, why
have you forsaken me?" Along the way, some of us make the
decision that the joy of love is not worth the pain. We usually
don't make this decision consciously. Instead we embrace a form
of religion that replaces the risks of intimacy with the security of
something impersonal. It's an unconscious rejection of love and
a form of unbelief disguised as orthodoxy. Sometimes the unbelief sneaks in through ritual and magic.

UNBELIEF THROUGH RITUAL AND MAGIC

Magic is the use of rituals, spells, charms, and the like to control people or events. It's manipulative, impersonal, and amoral,
if not immoral. The assumption is that with the right technique
you can manipulate "forces" in creation to serve you. Sometimes
when we think we are pursuing the voice of God, we may actually be attempting to use magic to get something we want.

Suppose I tell you to put this book down and think about God
for a minute. What is the thing that first comes to mind? Is it your
own particular church? Does a particular ministry or a sense of
duty present itself to your consciousness? Or do you begin to think
of the Bible or a set of absolute truths? Do you feel guilty for something you've done or something you should have done? I wonder
how many of you would have thought first of a *man*. If I would
have asked one of the original twelve disciples to picture God, a
man would have been the first picture to enter their minds. Immediately, they would have seen "the man Christ Jesus" (1 Tim. 2:5).

It is so easy to forget that God is a Person and begin to think
of him as a force or power, a duty or principle, something abstract
and impersonal—something that fills the room, even the universe, but has no face. God does have a face. It is the face of Jesus
Christ. And God is a very real person who relates to us as a Person, not as a force or set of moral principles.

Well-meaning teachers say, "Here, follow these biblical principles and your life will be full and happy." Tell that to the prophet

Jeremiah. His life could neither be described as full nor happy. God would not let him marry or have children (Jer. 16:1–4) and required him to face life with very few friends (Jer. 15:17). Ultimately God let Jeremiah "fail" in ministry. Jeremiah was faithful to God and faithful to his calling, yet he still lamented before God, "Why is my pain unending and my wound grievous and incurable?" (Jer. 15:18). God's *personal will* for the course of Jeremiah's life contradicts many of our trite formulas for the Christian life.

We have been saved that we might passionately love a Person. We have been redeemed to serve a Person, not a set of principles. We are called first to please a real Person, not perform a ministry. It's so easy to fall in love with principles and ministry, and fall out of love with a Person.

Here's where the magic comes in. When we fall out of love with God but continue to use the principles of the Bible in order to make our lives successful, we have entered the realm of magic. When we read the Bible morning after morning but don't allow God to search our hearts with his Word, we are practicing magic. It's so easy to fall into the habit of reading the Bible in the morning to get our "God stuff" out of the way, so we can get on with our real lives. At times, I have read the Bible in the morning with absolutely no sense of God's presence, totally bored with the whole experience, my eye on the clock waiting for my scheduled time to finally lapse, and then actually *felt good* when I was finished. I don't mean that I felt a sense of relief that the boredom was over—I felt satisfied with myself, with my discipline and perseverance, and I felt God was satisfied with me too. I thought my day would be better because I had read the Bible. That kind of experience is closer to ritualism and religious magic than to New Testament Christianity.

If you spent an hour with a person you really loved and were totally bored during that hour, would you feel satisfied with that experience? Do we ever feel good when those we love don't speak to us? The silence of God has been a problem for all saints. I'm not saying that we will never experience his silence in our "quiet times." After all, God is not obligated to answer every question we ask him. He will not automatically speak to us just because we open the Bible and read it for an allotted period of time. I'm not castigating anyone because they experience the silence of God. I'm saying that there is something very wrong in our relationship with God when we see, hear, and feel nothing from him, and yet leave our "time with him" feeling satisfied. That is simply not characteristic of any other meaningful relationship in our lives. It is, however, a characteristic of magic. Magic doesn't require moral behavior or personal intimacy.

When we continually persist in religious activity without any awareness of the presence of God, we are leaving the realm of personal relationship and entering the realm of magic. We should never be content with any habitual religious activity where we rarely experience the presence of God. He is a Person whose presence can be felt. If we are continually relating to him as a set of principles or as a duty, then we have left the realm of personal spiritual experience and entered into the mechanical realm of ritual and magic.

What should we do if our church experience or our Bible reading has become like this? Do we lengthen our private devotional times by half an hour, an hour? How long should we seek his presence? Hosea answers very simply, "Seek the LORD until he comes" (Hos. 10:12). Never be content with religious activity that is devoid of the presence of God. It will lead you places you don't want to go.

This is what happened to the Pharisees who diligently studied the Bible, but "never heard his voice" (John 5:37). Evidently, Jesus thought that the voice of God and the Bible were not the same, that it is possible to read the Bible and never hear the voice of God. Studying the Bible without hearing the voice of God led the Pharisees into a realm of knowledge devoid of godliness. It was the kind of knowledge that reinforced their prejudice and increased their religious pride. This kind of knowledge was like magic, because it gave them control over their followers without requiring them to actually hear the voice of God. If we allow ourselves to be satisfied with religious activity that has no presence of God in the activity, we too will find our pride growing and our prejudices strengthened.

Don't misunderstand me, we need discipline to pray and to meditate in the Bible. Listening to God speak through the Bible and talking to him in prayer are part of the very basic elements of our friendship with God. But we must never be content with hollow ritualism. The same goes for our church experience.

Some people's church attendance has more in common with ritual magic than with New Testament worship. For them, what is important are the elements of the service that have virtually nothing to do with worshiping. I know a lady who left her church because the new pastor didn't wear a robe in the Sunday service. I've seen people get up and walk out of a service because an extra instrument was added to the traditional piano and organ. The sad thing about this particular experience was that the presence of God was in the worship service, but the ritualism of the people who left would not allow them to feel his presence or hear his voice. The other day I heard about a pastor who had to leave his church because of the controversy he started when he had the piano moved from the side of the stage to the center. When he left, the piano was moved back to the side. Several years later he returned to the church and was shocked to see the piano once again in the center of the stage, but this time with no controversy. "How did you ever get the piano in the center of the stage?" he asked the new pastor. "Inch by inch," came the reply. People who will leave a church over the absence of a robe, the addition of a musical instrument, or the placement of a piano have been unwittingly taught by their leaders to find their security in ritual rather than in the presence of God.

I've been a pastor long enough to know that there is a wise way and a foolish way to introduce change. I also know that no matter how wise you are, change is going to be painful for many people. That pain could be greatly minimized if leaders made one of their primary goals to lead people to value the presence of God more than anything else in the worship service, especially more than the material elements.

Leaders also need to teach people that change is an inevitable part of life. Dead things don't change. Living things change because they grow. And growth means pain. Dead things don't have growing pains. Neither do dead churches. Part of the price of growing is pain and insecurity. Remember when you were still physically changing during your adolescent and teenage years? Not only your body, but your emotions were changing. You were going down a road you hadn't been on before. Remember how insecure you felt? But you accepted the pain and the insecurity because you wanted to grow. You didn't want to stay a child. It's the same way with a growing church. It is going down a road it hasn't been on before. Being a leader just means learning how to manage the conflict that comes from the pain and insecurity of growing. Of course, we could avoid the pain by simply refusing to change, but most of us would rather go to church than to a cemetery.

There is another form of magic I ought to mention that is in the opposite direction of mechanical study of the Bible and ritual church attendance. Some have referred to it as charismatic magic, or even charismatic witchcraft. Our culture so abounds with instant foods, instant credit, and instant pleasures that we can be duped into wanting instant spirituality. Sometimes we can be tricked into putting our attention on fleeces, dreams, visions, and impressions, while forgetting the basic elements of our friendship with God. There is no quick fix for our inability to hear God. When I ignore the Bible and prayer in favor of say, dreams and contemporary prophecy, I am asking God to give me knowledge that will benefit me in some way without requiring of me the disciplines that he requires of all his other friends. I am asking for magic. It can become witchcraft when I use dreams and prophecies against other Christians with whom I disagree.

It's very simple to explain how this happens. When someone neglects the Bible, they open themselves up to deception. They lose the ability to discern the nature of spiritual experiences. The dream that might prompt them to curse their opponents did not come from God, because he has already told us how to treat our enemies. We are to bless those who curse us (Luke 6:28). But since they are neglecting the Bible, they can't get the anger washed out of their hearts by the water of the Word. The devil takes advantage of this anger (Eph. 4:26–27) and leads them to prophesy against those whom God loves. Rebellion is like the sin of divination (1 Sam. 15:23), because it can literally lead the rebellious one into divination and magic. Rebellion led King Saul to the witch at Endor (1 Sam. 28:6–25).

So there are two ways we can be led into the realm of magic and ritual. One way is to do the basics—pray, read the Bible, go to church—without the presence of God. The other way is to forget the basics in pursuit of the instant and spectacular. Either way, friendship with God is left behind, and we enter into the realm of magic.

UNBELIEF THROUGH FEAR OF LOOKING FOOLISH

Before Robert came into my office and I saw that word PORNOGRAPHY, I had a *theoretical belief* that God speaks to us apart from the Bible. I came to this belief by reading the Bible, not by having any sort of supernatural vision or dream. But after the experience with Robert, I was different. In addition to a theoretical belief, I now had a *practical confidence* that God would speak to me. I was sure that this was something he wanted to do for all Christians. So shortly after the experience with Robert, I went to my home group meeting one evening and taught an overview of the book of Acts to about forty people. Throughout the overview I emphasized the numerous times God spoke in supernatural ways to his servants. Then at the conclusion of the group, I did something I had never done before. I told them that God was going to speak to us like that, *now.* "All we need to do," I said, "is to pray and wait upon the Lord. He will give us impressions or visions that will show us how we are supposed to pray for people in our group tonight." I encouraged everyone not to be afraid of failing and looking foolish. I emphasized the fact that none of us really knew how to hear God's voice that well. We were all just learners. The only way to find out the difference between an impression from the Lord and one coming from our own emotions would be to test our impression or vision in front of the whole group and risk looking foolish if we were wrong.

I had never attempted anything like this in public before, and as far as I know, neither had anyone else in the room. In spite of my inexperience, though, I was acting very confident. I prayed to God, asking him to display the revealing ministry of the Holy Spirit among us. We all bowed our heads and waited in silence for God to speak. I began to worry that I might have been presumptuous in telling everyone God would speak to us. At just that moment, I had an impression that someone in the room had pain in their left elbow. Was this an impression from God? I thought it was. I hadn't been thinking of body parts or diseases. The impression about the pain in the left elbow was an *interruption* to my thinking. It came like a small invasion. I thought maybe this is how "words of knowledge" came, like interruptions or invasions in your mind.

After waiting about five or six minutes, I asked if anyone in the group thought they had heard something from God. A young woman said she had seen a vision of the public school's administration building and underneath the building she had seen Proverbs 3:5–6. That Scripture text is about guidance. It must have meant that someone in the room that night was a teacher for the public school system in our city, and they had an important decision to make. The only problem was that I knew almost everyone in the room, and none of them were public school teachers. Then one of the two or three people in the room I didn't know raised his hand and said, "I am a school teacher here in the city, and I do have an important decision to make." We knew we were supposed to pray for him and that God would give him the wisdom he needed for this decision. Three more people reported similar specific visions or words that were all accurate.

I hadn't said anything about the "word" I had received. It didn't seem as specific or significant as the others. Yet I felt like I should announce my impression about the left elbow. Then I thought, "What if I am wrong?" What could have been more foolish than for me to tell the whole group that God speaks today and then announce an incorrect impression? I would look utterly foolish. I had told all of the people they needed to risk looking foolish if they wanted to find out what it was like to hear God's voice, and now I was looking for a way to convince myself that I was an exception to this rule. After all, I reasoned, if I, the teacher, announced a mistaken impression, it would take away confidence from the rest of the group to hear God's voice. If the one who teaches that God speaks today can't hear his voice, then everyone else will give up trying to hear it. That line of reasoning worked great. It allowed me not to give my impression, and to experience only a minimal amount of guilt for not giving it.

Later that night when we had gotten home, I confessed to Leesa that I was *sure* God had spoken to me about someone at the group that night. I told her I *knew* that someone had pain in their left elbow, but I was afraid to say it. She started laughing and told me that she had gotten the exact same impression. I went to bed that night confessing my fear of looking foolish and asking the Lord to give me one more chance. I also asked him to show me who had had the pain in their left elbow.

The next day a lady named Glenda walked through my office door. She had been in the meeting the night before. Immediately, I knew that she had been the one with the pain in her left elbow. "Glenda, were you having pain in your elbow last night?" I asked.

"Yes, severe pain. But the strangest thing happened. Before I left the meeting, the pain just went away. Why do you ask? Did you see me holding my elbow last night?"

The Lord had given me an impression about someone's pain, but my fear of looking foolish kept me from saying anything. The fear of looking foolish is not mine alone. It is a universal infection in the church today that keeps us from growing in our ability to hear the voice of the Lord.

For some of us, I think the fear goes deeper than simply looking foolish. Deep in our hearts, some of us fear that we really are fools. We don't feel that we have much of a contribution to make, and if we did try to make a contribution, that people would see we really are nothing but fools after all. So we devote a lot of energy trying to hide what we really are. Why risk exposing ourselves?

I will tell you how my friend John Wimber began to overcome this fear. A few years before he became a Christian, John had gone to an area in downtown Los Angeles to borrow money from a friend who was a drug dealer. While he was waiting for the friend, he saw a man walk by wearing one of those sandwich-board placards. On the front were written the words "I am a fool for Christ." John thought this was about the dumbest thing he had ever seen. He heartily agreed with the man, that he indeed was a fool. As the man passed him, John read the sign on the man's back. It said—"Whose fool are you?" The sign stunned John.

Years later he was sitting in a small Bible study, watching his wife being born again. She had begun to cry in front of everyone. She fell down on her knees and asked God to forgive her of her many sins. John's first thought was, "What sins? Carol is a good person." His next reaction was to be disgusted with his wife's emotional display. He said to himself, "This is the most *foolish* thing I have ever seen. I would never act like this." Then the picture of the man with the sandwich board from years ago came back into his mind—"I am a fool for Christ. Whose fool are you?" John's pride was broken. He realized that he had been a fool all these years—a fool for himself and for the devil. Now he was going to be a fool for Christ. Before he knew it, he was on his knees, sobbing, asking God to forgive him for his many sins.

In the end, aren't we all fools, really? What were we before Christ redeemed us, if not fools? Were we wise for rejecting Christ all those years? If we are not now fools, it is because of him, not us. The wisest people are those who admit they are fools apart from God's wisdom. When God gave the wisest man on earth, Solomon, permission to ask him for anything, Solomon asked for wisdom. His reason for the request, "I am only a little child and do not know how to carry out my duties" (1 Kings 3:7).

It doesn't really bother God that you and I are foolish, for he "chose the foolish things of the world to shame the wise" (1 Cor. 1:27). He doesn't mind us being fools, because he has a wisdom to give us that is not from this world. Every servant who has ever heard God's voice in a remarkable way has appeared a fool before the world. Noah built a useless ark. Jeremiah prophesied a Babylonian captivity for Judah when it appeared certain that Egypt would rescue Judah. Isaiah went naked for three years, and Hosea married a prostitute. Is it any wonder that Hosea could write "the prophet is considered a fool" (Hos. 9:7)? Even the apostles were made to look like "fools for Christ" in the world's eyes (1 Cor. 4:10). If all of God's great servants were fools apart from him, and were made to appear as fools after they came into his service, why should it be any different with us? Wouldn't we be better off just to admit we are fools and that we are going to look foolish by worldly standards? Remember Paul's warning, "Do not deceive yourselves. If any one of you thinks he is wise by the standards of this age, he should become a 'fool' so that he may become wise" (1 Cor. 3:18).

Trying to hear God's voice will probably make you look and feel foolish. As a father, I have watched my children try things and then fail. Sometimes I've been more proud of their foolish failures than their greatest successes. I wonder if God might not feel that way about some of our humiliating failures?

UNBELIEF THROUGH FEAR OF INTIMACY

There is a fear worse than the fear of looking foolish, and more effective in keeping us from hearing God's voice. I mentioned it at the beginning of this chapter. It is fear of the pain of love. Nothing, nothing hurts like love. The ones with whom we are intimate are the ones we love the most, and they are the ones who hurt us the most. Among all of our friends, no one hurts us like God. Never mind that when he hurts us, it is also for our good (Heb. 12:10). Never mind that some of the pain we blame on God actually comes from our own sin. It still hurts. God is sovereign. He can prevent pain if he wants to. He can keep us out of abusive marriages, keep our kids off drugs, save our loved ones from premature deaths. But instead, he lets some of us endure the torture from these and other painful things.

The sovereignty of God is scary in another way as well. If we get too close to him, he might send us somewhere we don't want to go, or make us do something we don't want to do, or be something we don't want to be—even the last place or thing we want to go, do, or be. We've all heard that dark voice whisper, "If you get too close to God, your worst fears will come true. He'll hurt you worse than you can bear." When we believe that voice, we lose some of our confidence in God and we look around for a substitute in which to trust. The substitute may be the Bible, theology, liturgy, church work, or just about any good thing. We can use all these things to keep God and others from getting close enough to hurt us. No one ever does this consciously. Our theology forbids it. No one could get away with saying, "I have decided to trust theology more than God."

I didn't say it, didn't know it, but I had done this. The signs were all around me. I had become more comfortable with principles than people, with ideas than intimacy. Principles and ideas don't hurt you like God and people do. And they're much easier to manipulate. The fact that I was an academic made it even easier for me to develop a nonrelational personality in the comfortable world of thought. Had I not been an academic, I could have just as easily hidden in church work or ministry. Fear of intimacy will always find a substitute suitable for your own individual personality. You'll never know you've chosen the substitute unless the mercy of God comes to you. And that mercy may come in pain ...

COCO AND BENNY

When we moved to Whitefish, we became best friends with Coco and Benny Bee. She was on the city council, and he owned and ran some radio stations. Benny had been a Christian for about four years, and Coco had been pursuing the Lord seriously for ten years or more. They weren't like any of our closest friends before. Most of our closest friends have been people with whom we were in ministry, either seminary professors or preachers— people with similar backgrounds and theology. Safe people. But there was an instant chemistry between the Bees and the Deeres in spite of our very different backgrounds.

We became such good friends that we saw each other almost every day. Benny and I became training partners at the gym. Coco helped Leesa decorate our new home. Leesa and I could drop by their home any time without calling. When I was in their home, if I wanted something, I just opened the refrigerator and got it. I didn't have to ask. Neither did they. Neither did we have to ask where we would spend New Year's Eve. It was a given that we would be together.

Before we came to Whitefish, Coco had beaten cancer— twice. Now she had been cancer free for several years. Then, in October 1994, it came back. Not to worry. We were here now. We knew about healing. We'd seen miracles. I'd even written about them. I believed God had sent me to the church in Whitefish to lead it into a greater experience of the power of the Holy Spirit. Now I believed he had sent me to get Coco healed.

We began assembling the troops. The church couldn't have responded better. We had sign-up sheets for twenty-four-hour prayer, even sign-up sheets for fasting. Each hour of the day someone was praying for Coco's healing and for anybody else who happened to be suffering at that time. Each day someone was fasting for healing. Surely God would respond to that kind of earnest sincerity. He wouldn't let a forty-three-year-old wife and mother of a teenage daughter die prematurely, especially one so loved and respected among the churchgoing and nonchurch-going folks in our community, would he?

It was a wonderful time in our church. So much love, unity, and faith. People even came to me privately saying, "Now we know why God sent you here." I felt God was going to heal Coco to give the community a wonderful testimony of the power and compassion of Christ. And besides, he wouldn't let our best friend die. He never *told* me she wouldn't die, and I never told anyone, not even Coco, that she wouldn't die. But just the same, my heart told me she wouldn't.

The new form of chemotherapy the doctors used almost killed Coco. After the first treatment, she refused any more chemotherapy. That was okay. We had a power greater than chemotherapy on our side. Six months to a year was the original prognosis. Six months later, she was still with us. She was miserable—felt like she had the flu all the time—but she was still with us. I developed a new theory about her healing. Maybe God was going to let her go right to the edge of death and then heal her. That would bring even greater glory to Christ.

In the meantime, I talked about Coco at every conference where I was a speaker. By the summer of 1995, people all over the country were praying for her, and even believers in other countries were interceding for her. By July she was bedridden. Paul Cain came to Whitefish a second time to pray for her. By the time he left, she was up again. It looked as if the healing had started. But it didn't last.

She couldn't eat. She lost weight. Her skin turned yellow. She got too weak to sing worship songs, one of her favorite things to do. So we went up to her room and sang worship songs for her. Though she couldn't sing, she would try to raise her hands in praise to God while we sang.

Then God did something very special for Coco. In August, he sent Don and Christine Potter and their friend Sheri McCoy-Haynes from Nashville, Tennessee, to serenade Coco with worship music. Don is the coproducer for Wynona Judd's music and her band leader. He is also one of the finest guitarists in America. You may have seen him on Oprah Winfrey in the fall of 1994. After Oprah interviewed him, Naomi Judd came on stage to surprise him. She said that Don was the spiritual glue that held their family together during their hardest time. Don and Christine had met Coco and Benny at a conference and had been praying for them ever since. When they heard how far Coco's cancer had progressed, they decided to come to Whitefish to help us through *our* hardest time.

For four days they serenaded Coco and prayed over her. One afternoon Don began a beautiful melody on his guitar. The room was filled with the presence of God. Then he sang a simple refrain, "His love is healing me." Over and over he sang. As he sang, the love of God kept increasing in Coco's bedroom. Benny was lying on the bed next to her. So was their seventeen-year-old daughter, Cassie. I was kneeling at Coco's feet. Leesa and our three children were sitting around the bed. We were all praying, worshiping, and sobbing. For the first time, I thought Coco might die. And for the first time, I thought it would be okay if she died. Either way God would win. I can't explain how or why I felt that. There was something about being surrounded by his love that made everything seem okay, even Coco's death.

On the night of September 15, 1995, all of Coco's family and best friends were gathered around her. We prayed for her and sang to her. Leesa and I kissed her good-bye at 11:30 P.M. She was in a coma. At 2:30 a.m., while her family was keeping vigil over her, she stopped breathing. They called me. I was there in five minutes, asking God to bring her back, but he didn't.

We buried Coco Bee the following Monday.

Everybody cried. I cried. I couldn't remember crying like that. For days I cried. My first instinct was to blame someone for the pain. But who? God, naturally. He could have healed Coco or raised her from the dead. He had done it for others. But my theology wouldn't allow me to blame God. I'd also read the book of Job. Nobody ever won by blaming God. Then could I be to blame? I could have prayed more, fasted more, been holier. But did Coco's healing really depend on my holiness? If that were the case, no one I had ever prayed for would have been healed. But some were, just not Coco. My opponents were the next candidates to blame. But who among my opponents desired Coco's death? They wanted her healed too. That only left the devil to blame, but was he stronger than God? And there I was, right where I'd begun, looking into the face of my sovereign, omnipotent God, asking him, "Why?" And he wasn't answering that question. I knew he had the answers for all of us. I knew the answers were different for each of us, for Benny, for Cassie, for Leesa, for me, for the church ...

I knew that my answer, or at least part of it, lay in the experience of God's love I felt when Don Potter sang in Coco's bedroom. I was sure of this. But no matter how often I asked God about it, I didn't get an answer. Finally I stopped asking, deciding that he would answer me when he was ready.

On April 15, 1995, almost seven months to the day after Coco had died, he did answer me. I was on an airplane descending through the clouds toward Amarillo, Texas. My eye caught the word Nashville in a book I was reading. Nashville caused me to think of Don Potter, and then my mind was led back to Coco and the scene of Don serenading us. For a brief instant, I was in that visionary state reliving the whole experience ...

Coco lay dying. And a part of me was dying with her. Don began to sing a refrain, "His love is healing me." We were losing her. His love wasn't healing anybody. Then it hit me—his love was healing *me*. It was *me* his love was healing. I had been hurt so much over the years that I had constructed a fortress around my heart to keep out all but a very trusted few who wouldn't hurt me. Somehow Coco and Benny got past that fortress. Through God's mercy, I guess. It was unrecognized by me at the time, but it was God's mercy nonetheless. And now Coco was hurting me. More than I had been hurt in a long, long time. And she was healing me. The fortress had cracked. And the part of me that died with Coco needed to die.

Perhaps that's why I had been sent to Whitefish—to be healed by a dying woman.

Who Hears His Voice?

20

The Kind of People
Who Hear the Voice of God

I was a senior in college, and the girl sitting beside me on the plane was a junior. I had just met her as we began the flight from Denver to Dallas on a cold, snowy December day. She was a psychology major, and I was a philosophy major who loved apologetics, that is, the part of Christian theology that specializes in intellectual arguments for the Christian faith. It didn't take me very long to find out that she was intelligent and that she wasn't a Christian. She was also living with her boyfriend.

Well, she had come to the right place. I must confess that, in all humility, I thought if anyone could shoot down her shallow arguments for resisting the Gospel of Jesus Christ, I could. She mentioned her favorite psychologist and his latest book. I had just finished reading it and critiquing it for one of my university classes. This was going to be easier than I thought.

An hour and a half later we were approaching Love Field in Dallas and I wanted to strangle her. Somehow or other she had managed to reject every single argument I had given her. She couldn't see the logic in any of my brilliant presentations. She even had the audacity to repeatedly say that she couldn't understand my crystal-clear explanations of the Gospel. I was totally exasperated and myself in dire need of a psychologist or a tranquilizer, or both.

I was rapidly becoming tempted to soften my intellectual approach and try something on the level of an old Humphry Bogart technique, "I never met a dame yet that didn't understand a slap in the face." Yet a slap in the face wasn't really consistent with the Gospel of love I had been so humbly presenting to this young woman. Actually, I was never really tempted to slap her, but my frustration was turning into anger, and I was beginning to dislike this young woman. I was thinking of her as an adversary to be beaten rather than a lost person to be saved. My anger was a certain sign I was not witnessing out of love, but out of a desire to win with the truth. It was also a revelation of my insecurity and immaturity. It would require many more years before I became open to these kinds of revelations. Later I would learn that it is compassion which seeks to understand, while pride seeks to win.

It was time for the plane to land, and my bungled attempt at witnessing was coming to a close. The experience was about to go down as a royal failure. Then the pilot announced that we could not land because of the back up in air traffic. We began to circle Love Field in a swirling snowstorm. I would have yet another chance. I had a very vague feeling I had done something wrong in my first attempt to witness to her. I didn't know it, but I had been speaking to her as though she were nothing more than a spiritual trophy to put in my evangelistic showcase. This time I decided on a new tactic. I would encourage her to talk, and I would listen. For the next thirty minutes I listened intently as she told me of her dreams and struggles and present unhappiness. She told me that she had been witnessed to often by students from churches and parachurch organizations. But none of it "took." I kept on listening. About forty-five minutes later, the plane began its descent into Love Field. Suddenly, she stopped talking and asked, "What do you think?"

What did I think? I had spent an hour and a half telling her what I thought, and it hadn't done any good. What more could I add? Before I knew it, almost involuntarily, a silent prayer for wisdom escaped my heart. I felt the compassion of Jesus for this young woman. With the compassion came a divine clarity so simple that it almost sounds foolish. I said to her, "Your problem is the same as mine—you are a sinner and you need a savior." She burst into tears, "I know," she sobbed. "It's true, it's true. You're right."

I began to understand something with that encounter. An hour and a half of apologetic arguments did not even come close to equaling the force of the simple statement, "You are a sinner and you need a savior." There was a *power* behind that simple declaration that was absent from all my carefully reasoned arguments. The power came because God had suggested those simple words to my spirit. At the time, I didn't have the wisdom or the maturity to ask *why* the power came. I just knew that it was there. That experience of power began to teach me, a philosophy major, the relative powerlessness of intellectual arguments. While they may occasionally remove genuine obstacles to faith, they are ultimately fruitless unless the Holy Spirit convicts the heart of sin.

What that experience *didn't* teach me was how to experience that power on a regular basis. I was still far too confident in my own abilities to enjoy the privilege of hearing God's voice with any frequency. God can and does speak to all kinds of people— Christians as well as pagans—whenever he pleases. But what most of us want is not just a sporadic encounter with his presence but a consistent meaningful experience of his voice.

"How can I get God to speak to *me*?" is a question I get all the time. All the ingredients to answer this question could be found in my experience with the young woman on the plane to Dallas, but I wasn't asking the question then. Many years later, when I set my heart to study this question, I meditated on the lives of all the people in the Bible who were famous for hearing God. I talked with contemporary people who had a reputation for discerning God's voice. And finally, I tried to pay close attention to my own successes and failures in hearing the voice of God. At this point in my study, it seems to me that there are three essential characteristics for hearing the voice of God speak to us: availability, willingness, and humility.

AVAILABILITY

If you study the life of Jesus, who heard the voice of the Father better than anyone else, one of the first things that will impress you is his "unreserved availability for God."[1] I had been a Christian for only about a year when I first noticed this characteristic of Jesus' life. I was reading the first chapter of Mark, where Jesus stayed up late into the night healing the sick and the demon possessed (vv. 32–34). After staying up half the night ministering to people, Mark tells us that "very early in the morning, while it was still dark, Jesus got up, left the house and went off to a solitary place, where he prayed" (v. 35). If anyone ever had an excuse for sleeping in, Jesus certainly had one that morning. But instead he followed his daily habit of seeking solitude with God (see also Luke 4:42; 5:16).

Early in my Christian life I used to use this passage to say that Jesus always *found time* for God. I don't see it that way at all now. When I look at the life of Jesus, I never really see him "finding time for God." Rather, I see a Son whose time belongs completely to the Father. Jesus was never in a hurry. He never needed more time. This is because he looked on his time as his Father's time. Also, he was completely available for his Father's desires. He only did what he saw his Father doing (John 5:19). And he was always in the right place at the right time in order to fulfill the desires of his heavenly Father.

I am continually amazed at the spontaneity and informality of the ministry of the Lord. Whether he was speaking to an unexpected crowd of over five thousand, as in the Sermon on the Mount, or to just one lost woman at a well in Samaria, he was always prepared and did just the right thing. He was never frantic, like the modern pastor who continually frets about how busy he is and then has to stay up late Saturday night putting together a "message" for Sunday morning. It is comical to imagine Jesus staying up the night before the Sermon on the Mount wondering what he was going to say to all those people. Yes, it is comical to imagine Jesus ever struggling for a sermon. His life is the sermon, and he ministered out of the daily overflow of his communion with his heavenly Father. He was able to do this because he was completely available to God.

Please don't think I am speaking about having a regular "quiet time." I am speaking about much more than this. I have known people who never missed their 5:30 A.M. quiet time of Bible study, and yet were meaner than junkyard dogs. It is possible to have a quiet time every morning and never be available to God. Unlike people who "find time" for God, who get their quiet time out of the way in the morning so they can go on with their real lives and forget God the rest of the day, people who are truly available to God see God as owning their day. He is free to reorder it at any time he chooses. They are not content simply to have a quiet time and get their "God stuff" out of the way early in the morning. Their satisfaction comes from experiencing his presence throughout the day and knowing they are pleasing to him.

Years ago I was in the process of developing a close friendship with a person who eventually became one of my closest friends. I was going through a difficult time and needed his help. As I was saying good-bye after lunch one day, I asked him how late I could call him that night. He said I could call him as late as I wanted to. I told him I didn't want to wake him up, so I needed to know what time he planned to go to sleep. Then he said to me, "It doesn't make any difference what time I go to sleep tonight. For you, I am a twenty-four-hour friend, seven days a week. Call me whenever you want. I'll be there." You see, availability is one of the primary characteristics of friendship. Friends are available to their friends.

Differing levels of friendship call for varying degrees of availability. There are some people to whom we will not give our phone number, but we will smile and speak to them if we meet them in a public setting. There are others who have only our office number. Then there are people who have our private home number. Of the people who have our private home number, only a few of them would feel free to use it any time of the day or night. These are our closest friends, the ones who can come in our back door without an appointment and be genuinely welcomed by us. Our closest friends are the ones who can interrupt our plans without causing us any irritation. The deeper the friendship, the greater the availability.

This is what God really wants with us: a friendship (John 15:15). Many of us try to satisfy God by meeting religious duties and obligations, but in our closest friendships, we go far *beyond* the sense of duty. We are available to our closest friends because we love them and want to be with them. In true friendship, availability is not a burden or an obligation. Instead, it is a joy and a privilege.

In a real friendship, availability is reciprocal. The people who have unrestricted access to me also give me unrestricted access to them. It works the same way with our heavenly Father. He is most available to those who are most available to him. To many Christians this idea won't sound fair. It may even sound like a "works" version of Christianity. They like to picture God being equally available to all Christians at all times. It is almost as if they conceive of God as a cosmic bellboy who exists to meet their needs and can be dismissed when they have no conscious need of him. But this is both a misunderstanding of grace and of the nature of personal relationships. God doesn't throw his pearls before swine. The ones who find him are those who seek him with all their heart (Deut. 4:29).

If we want a deep friendship with God, it is important to cultivate a state of mind where we view all of our time as God's time, a state of mind where we are totally available to him. It is necessary to do this because God speaks to us at the most inconvenient times. Sometimes he even lets his favorite servants spend time, energy, and money in organizing a mission journey. Then he waits until they get in the middle of that journey and forbids them to engage in ministry. Paul and his friends made plans to minister in Asia, but God wanted them in Europe (Acts 16:6–10). He let them "waste" time, money, and energy before he redirected them there.

It seems to me God almost delights in speaking to us at the most inconvenient times in order to test our availability. One of my most frequent prayers is that God would grant to me a warning before I say a critical word that he has not ordained to come forth from my lips or before I say a self-exalting word. I have great confidence in praying this prayer because it is one of the tasks of the Holy Spirit to convict us of sin (John 16:8). God frequently convicts me in regard to my speech. He lets me get to the point of no return in one of my self-exalting stories, then he gives me the warning that I am about to use my speech in order to make myself look better than I really am. When he does this I am suddenly caught between two alternatives: finding a new and awkward ending to the story so that I do not exalt myself, or disobeying God and finishing the story.

Only slightly less inconvenient is God's habit of waking you up at 3:00 in the morning. Sometimes he does this with a dream. You know it is important, and you know that if you don't write it down you won't remember it, but you are sleepy. Remember, if you are available to him, he will be available to you. Or it may not be a dream that disturbs you at night. It may be his Spirit that settles on you with a sort of nighttime clarity which makes sleep impossible. He will speak to you then if you will turn to him instead of to books or to magazines.

When Jesus first called his apostles, he made it clear to them that their first task was not ministry for him, but rather availability to him. Before Jesus chose his twelve apostles, he went up on a mountain and spent the night in prayer (Luke 6:12). In the Bible, mountains were considered the place of revelation. Moses went up on a mountain in order to receive the Ten Commandments from God. Jesus went to a place of revelation and spent the night in prayer in order to hear the names of the twelve apostles from his Father. Here is Mark's account of the calling of the twelve apostles:

> Jesus went up on a mountainside and called to him those he wanted, and they came to him. He appointed twelve—designating them apostles—that they might be with him and that he might send them out to preach and to have authority to drive out demons (Mark 3:13–15).

God chose the apostles for three purposes. First, "that they might be with him." Second, "that he might send them out to preach." And third, "to have authority to drive out demons" (Mark 3:14–15). Before they were ever to have the privilege or the power of preaching and ministering in the name of Jesus, they were to *be with him*. Availability to God, intimacy with Jesus, is the practical foundation for all of ministry. Preaching and witnessing only have power when they are an overflow of our intimacy with God. Availability to God is the first priority in ministry and the first requirement for hearing his voice.

There are both passive and active aspects to availability. There are times when we are simply to wait on the Lord (Jer. 42:1–7; Isa. 40:31 NASB). On the other hand, people who are available to God actively seek him (Matt. 6:33). How long should one seek the Lord? Thirty minutes each morning, an hour after lunch, two hours in the evening? Remember what I said earlier. We are to seek him until he comes (Hos. 10:12). Many people are content to spend thirty minutes or an hour, morning after morning, reading the Bible and praying, though they experience no real presence of God. These same people would never be content to speak to one of their friends for an hour without the slightest indication from the friend that he or she was listening to them. But years of practice have taught them to be satisfied by the performance of religious duties quite apart from the experience of God's presence.

Availability to God carries with it an expectation that he will speak to us. Habakkuk 2:1 says, "I will stand at my watch and station myself on the ramparts; I will look to see what he will say to me, and what answer I am to give to this complaint." The attitude of the person available to the Lord is, "Speak, for your servant is listening" (1 Sam. 3:10). If we make ourselves available to God, he will make himself available to us (James 4:8).

WILLING TO DO GOD'S WILL

Jesus' teaching continually amazed people. He even amazed his enemies. On one occasion his enemies were trying to discern the origin of his teaching. They knew he hadn't had any formal education or training, yet he spoke with an understanding that surpassed anything they had ever heard. Where did it come from? Jesus told them, "My teaching is not mine, but his who sent me. If any man is willing to do his will, he shall know of the teaching, whether it is from God, or whether I speak from myself" (John 7:16–17 NASB).

In saying this, Jesus gave the second prerequisite for hearing the voice of God. In effect, he was saying that spiritual discernment is based on our willingness to do the will of God. Those willing to do the will of God will recognize the source of Jesus' teaching. In other words, God speaks to those who are willing to do whatever he says to them.

One of the reasons Jesus heard the Father's voice better than anyone else was his utter obedience to this principle. He said, "By myself I can do nothing; I judge only as I hear, and my judgment is just, *for I seek not to please myself but him who sent me*" (John 5:30). When God sees that in our heart of hearts we are truly willing to do whatever he says, he will speak to us. Why should he speak to us if he knows that we will not do what he asks? I think God often refrains from speaking to us in his mercy because he knows we would disobey his voice and bring judgment upon ourselves.

Have you settled the issue of whom you are going to please in your short earthly life? Is the governing goal of your life the same as Jesus' goal? He said, "I have come to do your will, O God" (Heb. 10:7). Because this was the purpose of his life, Jesus could hear his Father when he spoke. Because pleasing God was his highest goal, he could endure the betrayal of friends and the rejection of his nation without letting any bitterness into his heart. He loved his friends and his nation, but the will of his Father was his first priority. Success in Jesus' ministry wasn't determined by numbers or by the faithfulness of his followers, but by his faithfulness in following the will of One who might lead him into pain and rejection. His reward was hearing the voice of the Person he loved the best and wanted to please the most.

You and I have a destiny in the kingdom of God. Our destinies are different, but they're both equally wonderful. And no one can keep us from fulfilling our destinies. No gossip, slander, betrayal, tragedy, not even the devil himself, can steal it. I'm the only one who can throw away my crown. You are the only one who can surrender your crown to another. But that will never happen as long as the issue of our life's goal stays settled in our heart of hearts. God will speak to us because he knows we will obey and because he knows we need his voice to obey. Even though, initially, the voice may not make sense.

Philip was in the midst of a revival in Samaria, a revival complete with signs and wonders. In the midst of that revival an angel of the Lord spoke to him saying, "Arise and go south to the road that descends from Jerusalem to Gaza" (Acts 8:26 NASB). You can imagine how little sense this command made to Philip. Why would God call the leader of a major revival to leave in the midst of a revival and go out to a desert road? It was amazing that an angel spoke to Philip, but just as amazing was Philip's response to the command to "arise and go." The very next verse says, "And he arose and went" (Acts 8:27 NASB). Eventually, it all made sense to Philip—*after he had obeyed the voice of the Lord.* However, he would never have heard the voice of the Lord, never received an angelic visitation, unless he had been willing to do what God had spoken to him.

Years ago I began to have the feeling that God was going to ask me to give up one of my hobbies. There was nothing wrong with this particular hobby. I told the Lord that I was willing to give it up, but he would have to ask me first. I am not into asceticism. I have never found it profitable spiritually to simply start denying myself things that are lawful just to get God's attention. When I have given up things without the Lord's leading, I have usually ended up in legalism and self-righteousness, and eventually in bitterness. This time I simply told the Lord, "I like this hobby very much, but if you ask me, I will give it up."

About six months later, early one Sunday morning while I was in that state between sleep and waking, I remembered a dream I had had during the night. In this dream I was talking to my friend Paul Cain. In the last part of the dream Paul said to me, "The Lord wants you to give up your hobby." (In the dream he actually named my hobby.) As I opened my eyes, I just barely remembered this dream. It was so faint that at first I thought I must have made it up. Then I thought, *No, I am remembering a true dream, but how do I know this dream was from the Lord. Maybe it came out of my legalistic conscience. Or maybe the devil gave it to me to lead me into legalism.* I was discovering that it wasn't going to be so easy to give up my hobby after all. Then I said to the Lord, "If that dream really was from you, I will give up my hobby. Just give me a sign. Let Paul Cain speak to me today about that dream."

It just so happened that Paul was in town that weekend. I preached in church that Sunday morning and afterwards Paul and I went to lunch with a group of people. After lunch he and I were alone in the car on the way to the airport. He said, "I had the most amazing clarity in my dreams last night. I had three dreams, and I remember every one of them."

I couldn't believe it! I stared straight ahead and said, "I had a dream too last night. And I also remember it."

"In fact, you were in one of my dreams, and I was speaking to you," he said.

"Uh, that sounds kind of like the dream I had. You were speaking to me in my dream too."

Then Paul said, "I suppose you want me to go first?"

"That would be helpful."

Then Paul told me some very encouraging things the Lord had said to him about me in the dream. When he finished, he hadn't said a word about my hobby. I looked across the car and asked, "Paul, is that all there was in the dream? This is important. I have to know if there was anything else."

"Well, I know how much you like this hobby so I wasn't going to say anything to you for a while, but since you asked, the Lord wants you to give up . . ." And he named my hobby.

At first I couldn't believe it. I was without excuse—I had to give up my hobby now. But my sense of loss gave way to joy when I realized the kindness of the Lord and the supernatural way he had spoken to me. I knew he would replace my hobby with more of his presence and that I would be the one to gain from all of this. I also felt a little proud of myself, at how quickly I had been willing to do his will.

With just a little more self-righteousness than I care to remember, I said to Paul, "So be it. I will give up my hobby. Is there anything else the Lord wants me to give up?"

Instead of answering me directly Paul asked, "Do you remember the story of the rich young ruler?"

"Of course I do."

"How did that story go?"

"The rich young ruler asked Jesus what he could do to inherit eternal life, and Jesus told him to keep the commandments. The rich young ruler said he had kept the commandments carefully from his youth up. He asked Jesus what else he had to do to get eternal life. That's when Jesus told him to sell everything he owned, distribute it to the poor, and follow him, and he would have riches in heaven."

Then Paul said to me, "Wouldn't the rich young ruler have been better off if he would have stopped after the first question?"

It took a minute for Paul's point to sink in. In the future the Lord would ask me to give up other things, but I didn't have the maturity or the character to say yes to those things now. He was only speaking to me about what he knew I was willing to do. It wasn't that I was rebellious, I was just immature. There are things you can ask a six-year-old to do that you can't ask a three-year-old to do. And there are things that you can ask an eighteen-year-old to do that you would never dream of asking your six-year-old.

Sometimes the Lord doesn't speak to us because we are actively rebelling against him. Often, however, it is not our rebellion that hinders the voice of God, it is our immaturity. As we grow up in him, we become more willing to do his will, and he will speak to us about larger areas of our lives.

HUMILITY—THE DIVINE VIRTUE

Next to Jesus, who was the greatest person of revelation in the Bible? The Bible tells us it was Moses. Miriam, the sister of

Moses, made the foolish mistake of seeing herself as a peer to her little brother Moses. The Lord rebuked her:

> When a prophet of the LORD is among you, I reveal myself to him in visions, I speak to him in dreams. But this is not true of my servant Moses; he is faithful in all my house. With him I speak face to face, clearly and not in riddles; he sees the form of the LORD. Why then were you not afraid to speak against my servant Moses? (Num. 12:6–8).

The Lord was telling Miriam that there was no one else like Moses when it came to hearing the voice of the Lord. In effect, the Lord was saying to her, "Miriam, Moses is not your little brother any longer. He is the only man on the whole earth with whom I speak face to face on a regular basis." In the very same chapter that proclaims that Moses is the greatest person of revelation in the Bible, it also says he was the most humble man on the face of the earth (Num. 12:3). Humility and the ability to hear God's voice go hand in hand. Every person in the Bible who had a great ability to hear God's voice was also a person of great humility.

Daniel was another person who heard the voice of God in remarkable ways. An angel came to Daniel with the following message, "Do not be afraid, Daniel. Since the first day that you set your mind to gain understanding and to *humble yourself* before your God, your words were heard, and I have come in response to them" (Dan. 10:12). And even Manasseh, one of the most wicked kings in the history of Judah, could get the Lord's attention by humbling himself:

> In his distress he sought the favor of the LORD his God and *humbled himself greatly* before the God of his fathers. And when he prayed to him, the LORD was moved by his entreaty and listened to his plea; so he brought him back to Jerusalem and to his kingdom. Then Manasseh knew that the LORD is God (2 Chron. 33:12–13).

What is humility? My favorite definition is found in Samuel's rebuke of Saul. Samuel said, "You were once small in your own eyes . . ." (1 Sam. 15:17). Being small in our own eyes doesn't mean we think we are worthless or that we have no abilities or good qualities. It does mean, however, that we have a profound distrust of our own abilities or goodness.

When the Lord came to Moses and commanded him to lead the Israelites into the Promised Land, Moses responded to God by saying, "Who am I, that I should go to Pharaoh and bring the Israelites out of Egypt?" (Ex. 3:11). Moses was expressing a profound distrust in his ability to accomplish this task. Gideon had a similar response to the Lord when the Lord called him to be a judge and deliverer of Israel (Judg. 6:15). It is not that either of these men thought they had no abilities or that they were particularly bad people. When they saw themselves in light of the character of God and his calling on their lives, they knew in their hearts they had neither the ability nor the character to accomplish his task.

Humble people know that neither physical strength (Prov 21:31), nor intelligence (Prov. 16:9), nor luck (Prov. 16:23) is decisive—instead, it is the Lord who will determine the outcome. Humility is a profound confidence in the mercy of God rather than in man's intentions or efforts (Rom. 9:15–16). A truly humble person knows that no matter how great their abilities or their character, they can do nothing apart from Christ (John 15:6). So humble people put their confidence in the Holy Spirit's ability to speak, not in their ability to hear, and in Christ's ability to lead, not in their ability to follow.

Another characteristic of humble people is that they are willing to associate with and serve people of lower position than themselves (Rom. 12:10; Gal. 5:13; and Phil. 2:3–4). No one was better at this than Christ (Phil. 2:5–11). God the Father is intrinsically humble. He loves to associate with the lowly (Isa. 57:15; 66:2).

One of the most frightening verses in the Bible is Psalm 138:6: "Though the LORD is on high, he looks upon the lowly, but the proud he knows from afar." In other words, God is intimate with the humble, but he keeps the arrogant at a distance. Humility is the pathway to intimacy with God, while arrogance leads to a spiritual desert. Religious pride is the worst form of arrogance. The sternest rebukes Jesus ever delivered were not given to the sexually impure but to the spiritually proud. Of all the sins that are most acceptable in the church today, religious pride tops the list. We reward proud leaders, laugh at arrogant humor, and look down on those outside our religious circle. Proud people don't really need God's supernatural revelation. Perhaps that's why there is so little of it in some parts of the church today.

Both the Lord and the apostles repeatedly emphasized the theme that God exalts the humble but opposes the proud (Matt. 23:12; Luke 14:11; 18:14; James 4:6; and 1 Peter 5:5). If we are ever going to hear his voice we must embrace humility. Jesus was humble in heart (Matt. 11:29) and so are all of his intimate friends. The proud may have leadership in our churches, but they are excluded from Jesus' circle of intimate friends.

The highest form of exaltation God can give is intimacy and friendship with himself. Will he make all of us awesome prophets? Will he give all of us a magnificent word of knowledge ministry? No, but he will give each one of us exactly what we need to be wise sons and daughters who make their Father's heart glad. He will give us enough of his voice to overwhelm our hearts with his affection. And he will give us his friendship.

If we make ourselves available to God, are willing to do whatever he tells us, and set our hearts to pursue humility, he will speak to us. When he spoke to me about the young woman on the plane to Dallas, all three of these things had come together for me. I had made myself available to him to be his witness. When the voice came, I was willing to say those words and no more. And my bungled attempt at witnessing caused me to lose confidence in my persuasive abilities, so I humbled myself and asked for help. Then the voice came.

But my loss of confidence was only momentary. Soon I regained it, and therefore had to wait a long time before I would hear the voice again.

21

Recognizing the Voice

Y ou're a sinner, and you need a savior." I've tried that line
many times since that December plane ride, but never with the
same result. Finally, I just discarded it. Without the power behind
those lines, they were just empty words.

At one time or another most of us have probably fallen for a
"get rich quick" scheme, both in the world of money and in the
world of the Spirit. It's human nature to want something valuable
without having to pay what the rest of the world does to get it.
That's why catchy formulas promising so much but delivering so
little have such a strong appeal. Actually, behind many of our
questions about God and his ways lies the hope that the answer
to something so profound may be in some simple, mechanical
formula—a subject we could master and even control for our
benefit.

I hear this false hope expressed in almost every conference I
attend where God's voice surprises and amazes a lot of people all
at once. This happened to about twelve hundred of us in Houston, Texas, in March 1993, at a conference sponsored by Calvary
Baptist Church.

Tim Johnson was attending that meeting where Rick Joyner,
Paul Cain, and I were speaking. At that time, Tim was an all-pro
defensive lineman for the Washington Redskins. At the close of
the 1992 NFL season, Tim thought God was leading him from the
Redskins to another football team. But he wondered if it was
really God speaking to him or might he just be reacting to some

changes in his circumstances. By the spring of 1993, he was almost certain God was opening a door for a move to another team that would be professionally and financially rewarding. However, Tim had begun to have such excruciating pain in his back that he could no longer jog, let alone run. It developed to the point that it threatened to end his professional football career.

Paul was introduced to Tim, but was not told by him or anyone else about his injury or his planned move from the Redskins. One night after Paul finished speaking, he began to give prophetic words to people. He asked "Where is Tim from the Washington *Rednecks?*" (Paul is not one of your more knowledgeable sports enthusiasts.) Tim stood up. Paul said, "Tim, you're in a place right now where promotion comes from the Lord. The Lord showed me in a very clear way that you have been in transition and you are thinking about a move. The Lord showed me you are not going to make that move right now because he still has something wonderful for you where you are. The Lord is touching the back of your neck and your lower back. You don't look like you have that kind of trouble. You look like you're in the picture of health. But the Lord is going to heal that pain. Let's thank the Lord for this."

That Easter Sunday, Tim woke up and went to the park near his house. He began to jog and had no pain. Then he began to run. Still no pain. He was completely healed of his back and neck problems. Remember that Paul had said the Lord was going to do something wonderful for Tim in Washington, D.C.? He stayed with the Redskins for the 1993 season and had his best year in professional football. At the end of the season he received a number of incredible awards. Among them, he was named the most valuable Redskin player by the Quarterback Club of Washington, D.C., an outstanding honor for a lineman. Had Tim left the Redskins, he would have missed a number of very rewarding things that happened to him.

After the meeting, everyone wanted to know how Paul knew Tim had back problems and how he knew that God was going to heal him. Paul said he had seen it in a vision. But how had he known the vision was from the Lord? This is the question I hear asked in every conference where people are surprised by the voice of God. Behind the astonished eyes of the questioner there is always the faintest flicker of hope for some simple formula, a quick and easy solution to recognizing the voice of God. The flicker fades when the answer begins by denying that there is any easy formula. When the answer turns to the themes of risk and humiliation, the astonished eyes become fearful eyes saying, "Maybe I'd better leave this hearing God business to the prophets." But don't give up. Let me offer you some guidelines.

RECOGNIZING GOD'S VOICE

How can you know it is God speaking to you and not your own emotions, or the devil, or the pressure you feel coming from others? When God doesn't give us an overt supernatural confirmation of his voice through prophetic ministry, or an angelic visitation, or the fulfillment of a supernatural fleece, how can we recognize his voice? What other kinds of help does God give us?

God's Voice Always Agrees with the Scriptures

All private revelation in any form ought to be checked against the Scriptures. I do not believe that God will ever contradict the Bible. He may contradict our *interpretation* of the Bible, just as he did Peter's interpretation of the Levitical food laws (Acts 10), but he will never contradict the actual teaching of the Bible. All prophetic words, impressions, dreams, visions, and supernatural experiences of any sort ought to be tested in light of the teaching of the Bible.[1]

God would never lead or tempt any of us to violate his Word (James 1:13). But what about those areas where the Scripture gives us freedom, things that may be permissible in general but not necessarily beneficial for us in particular? We all have freedom to marry in Christ, to change jobs, to buy houses, to encourage our children in certain occupations, to engage in various forms of ministry, etc. In these cases, how do we test the voice or impression that seems to be leading us in a certain direction?

God's Voice May Contradict Friends' Opinions

It is often said that the counsel of friends and trusted authority figures is important in discerning the leading of the Lord. And there are some texts that support this view (cf. Prov. 11:14). But often counsel from others is of only limited value when trying to discern whether an impression or dream we had is from God.

God sometimes leads people to do things that make no sense to their friends. Paul's friends urged him not to go to Jerusalem, knowing through a prophetic word of Agabus that imprisonment awaited Paul there (Acts 21:10–12). However, Paul refused their advice because he felt the Spirit was leading him to Jerusalem (Acts 20:22–23). Paul's actions made no sense to his friends. Yet it was he, not they, who was hearing the voice of the Lord.

In the 1960s a young British woman, Jackie Pullinger, shocked her family and friends by announcing that God was calling her to *go*. When they asked her *where* she was supposed to go, she replied that she didn't know, she was just to *go*. This made no sense to anyone, but Jackie was sure she was being led by God to leave her family and friends. She got on a ship and headed east. When she reached Hong Kong, she felt the Lord impressing her to stay there. She had no idea of what she was supposed to do in Hong Kong or how she would earn a living. But thirty years later Jackie Pullinger's story has become one of the most successful and miraculous missionary stories of our time. She led members of Triad gangs to Christ and successfully prayed for them to be delivered from various drug addictions. Thousands of people have been led to Christ, set free from drugs, and delivered from poverty through her ministry.[2] Jackie went against the advice of friends and trusted counselors, and she was right to do so.

When we are trying to discern whether or not the voice speaking to us is the Lord, we are not looking for advice in the natural. We do not simply want the *opinions* of others. We are trying to judge, not by our eyes or our ears, but by the Spirit of the Lord (Isa. 11:2–4). If others are to help us, what we need from them is true spiritual discernment, not reasonable advice. God expects us to learn to recognize his voice (John 10:3–4), therefore he will hold us, not our advisors, accountable for hearing his words (cf. 1 Kings 13:1–32).

God's Voice Has a Consistent Character

Another important facet of the voice that speaks to us is its character. Study the conversations of Jesus in the New Testament. Observe how he speaks to the woman at the well (John 4:7ff.), to the rich young ruler (Matt. 19:16ff.), or to his disciples on any number of occasions. The voice of Jesus does not nag or whine or argue. It is calm, quiet, and confident. It is not mean or condemning. Why do you think he would speak to us any differently?

Years ago a woman came to me who had been rebuked by an itinerant "prophet" who was not a member of any local church nor under any authority structure. He simply traveled from place to place telling aggrandizing stories about himself and taking donations for his "ministry." In the course of his rebuke he accurately named some of the woman's sins. He also screamed and shouted at her during his "ministry" to her. When she confronted him about his anger, he replied that he wasn't angry; he was just giving the message the way God told him to speak it. It was really God who was angry with her, the "prophet" claimed. After it was over, the woman was devastated.

Because this man had been accurate in naming some of her sins, she was inclined to think it was from God. She asked me if I thought this really was the Word of God to her. I told her I was sure it wasn't. I reminded her that the Lord didn't scream and shout at his children. The character of the voice speaking through the prophet demonstrated that it really wasn't the Lord Jesus speaking.

Many people mistake the condemnation and accusation of the devil (Rev. 12:10) for the conviction of the Holy Spirit. When the devil speaks to us about our sins, he makes us feel worthless and condemned. He nags and whines. His impressions make us feel we have always been this way and will never change. When we confess our sins, he tells us that we are not sincere, that we have done these things before and confessed them, and that we will simply end up doing them again. When the Holy Spirit convicts us, he confronts us with the reality of our sin, but he brings hope through the blood of Jesus.

God's Voice Bears Good Fruit

People frequently say that the major test of a prophet is whether or not his predictions come true. I don't think this is necessarily the best test, because many prophecies, if not the majority of them, contain a contingent element. Jeremiah teaches:

> If at any time I announce that a nation or kingdom is to
> be uprooted, torn down and destroyed, and if that

nation I warned repents of its evil, then I will relent and not inflict on it the disaster I had planned. And if at another time I announce that a nation or kingdom is to be built up and planted, and if it does evil in my sight and does not obey me, then I will reconsider the good I had intended to do for it (Jer. 18:7–10).

This is what happened to Jonah's prophecy over Nineveh. He had prophesied, "Forty more days and Nineveh will be overturned" (Jonah 3:4). Nineveh repented, and Jonah's prophecy did not come to pass.

When a prediction fails, there are at least three possibilities. First, the Lord may not have spoken the prediction. Second, the Lord may have spoken, but the human messenger may have misunderstood the timing of the event or misunderstood God's voice in some other way, just as we misunderstand the Bible on occasion. And third, it is possible that God has spoken and that the messenger has understood his voice accurately, but a response on the part of others has kept it from being fulfilled.

In addition to the contingent nature of prophetic words, there is another reason why the fulfillment of a particular person's prediction is not necessarily the best test of whether or not the Lord has spoken. It is possible for a prediction, even a sign or a wonder, to come true and not have been spoken by the Lord (Deut. 13:1–5). The word may have come true due to demonic power behind the word, due to some sort of deceitful manipulation by the speaker, or simply due to coincidence.

Finally, in the case of prophetic words to which no time limit is attached, it is hard for the fulfillment test to be applied in a very practical way. People had to wait some seven hundred years to see if Isaiah's prophecies about a suffering Servant would come true (e.g., Isa. 52:13–53:12). And some of his prophecies have yet to come true (e.g., Isa. 2:1ff.; 63:1–6).

I am not saying fulfillment is not a test of prophetic words. I am simply saying that it is not necessarily the *best* test of whether or not the Lord has spoken those words.

Jesus did not emphasize fulfillment as a test to discern false prophets and true prophets. Jesus said, "By their fruit you will recognize them.... A good tree cannot bear bad fruit, and a bad tree cannot bear good fruit" (Matt. 7:16, 18). Certainly, truth or fulfillment is part of the good fruit, but by using the word "fruit," the Lord is directing us to observe the effects of the voice speaking through the prophetic person. If that voice is from the Lord, it will produce good effects among the believing community—the fruit of the Holy Spirit: love, joy, peace, patience ... (Gal. 5:22–23). Obviously this is not a test that can be applied immediately, but then again, neither can the test of fulfillment in many cases. The test of fulfillment becomes practical only when a specific date is assigned to the words.

By encouraging us to look at the fruit of the voice, Jesus is giving us a general test of a person's life or ministry. If we really are listening to the voice of the Lord, our lives will be marked by the fruit of the Spirit wherever we go. If, however, we claim to be hearing from the Lord, and yet everywhere we go there is strife, dissension, and envy among believers, then it calls into question whether we are really hearing the voice of God.[3]

God's Voice is Different from Our Voice

I have already mentioned the importance of Isaiah 55:8–9. Read this magnificent passage again:

"For my thoughts are not your thoughts, neither are your ways my ways," declares the Lord. "As the heavens are higher than the earth, so are my ways higher than your ways and my thoughts than your thoughts."

According to this text, God's thoughts are radically different from our thoughts. On a practical level this means he will have a different perspective than we do on any particular situation. His ways are also radically different than our ways. This means he will have a very different way of handling a particular situation than we would. In other words, we are frequently going to find ourselves in conflict with God's perspective and methods.

Some might object that this is no longer true, because now we have the Bible to tell us God's thoughts and ways. But remember, having the Bible and *understanding* the Bible are two different things. The Pharisees and rabbis had the Bible. They had even memorized the prophecies about the first coming of Jesus—but when he came, they failed to recognize him as the Messiah. Isaiah had the Bible—at least, the Torah—when God spoke these verses to him. Furthermore, don't you believe God's understanding of the Bible might be significantly different from our understanding of the Bible? Don't you believe his ways of applying the Bible could be significantly different from our ways of applying the Bible? And we should also remember that not all of God's thoughts are contained in the Bible. What if he wanted to share one of his thoughts with you that he hadn't previously written down?

One of the practical consequences of Isaiah 55:8–9 is that frequently when God speaks to us, the content of his message will be different, perhaps even the opposite of our thoughts or our ways of handling the situation at hand. One of the tests I use to determine whether or not it is the voice of the Lord speaking to me is whether or not these thoughts are different from my own. Let me give you an example.

A friend of mine went to a series of worship services at a church known for prophetic ministry because he wanted to learn to hear the voice of the Lord better, and there were a number of speakers who were going to speak on this subject. One of the staff members announced that they were going to take an offering to retire the remaining mortgage debt on their building, about $130,000. He asked the audience to pray to see what God would have them give. My friend was sure he wasn't supposed to give anything to the offering for three reasons. First, he had already given more than his tithe that month. Second, he had no money to give. All he had left for the rest of the month was approximately $1,000, which was already designated for his mortgage payment. Third, he knew there was such appreciation for the ministry of this particular church that they would take up more than the $130,000 they needed to pay off their mortgage without his money. Yet when the person taking up the offering invited everyone to pray to see what God would say to them, my friend thought it was a good idea for him to ask the Lord anyway, even though he already knew the Lord's answer. He bowed his head and said simply, "Lord, would you have me give anything to this offering?"

Immediately the figure of $1,000 came into his mind. He said, "No, really Lord, would you have me give anything to this offering?" Again the figure of $1,000 came to his mind. His first response to the thought of $1,000 was that he had just made this up. But when he began to think about it, that solution made no sense to him. If he were making up an answer, he would have come up with the figure of zero. So he prayed the third time and the figure of $1,000 came to his mind again.

With his head still bowed, he tried to figure out why the Lord would ask him to make a sacrifice that made no financial sense to him. Isaiah 55:8–9 came to his mind, "My thoughts are not your thoughts and my ways are not your ways." The passage convinced him that it probably was the Lord speaking to him. He took out his checkbook and wrote out a check for $1,000. (I know this is a true story—I have seen the canceled check.) Then he prayed something like this, "Lord I am going to give this money because I really think you are telling me to. If, on the other hand, I am doing this out of some desire to be super-spiritual, or I am being deceived in some other way, I pray that you would protect me in my foolishness. As far as I know, in my heart, I am doing this now because I think it will please you."

The offering plate came by and in went the check for $1,000. After the service they announced that the amount of the offering had been $170,000—$40,000 more than the church actually needed to retire its mortgage. My friend was right; they hadn't needed his money.

He was sure that the Lord would give him back this $1,000 in some supernatural way so that he could make his mortgage payment on time, but that didn't happen. It took him about three months to catch up on his mortgage payments. (He wasn't violating the law or the terms of his mortgage contract in this situation. He simply had to pay the penalties provided for in his mortgage contract each month until he finally got caught up.) For several months my friend was puzzled by this whole incident. He continued to ask the Lord why he had wanted him to give the money, and why it didn't work out like he thought it should. It would be several months before he received an answer.

Now, you should know that before my friend went to that conference he had been praying for the Lord to speak to him. He had seen a number of prophetic ministers give amazingly accurate words of knowledge about people, and he wanted to be used in that kind of ministry. But every time he tried it, he failed. But not too long after he gave the $1,000, he began to experience specific revelatory words in his own ministry. They came with increasing regularity and accuracy. One day while he was praying, the Lord spoke to him about the whole incident at the conference. The Lord said to him, in effect, "You had been asking me for the ability to hear my voice in specific words of knowledge. I just wanted to see how *badly* you wanted to hear it." My friend was convinced that the whole experience had been a test from the Lord, a test he had passed. Before giving him prophetic words for others, the Lord had wanted my friend to prove he really did want to hear the Lord's voice, even if it cost him financially. The Lord had been testing him to see if his motive in hearing the divine voice was to please the Lord or to be prominent in ministry.

This example may sound strange to you, but certainly it is not any stranger than God sending his Son to be born in a stable and die on a cross. No matter how much Bible knowledge we acquire or how spiritually mature we become, God's thoughts and ways will still be far above ours. And he mainly shares his thoughts with the humble on a need-to-know basis. The proud, no matter how knowledgeable, usually don't penetrate the thoughts and ways of God because they are convinced that they already know them.

God's Voice is Easy to Reject

God's voice is not only different from our voice, but he himself frequently comes to us in ways that make it easy for us to reject him. He comes to us as a baby in a stable, when we were looking for a prince on a white horse. He comes to us in a shadowy dream, when we were looking for a solid text of Scripture. He only lets us prophesy in part and know in part (1 Cor. 13:9), when we want complete understanding.

"Why don't you speak more plainly?" we ask. Would it really do any good if he were to speak more plainly? He has already said much more than most of us want to hear. He commands us very plainly to love our enemies, do good to those who hate us, bless those who curse us, and pray for those who mistreat us (Luke 6:27–28). Who wants to hear these things, let alone obey them? The church can't even stop cursing those who curse us, much less bless them. Why should God speak more plainly to people who ignore his *clearest* commands? Why should he unlock the secrets of his kingdom to a church that seems bent on mutual destruction?

All too frequently our desire for God to speak more plainly is nothing more than our desire for him to lead us into greater comfort or prominence. It is so easy to want to bypass the things that are most important to God to get to the things *we think* are most beneficial to *us*—things that would contribute the most to our temporal happiness and success. We want to set the agenda. And the amazing thing is that God actually comes to us in a way that allows us to set the agenda and at the same time live under the religious illusion that he really is our Master after all. Why does he do this?

FRIENDSHIP—THE KEY TO RECOGNIZING GOD'S VOICE

God comes to us like this because he wants a relationship. But sometimes we only want results. He wants to talk. But we only want him to fix things. It's not that he is against results or minds fixing things. He actually enjoys serving us. But he wants to be more than a servant. He wants to be a friend. Though I fear sometimes we want only a servant.

Real friendships can't be forced. They must be chosen, and then pursued and purged of ulterior motives. Friends share secrets, and understanding of each other grows—so does trust and appreciation. If the friendship deepens, one day you wake up and realize that you love your friend for who they are, not for what they can do for you. In fact, they don't need to do anything for you. Just being with your friend is the highest joy. Yet the truth is that there is nothing you wouldn't do for your friend and nothing your friend wouldn't do for you.

Do you have any friendships like this? If you do, do you remember how they began? Didn't your friend come to you initially in a way that made it easy for you to reject them? At first you may have perceived your friend as a rival and felt threatened by them. Or perhaps, initially, you were just plain bored by your friend. But eventually you saw something in your friend that drew you back to them. You were not forced or manipulated. You chose your friend. If friendship is forced or manipulated, it ceases to be a friendship—the joy leaves and it becomes a burden. Real friendship is love, and love must be given freely or it is not love (Song 8:6–7).

As long as we're primarily interested in our friend for what they can do for us, we'll never have a true friendship. Relationships can begin this way and then develop into true friendship, but until the relationship is purged of our desire to use each other, we'll never have a true friendship. And yet it is our truest friends who will do the most for us. The paradox is that our friendship will never get to that stage unless we are always free to reject one another. The moment we feel coerced into the relationship because of something we need from our friend or something our friend might do to us if we fail them, that is the moment our friendship begins to die.

One of the great mistakes of the church is to offer Jesus to people solely on the same basis that a salesman offers a product to consumers. Come to Jesus—he'll save you from hell, fix your marriage, get your kid off drugs, heal your diseases, take away your depression, make you powerful in word and spirit, give you a good job and a nice house. Jesus certainly saves people from hell, and he can do all the other things too.

It's not wrong to come to Jesus initially for what he can do for us. The problem is that many of us never progress beyond this stage. What if he doesn't fix our marriage or get our kids off drugs? What if he lets us go bankrupt? If our primary interest in Jesus revolves around what he can do for us, then when he "fails" to meet enough of our perceived needs, we'll leave him or become embittered. Many of us in the church can't seem to get past the stage of desiring Jesus for what he can do for us. We are so dazzled by Jesus' ability to provide for us that we can't see the loveliness of his Person. He is infinitely wonderful in himself, worthy to be loved and adored even if he never does a single thing for us.

God gives us opportunities to demonstrate our real desire for Jesus by our attentiveness to his voice when it comes to us at the most inconvenient times, or in the fleeting and vague ways of dreams and impressions, or in "deceptive" ways that cannot be penetrated by the natural eye or ear—a rejected prophet, a baby in a stable, and a Son on a cross are all from God. "Yes, of course they're from God," you say. All Christians believe these things. They are in the Bible.

For years I, too, knew these things. I had even taught about them. Yet I managed to miss one of the major points of the "strange things"—they are *characteristic* of God's dealings with his people. That's why some of God's words, as Ken Gire observes, still "come in the most uncommon of ways that we will react against if we're not accustomed to the unaccustomed ways that God speaks."[4] His highest purposes are still being born in a stable, and he sometimes calls for sacrifices that make no human sense and are beyond our capacity to give.

God makes it easy for us to reject him because he wants us to choose him for himself alone. It is perhaps one of the universe's greatest mysteries that the Son of God *wants* a friendship with us. He will not force himself on us. We must choose him for our friend and then pursue him for the rest of our lives if we want that friendship to grow.

MARTHA OR MARY?

Jesus has a friend who is so important to him that he puts her on display at least three different times in his family picture album. We refer to the album as the gospels, but it's really a series of family pictures chosen by Jesus himself. He even included photos of his family's enemies.

Mary, the little sister of Martha, gets three prominent pages in the family album. She's not a blood relative, but she's a friend closer to Jesus than his own natural brothers or sisters. And each time we see her picture it's always in contrast to another picture, a picture of a behavior Jesus is telling us to avoid. The snapshot I want you to look at now is the most ordinary of the three—a record of a casual, unannounced visit by Jesus to the home of Martha.

> As Jesus and his disciples were on their way, he came to a village where a woman named Martha opened her home to him. She had a sister called Mary, who sat at the Lord's feet listening to what he said. But Martha was distracted by all the preparations that had to be made. She came to him and asked, "Lord, don't you care that my sister has left me to do the work by myself? Tell her to help me!"
>
> "Martha, Martha," the Lord answered, "you are worried and upset about many things, but only one thing

is needed. Mary has chosen what is better, and it will not be taken away from her" (Luke 10:38–42).

The contrast in this snapshot is not between two necessary types of believers. The first time I ever preached this text was to a preaching class when I was a student in seminary. I told my classmates that the story meant we were supposed to study the Bible. I've heard others say the story is about the service-oriented believer versus the contemplative believer, and that we need both types in the body of Christ. Jesus didn't give us this picture to tell us to study the Bible, or to tell us there are two necessary types of saints in the church. He is contrasting the two types of believers, telling us to avoid the one and follow the other.

First, there is Martha. Martha was not simply a "Sunday Christian" whose religion was a private affair, like the religion of so many churchgoers today. She was committed to hospitality and serving God. She opened her home to Jesus and all the disciples on a moment's notice. She could have served him a simple meal, but instead she began preparing a feast.[5] Martha was a "take charge" sort of person who was extravagant in her service to God. Now, you might be thinking, *We could certainly use more Marthas in the church today!* Right? Wrong. The Lord rejected Martha's service. It didn't please him. There's nothing wrong with extravagant service, but there was something wrong *in* Martha which caused her hard work to count for nothing. What was wrong?

Verse 40 says she was distracted. What's so bad about that? Distracted from whom? From the very Person she was serving. Martha allowed her service to Jesus to distract her from *him*. Sometimes our hard work can cause us to lose the very goal for which we are working. Like the mother who works all day Christmas Eve and half the night to prepare a feast for her family and relatives, but she's so tired the next day she can't enjoy the meal or the family. How many times have you heard someone say, "I'm so glad Christmas is over"? Distraction can turn something wonderful into a drudgery. But that's not all it can do. Listen to how Jesus explained it to Martha.

You might think that he was irritated or even angry with her. He wasn't. He was filled with affection for her. He said, "Martha, Martha . . . ." When the Lord repeats your name twice, it means that he loves you very much.[6] It also means he's about to give you a very serious rebuke. According to Jesus, Martha's distraction had very negative results. It led her to worry, which led her to be upset about *many things*. Think about the absurdity of this situation. God was sitting in Martha's living room, and she was worried and upset about many things! His presence was a pressure instead of a pleasure. Jesus was in her home, but Martha was bothered not blessed. That's what distraction does. It makes us oblivious to the presence of God and leads us into a realm of unnecessary turmoil. But those results are just minor in comparison with the other place it led Martha.

Martha asked Jesus, "Lord, don't you care that my sister has left me to do the work by myself? Tell her to help me!" Martha wasn't really asking the Lord a question. She was using a question to express her anger with the Lord. Like the time your little brother asked you, "Why are you so stupid?" He wasn't waiting for an explanation of genetics and heredity. He was expressing his anger toward you. Distraction makes us oblivious to the presence of the Lord. And when we try to serve God without his presence we become angry and bitter with him and his servants. We also try to use the Lord to control others—"Tell her to help me." Distraction can even lead to the arrogance of commanding God.

Martha's anger not only alienated her from God's presence, it put a wall between her and her sister. She was judging Mary, the one with whom the Lord was pleased. Being distracted from the Lord causes us to focus on our service, which then becomes the standard by which we judge the Lord's servants. No, we don't need more Marthas in the church. We don't need *any* Marthas in the church. We need Marys.

Mary was not in the kitchen, serving the Lord. She was in the living room, enjoying him. She was also violating the social conventions of her day. According to custom, she should not have been sitting in the room with all those men. Her place was in the kitchen, making dinner. Then after the men had been served, the women could eat. All of the disciples knew that Mary was out of place. Had she been sitting by Peter, we can be sure that he would have reminded her that she should be with the women. But she wasn't sitting by Peter or by any of the other disciples. She was sitting at the feet of Jesus. And if he was content to let her stay there, none of the others was going to walk over and ask her to leave. Then Martha burst in.

Mary couldn't understand Martha's anger. If she had been the one to answer Martha, she would have probably said something like, "Martha, how could you be in the kitchen when *he's* sitting in our living room. We don't know when he'll come this way again. I don't want to miss a word that he says. I don't want to depend on others to tell me what he said. How could you leave his presence unless he asked you to leave?" It wasn't that Mary was lazy or that she didn't want to serve Jesus. She would have been in the kitchen in a second if that's what he had wanted of her. But he didn't tell her to do that, so there was no way Mary was going to leave her seat at the feet of the Son of God.

Can't you just see Mary staring into the eyes of Jesus and hanging on every word? Can't you hear her heart expressing unspoken words of love to her friend, "Jesus, it means so much to me that you would let me sit next to you and listen to you. It means more to me than anything in the world."

But that's only half the picture. The other half is Jesus looking into the eyes of Mary, and his heart saying to hers, "Mary, it means just as much to me to be with you. And it means even more to me that you want to be here more than anywhere else." How many Christians do you know who would rather do nothing in life than sit at the feet of Jesus and listen to him? When Jesus finds someone like Mary, you can be sure he'll share the intimate details of his heart with that person.

Then Jesus explained to Martha and to all of us the meaning of the picture—". . . only one thing is needed. Mary has chosen what is better, and it will not be taken away from her." The phrase "what is better" is literally "the good part." What did Jesus mean by the good part? Part of what? Part of the feast that was being offered. Martha was offering Jesus a banquet. She didn't really understand that he was the host, the offerer, and the offering. He was the course in the banquet that Martha should have chosen.

Life comes at us like a huge banquet. There are so many wonderful courses to choose—husbands, wives, families, careers, vacations, possessions, friends—the list is endless. Mary looked at the banquet, and she chose the good course, the only necessary course. Out of all the courses only one is necessary. Only one is the key to life. Only one opens the ears to the voice of God. And Mary chose it.

The course she chose was friendship with Jesus. Call it devotion to God or loving God. Call it passion for Christ. It's all the same thing by whatever name. And Mary chose that course. And you and I have to choose it too. Friendship with God is the result of a conscious choice. Not to choose is to reject it. And it's the only necessary course because once we choose it, his friendship will determine the other courses we choose.

One more thing. Friendship with Jesus is the only course on the banquet of life that can't be taken from us. We can lose our mates, our families, our loved ones, our possessions, our health, even our minds in this life. But Jesus will never withdraw his friendship from those who choose him above all the rest.

Going to church, fellowshiping with other Christians, serving God in religious work can all be done outside the presence of God by good people who aren't really friends with Jesus. Just ask Martha.

FRIENDS KNOW FRIENDS

What does friendship have to do with recognizing God's voice? Look at the beginning of the story. What was Mary doing? Sitting at the Lord's feet, the posture of humility, and *listening to what he said*.

Mary is the kind of friend Jesus is seeking. She would rather sit at his feet and listen to him than anything else in the world. She doesn't want *anything* from him other than his presence. Some people want to hear the voice of God in order to be prosperous. Some want to hear so they can be successful in ministry. And some have a much purer motive—they want to hear so they can know the will of God and do it. They want to "find out what pleases the Lord" (Eph. 5:10). But Mary had progressed beyond these motivations and attained to the purist of all motivations. She had become like the Lover in the Song of Songs who called to his Beloved, "My dove in the clefts of the rock, in the hiding places on the mountainside, show me your face, let me hear your voice; for your voice is sweet, and your face is lovely (2:14).

Mary wanted to hear the voice of Jesus because to her it was the sweetest voice in all the world. She wanted to see his face because it was, to her, the most lovely of all faces. She simply wanted Jesus, and Jesus was enough for her. Being with him satisfied every need and every desire she had ever experienced. She was his friend. He was her friend. And Jesus shares his secrets with his friends.

Friendship with God has always been the key to recognizing his voice. Abraham was God's friend.[7] Therefore, when God was about to destroy Sodom where Abraham's nephew, Lot, lived, he asked, "Shall I hide from Abraham what I am about to do?" (Gen. 18:17). God told his friend Abraham about the destruction of Sodom so Abraham could plead for Lot's rescue. Moses was God's friend, and God revealed things to Moses he kept hidden from others (Ex. 33:11ff.).

We recognize the voices of our friends. I don't have a set of complicated rules for recognizing my wife's voice. Why should we think God would allow our friendship with him to be any less personal than our most intimate friendships? He won't allow his friendships to be reduced to a set of formulas or mechanical rules for discerning his voice.

Jesus said to his disciples, "I no longer call you servants, because a servant does not know his master's business. Instead, I have called you friends, for everything that I learned from my Father I have made known to you" (John 15:15). The reward of friendship with Jesus is knowing his Father's "business." Friends can trust each other with their secrets and plans. Of course, no one becomes the friend of Jesus without first becoming his servant. But Jesus wants more than our service. He wants our friendship.

Most Christians say that they too want to be friends with Jesus. They want to hear and recognize his voice. But what I actually find is that most of us are divided. We don't want *only* Jesus. We want Jesus and something else. We want Jesus and a good marriage. Jesus and obedient children. Jesus and a successful career. Jesus and a nice home. Jesus and good friends. None of these desires is wrong. It's just that it is very easy to see Jesus as the means for obtaining these things. It is very easy to desire Jesus as a means to another end, when he himself is the end of all things. This is what hinders friendship with God, and whatever hinders friendship with God, hinders our ability to hear and recognize God's voice.

Those who invest would love to know what the stock market is going to do next year. Those who live in an earthquake zone would love to know when the next major quake will happen in their area. And sometimes God does reveal these things. But the greatest revelation that God has to give is the revelation of his Son.

Jesus said, "Whoever has my commands and obeys them, he is the one who loves me. He who loves me will be loved by my Father, and I too will love him and show myself to him" (John 14:21). Did you catch the last part of that promise—"show myself to him"? Jesus promises his friends not simply a revelation of truth, or a revelation of the truths of the Bible, or even a revelation of the truth about himself. What he promises is a revelation of himself—the type of revelation shared between the closest of friends or the most intimate of lovers. Who wouldn't want to hear the words Mary heard spoken at the Savior's feet? Who wouldn't want to hear Jesus say that we had chosen the best course of the feast of life, the course that could never be taken from us? Who of us wouldn't want a relationship like that? And a revelation like that?

The Word and the Spirit

22

The Power of the Word
and the Spirit

In 1965 Jean Raborg was living the American dream. She had done everything right. She had been raised in a Christian home. Her mother had been the organist at Morningside Presbyterian Church in Phoenix, Arizona. She had married her college sweetheart, John, whom she had met at Arizona State University. Now they were living in San Diego, California. They had two wonderful children, a daughter Jeanelle who was nine years old and a son John who was six.

She was a popular home economics teacher in Kearny Mesa High School. She loved being a teacher, and she loved her students. The students could feel Jean's love and acceptance, and often came to her with their problems. It was common for Jean to pray for her students and even pray *with* them. In 1965 a public school teacher could still pray with her students without fear of losing her job.

Jean's husband had a promising career selling life insurance. He had already won some awards, and they had begun prospering financially. With their combined incomes, they were able to buy a lovely home on a hill in a suburb north of San Diego. They bought new furniture, and with Jean's decorating abilities their home looked like one of those show places out of *Home and Garden*. What more could any young couple want—a beautiful home, fulfilling jobs, a wonderful marriage, sweet children, and all of this in the midst of financial security?

In addition to all of this there was a vital, spiritual dimension to Jean's life. She was more than just a nominal Christian. She had loved Jesus with all of her heart since she was fourteen years old. When she was nineteen, she had an encounter with God that caused her to believe in the gifts of the Holy Spirit. She believed in a God who could do miracles. She and John had joined a church that believed in supernatural ministry. In spite of their work schedules, they were heavily involved in church work. Jean really had it all. She was married to the only man she ever loved. God had given her a wonderful family. She had never known depression or sorrow. She had prosperity and she had intimacy with God. She had a perfect life.

There was only one small problem in her perfect life. Jean was a perfectionist. She didn't know how bad her perfectionism was, and before 1965, it hadn't really caused her too much trouble. But now she found herself with more responsibility than she had ever had before. She was teaching 150 students every day. The more she loved those students, the more she took on their problems and their stresses. She put everything she had into her teaching. Also, the new house was not turning out to be the blessing that she had thought it would be. It was larger and required more effort to keep it clean than the smaller house they had before. There was the added worry about the new furniture—a worry that a nine-year-old girl and a six-year-old boy couldn't really share.

Jean began to come home in the afternoons physically and emotionally drained. It seemed that her own children were beginning to require more from her than she could give. In order to meet her own children's emotional needs, she frequently had to let the house go, and this bothered her. It seemed like it was all she could do to get a meal on the table for John and her children and then clear away the mess afterwards. John himself was burdened down with work he brought home at night. For the first time in her life, Jean began to have a problem sleeping. This didn't make any sense to her because she was so tired when she finally got to bed at night. But now it took her longer to go to sleep, and her sleep was fitful. When she woke up in the morning, she seemed almost as tired as when she went to bed.

Jean began to long for the weekends, not because she could rest, but because this gave her time to get her house in perfect order. And then there was their church. Jean and John were committed to their church. It was difficult for her to say no to the needs there. So instead of allowing herself to be refreshed on the weekends, she usually began Monday even more worn out than she had been on Friday.

As Jean approached exhaustion, she began to realize she could not handle all of her responsibilities—150 students a day, a new home, two children, and work in the church were drowning her. That is what it felt like to her—that she was being drowned very, very slowly. She felt she couldn't cut anything out of her schedule. She and John needed her income so they could live in their new house. And it was impossible for her simply to go to work and not be involved in the emotional lives of her students. She just wasn't that kind of person. And of course no mother could neglect her own children. That was out of the question. And how could she neglect the work of God in the church? No, she thought, it wasn't her schedule. It was something wrong with her.

She started to talk with John about the pressure she was feeling, but then she thought, *How could I worry John when he is already so overworked?* She thought about telling someone at church, but a *voice* went off in her mind telling her that no one should ever know that she can't really handle things—that she should just keep going and everything would be all right. She didn't know where this last impression came from, but she decided to obey it. She talked to no one about her exhaustion and the mounting stress that was drowning her. She decided to just keep going.

Jean did give up something, however. She had always been a lover of God's Word, and it was her daily habit to meditate on it. But she no longer had the energy or the ability to concentrate. For the first time in her Christian life, she stopped having what she called her "time alone with Jesus."

DESCENT INTO MADNESS

By February of 1965, Jean became desperate. She went to her family doctor, and the nurse led her into one of the examining rooms. In a few minutes Dr. Bowers came in. "Hi, Jean. What brings you here today?" the kind physician asked.

"Dr. Bowers, I am so worn out I can hardly put one foot in front of the other. It seems like every Monday morning I get on a big merry-go-round and go to school and take care of the students and do all of this and come home to my two little children and take care of them, and every Friday night I get off the merry-go-round. But when I get off, I try to do everything on the weekend that I have not been able to do all week. So it's like being on another merry-go-round. And then Monday morning comes, and I get on the big merry-go-round again. I just can't do this anymore," she sobbed.

"Jean, you are fatigued, and you are worn out. You are going to have to make some changes in your schedule. As soon as school is out, you are going to have to rest. You are not using the wisdom that God has given you. You are going to have to learn to arrange your priorities and let go of some things." Dr. Bowers gave Jean some medicine that would help her protect her immune system and give her a little more energy. She began to feel better, but she ignored the doctor's advice about rearranging her priorities because she really didn't understand what he meant.

The summer of 1965 came, and Jean closed up the Home Economics department. John had won an all-expense-paid vacation to San Francisco from his life insurance company. This was going to be a wonderful and restful vacation for both of them. On the night Jean was packing for the vacation she felt a sharp pain under her arm. Putting her hand under her left arm, she felt a large hard lump. She collapsed into a chair. A black despair fell over her. She thought of her best friend, Ann, who had died from cancer when she was twenty-eight years old and had left two beautiful little children behind. It had all begun when Ann found a lump just like this one.

Out of the darkness that enveloped Jean, a voice whispered, "You have lost weight, you are tired, you have a lump under your arm, and you have all the other symptoms Ann had. You *have* what Ann had, and it is just a matter of time before you join her." Jean had never known the kind of fear she was feeling now. It was paralyzing. She felt her legs going numb. She couldn't walk. The icy hand of fear gripped her heart and squeezed it so that the hope of the Holy Spirit oozed from her heart and was lying in a little pool on the floor beside her, and she was powerless to reclaim it.

The voice told Jean that she couldn't tell anyone. How could she tell John and ruin what few months they had left together? What good would it do to talk to God about this? After all, hadn't he permitted it? Maybe this was a judgment on her because she was failing so miserably in her responsibility as a wife, a mother, a teacher, and a Christian. No, it was over. There was nothing left except to waste away like Ann had done.

The vacation was a disaster. All Jean could think was, *I am dying. I am leaving these two beautiful children and my precious husband. I am leaving my beautiful home on the hill, and I won't be here to teach next fall.* She kept touching the lump, which seemed to grow every day. As it grew, Jean grew thinner and thinner. When she came back from San Francisco, she was no longer functioning.

Sometime that summer Jean started crying and couldn't stop. John couldn't understand it, and she couldn't tell him. Jean was having a breakdown, but since she had never known anyone who had had a breakdown, she didn't realize what was happening.

Somehow she made it to the end of the summer. Her principal told her she had been made head of the Home Economics department. Instead of causing her to celebrate, the news pushed her to the verge of hysteria.

Jean started teaching again, but she was an emotional wreck. Every time the students left the room, she broke into tears. After a couple of weeks of trying to teach, she went back to see Dr. Bowers. When he came into the examining room, she tried to tell him what was wrong, but all she could do was cry. Finally she raised her arm and pointed to the lump. "What is this?" she asked.

After examining her, Dr. Bowers said, "Jean, why didn't you come in here after you first found this?"

"I was too frightened."

"Well, you should have come in here because I could have alleviated all of your fears. This is not what you think it is. I want to do a complete physical on you, but I am almost certain that this lump is not malignant."

Later, after a complete physical, Dr. Bowers called both Jean and John into his office to give them his diagnosis. He told them that Jean did not have cancer. What she thought was a malignant tumor was nothing more than swollen lymph glands from using the wrong kind of antiperspirant. She was, however, sick and exhausted. Part of her weight loss was due to a problem with her female organs. Dr. Bowers said this could be corrected with minor surgery.

This news should have brought great relief to Jean, but when she heard about the minor surgery, she assumed that both the doctor and her husband were hiding the real facts from her. The voice told Jean that John and Dr. Bowers had conspired not to tell her right away about her cancer because she was so depressed and had been crying so much. In spite of the doctor's assurances, she was more convinced than ever that she had cancer and that the doctor was lying to her to keep her calm until the surgery.

Jean had been so confident and competent that she had never learned to ask for help. She was coming apart piece by piece, but she couldn't ask for help from God or her husband. That night she began to pound on the bedroom wall and cry hysterically. John had never seen Jean act like this. When he couldn't get her to stop, he slammed the front door in anger and escaped to his office.

The pounding on the walls had been Jean's inarticulate cry for help. John took her back to Dr. Bowers, who recommended she take two weeks off from school. Neither John nor the doctor understood the malignant lie that had spread in Jean's soul and the utter hopelessness that had come with it. She took two weeks off to rest, but continued to lose weight.

When she went back to teaching, one of the students in her class asked her where a certain ingredient was. She stared at the student for a minute, and then a blank look came over her face. Slowly the words, "I don't know, I don't know," came out of her mouth. It was as though something had switched off inside her. Everything she had ever known as an adult seemed to leave her, and she became like a little child. She heard herself saying, "I am leaving this room, and I do not think I will ever come back." Without any warning, she began screaming hysterically and ran for the door.

One of the teachers across the hall saw her bolting from the classroom and ran out to intercept her. She threw her arms around Jean, who was sobbing, "It's all over. It's all over." The colleague, Jane, calmed her down and got her into the car. She took her to Dr. Bowers, who immediately called a psychiatrist and made an appointment. By the time John got to the psychiatrist's office two hours later, Jean had still not been able to talk to the psychiatrist. All she could do was sit in his office and cry hysterically. The psychiatrist found that only drugs could calm Jean. He started her on tranquilizers.

Jean could not believe that she, a born-again Christian, had to take tranquilizers. She slid into an abyss of hopelessness. She never went back to the classroom. Her life consisted of tranquilizers and regular visits to the psychiatrist's office. She couldn't clean. She couldn't cook. She couldn't function. Her house meant nothing to her. Everything she had ever wanted meant nothing to her. She spent her days sitting in the livingroom and staring. She couldn't even comb her hair. John got her up in the morning, dressed her, and then combed her hair. He then got the children ready for school and went to work.

Jean thought she would be better off dead. She thought her family would be better off with her dead. These suicidal thoughts increased, and she began attempting to take her own life. Once she tried to jump out of John's car on a busy San Diego freeway. He was barely able to restrain her. The doctor put her on thorazine. John took her to work with him in the morning to keep her from harming herself. But Jean couldn't feel John's love, and the drug didn't really dull her pain. She felt enveloped by a suffocating darkness. She felt mentally, emotionally, and physically dead. The thoughts of suicide were constantly with her.

Jean's parents, Carl and Jesse Williams, were in anguish over their daughter's descent into insanity. Carl and Jesse had a vibrant faith in Christ and believed in his power to heal. Carl was the international treasurer for the Full Gospel Businessmen's Fellowship. He traveled a good deal with Demas Shekarian, its president, and had occasion to meet a number of well-known Christian evangelists. He and Jesse began to take Jean to all sorts of crusades and Christian meetings in order to have pastors and evangelists pray for her healing. Many of the most famous healing evangelists of the 1950s and 1960s prayed for Jean to be healed during this time, but nothing happened. She grew worse.

The American dream had unraveled fast for John and Jean Raborg. John had to hire a housekeeper to take care of his children *and* his wife. Jean's medical and psychiatric bills eroded their savings. She ran up thousands of dollars of phone bills calling her parents without John's knowledge. They no longer had Jean's income from teaching to help defray their expenses. They were headed for bankruptcy.

By February 1966, Jean simply couldn't function as an adult. John did everything for her. Her daughter Jeanelle, now eleven, had become the mother of the home. John had planned a birthday celebration for Jean the night of February twenty-second, after her appointment with the psychiatrist. When John came home from work to take her to the psychiatrist, Jean announced she was never going to see the psychiatrist again and that she was never going to take another thorazine tablet. John was in despair. He pleaded with her to go to the psychiatrist, "Jean," he said, "all of our friends have abandoned us. Our pastor never comes to see us. We have no one else to go to. Everyone has prayed for you, but it hasn't done any good. The doctor is our only hope." Finally, he persuaded her to keep her appointment. Dr. Dickson, her psychiatrist, asked Jean if she had been taking her medicine. She made the mistake of telling him that not only had she not been taking her medicine, but that she was never going to take it again. The psychiatrist promptly replied, "Then we will put you where you will take it." In spite of her protests, Jean found herself, on her thirty-sixth birthday, standing before the Mesa Vista Psychiatric Hospital.

The building was not at all what she had imagined. She found it physically beautiful. She thought, *Perhaps I can get some rest here after all.* The lobby was attractively furnished, and all the personnel seemed so kind and caring. She and John signed all the admittance forms. A nurse took them through a door, and they began to walk down a long corridor. The warmth she had felt in the lobby disappeared. They came to a stark metal door that had one small window in it. They walked through the door, and when it slammed shut, it automatically locked. Jean was on one side with a nurse, and she saw John on the other side through the little window. She had gone into the Intensive Care Unit.

Some patients were sitting in a corner watching television. Others were pacing back and forth, oblivious to their surroundings. Some simply sat motionless, staring into space. Then she heard screaming. Jean saw a patient tied down on a gurney, being taken to shock therapy. She called out for John, but he was not there. She called out to God, but he didn't seem to be there either. The attendants gave Jean an institutional nightgown and took all of her personal belongings, with the exception of her Bible. They led her into her new room. She stood there, stunned. The windows were barred. She was utterly alone. She stood in one spot and cried for two solid hours without moving. She was given more thorazine, and she slipped off into mental oblivion.

No matter what kind of therapy they tried on Jean, she didn't respond. She spent her waking hours in a daze. She began to want to sleep all the time. At four in the afternoon she would go to her bed and curl up in a fetal position. In the mornings, a nurse had to make her get out of bed.

A few times she seemed to come back from the darkness and pretend she was feeling better. On these occasions they let her go home for a visit. But when she got home, she would wander through her house from one bed to another, trying to sleep, but she couldn't. Her doctor would not allow sleeping pills at home because of her suicidal tendencies. Soon her visit at home would be over, and she would be back in the psychiatric institution. At least she could get the drugs there that allowed her to sleep.

John kept hoping that Jean would regain her sanity, but everyone else knew that she was not coming back home. Their children had given up hope. Her parents had given up hope. And Jean herself had given up hope a long time ago.

Jean knew she would never leave her prison again. The voice had come to her in her darkness and asked a simple question, *How could a Christian who loves God and believes in his supernatural power end up so far away from him in an insane asylum?* Then the dark voice had suggested the answer, *You have committed the unpardonable sin. You have blasphemed the Holy Spirit. You can never be forgiven. This is your judgment.* Jean believed the voice.

THE POWER OF THE SPIRIT

In October of 1968 Carl and Jesse Williams traveled to San Bernardino to hear a healing evangelist named Paul Cain. On the last night of the meeting Jesse stood up and asked Paul if he would pray for her daughter, who was locked away in a mental institution. Paul agreed and prayed for Jean. After the meeting Paul asked the Williams where their daughter had been institutionalized. They told Paul that the hospital was somewhere in the San Diego area, but they did not know its name or precise location. John had refused to tell Jean's parents where she had been institutionalized. Although his relationship to Jean's parents was extremely strained by now, he hadn't done this out of meanness, but rather out of despair. Almost every attempt by Christians to minister to Jean had not only not helped but had aggravated her condition. Each prayer for her healing had brought some hope and then bitter disappointment. In the end, both the institution and John agreed that Jean would be better off if she were totally isolated. John had cut off all contact between Jean and the outside world, except with himself. Paul told the Williams that he would continue to pray for their daughter.

Paul walked out of the meeting at midnight and went to his car. After two continuous weeks of meetings he was dead tired. On top of that he had a severe sinus infection. Paul thought it was ironic that the Lord had used him to heal various people over the last two weeks while he himself remained sick. He put the key in the ignition, but before he turned it he prayed one more time for Jean Raborg. As he prayed, he began to feel the compassion of Jesus for Jean. What started as a simple prayer became a torrent of words and emotions as he petitioned the Lord to deliver Jean from her madness. He wept as he felt the heart of Christ for her. As he was weeping, he looked up to heaven and the night sky turned into a giant television screen. On the screen, Paul saw Jean in the psychiatric hospital, and he saw things about her life before she went to the hospital. Then God spoke. It wasn't audible, but it couldn't have been any clearer if it had been audible. These sentences formed in Paul's mind: *If you will go to San Diego and pray for this woman, she will be instantly healed to my glory. And I will use this testimony to the end of her life to encourage women with hope.*

The next morning Paul drove to San Diego. He felt impressed to pull off the freeway at a certain exit in San Diego. He walked up to a pay phone without knowing Jean Raborg was just two blocks away at the Mesa Vista Psychiatric Hospital. The Williams had given Paul John Raborg's office and home phone numbers. First Paul called the office, but no one could find John. Then he called the home. Jean's daughter, Jeanelle, now twelve years old, answered the phone. Paul asked Jeanelle to give him the name of the hospital where Jean had been committed. Jeanelle replied, "I am very sorry, sir, but I cannot give you the name of the hospital. No one is allowed to see my mother but my dad."

"Jeanelle," Paul said, "I don't want you to disobey your father, but I would like you to stay on the phone for just a minute longer. You see, the Lord sent me here to help your mother. I am going to pray now. Please stay on the line. I believe the Lord will help me find your mother." Paul prayed, and in a few seconds he

saw the giant television screen again. This time he saw a San
Diego newspaper with a headline that read, "Mesa Vista."

"Jeanelle, I believe the Lord has shown me that your mother
is at Mesa Vista. I just need you to confirm this for me. Does that
name mean anything to you?"

"That's it, sir. That's it. The Mesa Vista Psychiatric Hospital."

"Thank you, Jeanelle. Honey, I know it has been a long,
weary road for you and your family. You have had to be so strong
while your mother has been so sick. I want you to know that God
is going to heal your mother, and she will be home in three days.
And when she comes home, she is going to be well and full of joy.
Good-bye."

Jeanelle put the phone down. How many times had she
heard people promise that her mother was going to be healed and
every time those promises had failed? But this time it was different. There was something different about that man's voice. And
how could he have gotten the name Mesa Vista?

Paul walked through the warm lobby of Mesa Vista Psychiatric Hospital and found the receptionist. "Hello, my name is
Paul Cain. I am a minister, and I'm here to see Jean Raborg." The
receptionist turned to look up Jean's room number. Next to Jean's
name were the orders, "To see *no one* but her husband." But
instead of forbidding Paul to see Jean, she inexplicably led him
down that long corridor and unlocked the door for him. Paul
walked straight to the nurse's station and asked for Jean Raborg.
She was in occupational therapy. For Jean, "occupational therapy" meant that she was folding bulk mail and stuffing
envelopes. This was the only thing they had found that she could
do. The rest of the day she simply wandered around in a thorazine daze. Jean heard her name called over the loud speaker
and shuffled toward the nurse's station. When she turned the corner, she saw Paul standing about fifty feet away at the nurse's station. *Dear God*, she thought, *who is that man? He looks just like an
angel. I see your glory coming from him. Oh, I wish someone like that
would come to visit me.*

"Jean, this man is here to see you," said the nurse. The two
walked to her room and sat down.

"Jean, my name is Paul Cain. You don't know me, but I know
you. What I am going to say to you now is going to be difficult for
you to understand. Jesus has sent me here because he loves you

and because he is going to heal you. I am going to pray for you today, and he will heal you, and you will be home in three days."

Before Paul had walked into the hospital, he had seen Jean's drugged condition and asked the Lord to grant her a clear mind while he talked to her. Now, when Paul told Jean that she was going to be healed, she felt there was something different about this promise than all the others.

"Before I pray for you, I want to tell you some things that will help you understand that God really has sent me for you. I can only stay a few minutes, and then I have to be on my way to Dallas. The first thing Jesus told me to tell you is that you have never committed the unpardonable sin, and he knows that you love him with all your heart."

Jean thought she was going to burst. "Oh, I do love him, I do love him—I love Jesus with all my heart!" she exclaimed.

"The Lord told me to remind you of something that happened when you were fourteen years old, Jean. You were in a summer camp in Oregon, and after a service one evening you threw a pinecone into the fire, and you asked the Lord Jesus to come into your heart, and you asked him to make you a missionary."

"Yes, sir! Yes, sir! But how could you have possibly known that?"

"I didn't know that, Jean. The Lord showed it to me, and he says he is about to make you a missionary, but not the way you thought."

Paul abruptly stopped speaking. He closed his eyes for a moment and then said, "Jean, I am having a vision right now. I see a man standing in an airline uniform, and he is a pilot. He is a friend of yours, a neighbor of yours. His wife's name is Pat. What's his name?"

"His name is Allan Lindemann. He is a captain for PSA in San Diego. He lives right across the street from us in University City."

Paul said, "You also have a neighbor named Marion?"

"Yes."

"In the future you are going to tell Pat and Marion what the Lord has done for you, and it will change their lives. I am having a vision of Allan dressed in his airline uniform, and you are giving him your testimony. He is going to believe in Christ through your testimony. Now let me pray for you."

When Paul prayed for Jean, she felt as if a giant heating pad had been put over her abdomen. Then she had a sensation of hot oil being poured over her and penetrating every fiber of her body. At the same time, she felt a cloud of oppression lift off of her. It was as though the Lord had turned on a faucet of joy inside her. "I'm healed!" she exclaimed.

"No, not yet, not quite yet," Paul said. "When I leave here, the madness is going to try to return. God is going to put a Scripture in your heart when I walk out of this door. That Scripture is going to seal your healing. When the evil voice returns to you, don't listen to it. Instead say, 'It is written,' and then quote whatever Scripture the Lord deposits in your heart when I leave. Quote that Scripture. The Spirit and the Word will heal you and will keep you healed, Jean. You will be home in three days, and you will be filled with joy. Good-bye. I will be praying for you."

THE POWER OF THE WORD

When Paul walked out of the door, Jean picked up her Bible. She tried to focus on the pages, but she couldn't yet read them—there was still too much thorazine in her system. Her mind began to cloud again. She could feel a numbness descending from her head. She put the Bible down, and she walked out of her door into a large rotunda where patients were permitted to walk. As she walked, a passage from the Old Testament came into her mind, Isaiah 41:10 (KJV): "Fear thou not; for I *am* with thee: be not dismayed; for I am thy God: I will strengthen thee; yea, I will help thee; yea, I will uphold thee with the right hand of my righteousness" At just that moment she felt an icy hand reach out of the darkness and grip her heart. She heard that evil voice begin to whisper, but instead of listening to it, she cried out, "IT IS WRITTEN—'FEAR THOU NOT; FOR I *AM* WITH THEE: BE NOT DISMAYED; FOR I AM THY GOD: I WILL STRENGTHEN THEE; YEA, I WILL HELP THEE; YEA, I WILL UPHOLD THEE WITH THE RIGHT HAND OF MY RIGHTEOUSNESS.'" The icy hand let go. The evil voice stopped. She quoted the Word again, and again, and again. Each time she felt the strength of God pouring into her body.

The next morning when her psychiatrist, Dr. Appleford, came to see her, he said, "Jean, what has happened to you? Why aren't you crying? Where did that smile come from? I have never seen anyone in all my practice snap out of depression overnight." Jean told him the story of what had happened when Paul visited her the day before. When Jean finished, her psychiatrist said, "Although I am a church member, I have never believed in miracles, but what I see before my very eyes is changing my mind. I am going to have you observed for a couple of days, and then I will make another evaluation." On the third day, a bright, sunny October morning in 1968, Jean Raborg walked out of that mental institution, never to return again.

John took her home to their new place, a small apartment. They had lost their beautiful home on the hill. They had lost their savings. But it didn't matter. None of their "stuff" had been able to give them joy or to protect them from the evil one. Now they had found the mercy of God. Or rather, the mercy of God had found them. His Word and His Spirit had set them free and given them back their lives with more depth and power than they could have imagined before Jean's descent into madness. Since they now lived in a poorer section of town, they didn't see their old neighbors anymore. But a few months later, she returned to a Bible study group in her old neighborhood to give her testimony of God's deliverance. Pat and Marion were profoundly impacted, just as Paul Cain had prophesied.

But Jean never got to talk with Allan Lindemann.

Soon after Jean's healing, the Raborg family moved from San Diego to Phoenix. Thirteen years after Jean's healing she was invited to come to Salt Lake City to share her testimony with a women's group. Jean flew from Phoenix to San Diego to meet her daughter Jeanelle, who was going to accompany her to Salt Lake City. In San Diego they boarded a PSA flight for Salt Lake City.

"Mom," said Jeanelle, "I wonder if Allan Lindemann could be flying this plane?"

"Oh, honey, I am sure he is retired by now." But to satisfy her daughter's curiosity, Jean asked the stewardess who the captain of the plane was that day.

The stewardess said, "His name is Captain Allan Lindemann."

Jean couldn't believe it. She sent Allan a message that she and Jeanelle were on the plane. The stewardess brought back a note from Allan, who asked if they would have coffee with him in Salt Lake City.

Normally Allan did not fly to Salt Lake City. His usual route was San Diego to San Francisco. He was filling in for another pilot on this day. At least this was the human reason for why he found himself in Salt Lake City in December, 1981. The real reason he was in Salt Lake City had been decreed by God and made known years ago in a mental institution. God was about to fulfill the vision Paul Cain had seen when Jean was healed.

At the airport restaurant Allan asked Jean what she was doing in Salt Lake City. "I am here to share the testimony of my healing," Jean said.

"Oh yes, I remember that prophet fellow had a vision of Pat when you were healed."

"That's right, Allan, but he just didn't see Pat in the vision, he saw you too."

"Really?"

"Yes, he saw me talking to you while you were in your uniform. That is how he knew that you were an airline pilot."

"That's amazing."

"Yes, it is amazing. It shows you how much God loves you, Allan, and how well he knows you."

From there Jean began to share the Gospel with him. Allan's eyes filled with tears. For the first time he understood that Jesus took his place on the cross and paid for all of his sins. That day, Allan Lindemann trusted in the Lord Jesus Christ to save him from his sins. He was born again right before Jean's eyes. "Allan, this is just like Paul said it would be in the vision he saw of you," Jean said. "You were wearing your uniform. You heard my testimony and the Gospel of the Lord Jesus and became born again."

Allan continued to cry. Finally he said, "What you don't know, Jean, is that this is the last day I will ever wear this uniform. I am retiring today. In just a little while I am flying home to San Diego, and I will take off this uniform forever."

The power of the Word *and* the Spirit saved Allan Lindemann and delivered Jean Raborg from the asylum.

A COSTLY DIVORCE

No one in the New Testament church would have regarded the above story as a unique, isolated event. They were used to seeing the power of the Word and the Spirit working together.

Somewhere along the way, though, the church has encouraged a silent divorce between the Word and the Spirit. Divorces are painful, both for the children and the parents. One parent usually gets custody of the children, and the other only gets to visit occasionally. It breaks the hearts of the parents, and the children are usually worse off because of the arrangement. Many in the church today are content to live with only one parent. They live with the Word, and the Spirit only has limited visiting rights. He just gets to see and touch the kids once in a while. Some of his kids don't even recognize him anymore. Some have become afraid of him. Others in the church live with the Spirit and only allow the Word sporadic visits. The Spirit doesn't want to raise the kids without the Word. He can see how unruly they're becoming, but he won't force them to do what they must choose with their hearts.

So the church has become a divided family growing up with separate parents. One set of kids is proud of their education, and the other set of kids is proud of their freedom. Both think they're better than the other.

The parents are brokenhearted. Because unlike most divorces, they didn't choose this divorce. Their kids did. And the Word and the Spirit have had to both honor and endure that choice.

In the meantime, how many more Jean Raborgs are languishing in asylums, waiting for the children to bring the parents together again?

Notes

Chapter 1: Surprised by the Voice of God

1. Cf. Romans 15:13, "May the God of hope fill you with all joy and peace as you trust in him, so that you may overflow with hope by the power of the Holy Spirit."

Chapter 2: The Problem of the Unreal Bible

1. Note that although James began by saying that the elders ought to pray for the sick, he concluded with an admonition to the *whole church*: "Therefore confess your sins to each other and pray for each other so that you may be healed" (James 5:16a). The whole church is to be involved in praying for the sick, not just the elders.
2. Dallas Willard, *In Search of Guidance* (San Francisco: Harper, 1984, rev. ed. 1993), 27.

Chapter 3: Jesus and the Voice of God

1. You can read more about James Robison's life and ministry in his exciting book *Thank God, I'm Free* (Thomas Nelson: Nashville, TN, 1988).
2. God gave prophetic words before the birth of the following children; Ishmael (Gen. 16:7–15), Isaac (Gen. 17:15ff.), Jacob and Esau (Gen. 25:21–26), Samson (Judg. 13:2ff.), Josiah (1 Kings 13:2), John the Baptist (Luke 1:11–20), and of course, Jesus (Matt. 1; Luke 1). Often, the very naming of children in the Old Testament was viewed as a prophetic word. The name of a child frequently signified an act of God or the role the child would play in God's kingdom. For example, the name "Saul" means "the one asked for." Saul was Israel's first king, the one the people *asked for* when they rejected God's kingship.
3. All these stories are found in Matthew 1–2 and Luke 1–2.
4. The references for the Virgin Birth (Matt. 1:22; Isa. 7:14); for the birth in Bethlehem (Matt. 2:4–6; Mic. 5:2); for the persecution of the Messiah (Ps. 22; Isa. 52:13–53:12); and the Egyptian sojourn (Matt. 2:15; Hos. 11:1).

5. I owe this insight to Frederick Buechner, who writes that God "comes in such a way that we can always turn him down" (*The Hungering Dark* [San Francisco: Harper, 1969], 14).

6. When the residents of Jesus' hometown referred to him as "Mary's son" (Mark 6:3), they were probably implying he was illegitimate. The normal custom would have been to refer to him as "Joseph's son." See W. L. Lane, *The Gospel According to Mark* (Grand Rapids: Eerdmans, 1974), 202–03. The religious leaders of Jerusalem also explicitly accuse him of being illegitimate in John 8:41.

7. Some theologians use the "kenosis" theory to explain the relationship of the humanity and deity of Jesus. Kenosis comes from the Greek verb *kenoo*—which means "to empty" or "to divest." Paul used it to describe the incarnation of Jesus in Philippians 2:7 (NASB), "but [he] *emptied* Himself, taking the form of a bond-servant, *and* being made in the likeness of men." Professor Gerald Hawthorne describes the kenosis like this:

> " . . . in becoming a human being, the Son of God willed to renounce the exercise of his divine powers, attributes, prerogatives, so that he might live fully within those limitations which inhere in being truly human.
>
> Divine attributes, including those of omniscience, omnipotence, and omnipresence, are not to be thought of as being laid aside when the eternal Son became human but rather thought of as becoming potential or latent within this incarnate One—present in Jesus in all their fullness, but no longer in exercise. Knowledge of who he was and of what his mission in life was to be were given to him as he developed by revelation and intuition, especially at times of crisis in his life, and during times of prayer and communion with his Heavenly Father" (*The Presence and the Power* [Word: Dallas, 1991], 208–9).

See also Roger Helland, "The Hypostatic Union: How Did Jesus Function?" *The Evangelical Quarterly* 65 (1993): 311:27, for a similar explanation.

Some of the earlier exponents of the kenosis theory actually claimed that Jesus *gave up* his divine attributes. This would mean that he ceased to be divine. This version of the theory contradicts the biblical teaching that the "fullness of deity lives in bodily form" in Jesus (Col. 2:9). Neither Hawthorne nor Helland are saying that he gave up his divine attributes, but that he voluntarily surrendered the use of them.

Professor Wayne Grudem rejects all forms of the kenosis theory. He raises an important question. How could Jesus have given up the use of his omnipotence and still have carried along all things by the word of his power (Heb. 1:3) or held the universe together by his own power (Col. 1:17)? For Grudem the answer lies in the Chalcedonian definition of the relationship of Christ's deity and humanity. The council of church leaders who met at Chalcedon in A.D. 451 issued a statement that Jesus was fully God and fully man—two natures, unmixed, in one Person. Grudem argues that even as a baby, Jesus was able to hold the world together and carry along all things by the word of his power because his deity was not limited by his humanity. In other words, becoming human did not necessarily require the Son of God to surrender the use of any of his divine attributes. For a fuller explanation see Wayne Grudem, *Systematic Theology* (Grand Rapids: Zondervan, 1994), 549–63.

It would be good for us to pause here and remind ourselves that we are walking on the holiest ground in Scripture, the incarnation of the Son of God. It is one of the most amazing mysteries in the universe. It is a mystery God was content to describe with metaphors like "overshadowed" (Luke 1:35) and "emptied" (Phil. 2:7). So none of us should be too confident in our abilities to explain all the details of this great event.

One thing is for sure. In becoming human, Jesus did allow his glory to be veiled while on earth and subjected himself to limitations he did not experience in his heavenly state. Both Grudem and Hawthorne agree that Jesus in his humanity is the model for our ministries as well as our moral lives. Both agree that in his humanity he depended on the power of the Holy Spirit to hear God and work miracles.

8. It is possible to argue that some of the miracles of Jesus were done out of his own deity. For example, when he turned the water into wine, John wrote, "He thus revealed his glory" (John 2:11). But even if this were so, the vast majority of Jesus' miracles are attributed to the power of the Holy Spirit or the Father working through Jesus' humanity. This is the testimony of Jesus (John 5:19) and the apostles (Acts 10:38).

9. Professor Hawthorne points out that even in the miracles of Jesus where the Holy Spirit is not mentioned explicitly, the references to the *authority* and *power* of Jesus reveal the conviction of the New Testament authors that Jesus is a prophet who is the bearer of the Spirit and consequently lives "in the environment of the Spirit" (Hawthorne, *The Presence and the Power*, 114).

10. Hawthorne, *The Presence and the Power*, 238.

Chapter 4: The New Testament Church and the Voice of God

1. Ezekiel 37:9, 14; John 3:8.

2. The Greek word translated "addressed" in 2:14, *apopheggomai*, is used in secular Greek to indicate a speech that was inspired by a god. See BAGD, 102.

3. See Gerald F. Hawthorne, *Philippians, Word Biblical Commentary Volume 43* (Waco, Texas: Word, 1983), 156–157 for a discussion of this passage. Also, see Peter T. O'Brien, *The Epistle to the Philippians, A Commentary on the Greek Text* (Grand Rapids: Eerdmans, 1991), 438–40 for a discussion on the meaning of the verb "to reveal."

4. There are three different expressions in Luke and Acts for the filling of the Spirit. The construction used in Acts 4:8, *pimplemi pneumatos agiou*, occurs eight times in the two books. It always refers to the Holy Spirit's empowering of individuals to give prophetic testimony to Jesus. Frequently this

prophetic testimony is in the face of a hostile audience. The references are Luke 1:15 with 1:41–44; 1:67ff.; Acts 2:4ff.; 4:8; 4:31; 9:17ff.; and 13:9.

5. For example, in the book of Acts, Luke never explicitly tells his readers that prayer is important. However, he emphasizes the importance of prayer again and again by telling us stories in which prayer is the key to the release of God's power. Prayer is mentioned explicitly or implicitly in eighteen of the twenty-eight chapters. In chapter 10 it is mentioned six times if you count the reference in verse 3 to the "ninth hour," which was the hour of prayer. The repetition of all these stories concerning prayer is meant to show us the power of prayer in all of life's experiences.

6. See John 14:26; 15:26; 16:13.

7. Acts 2:14–21.

8. Acts 11:16.

9. Acts 4:8–12.

10. Acts 5:1–11.

11. Stephen (6:8–7:60), Philip (8:5–13, 26–40), Agabus (11:27–30; 21:11), Ananias (9:10–19), and unnamed persons (4:29–31; 13:2; 19:6).

12. Some have argued that the gospels and Acts are simply *descriptions* of what happened, not *prescriptions* for how we ought to live. According to this view the historical books of the New Testament have more in common with modern newspaper accounts than with inspired theological works. The weakness of this argument becomes apparent when we ask ourselves why the Holy Spirit led the New Testament authors to describe certain events and pass over others entirely. Did the New Testament authors tell us stories in order to satisfy our curiosity or to change our behavior? No Scripture is merely descriptive. All of the examples of the Bible are meant to instruct us in godly living (1 Cor. 10:6; 2 Tim. 3:16–17). I have dealt with this objection more fully in *Surprised by the Power of the Spirit* (Grand Rapids: Zondervan, 1993), 111–14.

13. If the word "abnormal" seems too strong, substitute a word like "unusual." My point is still the same—we are making a comparison between inspired Scripture and our experience.

14. Both their stories are told in Acts 12.

Chapter 5: Presbyterian Prophets?

1. Someone might argue that his "misses" wouldn't produce good fruit. However, unlike the false prophets of the Old Testament, my prophetic friend admits his mistakes publicly and makes restitution for any wrongs he has caused. Good fruit usually follows our sincere repentance.

2. Deuteronomy 18:15–22 is frequently understood as referring to a succession of the prophets from Moses onward who would never make a mistake in their predictions. Several contextual factors militate against this interpretation. First, Moses did not say that God would raise up a line of prophets, but rather *a prophet* (v. 15). Second, Moses claimed that this future prophet would be *like me* (v. 15). Moses was not simply a prophet who foretold the future. He was the theocratic founder of Israel's religion

and the mediator of the Old Covenant. The qualifying phrase "like me" leads us to expect someone who is also a covenant mediator. Third, the epilogue to Deuteronomy, chapter 34, which was written in the time of Joshua or later, specifically states:

> Since then, no prophet has risen in Israel like Moses, whom the LORD knew face to face, who did all those miraculous signs and wonders the LORD sent him to do in Egypt—to Pharaoh and to all his officials and to his whole land. For no one has ever shown the mighty power or performed the awesome deeds that Moses did in the sight of all Israel (Deut. 34:10–12).

This means that not even Joshua was on a par with Moses, even though God promised to be with him as he was with Moses (Josh. 1:5). The significance of Deuteronomy 34:10–12, according to Patrick Miller, is that "one can hardly see 18:15–22 in terms of a continuing line of prophets through Israel's history. The only way to resolve the tension between chapters 18 and 34 is to project *into the future* the announcement that God will raise up a prophet ..." (*Deuteronomy* [Louisville: John Knox Press, 1990], 156–57; author's emphasis). Fourth, this was how the passage was interpreted in Judaism (see Peter C. Craigie, *The Book of Deuteronomy* [Grand Rapids: Eerdmans, 1976], 263, n.20). Fifth, in the New Testament both the Jews and the apostles understood this passage to refer not to a line of prophets, but to the Messiah (John 1:21, 25; 6:14; 7:40; Acts 3:22–26). Thus the context and later biblical interpretation favor the messianic interpretation of Deuteronomy 18:15.

If that is the case, then the false prophets mentioned in 18:20–22 may not be prophets who simply make a mistake, but rather pretenders to the place of Moses or to the messianic role. At any rate, Craigie cautions us against an inflexible application of 18:20–22. He writes,

> It would probably be wrong to take these criteria as rules to be applied rigidly every time a prophet opened his mouth. When a prophet announced God's coming judgment and called for repentance, it would clearly be pointless to wait first to see if the judgment actually came to pass, and then to repent (too late!). Rather the criteria represent the means by which a prophet gained his reputation as a true prophet and spokesman of the Lord. Over the course of a prophet's ministry, in matters important and less significant, the character of a prophet as a true spokesman of God would begin to emerge clearly. And equally, false prophets would be discredited and then dealt with under the law (*Deuteronomy*, 263).

Furthermore, there is no evidence in Israel's history that they ever put to death a prophet for a simple mistake in a prophetic utterance. For example, when David implied to Nathan that he wanted to build a temple for the Lord, Nathan said to him, "Whatever you have in mind, go ahead and do it, for the LORD is with you" (2 Sam. 7:3). But Nathan was wrong and later that night had to be corrected by the Lord (2 Sam. 7:4ff.).

If someone pedantically objects that Nathan did not preface his first prophecy with "Thus says the LORD ...," it should be noted that Nathan did speak in the name of the Lord, for he said, "the LORD is with you." Besides, would David have spoken to the prophet simply to obtain the prophet's human opinion? Why did people consult prophets in the Old Testament if not to receive a word from God? Nathan gave a wrong word, but he was not put to death. A wrong word was not automatically classified as a presumptuous word or a word in the name of false gods (Deut. 18:20–22).

3. For examples of prophets and miracle workers in every century see Paul Thigpen, "Did the Power of the Spirit Ever Leave the Church?" *Charisma*, (Sept. 1992): 20–29.

4. John Knox, *History of the Reformation*, vol. 1, ed. William Croft Dickinson (New York: Philosophical Library, 1950), 60.

5. *Dictionary of Scottish Church History and Theology*, ed. Nigel M. de S. Cameron (Edinburgh: T. & T. Clark, 1993), 65–66.

6. *Scots Worthies*, John Howie, ed. William McGavin (Glasgow: W.R. McPhun, 1846; orig. ed. 1775), contains a short biography of Wishart (pp. 27–38), as well as Knox's *History* (pp. 60ff.), from which the account above is drawn. In several quotations throughout this chapter I have taken the liberty of removing the Scotticisms as well as modernizing the spelling and grammar.

7. *Scots Worthies*, 28.

8. Jasper Ridley, *John Knox* (Oxford: Clarendon Press, 1968), 504. Ridley wrote, "The stories about Knox's prophetic powers, showing how his prophecies came true, were also circulated within a very few years of his death by Smeton, and were later repeated and elaborated by James Melville and many other Scottish Protestant writers" (ibid., 526).

9. *Scots Worthies*, 63; also *John Knox*, Jasper Ridley (Oxford: Clarendon Press, 1968), 517, 519

10. Ridley, *John Knox*, 519.

11. Robert Fleming, *The Fulfilling of the Scripture* (Rotterdam: no pub., 1671; orig. ed. 1669), 424.

12. John Howie, *The Scots Worthies*, ed. W. H. Carslaw (Edinburgh: Oliphant, Anderson and Ferrier, 1902; orig. ed. 1775), 120.

13. Ibid., 122.

14. Ibid., 121.

15. Ibid., 123, 131.

16. Ibid., 130.

17. Ibid., 124–25.

18. Ibid., 131.

19. Ibid., 132–33.

20. The term "Covenanter" refers to those who signed or supported the National Covenant (1638) and the Solemn League and Covenant (1643). These Scottish documents promoted Reformed theology and the spiritual independence of the church under the sole leadership of Jesus Christ. Generally the covenanters can be identified with Presbyterian theology and church polity. In addition to the works already cited by Knox, Howie,

and Fleming, see also Patrick Walker, *Six Saints of the Covenant*, 2 vols., ed. D. Hay Fleming (London: Hodder & Stoughton, 1901; orig. ed. 1724–32); and Alexander Smellie, *Men of the Covenant* (London: Banner of Truth Trust, 1960; orig. ed. 1903).

21. *Dictionary of Scottish Church History and Theology*, 104.
22. Fleming, 430.
23. Ibid., 431.
24. Ibid., 416, 418, 419, 432, 437–40.
25. Thomas Cameron, *Peden the Prophet*, (Edinburgh: James A. Dickson, 1981 reprint), 5. His story is also told by Alexander Smellie in his famous book, *Men of the Covenant* (London: Andrew Melrose, 1905; orig. 1903), 377–89; see also 331–35 for Peden's prophecy regarding John Brown. *Scots Worthies*, 502–15, also contains a brief account of his life. The fullest account is given by Patrick Walker, *Six Saints of the Covenant*, 2 vols. (London: Hodder & Stoughton, 1901; orig. 1724–32), 1:45–178; 2:119–55.
26. *Scots Worthies*, McGavin ed., 507.
27. *Men of the Covenant*, 1905 ed., 332.
28. *Scots Worthies*, 443–46.
29. *Men of the Covenant*, 1905 ed., 334–35.

Chapter 6: A Conspiracy Against the Supernatural

1. John Howie, *Scots Worthies*, ed. William McGavin (Glasgow: W. R. McPhun, 1846), 27.
2. Ibid., p. 27, footnote.
3. Ibid.
4. Patrick Walker (c. 1666–1745) was himself a Covenanter who was imprisoned and tortured for his faith. In 1724, Walker published the *Life of Alexander Peden*. Eventually, this work was combined with the biographies of five other Scottish Covenanters and published under the title *Six Saints of the Covenant*. The edition I have was edited by D. H. Fleming and published by Hodder and Stoughton of London in 1901. Before Walker wrote Peden's biography, he traveled over a thousand miles in Scotland and Ireland between the years 1722–1723, collecting facts about Peden's life. Walker was not an educated man, a fact betrayed by his grammar and style. He came under heavy criticism by a contemporary historian, Robert Wodrow (1679–1734). The attacks against Walker's accuracy were likely prompted by his poor style and his sometimes bombastic criticism of the established church rather than by real historical errors in his work. Walker's historical accuracy has stood the test of time. D. H. Fleming, who wrote the introduction to the 1901 edition of Walker's work, claimed "that a number of his marvelous stories can be corroborated from other works, some of which he never saw. His quotations are fairly accurate, and his dates are on the whole amazingly correct" (ibid., xxix). See also the positive evaluation by D. C. Lachman, *Dictionary of Scottish Church History and Theology*, ed. Nigel M. de S. Cameron (Edinburgh: T. & T. Clark, 1993), 851–52.
5. C. S. Lewis, *Miracles* (New York: Macmillan, 1978; orig. ed., 1947), 3.

6. Robert Fleming, *The Fulfilling of the Scripture* (Rotterdam: no pub., 1671; orig. ed. 1669), 422–3.
7. Ibid., 430, 473–74.
8. Ibid., 422–23, 452, 472–73.
9. Ibid., 474.
10. Ibid.
11. Ibid., 430.
12. Ibid., 423.
13. Ibid., 473–74.
14. Ibid., 474.
15. *Dictionary of Scottish Church History and Theology*, 325.
16. Samuel Rutherford, *A Survey of the Spirituall Antichrist. Opening the Secrets of Familisme and Antinomianisme in the Antichristian Doctrine of John Saltmarsh ...* (London: no pub., 1648), 42. The reference to M. Ioh. Davidson is to John Davidson of Prestonpans (also called Salt-Prestoun in old documents). He was the preacher on the day that the Holy Spirit fell on the ministers in St. Giles in March 1596, and started a revival. He had been at St. Andrews as a Regent or master of his college in the last days of John Knox. He was known for his prophetic words. See R. Moffat Gillon, *John Davidson of Prestonpans* (London: James Clarke & Co., 1936).
17. Ibid., 43ff.
18. For examples of the kinds of things that are happening in the church in China see Carl Lawrence, *The Church in China* (Minneapolis, MN: Bethany House, 1985).
19. Corrie ten Boom, *The Hiding Place* (Toronto: Bantam Books, 1974); and *Tramp for the Lord* (Fort Washington, PA: Christian Literature Crusade, 1974).
20. Corrie ten Boom, *The Hiding Place*, 202.
21. Ibid., 203.
22. Charles Whiston, *Pray: A Study of Distinctive Christian Praying* (Grand Rapids: Eerdmans, 1972), 9–16.
23. *C.H. Spurgeon: Autobiography*, Vol. 25, *The Full Harvest*, compiled by Susannah Spurgeon and Joseph Harrald (Carlilse, PA: Banner of Truth Trust, 1973), 60.
24. F.Y. Fullerton, *Charles H. Spurgeon* (Chicago: Moody, 1966), 206.
25. Charles H. Spurgeon, *The Autobiography of Charles Spurgeon* (Curts & Jennings, 1899), Vol. II: 226–27.
26. Ibid.
27. Os Guinness, *The Dust of Death* (Downers Grove, Ill.: InterVarsity Press, 1973), 299.

Chapter 7: God Speaks Through the Bible

1. The story of Monica's dream and her conversation with the bishop is found in Augustine's *Confessions* Book III:11,12. Augustine's experience in the garden is recorded in Book VII:12, and the death of Monica in Book IX:11.

2. For the details of Cowper's life (and references) see John White, *The Masks of Melancholy* (Downers Grove, Ill.: IVP, 1982), 142–46; and also the *Oxford Dictionary of the Christian Church*, 2nd. ed., 355.
3. Compare the analogies between the spiritual life and food in 1 Corinthians 3:1–4; Hebrews 5:11–14; and 1 Peter 2:1–2.
4. Daniel Goleman, *Emotional Intelligence* (New York: Bantam Books, 1995), 87–88.
5. C.S. Lewis, *Reflections on the Psalms* (New York: Harcourt, Brace & World, 1958), 114.
6. The Bible can be used destructively according to 2 Peter 3:16.
7. There are legitimate exceptions to this statement. There have been times in history, for various reasons, when it has been impossible for the ordinary Christian to read the Bible on a regular basis. Where modern governments have banned the Bible, God seems to speak all the more to his children in dreams, visions, impressions, and other ways.

Chapter 8: God Speaks Through Experience

1. C. S. Lewis, *The Problem of Pain* (London: Collins, 1940), 81.
2. Zondervan, 1996.
3. Ibid., 17.
4. In my book, *Surprised by the Power of the Spirit* (Grand Rapids: Zondervan, 1993), I discuss at length the various purposes of miracles (117–44; 219–27).
5. I illustrate this dilemma in *Surprised by the Power of the Spirit*, 53–54.
6. Please don't take this observation as a criticism of psychiatrists or antidepressants. I know wonderful Christians who at various times have benefited from counselors and antidepressants. I'm criticizing the hypocritical promise of something that the promisers are not themselves experiencing nor leading their followers to experience.
7. Psalm 119:26, 27, 33, 34, 36, 66, 108, 124, 135.
8. Zondervan, 1989.
9. *Windows of the Soul*, 172–73.
10. Ibid., 175.

Chapter 9: God Speaks Through Supernatural Means

1. Edith Schaeffer tells this story in *The Tapestry* (Waco: Word Books, 1981), 384–85. Peter Marshall, the famous Presbyterian pastor and Senate chaplain, also heard the audible voice of God when he was a young man. It saved his life. See Catherine Marshall, *A Man Called Peter* (New York: Avon Books 1971; orig. ed. 1951), 24.
2. Later Edith Schaeffer said, "Now Francis' answer to prayer and very special experience of hearing the Lord tell him to turn to this house could not be dashed to pieces by my spending the year complaining about the difficulty of living there! Nor, far more important, could I complain against

the Lord by failing to be thankful for what He had given in that particular shelter." Ibid., 385.

3. This story is in 1 Samuel 3:1–18.

4. Though the words spoken to our minds have divine authority, they do not have the same authority as the Scripture. See chapter 18, pp. 278ff.

5. Theologians can quibble endlessly over what is meant by "supernatural." I have no intention of entering their debate. Most have no difficulty using the term supernatural in reference to an audible voice or an angelic visitation. Some might argue that the "internal audible voice" described in this chapter is really not supernatural. Yet if that voice is from God, then it transcends our natural insights and must be described as supernatural. The real issue here is how to distinguish the "internal audible voice" from the voice of our own thoughts.

6. From the Christian perspective, see the article by Timothy Jones, "Rumors of Angels," *Christianity Today*, April 5, 1993, 18–22; Ann Spangler, *An Angel a Day* (Grand Rapids: Zondervan, 1994); and Larry Calvin, *No Fear! The Calling of Angels* (Fort Worth: Sweet Publishing, 1995). On the secular side, see the article by Nancy Gibbs, "Angels Among Us," *Time*, December 27, 1993, 56–65; and George Colt, "In Search of Angels," *Life*, December 1995, 62–79.

7. For the birth of Jesus, see Matthew 1:20, 24; 2:13, 19; Luke 1:11ff., 26ff.; 2:9–15. For his temptation, see Matthew 4:11 and Mark 1:13. For his resurrection, see Matthew 28:2, 5; Luke 24:23; John 20:12. For his ascension, see Acts 1:10–11.

Chapter 10: God Speaks Through Natural Means

1. Someone might think visions should be classified as supernatural rather than natural means of divine communication. I put them in this chapter with dreams, trances, impressions, sentence fragments, and single words because we all commonly experience these things in purely natural forms. Dreams often arise from our subconscious, and visions (or mental pictures) from our imaginations. Again, the real issue is how to determine the source of these experiences when they happen to us.

All forms of divine communication, whether from the Bible or from experience, have to be illumined by the Holy Spirit for us to benefit from the revelation. An unillumined Bible is as useless as winking at your lover in the dark. Even the audible voice of God cannot be understood apart from the illuminating ministry of the Holy Spirit (John 12:27–33). There is a sense in which we would be justified in calling any communication from God "supernatural" when it is illumined by God, whether it be a dream or a conversation with a friend. Any time the voice of God penetrates the heart, it is supernatural.

2. Sometimes the Bible uses both these terms interchangeably, e.g., Daniel 7:1–2.

3. Cf. Peter's experience in Acts 10:9–16.

4. Ken Gire, *Windows of the Soul* (Grand Rapids: Zondervan, 1996), 151–55.
5. The Greek word is *eidon* and can be used for both natural sight and spiritual perceptions, see BAGD, 220–21.

Chapter 11: Learning the Language of the Holy Spirit

1. This church is now thriving. I realize that some of the statements in this chapter may be offensive to some members who were there when I was. The last thing I want to do is offend any of them. I believe then and I believe now that the core of this church is made up of good, moral, sincere, Bible-believing Christians. The second point I want to make is that among the leadership I was the one most adamant that the most important ministry of the kingdom was teaching the Bible. I personally was not doing any significant work in evangelism or counseling or administration. The other pastors were basically carrying the counseling and administrative loads. All I was really concerned with was teaching. I was the one who had the major role in engineering the genetic code of the church, which I realize now was simply a cloning of my own personality and my own personal theology.
2. C. S. Lewis, *Screwtape Letters* (New York: MacMillan, 1961), 39.

Chapter 12: Facilitating Prophetic Ministry

1. If you're a hard-core skeptic, you might be thinking that Paul Cain could have looked up county records in Texas and Mississippi where my mom and dad were born, and gotten their birth names from those sources. Before you settle on that explanation, you might want to wait until the last chapter of this book.
2. Richard B. Gaffin, Jr., *Perspectives on Pentecost* (Phillipsburg, New Jersey: Presbyterian and Reformed Publication Co., 1979), 59, writes, "Apparently, the designation *prophet* is applied to those who exercise the gift frequently or with some regularity (e.g., Acts 21:10; 1 Cor. 12:28), while the gift can function temporarily in others on particular occasions (see Acts 19:6—also Acts 21:9; 1 Cor. 11:4ff.)."
3. Someone might object that Ananias and Sapphira were judged for not giving the full amount of money from the sale of their property, but Peter made it clear that they were judged for lying to God (Acts 5:4).
4. Exodus 14:31; 19:9; Joshua 3:7; 4:14; 1 Chronicles 29:25.

Chapter 13: "God Told Me to Tell You ..."

1. These possibilities are evaluated by Wayne Grudem in *The Gift of Prophecy in the New Testament and Today* (Westchester, Ill.: Crossway, 1988), 72–74, who concludes "the others" are all who hear the prophets.

2. These three things—love, testimony, glory—occur in the three contexts where the Spirit of Truth is mentioned in Jesus' last discourse with the apostles before the cross (John 14:17; 15:26; 16:13).

Chapter 14: Prophetic Pitfalls

1. It may sound strange to some that God would use an evil spirit to accomplish his purposes. However, all power belongs to God whether human, political, or spiritual. He used evil nations like Assyria and Babylon to discipline his people. Why wouldn't he use evil spirits for the same purposes? This happened to Saul several times (1 Sam. 16:14, 15, 23; 18:10; 19:9). It happened to David (2 Sam. 24:1 and 1 Chron. 21:1) and to others (Judg. 9:23; 1 Kings 22:19–23).
2. Terry Teykl, *Your Pastor: Preyed On Or Prayed For?* (Anderson, IN: Bristol Books, 1993).
3. *Windows of the Soul*, 216.

Chapter 15: Dreams and Visions

1. Cf. a recent article by Robert Moss, "What Your Dreams Can Tell You," *Parade* (Jan. 30, 1994): 13–14.
2. Some might object to my line of reasoning here by saying that Joseph probably didn't understand the meaning of either one of these texts. Or that even if he did understand the meaning, he would not have known that they applied to his son and wife. But neither of these objections has any force. The Holy Spirit is perfectly capable of bringing the most obscure passages to one's mind and leading one to apply them correctly.

   Let me give you an example of what I mean. Psalm 69:25 says, "May their place be deserted, let there be no one to dwell in their tents." Psalm 109:8 says, "May another take his place of leadership." Who would have ever thought that ultimately both of these passages referred to Judas, the apostle who betrayed the Lord? But Peter, standing up in the midst of the 120 disciples, declared that both of these passages had reference to Judas and, therefore, they must now choose another apostle to take Judas' place (Acts 1:20–26). When God wishes, he has no difficulty at all in taking any passage, no matter how obscure, and using that passage to guide his people into certain courses of action. In both of the passages I cited about the dreams God had given to Joseph, Matthew notes in each case that the dreams led to action which fulfilled the Old Testament prophecies about Jesus, namely Isaiah 7:14 and Hosea 11:1.
3. Cf. Hosea 12:10: "I spoke to the prophets, gave them many visions and told parables through them." See also Ezekiel 7:26: "Calamity upon calamity will come, and rumor upon rumor. They will try to get a vision from the prophet; the teaching of the law by the priest will be lost, as will the counsel of the elders." The absence of dreams and visions was often a

sign of God's judgment on the people, especially his displeasure with their corrupt leadership (1 Sam. 3:1; Lam. 2:9; Mic. 3:6, 7).

4. Other dreams that occurred in two different forms and represented decreed events are found in Genesis 37:5ff. The two dreams in Daniel 2 and Daniel 7 represented the progress of world empires beginning with the Babylonian kingdom.

5. Robert Moss, "What Your Dreams Can Tell You," *Parade* (Jan. 30, 1994): 13–14. What I find instructive about his article is that it appeared in *Parade* magazine, a weekly magazine distributed across the country in Sunday newspapers. This indicates that the editors felt there was enough widespread interest in dreams to justify a feature article on the subject.

6. Genesis 40:8; 41:16, 25, 28, 39; Daniel 1:17; 2:28; 4:18.

7. Daniel 7:28; 8:27; 10:8–17.

8. Genesis 41:11–13, 37–40; Daniel 5:12.

Chapter 16: God Knows the Proud from Afar

1. Jonathan Edwards, "The Distinguishing Marks of a Work of the Spirit of God," in *Jonathan Edwards on Revival* (Carlisle, Penn.: The Banner of Truth Trust, 1984), 137.

2. C. S. Lewis, *Mere Christianity* (New York: Macmillan, 1952), 109.

3. Ibid., 111.

4. Gordon Fee, *The First Epistle to the Corinthians* (Grand Rapids: Eerdmans, 1987), 146ff., argues that both the context and grammar of this passage demand such a corporate interpretation.

5. BAGD, 857.

6. Psalm 13:1; 28:1; 39:12; 83:1; 89:46; 109:1.

7. Quoted by C. S. Lewis in *Miracles* (New York: Macmillan, 1978; orig. ed. 1947), 81.

Chapter 17: Confessions of a Bible Deist

1. The Greek word is *diermeneuo*. See Acts 9:36; 1 Corinthians 12:30; 14:5, 13, 27; and BAGD, 194.

2. Shortly after this, Jesus appeared to his eleven disciples and said, "Everything must be fulfilled that is written about me in the Law of Moses, the Prophets and the Psalms" (Luke 24:44). Yet Jesus knew that the Bible would never become the sword of the Spirit in their hands without his supernatural touch. Therefore, "he opened their minds so they could understand the Scriptures" (v. 45). If this opening of the mind was universal and automatic to all believers, why do so many of us still misunderstand his Word? Why are there so many divisions in the body of Christ? Why are there so many vitriolic doctrinal debates among Christians?

The people who wrote the Bible believed that the Scriptures could not be understood apart from the illuminating ministry of the Holy Spirit. They knew that if God did not shine his light upon their hearts and upon his Word, they would never understand his voice in the Scriptures in any significant way. Psalm 119 is probably the greatest meditation in the Bible on the value of the written Word of God. The author of Psalm 119 prayed under the inspiration of the Holy Spirit, "Open my eyes that I may see wonderful things in your law" (v. 18). This was a man through whom the inspiration of the Holy Spirit was flowing so that he could actually write the Word of God. But even this man did not presume to understand the Word of God unless the Spirit of God opened his eyes. Again and again he appeals to God in this psalm to "teach" and give him understanding of the Scriptures (Ps. 119:12, 26, 33, 64, 66, 108, 124, 135). What understanding he has of the Scripture is attributed to God's work because God has taught him the Scripture (Ps. 119:102, 171).

In the middle of his second letter to Timothy, Paul stops, apparently realizing that Timothy may not have an effective understanding of what Paul is writing to him. Therefore, Paul says to him, "Consider what I say, for the Lord will give you understanding in everything" (2:7, NASB). Timothy's job is to consider; it is the Lord's job to give understanding.

By the way, I do not think that this is a blanket promise to all Christians. I think it is possible for many of us to "consider" individual passages of Scripture and completely misunderstand them or misapply them. Paul knew the heart of Timothy. He was the kind of person that the Lord would speak to if he would take the time to ponder the Scripture.

3. William Law, *The Power of the Spirit* (Fort Washington, PA: Christian Literature Crusade, 1971), 61, cited by Dallas Willard, *In Search of Guidance* (Ventura, CA: Regal Books, 1984), 198.

4. *Reflections on the Psalms* (New York: Harcourt, Brace & World, 1958), 57–58.

5. John Fletcher, *A Guide to Young Disciples* (Cheltenham: Richard Edwards, 1848), 1.

Chapter 18: Unbelief Through Theology

1. Donald Guthrie, *Introduction to the New Testament*, 3rd ed. (Downers Grove, Ill.: InterVarsity Press, 1970), 437, 558–59.

2. Fowler White, "Does God Speak Today Apart From the Bible?", in *The Coming Evangelical Crisis*, ed. John H. Armstrong (Chicago: Moody Press, 1996), 81.

3. Ibid., 87.

4. In the quote taken from page 87, White used the phrase "hear those words," but he must have meant "understand those words." The issue is not whether one hears an audible voice, sees a vision, had a dream or an impression, but whether one recognizes if the communication is from God rather than their own imaginations and whether one understands the communication.

5. Ibid., 83.

6. Ibid., 79.

7. Ibid., 78.

8. There are a number of errors in White's article to which I haven't made reference above. He attributes an appendix to me which I never wrote (88, note 17), namely "Appendix 7: The Sufficiency of Scripture and Distortion of What Scripture Teaches About Itself," in *The Kingdom and the Power: Are Healing and the Spiritual Gifts Used by Jesus and the Early Church Meant for the Church Today?* ed. Gary S. Greig and Kevin N. Springer (Ventura, Calif.: Regal, 1993), 440. In reality, Gary Greig wrote this appendix.

White also misrepresents my views when he writes, "He [Deere] insists that those means [i.e., the various ways in which God spoke in the Bible] are always connected with 'words of direction' from God without defining those words in other than personal and ministerial terms" (80–81).

I do not insist that the various revelatory phenomena in the Bible "are always connected with 'words of direction.'" Sometimes when God speaks to us it is to commune with us rather than give us direction (see chapter 15, p. 222–23).

White also accuses those of us who believe that God speaks apart from the Bible of diverting attention from the Scriptures and quenching the Spirit. Biblically, I wonder how he can do this, since quenching the Spirit is connected with despising noncanonical revelation. Paul wrote:

> Do not quench the Spirit; do not despise prophetic utterances (1 Thess. 5:19–20 NASB).

White even admits that this text "corrects the Thessalonians' overreaction" to false prophecies previously given to them (85). The overreaction is despising or denying the validity of noncanonical prophecy. But how can I be accused of that? I'm the one who believes in extra-biblical prophecy; the ones quenching the Spirit are the ones who don't believe in its validity.

And on a personal level, I wonder how White knows that I am "diverting attention from the Scriptures"? Am I giving the Bible less attention than White?

In my opinion, White makes another error when he appeals to the argument from the open canon (86). For a critique of this argument see above pp. 276–78.

Finally, it is surprising that White refers to God speaking apart from the Bible as a "new affirmation" and a "new view (77–78)." New to whom I wonder? Certainly it wasn't new to the biblical writers. Nor was it new to the Reformers and Scottish Covenanters. Nor is it new to the millions of believers who hear God speak regularly in their lives today. It may be new to White, but that wouldn't justify his unqualified use of the word "new" in his article, giving historically naive readers the impression that the church has remained closed to extra-biblical revelation until only recently. History, I think, teaches us the opposite.

At the conclusion of my last book I said that I intended to include a discussion of Ephesians 2:20 in this book. I have omitted this discussion since Sam Storms has already done it in *Are Miraculaous Gifts for Today?*

Wayne Grudem, ed. (Grand Rapids: Zondervan, 1996). See his response to Richard Gaffin, 78–81.

Chapter 20: The Kind of People Who Hear the Voice of God

1. I owe this phrase to Klaus Bockmeuhl, *Listening to the God Who Speaks* (Colorado Springs: Helmers and Howard, 1990), 53.

Chapter 21: Recognizing the Voice

1. Some might object that God commanded Abraham to sacrifice Isaac (Gen. 22). Although no specific command against child sacrifice had yet been inscripturated, the order to kill Isaac certainly went against the character of God revealed thus far in Genesis. But the command was a test, and God himself prevented Abraham from fulfilling it. We would be hard-pressed to come up with a true example of God actually commanding someone to violate the true meaning of biblical revelation. Jesus said no one was to violate the "least" of the commandments (Matt. 5:19) and "the Scripture cannot be broken" (John 10:35).
2. You can read about her exciting story in her book *Chasing the Dragon* (Ann Arbor, MI: Servant Books, 1980). Also see her book, *Crack In The Wall* (London: Hodder & Stoughton, 1989).
3. Note that I am saying we should expect real prophetic ministry to produce fruit *among those who believe*. When prophets speak to unbelievers or religious people who are in rebellion, as Jeremiah did, there may be little or no fruit from their ministry to these kinds of people. Here they may serve the function of demonstrating their audience's hardness of heart and announcing God's judgment.
4. Ken Gire, *Windows of the Soul* (Grand Rapids: Zondervan, 1996), 218.
5. The phrase, "all the preparations" (v. 40), is literally "much service" or "much ministry."
6. See Luke 22:31; Acts 9:4; and Matthew 23:37.
7. 2 Chronicles 20:7; Isaiah 41:8; James 2:23.

Bibliography

Bockmeuhl, Klaus. *Listening to the God Who Speaks.* Colorado Springs: Helmers and Howard, 1990.

Buechner, Frederick. *The Hungering Dark.* San Francisco: Harper, 1969.

Calvin, Larry. *No Fear!: The Calling of Angels.* Fort Worth: Sweet Publishing, 1995.

Cameron, Thomas. *Peden the Prophet.* Edinburgh: James A. Dickson. Reprint, 1981.

Colt, George. "In Search of Angels." *Life,* December 1995.

Deere, Jack. *Surprised by the Power of the Spirit.* Grand Rapids: Zondervan, 1993.

de S. Cameron, Nigel M., ed. *Dictionary of Scottish Church History and Theology.* Edinburgh: T. & T. Clark, 1993.

Fee, Gordon. *The First Epistle to the Corinthians.* Grand Rapids: Eerdmans, 1987.

Fletcher, John. *A Guide to Young Disciples.* Cheltenham: Richard Edwards, 1848.

Fullerton, F.Y. *Charles H. Spurgeon.* Chicago: Moody Press, 1966.

Gaffin, Richard B. Jr. *Perspectives on Pentecost.* Phillipsburg, New Jersey: Presbyterian and Reformed Publication Co., 1979.

Gibbs, Nancy. "Angels Among Us." *Time,* 27 December, 1993.

Gillon, R. Moffat. *John Davidson of Prestonpans.* London: James Clarke & Co., 1936.

Gire, Ken. *Windows of the Soul.* Grand Rapids: Zondervan, 1996.

Goleman, Daniel. *Emotional Intelligence.* New York: Bantam Books, 1995.

Grudem, Wayne. *Systematic Theology.* Grand Rapids: Zondervan, 1994.

Guinness, Os. *The Dust of Death.* Downers Grove, Ill.: InterVarsity Press, 1973.

Hawthorne. Gerald F. *Philippians.* Volume 43, *Word Biblical Commentary.* (Waco: Word, 1983).

———. *The Presence and the Power.* Word: Dallas, 1991.

Helland. Roger. "The Hypostatic Union: How Did Jesus Function?" *The Evangelical Quarterly* 65 (1993).

Howie, John. *Scots Worthies.* Rev. ed. Glasgow: W. R. McPhun, 1846. (Orig. ed., 1775.)

———. *The Scots Worthies.* Rev. ed. by W. H. Carslaw. Edinburgh: Oliphant, Anderson and Ferrier, 1902.

———. *Scots Worthies.* Edited by William McGavin. Glasgow: W.R. McPhun, 1846.

Jones, Timothy. "Rumors of Angels." *Christianity Today.* 5 April, 1993.

Knox, John. *History of the Reformation*, Vol. 1. Edited by William Croft Dickinson. New York: Philosophical Library, 1950.

Lane, W.L. *The Gospel According to Mark.* Grand Rapids: Eerdmans, 1974.

Law, William. *The Power of the Spirit.* Fort Washington, Penn.: Christian Literature Crusade, 1971.

Lawrence, Carl. *The Church in China.* Minneapolis, Minn.: Bethany House, 1985.

Lewis, C. S. *Mere Christianity.* New York: Macmillan, 1952.

———. *Miracles.* (New York: Macmillan, 1978; orig. ed., 1947).

———. *The Problem of Pain.* London: Collins, 1940.

———. *Reflections on the Psalms.* New York: Harcourt, Brace & World, 1958.

Moss, Robert. "What Your Dreams Can Tell You." *Parade,* 30 January, 1994.

O'Brien, Peter T. *The Epistle to the Philippians: A Commentary on the Greek Text.* Grand Rapids: Eerdmans, 1991.

Pullinger, Jackie. *Chasing the Dragon.* Ann Arbor, MI: Servant Books, 1980.

———. *Crack in the Wall.* London: Hodder & Stoughton, 1989.

Ridley, Jasper. *John Knox.* Oxford: Clarendon Press, 1968.

Robison, James. *Thank God, I'm Free.* Nashville, TN: Thomas Nelson, 1988.

Rutherford, Samuel. *A Survey of the Spirituall Antichrist. Opening the Secrets of Familisme and Antinomianisme in the Antichristian Doctrine of John Saltmarsh (et. al.),* London: 1648.

Schaeffer, Edith. *The Tapestry.* Waco: Word, 1981.

Smellie, Alexander. *Men of the Covenant.* London: Andrew Melrose, 1905. (Orig. ed., 1903.)

Spangler, Ann. *An Angel a Day.* Grand Rapids: Zondervan, 1994.

Spurgeon, Charles H. *The Autobiography of Charles Spurgeon.* Vol. 2. Curts & Jennings, 1899.

Spurgeon, Susannah and Joseph Harrald, comp. *The Full Harvest.* Vol. 25, *C. H. Spurgeon: Autobiography.* Carlisle, Penn: Banner of Truth, 1973.

ten Boom, Corrie. *The Hiding Place.* Toronto: Bantam Books, 1974.

———. *Tramp for the Lord.* Fort Washington, PA: Christian Literature Crusade, 1974.

Teykl, Terry. *Your Pastor: Preyed On Or Prayed For?* Anderson, In.: Bristol Books, 1993.

Walker, Patrick. *Six Saints of the Covenant.* 2 vols. London: Hodder & Stoughton, 1901. (Orig. ed., 1724.).

Whiston, Charles. *Pray: A Study of Distinctive Christian Praying.* Grand Rapids: Eerdmans, 1972.

White, Fowler. "Does God Speak Today Apart From the Bible?" In *The Coming Evangelical Crisis,* edited by John H. Armstrong. Chicago: Moody Press, 1996.

White, John. *The Masks of Melancholy.* Downers Grove, Ill.: IVP, 1982.

Willard, Dallas. *In Search of Guidance.* Ventura, Calif.: Regal Books, 1984.

———. *In Search of Guidance.* Rev. ed. San Francisco: Harper, 1993.

Subject Index

Scripture Index